Roy Bainton, author of *Honoured by Strangers*, *A Brief History of 1917: Russia's Year of Revolution* and *The Mammoth Book of Unexplained Phenomena*, among other books, served in the Merchant Navy and has travelled around the world three times. He has written extensively for newspapers and magazines and is a regular contributor to BBC Radio ·

Recent Mammoth titles

The Mammoth Book of Superstition

Roy Bainton

ROBINSON

ROBINSON

First published in Great Britain in 2016 by Robinson

Text copyright © Roy Bainton, 2016

1 3 5 7 9 8 6 4 2

p.303: Courtesy Nelson Mandela Foundation

A CIP catalogue record for this book
is available from the British Library

ISBN: 978-1-47213-748-7 (paperback)

Typeset in Whitman by Hewer Text UK Ltd, Edinburgh
Printed and bound in Great Britain by CPI Group (UK) Ltd, Croydon CR0 4YY

Papers used by Robinson are from well-managed forests and other responsible sources

Robinson
is an imprint of
Little, Brown Book Group
Carmelite House
50 Victoria Embankment
London EC4Y 0DZ

An Hachette UK Company
www.hachette.co.uk

www.littlebrown.co.uk

Dedicated to the memory of my friend,
Gerry 'Chiefie' Browning 1932–2016

A black cat crossed my path today,
Touch wood.
Two magpies came but flew away,
Touch wood.
A raven left me short of breath
Is he the messenger of death?
Touch wood.
The robin's hiding in a tree,
Touch wood.
Is that foul weather that he sees?
Touch wood.
No, it's all right, red sky tonight,
I'll heed the sailor's warning,
The moon is up and shining bright
There'll be sunshine in the morning.
Touch wood.

Contents

PART TWO: ORIGINS

PART THREE: THE DANGER ZONE

PART FOUR: THE COMFORT ZONE

Introduction
Stirring the pudding

Science of today – the superstition of tomorrow.
Science of tomorrow – the superstition of today.

Charles Fort (1874–1932), *The Book of the Damned* (1919)

I suppose this book could have opened with 'albatross' and ended with 'yew tree', but there are already numerous excellent, exhaustive and assiduously researched academic works which list superstitions from A to Z and there were too many seductive distractions along the way. It might seem that the alphabetic or encyclopaedic approach may be the only valid way to attempt a comprehensive overview of this subject, but although superstitions are here in abundance, this book is not a dictionary.

This is an expedition through the dark domain of these weird, comical and often inexplicable beliefs. This is more of a flight over the scattered territory of omens, rituals, curses, premonitions and general superstition, with random landings at the more thought-provoking locations, veering off at times into related cultural and religious areas which might promise interesting background. For example, what's the context for our dread of Friday the 13th? Is it a very old superstition? Does it have anything to do with the mysterious Knights Templar? Perhaps not, but the story of their downfall on that ominous date is interesting, so it seemed worthy of inclusion. Where did the Christian Church's rituals originate? Who was the Virgin Mary? Then there are superstitions about innocent animals – in particular, the cat. To get to the bottom of these pagan and Christian phobias it is worthwhile to look at examples of our cruelty to animals, driven by superstition, over the centuries.

There are thousands of superstitions worldwide, some peculiar to one village, town, region, country or culture, many others universal and familiar, and it is inevitable that some, perhaps your particular favourites, will slip through the net. If that is the case, I hope such an omission does not portend misfortune for either of us. You may place a curse upon me if this happens.

Superstitions are often, by tradition, accepted without knowledge of their origin or their context in history. For an inquisitive soul, digging in the subsoil around these bizarre eccentricities can sometimes steer one into a diversion, a winding little path leading to vague yet fascinating destinations with seemingly tenuous links to the subject in question. As you will discover, in my attempts to be as entertaining as possible, I have found these diversions irresistible. They can be dangerously dark in the unforgiving climate of religion, yet the survival of super-stition in a modern world can only be regarded as light-hearted fun, and most of my observations are carried out with tongue firmly in cheek. Well-read folklorists and academic researchers will no doubt spot any pitfalls I have stumbled into. For example, I almost ended up with the proverbial egg on face over the subject of the druids and mistletoe but was saved by the peerless erudition of the doyen of the history of British superstitions, Steve Roud.

Will the following pages have any effect on your social life? If so, what might that effect be? Here's one possibility. In 1972, on BBC TV's *Parkinson* chat show, Peter Sellers did an uncanny impression of fellow actor Michael Caine, saying, 'It takes a man in a tweed suit five and a half seconds to fall from the top of Big Ben to the ground. Now, there's not many people know that . . .' So once you've absorbed some of the more arcane and obscure data in these pages, you'll be able to reveal strange superstitions to friends and family and top off your contribution with, 'Now, there's not many people who know that.'

Tweed suits and Michael Caine aside, apparently even Peter Sellers was dogged by superstition. He refused to wear the colour green, saying it gave him 'strange vibrations'. If anyone appearing with him wore green, Sellers would refuse to work. Another later phobia for the great Inspector Clouseau was the colour purple. The film director Vittorio de Sica, when working on the Sellers movie *After the Fox*, had exploded in rage when a female script assistant walked onto the set dressed in purple. Sellers was intrigued, and once de Sica had told him that he regarded purple as 'the colour of death', Sellers adopted this superstition with a vengeance, eventually to the point that hotel staff had to ensure anything purple was removed from his room. Of course, many of us like to say this is all codswallop. Superstition at first seems that easy to dismiss. Yet it has tangled roots and links which lead to strange places; myth, legend, tragedy, paganism, witchcraft, all the major reli-gions. When we 'touch wood' we are touching something deep and mysterious.

This is certainly not the first book on the subject of superstitions and it undoubtedly won't be the last. For a writer, the subject is frankly overwhelming. From pole to pole and around the equator, everywhere one looks a bottomless pit of superstition and omens opens up. Fascinated by it all, bloggers, folklorists and academics continue to collect superstitions, many from their own culture or country, others casting an international net. These little rituals are so numerous and diverse that this book, which does not aim to be an academic treatise, can only skim the surface. Hopefully it will provide an entertaining flavour of what still lurks in the recesses of the human psyche, hidden behind a heavy curtain, in utter contrast to twenty-first-century technological reason. There is, however, a serious aspect to superstition because of religion. One bleeds into the other and those of us with a more secular outlook may treat superstition in a light-hearted fashion. Yet it seems a perverse reality in the twenty-first century that a similar attitude towards prominent branches of faith can produce a reaction far removed from the compassion and mercy such religions espouse. Therefore it is not without good reason that I have titled part three of this work The Danger Zone.

Even writers have superstitions. Goethe called them 'the poetry of life'. According to James Boswell's *Life of Johnson*, poet, essayist and moralist Dr Samuel Johnson (1709–1784), when out strolling past the railings on the streets of London, apparently trailed his hand or walking stick so that it clattered against each individual rail. Should he inadvertently miss one, the good doctor would make sure he went back and touched it with his cane. Johnson also confused those he visited with peculiar, baffling routines when walking up steps or going through doorways. Such odd behaviour, which falls under the heading of personal superstitions, is widespread. Ask anyone you know if they have a superstition and chances are they'll be wood-knockers, wish-bone pullers, folk in fear of broken mirrors whose umbrellas are never opened indoors. Over many centuries humanity has emerged from primeval darkness to unburden itself of so much eccentric mythological detritus, yet we're still crossing our fingers as we avoid cracks in the pavement.

To give it its full name, paraskevidekatriaphobia is a morbid, irrational fear of Friday the 13th. Friggatriskaidekaphobia describes the fear of things or events associated with the number thirteen. The term triskaideka is from the ancient Greek τρεισκαίδεκα for thirteen. Friday is Frigga's Day. Frigga (Frigg) was an ancient

Scandinavian fertility and love goddess, equivalent to the Roman Venus who had been worshipped on the sixth day of the week.

The 13th of September 1874 was a Sunday. Apart from that unfortunate number 13, surely any rational person would think there's nothing odd or superstitious about that day or that month or that year. However, they'd be wrong. There's an old superstitious rhyme with ends with 'The child that's born on the Sabbath day is fair and wise and good and gay.' The Scots believed that a boy born on a Sunday would become a minister in the church, and that those children born on the Sabbath day could converse with animals on Christmas Eve. If we take a closer look, we find that September has its origins in the Latin word septem, 'seven', because this was once the seventh month of the early Roman calendar. So what? Well, the number seven has a lot of superstitious baggage to contend with. Over the centuries some people, gamblers for instance, have considered seven to be lucky; others, unlucky. It remains a very powerful digit. Seven wonders of the world, seven deadly sins, seven days of the week, the seven golden candlesticks of Solomon's temple and the Jewish menorah. In ancient times it was believed that the seventh son of a seventh son would grow up with supernatural abilities, and that prophesy and healing would be the gifts enjoyed by the seventh daughter of a seventh daughter. And just to save you having to come up with a potentially frustrating feat of memory, what about Bashful, Doc, Dopey, Grumpy, Happy, Sleepy and Sneezy, the seven dwarves? But these are only a few of the superstitions connected with the number seven. What about that year, with the number 1874? Numerologists would have a field day with this. There's even supposed to be an angel with that number.

Superstitions, no matter how unsubstantiated they seem, cling like stubborn limpets to just about everything. In addition to September, if we examine every other day, week and month in the year we'll find a plethora of superstitions attached to them all. Old farmers believed a wet September promised a drought the next year. It is supposedly unlucky to post a love letter on the first day of September. Anyone hearing a cuckoo in September could expect a death to happen. And don't collect nuts in this month because you'll have company – that's when the devil is out looking for his nuts. The sheer number of superstitions is amazing. Another two volumes could be filled with these uncanny, ancient connections and there'd still be more.

So, on Sunday 13 September 1874, in Austria at Leopoldstadt, Vienna, composer and painter Arnold Schoenberg was born. He was triskaidekaphobic. Thirteen scared him rigid. Schoenberg, who developed the twelve-tone technique in music, was a fervent believer in astrology and an ardent fan of Hopalong Cassidy movies. (There are cowboy, Indian and horse superstitions, too.) It's hard to say when Schoenberg's triskaidekaphobia began, but composing his unfinished three-act opera *Moses und Aaron* in 1932, he pedantically counted the number of letters in the title – thirteen. So he dropped an 'a' and changed it to *Moses und Aron*. His fear of thirteen haunted him throughout his life. He believed he would die in his seventy-sixth year (7+6=13) and he was correct. He not only expired at that age in 1951 but managed to pass away on Friday the 13th of July at thirteen minutes before midnight.

In *Determinism, Chance and Superstitious Beliefs*, Sigmund Freud (1856–1939) examines the symbolic obsession some people have with numbers, but in general he hadn't much time for this sense of doom and gloom. In his 1901 work *Psychopathology of Everyday Life*, he sums it all up thus:

> Superstition is in large part the expectation of trouble; and a person who has harboured frequent evil wishes against others but has been brought up to be good and has therefore repressed such wishes into the unconscious, will be especially ready to expect punishment for his unconscious wickedness in the form of trouble threatening him from without.

Sometimes, in retrospect, omens and superstitions can be manipulated and moulded to fit the outcome of an event. The growing army of conspiracy-mongers on the internet love this bending of figures and dates. NASA's thirteenth Apollo mission was launched on 11 April 1970, at 13:13 CST from the Kennedy Space Center, Florida, from launch-pad thirty-nine (13x3). The mission was aborted on 13 April when an oxygen tank exploded. Of course, this proves nothing other than the existence of coincidences, yet the superstitious observer might have wondered how successful the mission might have been if they'd simply called the mission 'Apollo Fourteen'.

Many celebrities, rock stars and actors have their own superstitious eccentricities, which we'll examine. And as we've already seen, there's 'the big one', which fully deserves a chapter of its own. In 1982, at the age of thirty-four, Stephen King, with ten bestsellers under his belt, interviewed in South Carolina's *Spartanburg*

Herald, revealed his concerns over the number thirteen. 'I don't like it at all. Thirteen seems to have an enchanted hold on me. Maybe it's because of what I write. If you hit it big, then you get superstitious.'

Annually, the financial world loses over $900 million on Friday the 13th because even hard-nosed stock exchange traders appear not to be immune from the power of superstition, and many executives especially refuse to fly. American presidents Herbert Hoover and Franklin Roosevelt avoided eating at tables at which thirteen people were present. Almost 80% of high-rise buildings sidestep the dread of having a thirteenth floor. Many airports exclude gate thirteen and some hospitals avoid having a room thirteen. And if you think the number thirteen stands alone in this context, think again. Pick a number and there's a superstition attached.

Then there's superstition's sinister bedfellow, the omen. We may smile wryly to ourselves when we throw salt over our shoulder or inadvertently drop a spoon, but we're really exercising a primeval human custom that all the scientific and social progress of centuries has failed to extinguish.

Overshadowing all this with commercial persistence is astrology with its folksy, 'cross-my-palm-with-silver' impenetrable philosophy and obdurate ersatz 'science' which has continued to impress diverse devotees from Hitler to Ronald Reagan.

When I began writing this book, I was taken by the late Terry Pratchett's claim that he only had one superstition and that was to immediately begin another book as soon as he'd finished the latest – even if it was only with a few notes – because he couldn't bear not having 'work in progress'. I can go along with that. However, most superstitions seem to fly in the face of healthy scepticism; for instance, I possess a 'lucky' Sheaffer fountain pen, bought thirty-five years ago, which I use to map out every project and keep accounts. It must only be loaded with black ink. Without it, I can feel lost. Stupid, irrational? Maybe . . . yet many of us would have one superstition in common – avoiding walking under ladders. No one wants half a gallon of paint or a terracotta tile dropping on their head.

We live in an age of staggering technological progress, confirmed by the words appearing as if by magic on the screen in front of me as I tap away at these keys. Gone are those inky typewriter ribbons, carbon copies and crusty bottles of Tippex. The library of the world is just a couple of clicks away. I have over fifty (mainly abysmal) channels on my TV set, we've got NASA rovers trundling around on Mars, and yet . . . when I challenged the window cleaner this morning over whether or not he'd done the patio door, his wounded reassurance was 'Cross my heart and hope to die.' This has echoes of superstition. It may have some recent provenance with a children's poem, where that line ends with 'stick a needle in my eye' (kids can be cruel), but it more than likely originated as a religious oath based on the sign of the cross, generally accompanied by hand gestures such as crossing one's hands over one's breast and then pointing the right hand. In other words, 'God strike me dead if I'm lying.' Like knocking on wood and crossing fingers or sailors whistling for a wind, these oddities of human instinct persist.

Most of us like to think of ourselves today as level-headed, rational people who know that the earth is round, not flat, the moon influences the tides, comets are not harbingers of doom and many garden birds migrate to Africa. In juxtaposition to this rationality we have religion with its myriad persistent myths and legends and, in the no man's land between science and faith, stand portents and omens, as stubborn as ever.

When Galileo invented the telescope in 1609, the Renaissance was in full swing. Scientific discovery revealed many new truths, advances in medicine, mathematics and geography. Simultaneously, outside the studies, laboratories and the observatories of the Renaissance, indomitable superstition still consigned hundreds of innocent women and men, suspected of being witches, to be burned to a crisp at the stake. Folk were still crossing their hearts, kissing icons, predicting the future in animal entrails and stroking their lucky rabbit's foot. Today, we burn our suspected witches, political or otherwise, with the fire of derogatory ridicule and exposure in our all-pervasive media. Black cats and lucky charms won't keep you off Twitter or out of the tabloids.

In AD 400, Hypatia of Alexandria became the first woman to make a significant contribution to the advance of mathematics. She was the head of the Platonist school at Alexandria. Basing her teachings on those of Plotinus, the founder of neoplatonism, she absorbed his belief that there is an ultimate reality which is beyond the reach of thought or language. Plotinus doesn't say what this reality was, only that ordinary people were not able to understand or absorb the concept. But Hypatia seemed to understand why that might be the case, writing:

In fact, men will fight for a superstition quite as quickly as for a living truth – often more so, since a superstition is so intangible you cannot get at it to refute it, but truth is a point of view and so is changeable.

Hypatia may have been writing over 1,600 years ago but her view remains as valid as ever. A superstition is a belief which you can't defend. It stands outside philosophy and in many cases beyond religion. If you look up the word 'superstition' in a thesaurus, you'll find it listed with 'fallacy', 'delusion', 'misconception', 'falsehood' and 'irrational belief'. It's one of those areas of human behaviour which doesn't have an answer to Jack Nicholson's angry outburst in the film *A Few Good Men*: 'The truth? You can't handle the truth!'

If my neighbour thinks that those two magpies in her garden are lucky, she doesn't need to consult any statistics to support the notion. Two magpies are lucky, one isn't, end of story, even if she doesn't win the lottery that night. Putting your shoes on the table was always a cardinal sin to my parents. They didn't know why, or what that superstition's provenance might be; it was just a 'bad thing'.

Gamblers, for example, are the most superstitious people on the planet, yet with all their quirky beliefs, lucky shirts and Y-fronts, very few of them beat the bookies. Sir Francis Bacon (1561–1626) once had a job as chancellor (a post well suited to most gamblers) and observed, 'The root of all superstition is that men observe when a thing hits, but not when it misses.' As you will read later in this work, games of 'chance' almost prove that there is no such thing.

Today, the internet's interaction with terrorist threats, scams, bank account hi-jacks and frauds, the way we approach the subject of security almost borders on superstition. We imagine when we've downloaded the latest anti-malware or security package that this computer-generated good luck charm will keep the wicked away from us. But it doesn't. Nor will hanging a string of cyber garlic above your laptop stop that Nigerian vampire who claims to be the chief auditor at the Bank of Burkina Faso from offering you 10% of $25 million he wants to free up from a dead oil man's account. The great American writer, Helen Keller (1880–1968), astutely observed, long before Microsoft, Google or Yahoo!, that:

Security is mostly a superstition. It does not exist in nature, nor do the children of men as a whole experience it. Avoiding danger is no safer in the long run than outright exposure. Life is either a daring adventure, or nothing.

It would be a mistake, however, to assume that superstitions stand in the way of an adventurous life. Many high achievers, artists, explorers, politicians and celebrities are among some of the world's most superstitious people.

London artist and designer Shing Tat Chung studied at the Slade School of Fine Art and Frankfurt Städelschule. He completed his masters in design interactions at the Royal College of Art. His multidisciplinary work explores the often hidden effects of superstition on societies and infrastructures. Shing Tat Chung's innovative projects aim to raise discussion and debate around our irrationalities. To test the superstitious nature of those working in high finance, he set up an innovative experiment in the markets, explaining:

> We always imagine technology to eliminate human errors but what happens when they begin to operate with human characteristics? The 'superstitious robot' was created with these human traits, to trade purely on superstitious beliefs. It makes decisions based on numerology and in accordance to lunar phases. So, for example, it has the fear of the number thirteen and of a full moon. The algorithm also generates its own lucky and unlucky superstitions. Just as we are hardwired to search for patterns superstitiously to give us the illusion of control, the algorithm, on completion of a trade, searches for ulterior patterns to give rise to new superstitions. It ranks and de-ranks these superstitions throughout the year. These algorithmic-produced superstitions are then used as new logic in trading. The accumulations of superstitious beliefs enable it to open 'short' or 'long' positions.

The experimental fund, in which anyone could invest a mere £2 in the hope of a positive result, ran for a year from July 2012. At the close of business it registered minus 16.18%.

Is superstition dangerous or just a bit of quirky, instinctive fun? Whether or not this book will answer that question is down to the reader. However, I was amazed when I began researching this subject to discover just how prevalent omens, superstition, sooth-saying and prediction are in advanced societies around the world. I considered Albert Einstein's observation:

> Scientific research can reduce superstition by encouraging people to think and survey things in terms of cause and effect. Certain it is that a conviction,

akin to religious feeling, of the rationality or intelligibility of the world lies behind all scientific work of a higher order.

Genius though Albert was, I doubt my mother would have had any truck with his views when the annual making of the Christmas puddings came around. We were all firmly instructed to have a stir. This was only on Sundays, hence the term 'stir-up Sundays'. The pudding had to be stirred from east to west, in honour of the three wise men (a pagan version of the stirring direction was made to avoid offending the 'sun god'), we'd add at least one silver sixpence to ensure prosperity in the coming year (with the added potential thrill of either breaking a tooth or choking to death during the Queen's speech) and, while stirring, we all had to make a secret wish. I can't recall if any of those wishes materialised; prosperity certainly didn't, but I did get my first record player for Christmas in 1957.

Right now I'm looking at the rich ingredients, namely the superstitions in this book, all ready for a good stir. As it's a Tuesday as I write this, I hope it all turns out well and, as I've just been to the barber's for a trim, there's another superstition that applies. Getting your hair cut on Tuesday is best for the wealth of the person doing the trimming. No wonder my barber's always smiling. I hope it works for writers, too.

Part one

Wild West

———

White rabbits

You'll find superstition a contagious thing.
Some people let it get the better of them.

Curt Siodmak (1902–2000), screenwriter (*Donovan's Brain* and *The Wolf Man*)

'White rabbits, white rabbits, white rabbits.' There, as it's the first day of the month today, I've said it. Harmless, silly, irrational. Yet, who knows? It just might make for a lucky month.

The western hemisphere is as jam-packed with superstitions and omens, along with the somewhat sexist term 'old wives' tales', as anywhere else on the globe. A great number of these have obvious roots, such as walking under a ladder, based on common sense, although even this has a tenuous background in religion. Others are more peculiar.

After a particularly bad run of family luck due to various serious illnesses that ended in the death of my daughter, my grief-stricken son in law commented, 'Anyone would think we'd killed a nest of robins.' I pondered over that remark for some time. I subsequently discovered that the robin is one of many birds lumbered with superstition. The Irish believe that anyone who kills a robin will have a life full of misery. If a robin flies into your house, it's a sign someone close to you will die. We didn't kill any robins and nor did one fly into the house so our lousy luck must have resulted from something else.

Because of our geographic position, edged in a corner of wide, harsh ocean in north-western Europe, with the ancient culture of Scandinavia a short longboat trip away to the east, the British Isles has acted as a powerful magnet for superstitions for thousands of years. We've been invaded by Celts, Romans, Vikings and Normans, and in the past century we've welcomed thousands from India, Pakistan, the Caribbean and parts of Africa. Today we're playing host to a massive influx of new migrants from countries in the European Union, such as Poland and some former Soviet states. All of these cultures will keep adding to our staggering stock of superstitions. We will find many of theirs bizarre, just as they will regard a number of ours with equal puzzlement. People with a deep religious faith often claim to have unburdened themselves of superstition. Yet – pagan or Christian – many of these small rituals, practices and omens are deeply rooted in the legacy the founding fathers of their faith have left them.

On the first day of the month in the UK, it supposedly brings luck to say 'white rabbits' three times before saying anything else. It was common for some WWII RAF bomber crews to exclaim 'white rabbits' when they awoke each day. Where did this strange idea come from? This, one of the most perplexing traditions, demonstrates what confronts us when we search for a superstition's origin.

The 'easy' solution is that the rabbit is a lively breeder and he moves ahead at a decent speed. So as an emblem of birth and going forward, our cute bunny ticks the box. But could this be connected to that other floppy-eared thumper, the hare? Why is 'white rabbits' said three times? In various churches, cathedrals and syna-gogues throughout Europe and even in the Far East, three hares is a circular motif which appears in sacred sites as well as in the churches of south-west England, especially where tin-mining took place. The miners, who needed all the luck they could muster, took three hares as their craft symbol, yet they became known as the 'tinner's rabbits'.

This symbol even appears as early as the sixth century in cave temples in China during the Sui dynasty. Three hares, three rabbits. But why white rabbits? Why not brown? Could it be that historically, in a spiritual sense, white has always been regarded as representing purity, innocence, wholeness and completion? (If so, why is it bad luck to leave a white tablecloth on the table overnight?)

The three hares in churches are said to represent the holy trinity – father, son and holy ghost. Like many of the subjects in this book, the mystery remains deeply buried in our long past. It seems that almost everything, animal, vegetable or mineral, is encrusted with myth, legend and superstition. Perhaps when we attempt to excavate this boneyard of auguries it might tell us something about ourselves, our past, present and our future.

Is there a need for superstitions?

We have a choice with omens and superstitions. We can laugh them off or dismiss them, as the Chinese military philosopher Sun Tzu (544–496 BC) instructed: 'Prohibit the taking of omens and do away with superstitious doubts. Then, until death itself comes, no calamity need be feared.' Centuries later, the lofty Scottish anthropologist Sir James George Frazer (1854–1941), in his magisterial master-piece on ancient religions and magic, *The Golden Bough* (1890), wrote, 'If mankind had always been logical and wise, history would not be a long chronicle of folly and crime.' However, history without folly and crime would be a bit dull.

As an alternative to any dismissal, we can continue to approach superstitions and omens with a divided mind; one eye on the arcane, ancient mystery of their existence, the other on the possibility that, in our shiny modern world, this is all just a bit of outlandish, entertaining fun.

Superstitions have other functions. We need to feel secure in a rapidly chang-ing world. The often religious roots of superstitions can make them seem like anchors; universal laws. We can't simply do anything we fancy. There needs to be a rule book. For many of us, superstitions act like mental brakes, making us pause and think. Omens about good or bad luck and our belief, no matter how silly, that lucky charms might work, seem to offer some vague idea that we can influence our future. To quote Sir James George Frazer again, in *The Golden Bough*, 'Every man is more or less his own magician.'

Many of our British and European superstitions, rooted in the medieval world of paganism, mythology and the early Church, are usually adaptations of earlier folk beliefs revised to fit Christian morality. These travelled easily with migration, and in the USA and Canada they survive to this day, often returning to the source with added sophistication.

A good example is the tradition of Halloween that, as All Hallows' Eve, tradi-tionally employed humour and ridicule to confront the power of death. Of course, today – unless we're very old and infirm or hit by some unexpected tragedy – we don't need to confront death in the same way as our medieval forebears did, in a world of darkness and plague where you'd have been lucky to live past forty.

Today, Halloween has become a western festive night for children, the opportunity to engage in a bit of spooky fun and dressing up. Scholars are divided on whether this has pagan or Christian roots, but in recent decades it has returned across the Atlantic to the UK in all its new, colourful American livery.

When I was a kid (admittedly a long time ago) I don't recall seeing pumpkins in the corner shop in late October, and the same goes for trick-or-treating. In the early 1960s I recall learning Chuck Berry's song 'Trick or Treat' and wondering what the hell he was singing about. In any case, at that time of the year we short-trousered, dirty-legged urchins were too busy with our 'penny for the guy' begging in preparation for bonfire night on 5 November. Today, by late September, supermarket shelves are weighed down with pumpkins, heaving with witches' hats, skull masks and black robes (in the aisle next to the mince pies and Christmas puddings), thanks to the attraction of Halloween as represented in Hollywood movies. As for the 'celebratory' burning of Guy Fawkes, the once rigorously held custom of 5 November now spreads nightly from Halloween into December, with many of the participants having little knowledge of its true origin and even less respect for what was once a one-night tradition.

Categories of superstitions

These are usually connected with our ideas of good luck and bad luck. Many people have their own personal rituals; for example, keeping a combination of 'lucky' numbers for entering the lottery. You may have a personal lucky charm, such as a St Christopher medallion, perhaps a horseshoe nailed above your door. A gypsy might sell you a sprig of 'lucky' heather (but not, as we'll discover, if you're in Scotland, where such a talisman means bad luck). You may feel yourself to be totally devoid of superstition, yet still pull that wishbone after Christmas dinner or make a silent wish when a black cat crosses your path (provided you're not Chinese).

Personal superstitions can also involve the interpretation of a range of myths, omens and legends with roots going back to pagan times. These are often stylised and customised over decades of family tradition. Maybe granddad was wearing a blue shirt when he won the football pools back in 1959 – so let's wear something blue when we buy our lottery tickets. That tie you wore at that job interview – the job you actually got – why not wear it for occasions where you're desperate for good luck? Stepped in that heap of dog poo? Is that a lucky omen masquerading as a mental consolation for the fact that everyone except a cloud of flies is avoiding you and you're about to spend an hour scraping Fido's foul emission off your new lucky trainers?

CULTURAL SUPERSTITIONS

These vary enormously all around the world. Often, depending on the national culture in question, what may be a traditional superstition in the west might have a totally opposite interpretation elsewhere. For example, if you possess a pair of lucky gambling trousers in the UK, you'd not be too concerned about the way you put them on. But in Turkey, to put on trousers by standing up is the sign for poverty. Black cats may sometimes be lucky in the USA and parts of Europe, but luck means white cats in the Far East.

Behaviour and manners are often radically different in many nations and are influenced by myth, magic and especially religion. In Greece, it is Tuesday the 13th of the month that is considered unlucky, not Friday the 13th. If you enjoy sushi, be careful with your chopsticks. In Japan, chopsticks should not be stuck upright into food, especially rice. Chopsticks are only stuck upright into rice in the bowl on the altar at a funeral. In the UK and the USA, crossing your fingers encourages good luck. But not in Germany. There the equivalent is '*Daumen drücken*', literally: 'to press your thumbs', and it has a very different connotation – it means you're lying and have no intention of standing by any promise you have made.

RELIGIOUS SUPERSTITIONS

There are an estimated 4,200 religions on planet Earth. Islam, Christianity, Judaism, Hinduism and Buddhism lead the field. Within these faiths, there are dozens of opposing sects and factions. In India alone there are eight dominant religions, and in China, despite the efforts of Chairman Mao and the Chinese Communist Party, religion could not be stamped out, where today there are at least five variations of religious faith. This all adds up to a lot of legends, myths, deities, scriptures, holy books, relics, temples, churches – and superstitions. There's even a more recent western 'religion' known as New Age, which basically believes we're all gods.

Some people can go to church every Sunday throughout their lives and the power of their faith and adherence to the scriptures may obliterate any superstitious habits. Yet a great number of our western superstitions have Christian connections, even though some fundamental branches of Christianity regard these as a satanic aberration. But superstitions are connected to the same needs and desires which preoccupy those with a strong religious faith. Determined atheists and agnostics will imagine they are intellectually removed from what they regard as mythical mumbo-jumbo, yet they may well stand in silent respect at a passing funeral cortège, knock on wood or catch their breath at the sight of a black cat. Islam claims to have banished superstition completely.

I was brought up as a Catholic (and am today in the 'irretrievably lapsed' category), and, during my teenage years in the Merchant Navy, my mother always insisted I travelled with my St Christopher medallion around my neck. In respect of her memory, my wedding ring, bought in 1966, is a St Christopher signet ring. I don't think it stopped the big end blowing in my Ford Sierra on the M1 in 2002 (or subsequent other motoring mishaps), but as an aviophobic with an extreme dread of flying, perhaps I should thank this mythical third- century martyr for every safe take-off and landing. As we'll see, belief in the power of holy objects is one of the broader areas of superstition, which remains the engine which drives many religions.

Omens, old wives' tales and portents

We need here to look at the definitions of three related terms. According to the *Oxford English Dictionary*, the definition of 'omen' tells us it's a noun, an event regarded as a portent of good or evil: e.g. 'the ghost's appearance was an ill omen' or 'a rise in imports might be an omen of recovery'. It has prophetic significance: 'the raven seemed a bird of evil omen.' It comes from the late sixteenth century, from the Latin *ominosus*.

The definition of 'superstition' is again a noun, an excessively credulous belief in and reverence for the supernatural: e.g., 'he dismissed the ghost stories as mere superstition'. It also represents a widely held but irrational belief in supernatural influences, especially as leading to good or bad luck, or a practice based on such a belief: e.g., 'she touched her locket for luck, a superstition she'd had since childhood'. The word comes from Middle English and from Old French or from the Latin *superstitio(n-)*, from super ('over') and stare ('to stand'), perhaps from the notion of 'standing over' something in awe.

A close relative of these terms is the old wives' tale, an epithet indicating a supposed 'truth' which is really a superstition and probably (but not always) untrue and subject to ridicule. This fits the idea of the urban legend, folklore passed on from the old to a younger generation. It doesn't say much for the contemptuous way older, often single, women were regarded in antiquity, and the feminine aspect can be gauged by the fact that most of these tales address traditional female concerns, such as pregnancy, social relations, health, herbalism and nutrition.

In defence of 'old wives' everywhere, it's worth pausing here to examine ten of their 'tales' which are actually true.

Wise old wives – cleverer than you thought . . .

1. Chicken soup and health: if you're suffering from a bad cold, according to Dr Stephen Rennard of the University of Nebraska medical centre in Omaha, chicken soup reduces inflammation as it slows down the activity of white blood cells, relieving some of the symptoms.

2. Childbirth: if a mother experiences a long, strenuous labour, the result is often a baby boy. It appears scientifically correct that we blokes give our mothers far more painful trouble coming into the world than our sisters do. It's something to do with our size and our big heads. In Ireland in 2003 a medical survey revealed that labour complications were more prevalent for women giving birth to boys, with an increased number of emergency caesareans.

3. 'An apple a day keeps the doctor away': this Welsh proverb first appeared in print in 1866. Originally it was in the form of a rhyme: 'Eat an apple on going to bed and you'll keep the doctor from earning his bread.' There's nothing wrong with this – as part of your five-a-day fruit and veg routine, it works. In 2013 a medical survey came to the conclusion that if all the over-fifties in the UK chose to eat that single apple daily, it might stave off or even prevent up to 8500 strokes or heart attacks a year.

4. Chocolate relieves premenstrual cramps: apparently it does, according to a study by the University of Chicago. It's nutritious and one of its antioxidants, anandamide, is an endogenous cannabinoid neurotransmitter, which sends chemical messages between nerve cells (neurons) throughout the nervous system. Like cannabis, this affects brain areas that influence pleasure, memory, thinking, concentration, movement, coordination and sensory and time perception. Anandamide gets its name from the Sanskrit word *ananda*, meaning 'joy', 'bliss', 'delight'. It may calm you down, reducing anxiety. Chocolate is only naughty if you eat too much of it – and don't give it to your dog.

5. Ladies – want to avoid pregnancy? It may spoil that magic moment, but make him take a hot bath. A good hot soak for a bloke can lower that male fertility factor. So if he comes over all amorous, make sure you've paid the gas bill and the boiler's working.

6. Pregnant and experiencing repeated heartburn? The old wives maintained that this guaranteed the arrival of a very hairy baby. Once again, they weren't far wrong. At Johns Hopkins University in 2007 they surveyed this bit of archaic wisdom and discovered that babies born to mothers with excessive heartburn did indeed produce offspring with more than their expected share of hair.

7. Full moon: an old wives' favourite. 'Howling at the moon' sums up the way many people think that earth's satellite affects people. But there's more than a grain of truth here, too. The moon is a powerful astronomical influence not only on the tides but on animals and people. Lunar patterns during a full moon have been shown to have some effect on the birth rate, fertility and our sleep patterns. And although the term 'lunatic' is not politically correct, we can see where it came from.

8. Hair of the dog: if you're a drinker, you'll know all about the horrors of a hangover. And in the head-throbbing morning, if you're not driving, you can indeed alleviate the symptoms with a small measure of what made you drunk the night before. But it's a dangerous exercise – a potentially vicious cycle. The best way to keep the boozy pain at bay is by drinking a pint of water before you go to bed. It works, although you'll make more than a few trips to the bathroom.

9. Cheese for supper and dodgy dreams will follow: this is true for a lot of us. A few pints of Stella to loosen your self-control can mean a *quattro formaggi* pizza on the way home from the pub. Clocking in at about 750 calories on top of the beer, it can do all sorts to your sleep pattern. But some scientists claim that cheese's psychoactive fungal elements can indeed affect your dreams, although not always necessarily in a bad way. The one to look out for, according to a British Cheese Board survey in 2005, might be stilton.

10. Eat some fish – it's good for your brain: I grew up in a fish city – the port of Hull – and fish and chips was on our table every other night. Seems again that the old wives were right. According to a Harvard school of public health study, published in 2006 in the *Journal of the American Medical Association*, pregnant women who ate plenty of fish had babies who did well in tests at six months old, because the omega-three fats in fish are important for optimal development of the brain and nervous system. And if you eat fish three times per week, this reduces by more than one-third the chances of dying from heart disease.

Omens and portents are big bucks

Mankind's age-old entrepreneurial spirit has always meant he can make money from just about anything. If the word 'designer' is attached, and the brand is right, people will willingly empty their wallets. The situation is no different with the paranormal and spiritual market. Touring mediums fill theatres at twenty pounds a ticket. You can buy any number of lucky talismanic products online or from various magazines. Tarot readings are increasingly popular.

I recently tried out a free reading by a famous online psychic and opened up a Pandora's box of daily emails imploring me to pay for stage one of my future knowledge and, as I didn't respond, the ensuing emails began to suggest that something cataclysmic was about to happen, something I should know about, according to my star sign, and that – for a fee – could be revealed. Many people receiving this cyber sales pitch could fall for it and pay dearly. None of this is necessarily bad, unless you are a member of some serious religious sect.

How a person chooses to spend their money is their business. Yet if there were some way of containing fresh air in suitable receptacles and selling it back to a diesel-choking population, there would already be a string of high-street outlets (Air4U?) doing just that. In the UK you can pay as little as £3.99 for a bottle of wine. However, I recently paid £6 for a bottle of water in a Birmingham restaurant. To my generation, the commercial gentrification of humble H_2O remains one of capitalism's craftiest cons, yet in some countries – Germany, for instance – if you raise a toast using water you're wishing bad luck on your drinking friends. Therefore, if you're eating lunch or dinner, push your plate aside for a minute and consider the following slightly tenuous diversion from superstition as an example. (You may think I'm straying from the subject, but there is a point.)

Try to imagine the eighteenth-century annual balance sheet of the entrepreneurial John Hunt of Goswell Street in London. He distributed flyers advertising his services as 'Night man and rubbish-carter'. In Manchester, men making a living in the same business were called 'night mechanics'. They collected human ordure, dug out cess pits and made sure everyone's urine did not go to waste. I suppose at least they didn't need to let their family know when they'd arrived home after a shift – they would have smelled them coming from the top of the street.

The excrement was valuable on the land (and is still big business in parts of China) and the human urine had many more profitable uses. It was used for tanning leather and most launderers preferred it to soap for cleaning and whitening clothes. It was used as a tooth whitener, applied to battle wounds and was important in warfare because of the saltpetre used to make gunpowder. As we expel enough in our lifetime to fill a swimming pool, it seems a shame so much pee is wasted today.

There are a number of superstitions concerning bodily waste but they mainly apply to animal and bird droppings – although in China the darker human faeces are associated with evil, disaster and bad fortune. Robert Boyle (1627–1691), the father of chemistry, told patients to drink a draught of their own issue every morning while it was still warm. Boyle's friend and contemporary was Thomas Willis, England's costliest doctor (although he treated the poor for free), and he had such faith in drinking your own that he recommended to a well-heeled lady that she should imbibe her own warm urine against 'extreme sourness' in her throat. In 2011 it was reported that a surgeon in Beverly Hills practising liposuction had been using his patents' extracted fat as 'lipodiesel' to run his own and his girl-friend's SUV. Because he was breaking state laws on medical waste, he decamped to South America.

One would have thought that there's enough money to be made in plastic surgery to afford the odd tank of diesel.

So what has this malodorous diversion to do with superstition? It's about making money from our humanity. While I am in no way comparing profits gained from superstition and prediction to effluent, the growing astrological lucky charm and prediction markets deal with our cerebral issues, while others have profited from what comes out of the other end.

You may be surprised that there are quite a lot of superstitions attached to just about every human extremity, from your hair down to your toenails. The Greeks and Romans once thought that the gods interfered with bodily functions. If you're superstitious and have money to spare, you can hedge your bets by investing through AstrologicalInvesting.com, where I imagine them to start the day with a superstition: 'Find a penny, pick it up, all the day you'll have good luck'.

According to the entertaining website doubtfulnews.com, specialising in news of 'alt. med/anti-vax, cryptozoology, hauntings, paranormal, UFOs, psychics, superstition and money-making schemes and generally questionable claims':

Despite a few cases in which psychics were sued or prosecuted for alleged fraud, overall the psychic services industry is thriving; it has grown 2.2% from 2009 to 2014 and is projected to grow another 3% in the next four years, according to research firm IBIS World. The $1.9 billion revenue industry consists of astrology, mediumship, palmistry and numerology, among other services.

In some businesses, good luck symbols are aimed at bringing attention back into focus. In the more adventurous corners of the new, commercial hipster world, superstition is often regarded as 'cool'. These symbols supposedly help you to think more carefully, enhancing your corporate life. But once in a while, superstition can give big western businesses more than a few headaches, especially when far away from their homeland comfort zone, facing an unexpectedly united front of superstition, feng shui and numerology.

In China there is a firm belief that humanity is linked to the earth and everything is interconnected to achieve a harmonic balance. If a business fails in China, it can often be blamed on bad feng shui. Architects have to respect the landscape so that new buildings blend in. This ensures the flow of chi, a positive energy. So when the Disney Corporation's chief designer, Tom Morris, faced the challenge of building Mickey's kingdom, Disneyland Hong Kong, on reclaimed land in Penny's Bay, Lantau Island, the ancient art of feng shui was required.

Goofy must have been scratching his head when feng shui, numerology and superstition took over the blueprints. Disney had to incorporate the five elements of feng shui (water, wood, fire, earth and metal) into the site, so you'll see a lot of water at the Hong Kong branch, which opened in 2005. A geomancer had to be employed. Geomancy is divination by means of figures or lines or geographic features. Then the local Hong Kong feng shui experts came on board. The main entrance gate's position was not spiritually pleasing so the Chinese had it moved twelve degrees to maximise a positive flow of chi energy. As each building was completed, a ritual of burning incense was carried out. There was even a superstitious element to the path visitors would walk from the adjoining train station. They had to create a curve in the walkway so that good fortune couldn't easily escape the site. Then there were 'no fire' zones, in which you couldn't build a kitchen.

If all this wasn't enough to have a Californian architect tearing his hair out, along came the numerologists. If you speak Cantonese, you'll realise that the pronunciation of the number four sounds very similar to the word 'death'. It's considered very unlucky, so throughout the park no buildings have a fourth floor. But in Cantonese and Mandarin culture, if you're looking for wealth and prosperity, the number eight is fine. In fact, if you say the number 2238 in Cantonese, it sounds eerily like 'becoming wealthy with ease'. Therefore one of the Disney restaurants is decorated with 2238 lotus blossoms. A hotel ballroom on the site was built to measure 888 square feet. It's hard to say what that old son of fun, Chairman Mao, would have made of all this, but one thing would please him – there's a lot of the colour red at Hong Kong Disneyland – red represents prosperity.

One thing you never give as a gift in China is a clock – it's a bad omen, prefacing a possible funeral. So if you need to know the time at Hong Kong Disneyland, better wear your watch – there are no clocks to be seen. Finally, if a man dons a green hat in Hong Kong it's an admission of adultery, so if you're looking for some Robin Hood-type headgear over there, you'll not find any in Uncle Walt's onsite stores.

Following that diversion to the other side of the world, it's time to examine just how superstitious the British are. I was extremely fortunate in this instance to make contact with Professor Richard Wiseman, of the psychology department at the University of Hertfordshire. Professor Wiseman's work in the area of superstition, luck and the paranormal, and his numerous books, have proved invaluable in my research. I was delighted, therefore, when he generously gave me permission to include here his fascinating 2003 UK superstition survey. Over a decade later, we can only wonder what a current survey might reveal, but these edifying results are extremely interesting.

UK superstition survey

THE RESULTS DESCRIBED ARE BASED ON INFORMATION PROVIDED BY THE 2068 PEOPLE WHO PARTICIPATED IN A NATIONAL SUPERSTITION SURVEY DURING 2003 NATIONAL SCIENCE WEEK.

1. The current levels of superstitious behaviour and beliefs in the UK are surprisingly high, even among those with a scientific background.

Touching wood is the most popular UK superstition, followed by crossing fingers, avoiding ladders, not smashing mirrors, carrying a lucky charm and having superstitious beliefs about the number thirteen.

2. Superstitious people tend to worry about life, have a strong need for control, and have a low tolerance for ambiguity.

3. There has been a significant increase in superstition, possibly as a result of current economic and political uncertainties. This is especially true of people with a high need for control and low tolerance for ambiguity.

4. The Scots top the UK superstition table, followed by the English, the Welsh and Northern Irish.

5. Women are more superstitious than men and young people more than old.

6. The many bizarre personal superstitions collected during the survey illustrate the extent of modern-day superstitious behaviour.

General levels of superstitious behaviour and belief

Respondents were asked to rate the degree to which they were superstitious, and whether they carried out the following superstitious behaviours:

Saying 'fingers crossed' or actually crossing fingers.

Avoiding walking under a ladder because it is associated with bad luck.

Being superstitious about the number thirteen.

Being anxious about breaking a mirror because it is thought to cause bad luck.

Saying 'touch wood' or actually touching or knocking on wood.

Carrying a lucky charm or object.

The results indicate very high levels of superstitious beliefs and behaviour.

Seventy-seven per cent of people indicated that they were at least a little superstitious and/or carried out some form of superstitious behaviour, and 42% indicated that they were very/somewhat superstitious. To help place these figures in perspective, a 1996 Gallup poll reported that 53% of Americans said that they were at least a little superstitious, and only 25% admitted to being very/somewhat superstitious.

People were also asked to indicate if they had a background in science. Interestingly, even 25% of people who indicated that this was the case said that they were very/somewhat superstitious. The rank order and percentages of people endorsing these behaviours and beliefs are shown in the table opposite:

Rank	Superstition	Percentage of people endorsing each superstition
1	Touch wood	74%
2	Fingers crossed	65%
3	Avoiding ladders	50%
4	Smashing mirrors	39%
5	Carrying charm	28%
6	Number thirteen	26%

WHAT SORTS OF PEOPLE ARE SUPERSTITIOUS?

The survey examined the possible relationship between superstitious beliefs and whether people:

worry about life, e.g., do you agree/disagree with the statement: 'I tend to worry about life'?

have a strong need for control, e.g., do you agree/disagree with the statement: 'I get quite anxious when I'm in a situation over which I have no control'?

do not like ambiguity in their lives, e.g., do you agree/disagree with the statement: 'I believe that there is a clear difference between right and wrong'?

The results were striking. People who tend to worry about life are far more superstitious than others – 50% of worriers were very/somewhat superstitious, compared to just 24% of non-worriers. People who have a strong need for control in their lives are far more superstitious than others – 42% of people indicating high need for control were very/somewhat superstitious, compared to just 22% of people indicating low need for control. People who have a low tolerance for ambiguity are far more superstitious than those with a high tolerance – 38% of those with low tolerance were very/somewhat superstitious compared to just 30% of those with high tolerance.

Changes in superstition

The survey examined whether economic and political uncertainties may have caused people to become more superstitious. The results suggest that this is indeed the case.

Eighteen per cent of people indicated that they have felt much/slightly more anxious over the past month when they carried out superstitious behaviour reputed to bring bad luck (e.g., walking under a ladder).

Fifteen per cent of people indicated that they have carried out superstitious behaviour meant to create good luck much/slightly more frequently over the past month (e.g., carrying a lucky charm). Of these, the vast majority were those who described themselves as worrying about life, having a high need for control, a low tolerance for ambiguity and being superstitious. For example, 91% of the people who said that they had become more anxious over the past month when breaking superstitions expressed a strong need for control in their lives. Likewise, 92% of those who had increased their superstitious rituals had a low tolerance for ambiguity.

Regional differences

The Scots top the superstition table, with 46% saying that they are very/somewhat superstitious, compared to 42% of the English, 41% of the Welsh and just 40% of the Northern Irish. Crossing fingers is especially popular in Scotland (72% vs UK national average of 65%). Avoiding ladders is especially popular in Wales (57% vs UK national average of 50%). Associating broken mirrors with bad luck is especially popular in Northern Ireland (46% vs UK national average of 39%). Touching wood is especially popular in England (84% vs UK national average of 74%).

Gender and age differences

Women are significantly more superstitious than men – 51% of women said that they were very/somewhat superstitious, compared to just 29% of men. When it came to individual superstitions, far more women than men cross their fingers (75% of women vs 50% of men), and touch wood (83% of women vs 61% of men).

These findings replicate other research concerned with belief and gender, and may be due to women having lower self-esteem and less perceived control over their lives than men.

People become less superstitious as they age – 59% of people aged between eleven and fifteen said they were superstitious, compared to 44% of people aged between thirty-one and forty and just 35% of the over-fifties. These findings do not suggest that superstitious behaviour and beliefs will be consigned to the past. Instead, they are strongly held by the younger members of society.

Personal superstitions

The survey also asked people about their personal superstitions. Over 500 people responded (approximately 25% of all respondents), and many people described how they wore lucky clothes to exams and interviews, used their lucky numbers when choosing lottery numbers and saluted magpies. Some of the more unusual superstitious behaviours and beliefs were:

I always avoid staying in the bathroom once the toilet has been flushed.

I always draw a smiley face in a free pint of Guinness.

I always leave a house by the same door by which I entered.

I never have the volume on my car stereo set to volume thirteen.

When a clock has matching numbers, such as 12:12, I have to say 'one-two-one-two' out loud.

Whenever I see a hearse, I touch my collar until I see a bird.

This range of behaviour supports the notion that new superstitions are constantly developing and evolving, and that there is no reason to expect superstition to decline in the near future.

The survey questions and possible response options are available online at www.luckfactor.co.uk/survey. This website will remain active and continue to collect additional data. My thanks to Dr Jed Everitt, Dr Caroline Watt and Dr Emma Greening for their help in designing and running the survey. I would also like to thank the British Association for the Advancement of Science for supporting and helping to promote the project.

Superstitions: do they work?

I've done it myself – instructed an actor or musician friend as they're about to go on stage, 'Break a leg', or told them that I've got my fingers crossed. Doing so, am I actually bringing them some luck? The connections between superstition and luck are found in cultures around the world. They often stray into a positive area of psychology in which research has shown that, for example, a good luck charm in certain situations may indeed improve performance. The charm, whatever artefact it may be, does not necessarily have to be linked to the event.

In Germany, a team of psychologists at the University of Köln carried out experiments where they set tasks involving motor skills and memory. This project studied the effect of behaviour and 'object superstitions' – which rely on good luck charms – among college students. In the initial experiment students were given a ball to putt on a golf course. Those who were quietly told that theirs was 'a lucky ball' out-performed the others.

Another experiment featured a cube containing tiny balls and a slab with holes. The goal was to get as many balls in the holes as quickly as possible. The students she were told by the controller that he was 'crossing his fingers' for them did better than the others.

In the final two experiments, each participant brought their own lucky charm, but not everyone was allowed to keep them for a test that followed. It included an anagram and a memory exam. Surprisingly, the students still in possession of their charms had better results than those whose charms had been withdrawn. In a survey of the participants' attitudes, researchers found that those with lucky charms felt more confident. In effect, superstition had boosted their confidence. The university's report on the experiments concluded that 'Engaging in superstitious thoughts and behaviours may be one way to reach one's top level of performance.'

A respected physician and practising Buddhist for more than twenty years, Dr Alex Lickerman is the author of the successful and stimulating book *The Undefeated Mind*.

In his blog, *Happiness in this World* at www.psychologytoday.com he comments on the results of the University of Köln experiment:

Superstitions are typically seen as inconsequential creations of irrational minds. Nevertheless, many people rely on superstitious thoughts and practices in their daily routines in order to gain good luck. To date, little is known about the consequences and potential benefits of such superstitions . . . A belief in a force external to ourselves that can be invoked to help us may not be merely comforting, then. It may be a powerful psychological lever we can pull to access forces within ourselves that actually affect our ability to achieve what we want – even if our belief is incorrect.'

When we decide we've done all we can in a tight situation and we're feeling vulnerable, that's often the time when superstitions seem attractive. It's well known that US soldiers, like most soldiers around the world, have their odd superstitions. When you're in battle, anything you can hang onto for luck is worth considering. Apparently soldiers in Afghanistan took against uttering what they named the '"A" word' – 'apricots'. No one was entirely sure why, but they wouldn't go near the fruit or eat them. They thought they brought bad luck. However, further research throws a little light on this. The superstition allegedly started in WWII, when marines found that every tank that had apricots on board inevitably broke down. A similar superstition now also applies to a brand of candy, Charms.

You unearth superstitions in the most unlikely places. One of the greatest of American authors and broadcasters, Louis 'Studs' Terkel (1912–2008), conducted over 5000 radio interviews over forty-six years with ordinary Americans. His book, *The Good War*, won a Pulitzer Prize. In his book about the depression, *Hard Times*, among the many people he interviewed was the social realist painter from Virginia, Robert Gwathmey (1903–1988). In an age when smoking was common, Gwathmey's home town Richmond was the tobacco capital of the USA. But despite the hold of the cigarette on America, the big depression hit Virginia, too. Gwathmey said that many local people committed suicide and even those who survived, often very religious people, became very superstitious. He recalled that people began sitting around the Ouija board asking if their bank was about to become insolvent.

Flights of fancy

If black boxes survive air crashes, why don't they make the whole plane out of that stuff?'

George Carlin (1937–2008)

Late one January night in 2011, after boarding a flight from Prague to East Midlands airport, when the Czech temperature was 20 below, as we sat on the runway the pilot announced over the speakers, 'I have a light on my console here that says there's something not working with the forward landing wheel. Could be iced up . . . we're not sure. We'll await an engineer's inspection before taking off.'

Half a nail-biting hour passed with no inspection, and then the pilot announced glibly, 'Oh, that light on my console's gone out now. So we can take off.'

Terrific!

Don't bother to see if that landing wheel's kaput! Let's go anyway! Landing at East Midlands was the biggest relief ever. Yet why worry, when a 2006 Harvard study found the odds of dying in a plane crash to be one in eleven million? The odds of being involved in a shark attack are one in 3.1 million, and the odds of dying in a car accident are one in 5000. Therefore I ought to be rigid with fear every time I drive the car but those odds never cross my mind. As for sharks, I've made a firm decision to stay out of their way.

I may not be alone in this. I hate flying. Everything about flying brings out that latent irrationality that I like to think is not part of my psyche. Unfortunately, in the twenty-first century, if you need to go to any major world city in any country other than your own, it's a plane journey. In the good old days, you would book a steamer to New York and travel in relaxed style for five days or more with a comfortable cabin, good food and little, if any, fear of dying in peacetime. Even if the ship did a *Titanic* or a *Lusitania*, there could be an outside chance of a seat in a lifeboat and you could dine out on the story for years. None of this is possible in a 747.

Today, if you had the time to spare, you could travel from Manchester to Berlin by train. The trouble with that is the cost. On Britain's Cosa Nostra-run, private rip-off railways it is cheaper to fly to Berlin than book a standard-class, single ticket to Euston from Manchester. And if you did take the train to Berlin, there'd be maybe two more train journeys across Europe.

Otherwise, the train is quite civilised and totally unlike air travel, with the sheer tedium of getting through the airport made worse thanks to the recurring insanity of unknown distant entities who want to kill me with a bomb or a hijack simply because I don't worship their god. And then there is the aircraft itself. Every time I see an airliner take-off or land it gives me the shivers. All that flimsy pressurised metal, tons of it, shouldn't be in the air. There's the horror when the wheels leave the tarmac and I'm grinding my teeth into powder. Then comes turbulence and finally it feels like someone is forcing knitting needles into your ears as you descend. Those landing wheels never look strong enough to stand that impact on the tarmac. And now you can't even smoke a soothing cigarette before the potential crash.

Is it any wonder, then, that air travel is burdened with so many rituals and superstitions? I refuse to indulge in any because, if your number's up and a plane crashes, you're dead. Forget all the arm-waving semaphore of the well-meaning flight attendants, telling us where the exits and the oxygen masks are. With that safety belt locked you're imprisoned in a hypothetical metal coffin 35,000 feet above unforgiving terra firma.

However, there are thousands of regular air travellers for whom good luck, life-enhancing rituals and superstitions are as much a part of the journey as checking-in luggage. Yet even before anyone boards a plane, there's some funny administration stuff going on which further dents an aerophobic's confidence. Many airlines are wary of scheduling a flight number thirteen. And there's that question lots of pilots, air crew and passengers find interesting – does the airport have a gate 13? We seem to have them in the UK at Heathrow and Gatwick, but you'll not find gate thirteens at places such as LaGuardia (although gate fourteen is also missing), Tampa, Sarasota-Bradenton, Cleveland, and JFK (terminals three, five, seven, and eight – although seven has an 11A so the numbers end on twelve).

Some airlines dismiss irrationality, but only just. In Europe, Germany's Lufthansa uses a gate thirteen and has a daily flight number LF-013 between Hamburg and Frankfurt. That's all very sensible, but even the no-nonsense Germans are wary of a bit of superstition. When it comes to seating on their planes, there's no row thirteen; it goes straight to fourteen and, if you're flying with them to Italy or Brazil, you'll not find a row seventeen, because in those countries the unlucky number is seventeen.

If you are superstitious about those two numbers, your fears would have been confirmed in November 1987 when Continental Airlines flight 1713 crashed while taking off in a snowstorm from Denver, Colorado. Other companies follow Lufthansa's example in avoiding a row 13, such as Continental Airlines, Iberia, Ryanair and Air France. Overall, approximately 25% of the world's airlines have no seating row thirteen on their planes.

In some respects, the airline industry, like any other commercial travel organisation (trains, buses, ship), has no choice but to rely on all numbers. How would you do a timetable otherwise, after all? Yet when some numbers come into unwelcome prominence, they have to be dealt with. American Airlines Flight 191 crashed in Chicago on 25 May 1979, killing 258 passengers and thirteen crew plus two people on the ground. This was the deadliest aviation accident in the USA, hence another unusable flight number.

You may not find many flight 911s since the 2001 attack on 9/11. On that fateful day, other flight numbers would be pulled after American Airlines eleven, United Airlines 175, American Airlines seventy-seven, and United Airlines ninety-three were all victims of the murderers.

And even when all the passengers and crew survive a disaster, as when heroic pilot Chesley Sullenberger landed his disabled plane on New York's Hudson River in 2009, US Airways retired its flight 1549 designation.

Yet avoiding these numbers is not totally down to superstition; this is the kind of respect we would expect from decent human beings. As for those ordinary cases in which there is a hint of old-fashioned superstition, we can regard corporate behaviour in marketing terms as a bit of thoughtful customer care. If only a small percentage of your customers are superstitious, it's still good business to recognise the fact and keep them happy and all the fearless flyers can feel superior.

Taking superstition face on is Finnair's flight 666 that flies with no qualms on Friday the 13th. From Copenhagen to Helsinki, taking off on Black Friday, ought to be the unluckiest flight ever, but it's fine. You can't keep those Vikings down. This is a superstitious person's dream ticket; the biblical number of Beelzebub, 666, and you're flying to a destination with the airport code HEL.

So what can you do to stay lucky and alive in the air? Here are some of the most popular solutions.

- Many people, as they're boarding the plane, like to lean over and touch or pat the fuselage. If you're bold and athletic enough and no one stops you, you might try and kiss the plane.
- Some passengers, according to flight crews, are known to perform a few little 'good luck' dance steps before entering the plane.
- There is a good luck tradition followed by construction workers at airports who have been known to put a cedar tree on top of a completed control tower. According to Native American tradition, the cedar stands for protection, repelling negative energy, encouraging healing, purification, money and the warding away of evil spirits. Middle East Airlines, the flag-carrier of Lebanon, first flew in 1945. The cedar tree in the airline's livery is the symbol of Lebanon and some decades ago one was presented to Heathrow as a goodwill gesture by MEA and can still be seen growing outside the terminal.
- Some people wear the same lucky shirts or suits on each flight.
- Pilots often carry pictures of their wife and children tucked into their cap.
- If a pilot wants to comment on good weather conditions, he should address only the sun but not the general weather itself.
- If you're a pilot you should never have a photograph of yourself taken in front of your plane prior to a flight.
- Some pilots ritually smoke half a cigarette before the flight and smoke the other half once it's over. If they don't smoke, they might eat half a sandwich and finish it when they land.
- There are still pilots who are known to take a pee on the aircraft wheel in a primeval way before flight to show the plane who's boss.
- It is bad luck before a flight to point at the sky. As on ships, whistling is discouraged.
- Some people pray before a flight but it's not advisable to let other passengers see you do it.
- American gamblers who like lucky numbers like the idea of flying with Southwest Airlines flight 711 from San Antonio to Las Vegas as apparently

711 is a lucky number. It is also one of the 'angel numbers'. Angel number 711 is regarded as a powerful, spiritual messenger from the spiritual realms.

- Alaska Airlines, which flies many Canadians from Las Vegas, gave its flight to Bellingham, Washington, the number 649 (Canada's lottery is called Lotto 6/49).
- Many fliers travel with a talisman or good luck charm, anything from a lucky piece of jewellery or worry beads to a teddy bear.
- Spotting a rainbow is a good omen.
- Some passengers (and even pilots) like to listen to the same music every trip – sometimes one particular song for taking off and another for landing.
- It is common for a percentage of passengers to burst into a round of applause when the plane finally lands. The crew and other passengers are unimpressed and think we're mad.
- Some flight attendants think that if the first passenger to board the plane is a man then everything will be OK.
- If a steward accidentally spills drink on a flight they believe this means luck in the form of money.

The above is not an exhaustive list and you probably have your own rituals. But for me – despite avoiding superstition – flying remains a terror.

Top superstitions

Walking under ladders, crossing fingers, avoiding breaking mirrors, touching wood and black cats (and a few others) are more or less global superstitions. A whole later section of this work will be devoted to the tricky area of origins.

It's worth mentioning, too, that in a large country like the USA, the same superstition often has variations depending upon which state it occurs in and the dominant ethnic heritage of the area. For example, African Americans have many superstitions of their own, some brought from Africa in the age of slavery, others adapted from European folklore. As we would expect, Native American superstitions are complex and numerous, and with their own ancient origins, blend in with myths, legends and deep spirituality. They often stand outside the mainstream.

Superstitious Europe

Attempting to present any kind of comprehensive overview of superstitions across Europe is like trying to round up several flocks of wayward, uncooperative sheep with a tired and disinterested dachshund. There are dozens of sources for these superstitions. Often these are additional features on various national tourist agency sites. Such information takes the form of what to do in particular situations. For example, they may warn you against toasting a dinner party in Germany with a glass of water or answer the conundrum, why is that cheerful Turkish gentleman scratching his arse as he speaks? Many patriotic bloggers also like to highlight their country's idiosyncrasies by enlightening potential visitors about their nation's wilder beliefs and rituals.

Even when one narrows a batch of superstitions down to one country, it becomes clear that versions of any one particular practice can vary from region to region, village to village, even family to family. Therefore this round-up of Europe, from France across to Russia via Scandinavia and down through the Balkans to Turkey and Greece, only skims the surface of a deep well of peculiar beliefs. As to how current some of these are, perhaps this can only be established by visiting the territory in question. Yet if nothing else, these are an entertaining window on a bizarre landscape of apparent irrationality which remains a wider cultural domain that we all still inhabit, despite our imagined sophistication.

FRANCE

The French have some original and colourful superstitions. For example, their sailors have a red pom-pom on their jaunty berets and touch the pom-pom for good luck. No doubt the debonair Gallic matelot doesn't mind this at all. Like many other western nations, the French believe that stepping in dog poo is good luck, provided it's with your left foot.

There's a grim tradition concerning bread. In medieval times, when bakers made bread for an executioner, the loaf for the man with the axe (or the guillotine) was placed upside down on the table, so that everyone knew it was exclusively his.

Today, superstition dictates that placing a loaf of bread upside down on the table is regarded as an omen of bad luck.

Belgium

Belgium is a bit of a melting pot when it comes to superstitions. It could be regarded as a borderland between Latin Europe and the more dominant German culture.

Belgium has two distinct communities with their own language. Forty-one percent of Belgians are the French-speaking Walloons; the other 59% are Flemish, who speak Dutch. There is also a minority of German speakers. Expect some odd superstitions, then, such as if your derrière is itching, you'll soon be eating a pie. Whistling is good luck, because as well as possibly bringing money, it could also land you a lover; better still, if it's a man, he might be wealthy. On New Year's Eve, when you've finished eating, it's good to pick up a plate and place a coin beneath it for good luck. Make sure you're well insulated if you go out to pick some poppies. Picking these flowers in Belgium is said to cause lightning.

No doubt some house-proud Wallonians would dispute this, but one of their superstitions claims that when you're sweeping up, you shouldn't brush the dirt out of the building, as you could be sweeping your luck away . . . in which case, thank heavens for the hoover.

An old Belgian belief refers to childbirth – if a child is born with the placenta on its head he or she will grow up lucky. However, once your baby's grown up and it's time to dispose of the cradle, whatever you do, don't throw it out. All manner of bad events could be the result.

Repairing a piece of white clothing? Don't use black thread – that signifies death (although any seamstress or tailor doing this would soon be out of a job . . .).

Netherlands

We usually feel a bit ragged on New Year's Day, but there's a Dutch superstition that suggests that, whatever you're doing on the first day of the year, you'll end up doing it all year long. Another Dutch new year belief concerns the hair colour of the first visitor you have to your home on that day. If they're dark-haired, that's good. Blonde? Bad luck.

If you're having a dinner party in Holland, don't start a sing-song around the table. Apparently, that's tantamount to asking the devil for your meal.

You can cut a lock of your hair in Holland, and set fire to it. If it burns brightly for longer than expected, you'll live past seventy. If it burns shortly, well, you get the picture . . . and if the church bells are ringing and you happen to be pulling a silly expression in the mirror, stop it, or you'll stay like that.

We're already familiar in other lands with the significance of robins, crows and magpies, but the Dutch expect good luck if they spot a pair of swallows or two storks. No doubt that the Netherlands, with such large areas of wet flatlands, will be popular with large, long-legged, long-necked wading birds.

The Dutch, like the rest of us, also knock three times on wood. Another popular belief is that if you know a sick person and attach a piece of cloth to a special tree, known as a 'fever' tree, this will make the fever vanish. This has a connection to St Willibrord (658–739), known in the Netherlands, Belgium and Luxembourg as the Apostle to the Frisians. He became the first bishop of Utrecht and died at Echternach, Luxembourg. On Whit Tuesday each year, an enormous dancing procession is held in Echternach, which is a major tourist event.

GERMANY

Germany's a superstition wonderland, but perhaps not if you're an elderly woman. It may come across as a piece of Teutonic misogyny but Germany has a couple of odd beliefs related to old ladies. They appear to be regarded as evil. Whatever one does, don't walk between two of them on the road – that's very bad luck.

You arrive at the pub, look around and see where your friends are sitting. Do you wave? No way. You knock on the table. This is known as 'knocking on the *stammtisch*'.

Traditionally, the *stammtisch*, the table used by the pub regulars, was made of oak. Legend has it that Satan can't touch oak, as it's considered to be a holy tree, and to prove you weren't Beelzebub, you gave it a knock. No one wants a devil at the bar. (Unless he's going to get a round in.)

So, the wedding is over, and before you can enjoy your honeymoon, the German tradition of wedding stockings requires the happy couple to sit down on the marriage bed. The bridesmaids and the best man (or men) have to turn their backs on the bride and groom, then remove their socks and stockings and throw them to hopefully land in the bride and groom's faces. Whoever's (hopefully washed) hosiery hits the happy couple first will be the next to marry. At a housewarming party, it is traditional to give a gift of bread and salt to ensure your new hosts will never be hungry in their new home. Then there's theatrical spitting. We know about the English and American traditions for Thespians, such as 'break a leg' and not mentioning 'the Scottish play'. However, once they're in costume, Germans spit on each other's left shoulders. If you're averse to dredging up some gelatinous phlegm, the alternative is to exclaim 'Toi Toi Toi!' Apparently, way back the devil did a dodgy deal with a knife smith, so to give a household a present of knives is tantamount to wishing them injury and death. Chances are they'll already have all the cutlery they need, but it's OK to give them a knife token. As you would expect in a civilised society, there are rules about disposing of animal remains. But in Germany, if your dog expires, there's an old superstition which maintains that if you bury Fido under your front doorstep, then his canine ghost will forever protect your house. Lucky coins and a watery toast: this seems to be universally popular. If you've bought someone a gift of a new wallet or purse, always ensure there's a coin in it so that they'll never be poor. In Germany, you should never toast anyone, at a wedding or any other occasion, with plain water. This sinister superstition translates as wishing death on friends.

POLAND

Poles knock on wood and many of their other superstitions are also more or less identical to those in the UK and the USA.

However, when it comes to marriage, the day before the wedding the bride should put her shoes on the window sill to guarantee good weather for the big day. The bride's bouquet should not contain roses as thorns symbolise a cut to the heart. There should be money placed in the bride's shoes to assure wealth. There's an old belief that if the bride wants to rule in the forthcoming life of bliss, she should save a tiny patch of the material from her dress and drop it onto the groom's shoes as they are kissing in front of the altar. At that moment, she'll gain dominant domestic power for the future.

The good old chimney sweep, where would we be without him? If the Poles see one, they must grab a button on their clothes for good luck. Want more good luck? Blow on your fingers.

It's probably something many would like to do, but Poles give students good luck by kicking them as they enter the examination room.

Ladies – if you're in Poland and wish to avoid bad luck don't put your handbag on the floor (you'll lose your money) or arrange your wedding in the month of May. It's bad luck if a woman is the first person to enter your house at Christmas. (It's a good omen if a man is the first to cross the threshold.) At your Christmas Eve supper, you must sample each of the traditional twelve dishes. The more you eat, the more pleasure you'll store up for the year ahead.

RUSSIA

Russia may not be part of the European Union, but Russia west of the Urals considers itself part of Europe and they never miss the Eurovision Song Contest. The Levada Centre is a Russian independent, non-governmental polling and sociological research organisation. It is named after founder Yuri Levada, the first Russian professor of sociology.

It was reported in the *Moscow Times* on 19 March 2013 that the Levada Centre had carried out a survey which had revealed that, since 2000, although over half the population believed in God, Russian superstitious beliefs in things like omens, prophetic dreams and astrology had declined. Fifty-two per cent of respondents surveyed said they believed in prophetic dreams, compared to 57% in 2000. Belief in omens was 43% compared to 51% in 2000. Only 28 percent of respondents believed astrological predictions, compared to 33% in 2000, when 31% of Russians believed that aliens occasionally visited earth. That figure dropped to 26%. The breakdown showed that Moscow residents are more likely to expect aliens, with 41%.

In some ways this poll might seem surprising, because one might expect that figures would be higher following seven decades of enforced anti-religious, nuts-and-bolts Soviet realism. Yet Russians have dramatically changed their views, as

Lavada's poll on the popularity of Stalin demonstrates at www.levada.ru/eng/stalin. A Levada survey from late 2006 found that 47% of Russians viewed Stalin as a positive figure and only 29% as a negative one.

Russia is a massive country and, as one goes further east, the ethnic diversity reveals many cultures, religious beliefs and rituals. The peoples of Chechnya or Siberia are radically different in this respect to the stock image westerners have of the Russians of Moscow and St Petersburg. Many Russian superstitions about salt, whistling, shaking hands over a threshold, knocking on wood or sitting at a corner table echo those in the nearby states which were once part of the Soviet Union. Yet there are still some home-grown peculiarities.

For birthdays and celebrations, we all know that a bouquet of flowers is always well received. However, in Russia, make sure they're filled with an odd number of flowers, because Russians will tell you that bouquets with an even number of flowers are for funerals. Spitting over your shoulder for luck avoids a curse. Those Russians who don't always follow the universal knock-on-wood might spit three times over their left shoulder (or do both). As the unsavoury act of spitting becomes less acceptable, you can always substitute this by making the spitting sound 'fu-fu-fu'.

It gets very cold in Russia, so it makes sense never to sit down directly on cold ground or any icy surface, but it also apparently makes you infertile, especially if you're a young woman.

It may be your friend or relative's birthday tomorrow or next week, but don't ever wish them 'Happy birthday' before the actual day – that's bad luck.

In a country where many people have similar names, such as Vladimir, Dimitri, Ivan, Svetlana, Masha or Natasha, it's nice to know that if you meet someone with the same first name then that's a good omen. You could find yourself in a meeting with two people of the same name – if so, make a secret wish and keep it to yourself.

Drinking alcohol in Russia is accompanied by many small rituals. One rule is that it's bad form once you've opened a bottle of vodka not to empty it. Regarding empty bottles, be they vodka or wine, there's a strong, 200-year-old superstition about these. You must always put your empties on the floor. There's a French connection here. Back in 1814, no hostile army had reached Paris in 400 years, yet the Cossacks drove the invading army of Napoleon Bonaparte all the way back to France. Initially, Parisians found the Cossacks terrifying. The Russians noisily occupied restaurants and hammered on the tables yelling '*Bystro!*' which is the Russian word for 'quickly'. Since then certain smaller restaurants have become known as 'bistros', although many French linguists will challenge this origin. The hard-drinking Cossacks soon realised that Parisian restaurateurs charged customers per empty bottle left on the table rather than per bottle ordered. An easy way around this was to hide the empties under the table. Upon the Russian army's return home, they took the custom with them.

AUSTRIA

Some of Germany's superstitions can be found in her neighbour's home, too, but the Austrians have a few peculiarities of their own.

If you wake up after having dreams, don't start telling your partner about them before you've had a glass of water. It's bad luck. Over on the Atlantic coast the Portuguese always believe that you must enter or leave a building with your right foot, and the same applies in Austria. If your luck has truly left you and you need some Austrian good fortune, slice up some raw garlic, mix it with a pot of yogurt and down the lot. (You'll be lucky if you don't throw up . . .)

The Austrians are also superstitious about bragging. If you're pretty good at what you do or a great success in any endeavour, don't talk yourself up. It's bad form.

When the new moon comes out, don't stare at it too long because you might sneeze. Result? You guessed it – bad luck. Finally, don't sneeze before you've started your breakfast.

CZECH REPUBLIC

The Czechs are careful how they slice their apples. You need to cut horizontally through the core for good luck. If the seeds are revealed to form a five-pointed star, that could mean death. Maybe an apple a day in Prague doesn't keep the doctor away, after all. If your chickens lay eggs on Christmas Day, that's good news and it's an auspicious day to bake bread.

If you're at a dinner table and realise you've forgotten an appointment, ignore the clock and don't leave early – you could be dead the following year.

Czech beer is some of Europe's finest but you need to treat it with respect. Never refill your glass with a different brew. Always use a fresh glass. And once you've downed a few Pilsners, you can attract good luck by throwing a shoe over your shoulder (but watch out if your mate's standing behind you). Czechs see good luck in breaking glasses and a newly married bride will smash a plate – it's her husband's job to brush up the mess and they should hang on to a couple of shards for good luck. Spiders are lucky if they choose to crawl around your house, and don't get all romantic by writing a love letter on Christmas Eve – Santa might bring you bad luck.

SLOVAKIA

Easter in Slovakia sees an odd rural superstition in villages involving young men and women. The lads pretend to hit the girls, then throw water at them. The man then receives a gift from the damp girl, a decorated egg and a ribbon, or maybe some loose change and a handful of sweets.

There's a touch of *The Wicker Man* at the end of a Slovakian winter. The Slavic goddess of death, Morena (or Morana), is the stuff of nightmares. Burning or drowning a straw effigy of Morena to celebrate the end of winter is a folk custom that survives in Slovakia, Poland and the Czech Republic. It represents victory over death, the end of the dark days of winter and a welcoming of the spring rebirth. The usual regard for spiders insists that they're lucky to have around, but it helps your good fortune to carefully pick them up and put them outside.

At Christmas, the Slovak tradition is to put fish scales under dinner plates for good luck.

ITALY

As elsewhere, Italians see a bird entering your house as bad luck, although a cat sneezing is the opposite. In a country which has the HQ of the Catholic Church, there are plenty of nuns around and seeing one of the sisters is lucky, providing you touch something metal to preserve the good fortune. Similar to knocking on wood, this practice, which is known as *tocca ferro*, suggests you touch iron if you think that something bad is going to occur. There's a regional variation where Italian men, protecting their vital assets, may tap their testicles in a routine known as *tocca palle*. (As most women elsewhere will probably testify, this is hardly a superstition with most men – just an embarrassing habit.)

If an Italian is unmarried, they should steer clear of anyone sweeping up who is wielding a broom, because if the brush touches their feet, they'll never get married or be swept off their feet. Another way to ward off bad luck is *le corna* – the sign of the horns. Make a fist and then unfurl only your index and little fingers to point them at the ground . . . you might look like an LA gangsta rapper but at least you'll be lucky.

SPAIN

Spain's unlucky day is Tuesday the 13th. A legend has it that this day was also the one when everyone started speaking in unintelligible tongues on the Tower of Babel.

Spaniards have their version of an old WWI superstition – the 'third light'. It is considered unlucky to take a third light, that is, to be the third person to light a cigarette from the same match or lighter. This superstition may have originated among soldiers in the trenches of WWI when a sniper might see the first light, take aim on the second and fire on the third.

Never ask someone to pass you the salt – it must first be placed on the table for you to pick it up.

It must get smoky in some Spanish dwellings, as chimneys are supposed to be capped to keep the devil from slithering down your flue.

If you see a cricket – or, better still, hear one – that's a good omen, but if you're moving house, leave your old sweeping brush behind and buy a new one.

PORTUGAL

The Portuguese always believe that you must enter or leave a building leading with your right foot because your left is unlucky. It's also bad luck to leave your hat on a bed. The superstition about your ears burning if someone talks about you is narrowed down to heat in your left ear, signifying that someone is talking about you in an uncomplimentary fashion.

There could be a widow about to get married if the sun shines during a rainstorm.

Don't worry about losing your co-ordination when you've had a few – if you spill wine on the table in Portugal, that's going to be a happy house. But don't walk backwards – that's the way Lucifer perambulates.

ICELAND

With its volcanic landscape and heritage of sagas and Norse myths, this is undoubtedly a land of superstitions. One says that if you spot a cow licking a tree, expect it to rain. And rain is good if you're moving house, because doing so on a rainy day is bound to bring you good luck in your new home.

Here's a truly odd one; if you're knitting a scarf or a new sweater, don't get your needles out on the doorstep in late winter. Knitting on your doorstep will only lengthen that already very cold season (why you'd want to sit on your doorstep knitting in an Icelandic winter is a mystery.)

It's Sunday morning and, just before breakfast, you sneeze three times – that's good, because you might have some money coming in before the week is out.

Understandably, considering Iceland's geographic location, much of their superstition revolves around the weather. For example, if during late autumn you see an Icelandic sheep grinding its teeth, then you might be in for a storm. Cows and sheep figure largely, so look out for the colour of a calf born during winter – if the little bovine babe is white, then the winter's about to get even worse.

It's worth mentioning that, like the Danes with their *nisse* (little people) and trolls, over half of Iceland's population believe they share the island with a hidden population of elves known as the Huldufólk, as well as ghosts and dwarves. Currently, roads and pathways are still subject to alteration if local government planners haven't taken Huldufólk rights of way into consideration.

NORWAY

Norwegians keep an eye on their frozen lakes and waterways on May Day because – as obvious as it seems – if they're thawing slowly, this promises a late spring; sound common sense.

Traditional Norwegian risgrøt – rice porridge – is known as 'Christmas porridge'. It's eaten at lunch during the day on Christmas Eve. White rice is cooked in milk for nearly an hour with salt added and perhaps sugar with a dash of vanilla. The kind Norse folk leave a bowl of this delicacy outside their front door for the trolls (these being not the big scary ones lurking under bridges but cute, elderly, little characters who live in your barn).

If the sun is out, try not to whistle in its direction or you'll have rain on the way. If you say 'Tvi, tvi' to someone, you're wishing them good luck. This is an odd superstition inasmuch as 'Tvi, tvi' was originally a curse, but the idea is that if you're already cursed in a nice way, no one else can curse you any further and the devil with leave you alone. 'Tvi, tvi' also doubles in Norway for 'break a leg' in theatres.

Like the Icelanders, the Norwegians have a superstition about knitting too. A girl shouldn't knit her boyfriend a sweater because this means he might leave her.

Norwegians with an interest in meteorology keep a keen eye on the rowan trees. If the trees are heavy with berries that year, that promises a lighter snowfall for the winter. This is because the good old rowan shouldn't have to carry more weight than a good crop of berries.

SWEDEN

Small arthropods belonging to the subclass Acari, mites are good luck in Sweden. As to which class of this little creepy-crawly brings luck – perhaps the red one, *Tetranychidae sp*, it's hard to say. But if you spot one on its own (not two or three), then good luck is on the way.

Again, Friday the 13th is a bad day in Sweden and not a good day to step on cracks in the pavement.

Sneezing signifies that someone, somewhere, who doesn't like you has mentioned your name, so to prevent this having a bad effect, you simply have to say '*Prosit!*'

When Swedes knock on wood they exclaim '*peppar, peppar ta i trä*' which translates as 'pepper, pepper, touch wood'. Other nations regard walking under ladders as plain bad luck but the Swedish version of the superstition comes with a precise time limit – three weeks. Gypsies may try selling us bunches of 'lucky' heather but they'd register no sales in Sweden, where this attractive plant means death.

FINLAND

Finland, lovely Finland, country of many islands, trees and odd superstitions.

The evening of 23 June, St John's Eve, is the eve of celebration before the feast day of St John the Baptist. This roughly coincides with another sacred Scandinavian festival, Midsummer's Eve (It was called in the past *Ukon juhla*, Ukko's celebration, after the Finnish god Ukko, until the Christians came along). Bonfires are lit. Single women collect seven different flowers and place them under their pillow to dream of whichever lucky beau they might marry.

Don't kill spiders in Finland – as elsewhere, this brings bad luck. If you've been reading a book, don't leave it open laid upside down because all the knowledge in it might vanish. If you've a loose thread on your clothes or a tickly nose, someone is thinking of you.

Heaven help you if you have a bad cold because four sneezes in a row works this way: sneeze number one, good. Number two, bad, number three, wealth, number four, illness (although by then you'd have realised you were off colour).

There are a couple of odd superstitions which are obviously not as ancient as some in the region. One is to do with red cars. Apparently, once you've seen a hundred, the number plate of the last one contains the initials of your future partner. There are also some superstitious angles to drinking frothy coffee in Finland. Look out for a bubble drifting toward you, because you're due for some money. If it moves away, forget it.

DENMARK

Cold winters and long dark nights make for plenty of superstitions. The state-funded Danish Council for Independent Research set aside 2.5 million kroner ($428,000) for a Ph.D. project to look into the under-earthlings rumoured to inhabit the island of Bornholm.

A Gallup survey in 2008 revealed that 37% of Danes believe in the existence of ghosts or spirits. Two-thirds of those surveyed said that ghosts and spirits are real and believed that they can be contacted.

The superstitions around national flags occur around the world and Denmark's must never touch the ground when it is lowered, nor must it ever be hoisted at night. Why? It means you're paying homage to Lucifer.

Denmark's maritime heritage has its superstitions, such as the one that asserts that if a black-and-white crow (known as a pied crow) is seen flying in the direction of the ocean, it could indicate that your next lover could be a sailor . . . or a mermaid (or simply someone on a cruise?).

As with the Norwegians, Danes like to leave out some Christmas porridge for their little folk, the *Nisse*. If you have any old, cracked or broken crockery in your house in Denmark, you save it for New Year's Eve to be thrown on your friends' and neighbours' doorsteps; apparently it brings them luck for the coming year.

LITHUANIA

There's a different angle to broken mirrors in Lithuania. Although it's bad luck to stare into a smashed mirror (it has an adverse effect on your beautiful good looks), it's good luck to gaze at your image in the broken pieces.

Got a spot on your nose? It means someone doesn't love you anymore.

Bird droppings and various poo are good luck. Step in any old crap (it needn't be a dog's) and you're laughing, as you'll be if a passing bird drops a load on your head or shoulders.

If you arrive at a house and knock on the door, when it's opened don't shake hands with the occupant across the threshold. On the way there, don't step on any manhole covers. That's bad luck. If you do, either spit three times over your shoulder or, alternatively, whoever's with you can knock you once on the back and negate the bad luck.

Never light anything, such as a cigarette, from a candle. If you do, you're condemning a sailor to death. If you want to put off getting married for seven years, just sit at the corner of a table.

LATVIA

We all know this feeling; you've left home but you've got a nagging feeling you've forgotten something. Go back, look in the mirror and you'll be reminded of what it was.

There's a crude variation on the old superstition about having a wallet with a coin in it. In Latvia, if your wallet is empty, this is an invitation to the devil to come and take a dump in it. He'll also turn up if you whistle in your bedroom or lounge.

Like Finland, Latvia celebrates 23 June, St John's Eve, before the feast day of St John the Baptist. Midsummer is very significant and important in the Baltic area and many of the old pagan rituals survive. If you fancy getting really drunk very quickly, then the best way to do it in Latvia is to wear your clothes inside out. But don't put your gloves on the table.

On New Year's Day, the luckiest meal you can have is fish. Save the scales from the fish and put them in your wallet (but check Lucifer hasn't been there first), because the fish scales ensure more money in the coming year.

It seems unusual to many of us for anyone to buy a present of a pair of scissors or a knife, but if you get such a gift you should reimburse the money spent on the gift to avoid bad luck.

ESTONIA

Like the Latvians, the Estonians regard whistling indoors as a bad omen. But here's a real curiosity. If you're in conversation with someone and you both happen to say the same thing simultaneously, you should both make a wish, then hook your little fingers together, count three and say 'Adam' or 'Eve'. For the wishes you've just made to come true, you must both say the same thing.

Don't shake hands on the doorstep.

If you're single and eating a cake, don't drop a slice or you'll not get married. A newly married bride should go through her home dropping money and ribbons in each room to ensure the happy couple a pleasant future. Don't lay your handbag on the floor – that's lost money; and if you drop a knife this means a male person is about to visit.

BELARUS

There's some peculiar superstitions about legs, stumbling and birthdays in Belarus. If your birthday falls on an even day and you trip or stumble with your left leg, that's good luck (as it is with the right leg on an odd day). But bad luck comes if your birthday's on an even day and you stumble with your right leg (or left leg on an odd day).

In Belarus they share Estonia's superstition about speaking the same thing simultaneously, but with an added twist; you should touch something black, make a wish, then ask the other person when they think that wish might come true.

If someone is leaving home on a journey, don't clean the house until they let you know they've reached their destination. Having a clean-up before they get there could mean that they'll not return. No doubt the house will end up in a right old mess if the departed get lost or happen to be astronauts.

UKRAINE

Itchy palms and the expectation of money – a superstition familiar in many cultures, but in Ukraine there are added elements. If your left palm itches, expect some cash. If your right palm itches, that means you're going to spend some.

If you're expecting a baby in Ukraine, don't get a room ready or buy the child clothes in advance. You're supposed to leave all that until they are born.

Dogs, priests and old ladies loom large in Ukraine's folklore, and especially in the morning. If you pass an old woman carrying an empty bucket (an uncommon sight, but be vigilant; perhaps there's some significance in the bucket being empty), or early in the morning you come across a dog you've not seen before or if a priest passes by, don't say anything to any of them or the rest of the day you'll experience rotten luck.

If you're about to move into a newly constructed house, you need to please the spirit of the house by sending a cat in there first.

Make sure you don't brush your breadcrumbs into your bin. Throwing bread-crumbs away may result in you being hungry. Breaking dishes might be noisy and expensive, but dropped crockery is good luck in Ukraine.

Pay all your debts off by 31 December or (perhaps logically) you'll be in debt the following year.

Here's a nice one: someone is about to go on a journey and leave the house. It maybe a long trip or only for a few days, so before that person leaves, everyone shall sit for a minute's silence.

ROMANIA

We're into deep superstitious territory here. As Transylvania is part of Romania today, we're in a land of castles, deep wooded valleys and mysterious mountains. One Romanian superstition considers it lucky if your name has seven letters in it, which must have pleased local celebrity Dracula. There are a lot of superstitions, as you'd expect, to do with garlic, which we'll examine later in this work.

If you're having some wine, pour a drop on the ground – it's for the souls of the dead. When your new baby arrives, to prevent the infant being cursed, a red bracelet or a loop of red string should be placed around the nipper's wrist.

Here's one reminiscent of Finland's 'a hundred red cars' superstition: if a girl counts a hundred white horses, she will marry the first single man she meets.

Bouquets with even numbers are for funeral ceremonies or cemeteries, so you should never give four, six or eight flowers to a person.

Romanians consider both Tuesday and Friday the 13th to be unlucky, and to add to the gloom, it is said that every Tuesday has three hours of potential bad luck and it's a bad day to wash your hair. Which three hours these are remains unclear, so be careful.

Don't blow out a Romanian candle – that's bad luck; pinch it out with your finger or a sailor might die.

It means good fortune to spill your coffee.

Going on a journey? If so, sit on your suitcase for a while first because that proves you're going to enjoy the trip. If you want to wish a friend good luck, buy them a new pair of gloves. Oddly enough, if you're looking for a good relationship with your mother in law, then eat the corners on a slice of bread.

Itchy nose? You're going to a party. And no whistling in the home – that's bad luck.

HUNGARY

A national holiday falls on 15 March. It stands for democracy and freedom, commemorating the Hungarian revolution of 1848, which became a war for independence from Habsburg rule. The revolution was subdued by Russian forces. Since 1848, in memory of soldiers killed, no Hungarian will raise a toast with beer.

It was originally decreed following the revolution that a beer toast would not happen for 150 years. That period may have elapsed but no doubt the tradition will continue.

Whereas the Latvians get drunk quicker by wearing their clothes inside-out, for good luck you can do the same in Hungary – you'll get lucky but stay sober.

An attack of the hiccups signifies someone is talking about you.

A cactus as a house plant brings bad luck, as does cutting your child's fingernails or toenails before they're twelve months old (if you don't want your offspring to grow up to be a criminal). If you're visiting a new baby, it's essential that you sit down. Apparently, if you remain standing, you're stealing the baby's dreams. And whatever you do, don't kiss a baby's foot; it may have an adverse effect on the child's walking ability later on. The pain of labour in childbirth was even greater when it was customary for men to aim their gun above the poor mother's head and fire a shot to scare away evil spirits.

As elsewhere, the ubiquitous chimney sweep's appearance in Hungary is good luck, as is seeing a passing wedding procession.

SLOVENIA

In Slovenia, it's bad luck to see an owl or a black rat and a bad omen to kill a spider, but good luck to see one. There are other good-luck animals to keep an eye open for: pig, dove, pigeon (the last two suggest a child is on the way) and . . . an elephant. Considering the extent of the elephant population outside zoos in Slovenia, it would indeed be lucky to see one, but you could benefit from coming across a smaller creature; it's good luck to spot a ladybird. The poor black cat's appearance is a bad omen, but a white cat is lucky.

Seeing your headless shadow on the wall suggests death for someone. That's a strange one indeed – seeing your shadow *without a head*?

If you hear a cuckoo's call and have money in your pockets, that's a good financial omen.

Make sure your neighbours refrain from any household DIY on New Year's Eve, because if you hear the sound of hammering, someone will die in the coming year.

CROATIA

The number thirteen is not considered unlucky in Croatia. However, don't think you can get away with brushing your hair while still in bed. That's bad luck.

What seems to be the biggest area of superstition in Croatia revolves around the *propuh*. This is the draught. Whereas many nations would have no objection to opening their windows on a warm day and letting the breeze blow through the house, it would be bad form here. All manner of ailments are attributed to draughts, up to inflammation of the brain and muscular aches and pains.

Whether the following are superstitions or examples of common sense, you can decide: after a shower you must immediately dry your hair. Don't sleep with wet hair or go outdoors with a wet head. During the autumn, don't expose the back of your own or your child's neck to the wind but cover them with a scarf or a hood. Don't pad around the house in bare feet – always wear slippers and socks, even in summer. Don't, in the same room, open two opposing windows at once, because the *propuh* cross-breeze represents the worst danger and this is a very bad omen.

Don't cut your nails on Sundays.

Other superstitions are familiar, such as paying a small fee for the gift of a knife and not condemning a hapless sailor by lighting your cigarette from a candle. You'll not be too happy if you're left-handed in Croatia – you've been touched by the Prince of Darkness.

SERBIA, BOSNIA AND HERZEGOVINA

As we move along the Adriatic coast the superstitions become more bizarre. For example, accidentally putting your underwear on by mistake inside out – that's a good omen, as is placing garlic in your luggage to ensure you get through customs. If you inadvertently bite your tongue or the inside of your cheek here and you have a grandma, that's good news, because it means she's baking you a cake. Don't whistle indoors or you'll invite rats into the house.

In most cultures, having long, elegant fingers would be a plus – you'd make a fine pianist or guitar player – but here those long digits signify you're destined to be a thief, and if you have a widow's peak hairline then, yes, you'll lose your partner. Most of us, on seeing a new baby, would issue a compliment as to how attractive the child is. After all, babies are beautiful. Not in Serbia, Bosnia and Herzegovina – you should designate the baby as 'ugly' because if you don't the kid will have bad luck throughout life.

ALBANIA

The Albanians tend to drink Turkish coffee and, as it leaves a nice sediment of grounds in the cup, then this residue is just the thing you need for telling fortunes, in the same way as reading tea leaves exists in other countries, especially in the UK. As we're near to Greece with its long and mysterious classical history, in Albania the 'evil eye' crops up in superstitions. This suggests that if someone has a grudge against you, they can inflict a curse just by an evil glance. This has resulted in the odd custom of attaching cuddly toys to buildings in order to divert the gaze of the person trying to give you the evil eye. It means that they could be distracted by looking at the toy and therefore the aim of their wicked gaze won't affect that building's occupants.

BULGARIA

Bulgaria has some amazing superstitious customs, such as *Baba Marta* (the 'Granny March'), beginning on 1 March to celebrate the start of spring. Families and friends give one another red-and-white wrist bands which they can only take off once they've seen a blossoming tree or a stork. There is also *nestinarstvo*, fire dancing, in villages in the area around the south-eastern city of Bourgas. This occurs mainly on 21 May, the holiday of St Konstantin and Elena.

Bulgaria's a long way from the USA yet the Bulgarians have a superstition which seems related to the American 'splitting the pole' (see p. 58). This occurs when two people are passing on opposite sides of a tree. They must say 'Hello' to one another to prevent an argument.

As in Ukraine, the cat plays a part when you're about to occupy a new house, but with a twist. Let the cat in and wherever it decides to curl up and lie is where you should put your bed. (This could be a problem in the kitchen, but rationality and superstition rarely occupy the same room.)

There's an old English superstition about not sewing buttons on clothes while they're being worn; Bulgarians believe that sewing a dress whilst it's being worn is also bad luck.

If you're in the process of talking to someone and you accidentally drop something, this could signify that you're lying.

For special days in a Bulgarian's life, such as starting a new job, leaving school, getting married or leaving on a long journey, a cup of water should be thrown outside the house in the direction of the lucky person, with the exclamation, 'All the things will run smoothly like water flows.'

If someone offers you the last piece of bread, meat or cake on the table, take it. But don't take the last portion without it being offered; it becomes known as the 'shame piece' (in Germany, not eating the last piece at all results in good luck).

MACEDONIA

As in nearby Bulgaria, there's a superstition relating to the last piece of food, but Macedonians believe that if you *don't* eat the last piece of food on the table, you'll attract bad luck. Knocking on wood three times is good luck here, too.

Curious religious customs abound. Lent is a Christian religious observance beginning on Ash Wednesday and lasting approximately six weeks until Easter Sunday. In Macedonia, on the night before Lent begins, the oldest family member ties an egg to a length of string (how do you do that?) and, as it's swinging about, other family members try to catch it in their mouths. If they do, that's good luck (particularly if it's been hard-boiled). Then they take the shell and drink water from it to defeat evil spirits. Additionally, burning the string will enable them to count the number of years they will live. On the last Monday before Easter, they don't take money, belongings or clothes out of their houses because this could send good fortune away. On the first Friday in Lent, should a girl take some wheat from a church and place it beneath her pillow, she'll dream of her future husband.

As mid-winter approaches, 20 December is regarded as the time when days begin to lengthen. Pull your child's head upwards (keeping an eye out for any passing social worker) because superstition suggests this will make your little one grow more.

GREECE

With its various regions and scattered islands, the ancient 'land of the evil eye' has many superstitions that seem to alter from village to village. Killing bats is bad luck – and yet a bat's bones are considered lucky. Some islanders carry fragments of bat bones around with them as charms. Yet go to the next island and the bat is nothing less than a dreaded curse to be entirely avoided. It's Tuesday the 13th that is unlucky. One symbol of good luck and well-being is the pomegranate. If a Greek visits a friend's house on New Year's Eve, they might smash this fruit on the doorstep to bring the house good fortune (but a very slippery doorstep).

As for the evil eye, this superstition covers a lot of bases in Greece. Anyone can give you the evil eye. They may compliment you on your new twenty-four-piece dinner service, then minutes later you could drop a couple of plates; the compliment was a cover for the evil eye. Maybe they're admiring your new dress or shirt over which you immediately spill red wine. They've given you the evil eye. To protect against this, you need to possess something of the colour blue (yet, perversely, people with blue eyes are often thought to be responsible for casting the evil eye). Beware; one never knows when it will strike next, and, meanwhile, keep a look out for a crow – he's bringing bad news, rotten luck and death.

TURKEY

There are so many superstitions in Turkey that it would take several pages to list the full number – and many are extremely odd. In this region, as in the Balkans, we are in the borderlands of differing cultures and religions dating back many years and superstitions take on new forms.

For example, you're in a good mood, telling friends or family all about the great things that are happening in your life. There's something you should do as you're speaking. Scratch your bottom. It'll stop your good luck turning bad.

One thing you'll find in Turkey is a small, eye-shaped blue, white and yellow amulet – the evil eye (*nazar boncuğu*). You'll see it everywhere – cars, taxis, the sides of buses, buildings that have it built into their foundations and babies who have it pinned to their clothes. It appears in shops, doorways, everywhere. It can be worn as an earring, a bracelet or necklace. Nothing can harm you as long as you are protected with the *nazar boncuğu* because it will absorb the bad energy.

There are lots of similar superstitions to those found in eastern Europe. Don't crack the bones in your fingers because you'll be talking to Satan. Don't cut your nails at night. And here's an odd one: if you're chewing gum at night in Turkey, you're actually chewing the flesh of the dead.

Finally, let's nip back up north to . . .

IRELAND

When a country has the attractive plant a shamrock as a special national emblem you can guarantee there are plenty of accompanying superstitions. It's from the colour of the shamrock that Ireland has earned its attractive name, the 'emerald isle', although even without the shamrock it's a very beautiful, green country.

So, in Ireland, don't stand up quickly at the table because your chair might topple over and that's a grim omen indeed. In England, it was usual when a funeral cortège passed by for a man to remove his hat or at least pause on the pavement in respect. In Ireland, you're supposed to walk along with the cortège for a few steps – four at least – to prevent bad luck.

There are Irish superstitions about birds, such as the robin, which we'll deal with elsewhere. The magpie has an extra dimension. In England they talk about 'one for sorrow, two for joy,' but should you open your door and find one of these black-and-white feathered friends facing you in Ireland, and he actually looks straight at you, you may as well call the undertaker.

And if you're in Cork, take a trip to the castle and kiss the Blarney Stone, a block of carboniferous limestone built into the battlements. It'll invest you with eloquence.

Finally, let us not forget the leprechauns, solitary creatures who spend their time making and mending shoes and have a hidden pot of gold at the end of the rainbow.

From sea to shining sea: the USA

THE GREAT SPIRIT: NATIVE AMERICA

Centuries before Columbus was even a glimmer in his father's eye, long before the Vikings stumbled onto Greenland's shore, North and South America had their own well-established indigenous populations, the majority of whom would eventually be mistakenly designated 'Indians'. Apparently, the Spanish monarchs sponsoring Columbus's voyage issued him with a passport in Latin which dispatched him on their behalf *ad partes Indie* ('toward the regions of India'). Thinking he'd reached the Indian Ocean in 1492, from then on he referred to any alien culture he came across as Indians.

Watch any tourist documentary on the American west today and you'll see sun-dances, pow-wows and all manner of lively, colourfully costumed Native American festivals alive with ancient spirituality. Yet few will realise that, until 1978, American Indians on reservations had no religious rights. Washington's argument was that native peoples were sovereign nations by treaty (a position which disregarded the historical fact that the same government had regularly broken those same treaties.) As sovereign nations they were not to be granted the freedoms and fundamental rights that American citizens enjoyed. This meant specifically that they were barred from practising any rituals or traditional ceremonies. This manipulation of the law was borne out of a deep fear of Native American uprisings, tragically epitomised by the massacre of Lakota men, women and children at Wounded Knee, on 29 December 1890, as they assembled for a ghost dance, a spiritual practice.

After bitter campaigning, this changed with 1978's American Indian Religious Freedom Act and its a subsequent amendment. The US government would 'protect and preserve for American Indians their inherent right of freedom to believe, express, and exercise traditional religions and possession of sacred objects and the freedom to worship through ceremonials and traditional rites.'

As the slave masters had done with captive Africans, white, English-speaking America attempted by cruel force to obliterate all native culture and language and impose Christianity upon the indigenous peoples. In some cases it worked, but the spiritual beliefs, superstitions and cultural practices which had developed over thousands of years could not be annihilated in a mere century. Railroads, gold mines, ranches and logging camps may come and go, but a people's ancient culture is far more resilient, a fact which the eternally oppressed Jews have amply proved.

To the Native American, the material world is responsive and intelligent. Animals and birds – even reptiles – are capable of hearing man's prayers. In fact, the animal kingdom can exert its own influence over mankind's future. Yet belief goes way beyond these living creatures and extends to the earth itself. A waterfall or a river, a placid lake, the dwelling places of spirits, each of these possesses a soul and will listen if spoken to. Rocks, mountains, trees . . . all are sentient entities. They can be a source of good or evil influences and each can be appeased with offerings or prayers. There is nothing inanimate to a Native American who still upholds this faith that is incapable of giving him benediction. The animal kingdom is closely linked with mankind and every animal has its own mythical monarch which exists beyond the sight of man. The giant eagle, the great buffalo, giant crows, wolves, bears, cranes, all rule their kind from the spirit world.

Today there are 562 federally recognised Indian tribes, bands, nations, *pueblos*, communities and native villages in the USA, and it's quite a challenge to keep track of the varying superstitions. There are 229 nations located in Alaska alone; the rest are located in thirty-three other states with a great deal of ethnic, cultural and linguistic diversity. The following brief selection serves to offer you a basic idea of the scope.

Standing inside a circle will keep away evil spirits.
Dances are performed in a space which is called the ring and it is considered sacred. The ring is for much more than dancing: babies are introduced to their culture, heroes are honoured or money is given to someone in need. Dancers, taking a break, may indulge in a sing-song.
When night falls, it is preferable to sleep facing east.
To ward off evil, surround your dwelling with salt.
If you hear a rooster crowing at night, that means bad news.
Seeing an owl during daylight or hearing one hoot near your own or someone else's home signifies a death is near, although the Navajo see the owl as a good omen. Cedar trees near your home are good luck.

The Cherokee have numerous superstitions, including those concerning the number four, representing the four directions (north, east, west and south). The four directions are also associated with certain colours. The number seven represents the seven clans of the Cherokee people: Bird, Deer, Wolf, Longhair, Wild Potato, Blue and Paint. They also think the owl, always regarded as a messenger, is the bearer of bad news or brings bad luck.

The Lakota believe that when a swallow flies low to the ground there is a storm on the way. When a crow or raven flies in circles it's going to be windy. The Lakota also think that when a butterfly touches you, one of your family members from the spirit world is missing you and is thinking of you. If a ladybird touches you and then flies away, it is travelling to your future partner, husband or wife. Another Lakota belief concerns childbirth: when the birth is imminent, the oldest and wisest of the women has to be present and it is good to have your baby delivered by someone with a good personality so that the child will inherit that desired characteristic.

There are superstitions regarding feathers that differ between tribes, depending on the kind of bird the feather came from. Many Indians use feathers only as decoration. Plains Indian warriors were awarded a feather when they were particularly brave in battle. The magpie, a bold and fearless bird, is considered to be a friend and helper and in some tribes wearing a magpie feather represents bravery.

There is an ancient myth among the Lakota in South Dakota that tells of the occasion that the animal kingdom decided they would all have a race. It was to decide if two-legged animals had the right to eat the four-legged ones or vice versa. Apparently, a buffalo led the field with a magpie sitting between his horns. As the buffalo approached the finish line the cheeky magpie shot from his head and won the race. That's why his boldness and guile are so admired.

For the Cherokee, cedar, pine, spruce, laurel and holly trees have very special powers because their leaves remain green all through the year. They believe these plants are important in medicine and ceremonials and did not sleep for seven nights during the creation of the world.

When borrowing someone's pocket-knife, hand it back as it was presented to you. If the blade was open, open it on its return.

It is bad luck to walk across someone's grave.

Houseplants give off positive energy.

Pregnant women should avoid being near anyone who has died – when someone is laid out or a funeral.

There are traditional superstitions regarding the dead. For example, some Native American traditions believed that noisy hooting owls at night were a bad omen, and saw the bird as a symbol of death. Children would be told of the ubiquitous bogeyman and this meant they had to stay indoors at night, not to cry, lest the owl come and carry them off. The birds were supposed to be able to carry messages from the dead and give warnings from the here-after. Even their appearance was suspect; the circles around their eyes were claimed to be made from the fingernails of ghosts.

Got my mojo working: African-American superstitions

From a European perspective, for my generation – so-called 'war babies' – much of our understanding of African-American culture has been formed from the mid-1950s onwards by popular music and entertainment. Now, in the twenty-first century, as discrimination and victimisation refuse to die and the struggle for full civil rights continues, the veil has been lifted and we're much more aware of the challenging nature of black life in America. So to understand the way in which deep-rooted beliefs, omens and superstition in African-American culture were slowly revealed to us, arguably via popular music, it may be worth looking back a few decades.

In the early post-war decades we could have been forgiven for believing there were only three leading black movie actors: Sammy Davis Jr., Sidney Poitier and Harry Belafonte. Al Jolson's burnt-cork face and melodramatic bellowing no doubt made most cinema-goers think that he was what black America was all about, extolling the murderously intolerant South with 'Dixie', waxing lyrical over 'Swannee River', 'Mammy' and 'Sonny Boy'. However, Jolson was an active campaigner for civil rights and hundreds of black Americans attended his funeral. Of course, before WWII Louis Armstrong came to prominence, but much of America's black jazz and swing music had, in the main, been hijacked by white bandleaders such as Paul Whiteman, Tommy Dorsey and Woody Herman. For

ordinary Britons, for example, the black population of the USA (with the exception of Paul Robeson) were more or less caricatures. People didn't see them in the
same way they saw whites. Black-face Minstrel shows, so-called 'swivel-eyed
coons', dancing with waving hands exclaiming 'Yass, boss!' were little more than
light relief. None of the film *Gone with the Wind's* black actors, one of whom, Hattie
McDaniel, won a supporting actress Oscar, were allowed to attend the film's
Atlanta premiere. Slavery may have ended with the Thirteenth Amendment to the
Constitution after the Civil War, but in the 'land of the free', African-American
culture was locked down beneath a rigorously applied racism.

The way many British teenagers learned about the culture was through music,
but until the 1950s, when radio was king across the Atlantic, we had little idea of
the state of the USA's popular music scene. We now know that black music on
American radio was shunted off into an airwave ghetto and any recording by a
black artist came under the heading 'race music'. In general, white people didn't
listen to black radio and vice versa. Then someone in the record industry found all
this too tedious and decided it was time for change.

The main trade paper for the US music industry has always been *Billboard*. Paul
Ackerman joined the paper's staff as music editor in 1934. He was an erudite,
educated man who had a degree in English literature. His special subject was the
lake poets. Ackerman was admired by his staff and especially by another eloquent
journalist working for *Billboard* in 1949, Jerry Wexler, a man who would become
one of the recording world's great legends. By 1949 Ackerman was becoming tired
with the designation of African-American recordings as race records or the equally
tasteless 'sepia'. The titles of record chart genres in *Billboard* at that time seem
quaint today; 'hillbilly' and 'folk', for example, seemed to be a catch-all for all
manner of music with a rural or 'down-home' feel.

One June weekend in 1949, this all changed. Ackerman pondered over 'hillbilly'
and 'folk' and came up with a new designation; 'country & western'. Jerry Wexler
went home for the weekend, and when he returned to work on the following
Tuesday, he reported to Ackerman with his idea to replace 'race' and 'sepia':
'rhythm & blues'.

With the fearless actions of US radio DJs such as Alan Freed, who dared to play
black records on the white airwaves, the heaving dam of black talent burst. The
Billboard charts soon filled with new names like Fats Domino, Little Richard and

Ray Charles. It would take another decade for British musicians to rip down the next barrier and show young white Americans that they also had the blues, courtesy of Muddy Waters, Howlin' Wolf and John Lee Hooker.

Yet once we attempted to decipher the arcane lyrics and phraseology of these exciting artists, each verse often left us scratching our heads. What did 'Tutti Frutti' mean? Why were women implored to 'shake their money maker'? How do you 'pitch a wang dang doodle'? What was a 'mojo hand', a 'nation sack', 'hot foot' powder or 'hoodoo'? It was all immensely entertaining, yet became more and more mysterious. What on earth was a 'hoochie coochie man'? Who or what was 'John the Conqueroo'? Exactly what was blues singer Robert Johnson doing down at the crossroads, and why did he have a 'hell hound' on his trail . . . and so we asked, *what are these guys singing about?*

The answer was superstition.

Many of the centuries-old supernatural and magical rituals of African-Americans, although fading away, came to America from Africa through slavery. Much of the slaves' cultural heritage was beaten or whipped out of them. Even the drum was banned, seen as a primitive threat which could send rebellious messages. Yet even as the hypocritical slave masters bombarded their 'property' with a strange belief called Christianity, an obstinate, heady mix of ritual, superstition and the supernatural survived.

In Louisiana, where the predominant language was French, a melting pot of these folk beliefs, with a good dose of Catholicism stirred in, was blended with an ancient religion from West Africa, vodoun. Eventually, we came to know this mysterious melange as voodoo. Parallel to this, but not to be confused with voodoo, is hoodoo.

Whereas voodoo can be regarded as a religion, hoodoo represents the tenacious survival of ancient links to Africa's superstitions and beliefs. Hoodoo is not as widespread today as it was in the first half of the twentieth century, although it still has its adherents among some African-Americans throughout the southern states. It was regarded as a supernatural force to help promote health, wealth and luck. The fundamentalist wing of Christianity has in the past seen both voodoo and hoodoo as something approaching Satanism or black magic. Yet those practising in both traditions would see themselves as Christians. Many of the rituals and superstitions often had a biblical base. Looked down upon by the Baptist church, in the same way that religious southerners still regard the blues as 'the devil's music', these ancient traditions linger on as enticing elements of popular culture below the Mason-Dixon line.

What would New Orleans be without its Voodoo Museum on Dumaine Street or the *gris gris* music of Dr John, inspired by a legendary Louisiana voodoo practitioner of the early 1800s? A *gris gris* is a Voodoo amulet originating in Africa which is believed to protect the wearer from evil or bring luck.

What would Mississippi and Tennessee be without black cat bones (a hoodoo charm associated with blues music), the singing river (known throughout the world for its mysterious sounds at night, a strange, humming music), or Mississippi's Natchez Trace dancing witches? Mississippians say the witches gathered here to dance and, wherever their feet touched the ground, the grass withered and died, never to grow again.

These and many more superstitious subjects have added an extra depth of exotic mystery to movies such as *The Skeleton Key* (USA, 2005), which deals with hoodoo, the 1987 horror *Angel Heart* (USA) starring Robert De Niro, with its voodoo, fortune tellers and Lucifer himself. Voodoo, witches and fortune telling also dominate in 1997's *Eve's Bayou* (USA).

As in European history, where the figure of the witch was usually female, in African-American superstitious culture the healing or 'conjure' woman, female root worker, sometimes known as Mambo or Voodoo Queen, goes way back in black literature. In 1789, Olaudah Equiano wrote *The Interesting Narrative of the Life of Olaudah Equiano* and in Charles Chesnutt's *The Conjure Woman* (1899) he covers similar subjects against a bizarre supernatural background. Jewell Parker Rhodes's *Voodoo Season* from 2005 features a voodoo priestess. Zora Neale Hurston (1891–1960) covered African, Caribbean and American cultural practices in her works, such as *Jonah's Gourd Vine* (1934) *Mules and Men* (1935), *Tell My Horse* (1937) and, to a lesser extent, *Their Eyes Were Watching God* (1937), which was made into a movie in 2005 starring Halle Berry. Literary giants such as Alice Walker and Toni Morrison have also featured superstition and African slave rituals. Here are a few of these beliefs which have survived.

'Splitting the pole' gives you bad luck. This seems particularly popular. While out walking with anyone, never let a pole – such as a streetlamp, telegraph pole or street sign – break the plane between you. You should walk on the same side of the pole. (A variation offers a solution – if you make this mistake, say 'Bread and butter!')

Itchy palm: you are going to receive money soon.

Step on a crack: can break your mother's back.

Don't put your purse on the floor or you'll stay broke.

If your ear is ringing, someone is talking about you.

Don't cut a baby's hair before his or her first birthday.

Sunshine, rain and thunder at the same time: the devil is beating his wife.

If you keep making funny faces, one day it will get stuck that way.

Don't talk on the phone or turn on the TV in the middle of thunder and lightning.

Don't go to the zoo when you are pregnant. Your baby will come out looking like a monkey (this probably also has racist roots).

Dreaming about fish means that someone you know could be pregnant.

Animals know when you are pregnant.

Never buy your man shoes as a gift (he'll walk out of your life with them).

If you allow children to sweep the floor, they will sweep up unwanted guests.

When you cross the railroad tracks, touch a screw for safe crossings.

Never put your hat on a bed; it can mean bad luck or even death.

Now we're cooking! A few of these superstitions have lived on while others, by their very quaint, folksy nature, may well have fallen by the wayside. The splendidly named Vergilius Ture Anselm Ferm (1896–1974) was a prolific author of detailed encyclopaedic works on morals, philosophy and religion. In 1965 he penned the indispensable *A Brief Dictionary of American Superstitions* and it makes for fascinating reading. I am indebted to the publishers Philosophical Library for their permission to include some of Mr Ferm's unusual collection of superstitions.

He includes essays on amulets, astrology, athletes, bees, Bible divination, birds, brides, card games, cures, dreams, the inexorable Friday the 13th, the moon, omens, palmistry, phrenology and other arcane terms worthy of further research, such as: cledonism: the art of divination from words used occasionally. Cleromancy: the art of learning the unknown by casting lots. And my all-time favourite, coscinomancy: the art of learning the unknown by consulting a sieve! It's difficult to decide which of the noble Vergilius's superstitions to leave out, but here's a sample.

AMERICAN GOOD LUCK SUPERSTITIONS

Wear old clothes for luck.

Knock on wood; this seems universal.

Snap your fingers.

Always carry an acorn with you.

Drink at a fountain.

Here's a couple of odd ones: give a coin to a cripple and touch the hunch of a hunchback (one might hope that in both cases the afflicted person agreed to your venal intrusion, but at least the cripple got paid . . .).

When you sneeze, sneeze three times.

Another world favourite is attaching a horseshoe over a door.

Stick a pin in the lapel of a friend's coat.

Carry a crust of bread in your pocket.

Throw coins to a beggar or into a fountain.

Carry a rabbit's foot or a penny in your pocket.

Watch for shooting stars until you see one.

Bow nine times at the moon while shaking silver coins in your pocket (if nothing else, this will get you noticed . . .).

AMERICAN BAD LUCK SUPERSTITIONS

Finding a pin or spilling sugar.

Buttoning your coat the wrong way.

Hearing the sound of an owl.

Singing while playing cards.

Hopefully, you weren't born during an eclipse.

Don't wear skirts that have buttons and don't brag about your good fortune or lend anyone an umbrella or a handkerchief.

Don't light three cigarettes from one match.

Don't drop a card (any sort of card) on the floor or look into a mirror by candlelight.

Don't let soap slip out of your hand to the floor. (This has proved especially accurate in most male prisons.)

It is also regarded as unlucky to stand a slice of cake edgewise if it then falls over.

Washing blankets in months with an 'r' in their name. Never take the last piece of bread on a plate. The last two certainly have a flavour of the Great Depression; bad luck if you encounter a beggar shortly after leaving home or get trodden on the toes by a cripple. Cripples and beggars seem to get a raw deal here.

AMERICAN BETTER-HEALTH SUPERSTITIONS

These seem to have a certain peculiar antiquity. If they were ever in regular use, then twentieth-century America must have been a pretty unsavoury place at times. For example, you can get rid of warts by killing a cat and burying it in a black stocking. Well, you might lose your wart but it'll be nothing to the Twitter storm, the hate mail and the subsequent prosecution by the RSPCA.

For sore eyes apply an ointment made from crushed bedbugs mixed with salt and *human* milk. On reflection, it would seem (a) that sore eyes are preferable, (b) it's time to fumigate your bedroom and (c) at least take a crash course in social etiquette before approaching any lactating mother. Alternatively, come to your senses and book an optician's appointment.

To cure the common cold, drink whiskey, wrap a dirty sock around your neck, tie some fish skin to your feet or rub onions and molasses onto your chest. All that can be said for this one is heaven help you if you have sore eyes at the same time. In any event, once the onions and fish skin kick in, you're going to be lonely, therefore this seems one of those remedies best suited to someone who lives alone.

A cure for a child's cough could be gained by passing the child three times under a horse. One would hope that the equine consultant would agree to remain still and was not incontinent.

Now things become even more bizarre: relieve or prevent cramps by wearing an eel's skin on your bare leg or tie cotton string around an ankle. Relieve lung infections by putting onions on your chest. (Onions and fish again. There may just be something in it – onions are excellent sources of vitamin C, sulphuric compounds, flavonoids and phytochemicals, and no doubt there's a bit of omega-3 in that eel skin. Just don't sit next to anyone on the bus and stay away from the cinema. Not sure about that cotton string, though.) And we're not done with eels and vegetables just yet.

To ward off rheumatism, carry a peeled potato in a pocket or buckshot in your hip pocket and wear an eel skin around your waist. Ah, the old buckshot ploy . . . Cure lameness by applying skunk grease and colic with wolf dung mixed with white wine. *Skunk* grease? At least there'd hopefully be some white wine left. You'd need it.

Cure earache by inserting the warmed fat of a fox into the ear. For general aches and pains, apply a poultice made from cow manure. There may well be a general shortage of wolf dung, fox fat and buckshot, but don't despair. A quick car ride into the countryside and you'll eventually find a handy cowpat. But if you're caught in a fire, don't panic – you can heal burns by applying mashed potato.

If, after all these arcane remedies, your health doesn't return, provided your head points east, at least you'll have an easier death.

One thing's for sure, in collecting these oddities, Professor Ferm must have visited some strange places and even stranger people. Without his questing nature for the unusual, these little guides to good fortune may have vanished into history.

Days of dread

Next to walking beneath a ladder and knocking on wood, Friday the 13th is probably one of the widest-held beliefs throughout the modern world. Its tangled yet dubious origins will be dealt with later in this work. The number thirteen itself has its own engaging baggage, as we shall see, and Friday, as a day, doesn't get a good press historically, but on closer inspection it doesn't appear any more portentous than the other six days of the week. Yes, there have been 'unlucky' Fridays, but each year we also have a 'Good' Friday. It's generally also a good day because it's usually the end of the working week for most people. A good night to relax, have a drink. And we all like Saturdays. However, because many determined doomseekers over the last hundred years have trawled relentlessly through history to shore up the dread attached to this day, we are led to believe that as an augury of despair Friday the 13th is very ancient indeed.

However, in the comprehensive and meticulous study of British superstitions, the *Penguin Guide to the Superstitions of Britain and Ireland* (2003) and its entertaining and popular follow-up of 2004, *A Pocket Guide to Superstitions of the British Isles* (Penguin), Steve Roud blows apart Friday the 13th's claims. He informs us that 'although Fridays have been regarded as unlucky since medieval times, it is quite certain that the fear of Friday the 13th is a Victorian invention.' And he gives us a year – 1852. So, as with all myths and legends, this one suffers from what I call the dirty snowball effect. The story rolls down the steep decades, picking up enough demonic detritus as to even adversely affect the financial world and the airline industry. We could stop here, at this reality crossroads, but the mass of Friday the 13th lore is nothing if not entertaining, and so we'll press on.

To give it its full name, friggatriskaidekaphobia is a morbid, irrational fear of Friday the 13th. Friday is Frigga's Day. Frigga (Frigg) was an ancient Scandinavian fertility and love goddess, equivalent to the Roman Venus who had been worshipped on the sixth day of the week.

While I was compiling this chapter, many friends reminded me of another auspiciously doomy day which they thought may be a challenge to unlucky thirteen. Therefore, let's get the Ides of March out of the way. As a measure of historical significance, in a UK footballing analogy, Friday the 13th would be Manchester

United and the Ides of March a Sunday Boy's club from Cleethorpes. Match result? Friday: 25, March: 0. So for the Ides of March even to be included, we can blame the bard of Avon. In his play *Julius Caesar*, Shakespeare has a soothsayer warning the Roman Emperor 'Beware the Ides of March'. Caesar, far from impressed, responds, 'He is a dreamer, let us leave him'.

Our current 15 March corresponds to the Ides of March in ancient Rome, and we need to know what an ide is. As words go, it's an oddity, described by the *Oxford English Dictionary* as 'from late Old English: from Old French, from Latin *idus* (plural), of unknown origin'. Other sources inform us that ides comes from a Latin word which means 'to divide'. The *OED* adds that it was, 'in the ancient Roman calendar a day falling roughly in the middle of each month (the 15th day of March, May, July and October, and the 13th of other months) from which other dates were calculated.' From the Roman word *kalends*, the first day of the month, we get our modern word 'calendar'. One of the original purposes of the ides was to mark the full moon, but there was such a difference between calendar months and lunar months that the method became too confusing and went out of fashion. It's almost worth quoting Michael Caine again here: 'There's not many people know that.'

As with any day of the year, no doubt throughout history there will be no shortage of terrible things which have happened on 15 March. It wasn't a particularly good day for kings and emperors. Long after Julius Caesar's demise in 44 BC, in AD 493, following the fall of the western Roman empire, the first barbarian King of Italy, Odoacer, was halfway through a gleeful dinner party when his host, Theoderic the Great, King of the Ostrogoths, decided to kill his guest. No one complained about the soup being cold after that.

The writing was also on the wall for Tsar Nicholas II on 15 March 1917, when the Bolsheviks forced his abdication. In July the following year he and his family were all executed. On that day in 1937, the great writer of extremely scary horror stories, H. P. Lovecraft, died. He was a man who invented his own, dark and terrible fictional mythologies, yet wrote in his 1920 short story *The Temple*, 'It is only the inferior thinker who hastens to explain the singular and the complex by the primitive shortcut of supernaturalism.'

On 15 March the Syrian civil war kicked off in 2011.

And I know it doesn't count, but it was also on 15 March 1996 that a carelessly driven Vauxhall Cavalier ploughed into the back of my stationary Ford Mondeo when I was halted at traffic lights near Bournemouth. There's mystical fate for you . . . with a lingering hint of whiplash.

Yet 15 March isn't all doom and gloom. There's not many of us who don't love Father Christmas and 15 March AD 270 was the birthday of St Nicholas. On this day in 1892 Liverpool Football Club was formed. In 1912 the great bluesman Lightnin' Hopkins came into the world.

For Catholics, 15 March is the day of St Longinus, the legendary Roman soldier who thrust his spear into the side of Jesus on the Cross, completing the 'five wounds of Christ'. This act sparked a depressing chain of events, as the head of his spear, which became known as the Holy Lance, would be fought and squabbled over by kings and emperors for 2000 years due to its supposed mystical powers. It spent WW2 in the hands of Adolf Hitler but it didn't do *der Führer* any good, and today the so-called Spear of Destiny is back in the Imperial Treasury in Vienna.

So, there we have it. The Ides of March – Friday the 13th's poor relation.

Time to take the first bite into the great, big, rotten apple of Black Friday. This day and its number of extreme superstition have many elements, so perhaps it makes sense to break these down and deal with them in sequence.

Thirteen: (un) lucky for some?

This is the kind of madness thirteen inspires: We sometimes say 'I'm all at sixes and sevens'. Think about it: 6+7=13. According to Christian tradition, Jesus died on a Friday. I've just had a scary thought. I'm writing these lines on Friday the 13th November. My house is number thirteen in our street. I was born in the month of April – the fourth month and 1+3=4. On my thirteenth birthday a teacher at the nautical school I attended told me somewhat aggressively that my dismal grasp of mathematics would ensure that I'd achieve very little in life. At that time our family had moved house thirteen times.

If I had the patience to dig deeper into my past, no doubt other negative thirteens would come up. Maybe we could all go through the same exercise, and superstition would swamp us to the point where we'd stay in bed all day for thirteen hours with the curtains closed. But what a portentous number this is.

According to Donna Henes, a shaman and expert in rituals who writes a Huffington Post blog, thirteen is a 'female number' for some mythologists. A woman has thirteen menstrual cycles a year. 'When Chinese women make offerings of moon cakes, there are sure to be thirteen on the platter,' writes Henes. 'Thirteen is the number of blood, fertility, and lunar potency. Thirteen is the lucky number of the great goddess.' Babylon's ancient Code of Hammurabi omits number thirteen when listing laws. Egyptians considered the afterlife to be the thirteenth phase of life. The cat was revered in ancient Egypt and legend has it that cats have nine lives. One cat, however, goes on for ever – Kaspar the cat in the Savoy Hotel, London.

For almost ninety years the Savoy has offered dining parties of potentially 'unlucky' thirteen the company of a fourteenth guest, Kaspar. It all began in 1898 with the kind of guest you'd expect at the Savoy, South Africa's 35-year-old diamond magnate Woolf Joel. He was host at a planned dinner for fourteen. Then one guest cancelled. Joel doesn't appear to have been superstitious, but one of the guests was. It was suggested that, with thirteen at the table, the first person to leave could be facing death. You don't scare a diamond magnate that easily, and Woolf Joel ignored such a portent and the dinner went ahead. A few weeks later he was shot dead in his Johannesburg office by a blackmailer. Karl Frederic Moritz Kurtze, masquerading as Baron Kurt von Veltheim, was an all-round bad egg, a sailor, con-man, thief, a blackmailer, serial bigamist, several times a deserter, an extortionist and a murderer. He spent his final twenty years in a UK jail.

A far cry from KFC, Pizza Hut or McDonald's, the sophisticated Savoy took Joel's death seriously, so that whenever a party of thirteen was booked, an extra guest, usually a member of the Savoy staff, was offered. However, having a lower-class stranger rubbing shoulders with the high and mighty didn't work. Opulent guests felt unable to freely exchange sensitive information. Enter the feline saviour, Kaspar. In 1926, Basil Ionides (1884–1950), an important Art Deco designer and an architect of the rebuilt Savoy Theatre in London, sculpted Kaspar the Art Deco cat, who to this day makes up a table of fourteen with a napkin round his neck. Waiter! Sardines all round . . .

AMERICA: THE LAND OF THIRTEEN

In Asheville, North Carolina, you'll find the Stress Management Center and Phobia Institute, run by Donald Dossey, Ph.D., CEO. (www.drdossey.com) The centre offers counselling on 'financial strain, worries about monetary disasters, and stress over the uncertainties of the economic future – job loss, home foreclosure, bankruptcy, plummeting stock and retirement values. Dr Dossey offers counselling to overcome various phobias. His website references the fear of Friday the 13th, estimated to affect up to 21 million people in the USA.

Money is always worrying. Take the US one-dollar bill; this is a conspiracy theorist's delight. It has thirteen of each of the following: stars, arrows, and the pyramid with its all-seeing eye, which has thirteen steps indicating the original thirteen states. The bill has thirteen stripes, thirteen olives and thirteen leaves. Turn the bill over and there's more stars, arrows, berries, stripes and leaves – there's thirteen of each in the Great Seal of the USA. If we count the letters in its mottos, both *annuit coeptis* and *E pluribus unum* have thirteen.

Thirteen on the notes is one thing, but the fresco painted by Greek-Italian artist Constantino Brumidi in 1865, *The Apotheosis of Washington*, visible through the oculus of the dome in the rotunda of the Capitol Building, has the first president surrounded by thirteen maidens representing the states plus the goddesses of victory and liberty. Liberty must have turned a blind eye. Washington himself had been a slave owner for fifty-six years, his estate's enslaved population numbering 318 people. However, his will stipulated the freeing of his slaves upon his wife's death, making him the only slave-holding founder to put provisions for the freeing of slaves in his will.

In the eighteenth century, thirteen states rebelled against the British crown. If you count the stripes on Old Glory, the US flag, you'll find thirteen: seven red and six white. The stripes represent the thirteen British colonies that declared independence from Great Britain. The Confederate flag or, more accurately, the Second Confederate Navy Jack (used between 1863 and 1865), had thirteen stars representing the Confederate states which fought against the original thirteen states of the union. However, by the end of the civil war more than twenty union states were involved.

It would be possible to go on in this numerical vein ad infinitum, but that would be tedious. As for the dreaded day, Friday the 13th, this has only developed into its current paranoid status since the end of the nineteenth century. Yet, if nothing else, thirteen is an entertaining number, as the following story will illustrate.

Welcome to the Thirteen Club

Knickerbocker Cottage was a popular hostelry located at 456 on Sixth Avenue and Twenty-Eighth Street in New York. Part of the building was originally known as the Varian farmhouse. In 1910 it became the Mouquin Restaurant and Wine Co. Remnants of the building still survive today.

On 13 September 1863, Captain William Fowler of the Union Army bought the premises which he would run with his sons. When it comes to stonewall defiance of the number thirteen and its attentive bad luck, Fowler led the field. He was educated at New York City's Public School No. 13 until thirteen years of age. He then spent some time in the printing industry. Not a man to be hemmed in, he swapped the printing press for an outdoor life in construction and took part in the erection of thirteen of the city's notable buildings. As the civil war began, after assuming command of a hundred union volunteers on 13 April, 1861, he fought in thirteen major battles during the conflict until he was wounded. This led him to resign his military position on 13 August 1863. He bought the Knickerbocker Cottage a month later on 13 September. He ran the establishment for twenty years before finally selling it on Friday 13 April 1883. According to some sources, such as the New York Historical Society, Fowler enjoyed membership of thirteen societies, some secret, including the Ancient Arabic Order of the Nobles of the Mystic Shrine, founded in 1870. It's going strong today with 350,000 members, now known as Shriners International, a fraternity based on fun, fellowship, and the Masonic principles of brotherly love, relief and truth. The organisation is best known for the Shriners Hospitals for Children and the red fezzes that members wear. Among these various memberships was an enterprise Fowler founded in 1882, the Thirteen Club. With the dreaded number thirteen having such prominence throughout his life, the ebullient Captain decided to face up to 'the curse' and give it a humorous run for its money.

So, after a year spent persuading a dozen brave souls to join him, in room thirteen of Knickerbocker Cottage on Friday 13 January 1882 at 8.13 p.m., thirteenth member Captain Fowler assembled his guests for an inaugural dinner. On their way to the table, where thirteen candles were lit, each man had to walk under a ladder. Above this was draped a banner bearing the old gladiatorial declaration 'morituri te salutamus' ('those who are about to die salute you'). Fowler had really thought this through; guests noticed the cruets in which the salt cellars were tipped on their side. Firm instructions were issued that salt should not be thrown over shoulders. Lobster salad was served formed into the shape of a coffin.

Thus did the intrepid Thirteen Club begin its impudent challenge to superstition, with many similar meetings to follow. As membership eventually grew to 400 members, they still sat at tables of thirteen diners, and defiantly added whatever new superstitions they could each year, such as bringing umbrellas and happily opening them indoors and deliberately breaking glasses.

In January 1883 the club's first annual meeting took place and, according to the New York Historical Society, its subsequent report gave the dreaded demon of number thirteen a decisive middle finger, boasting:

> Out of the entire roll of membership . . . whether they have participated or not at the banquet table, NOT A SINGLE MEMBER IS DEAD or has even had a serious illness. On the contrary, so far as can be learned, the members during the past twelve months have been exceptionally healthy and fortunate.

In an age when such enterprises represented entertaining and exclusive fun for prominent, well-heeled figures, it's hardly surprising that Captain Fowler's fellowship would attract men of substance. Among the Thirteen Club's more famous honorary members were no ffewer than four American presidents: Chester A. Arthur (1829–1886), twenty-first president of the USA; Grover Cleveland (1837–1908), who served two terms, making him the twenty-second and twenty-fourth president; and also the twenty-third president, Benjamin Harrison (1833–1901). The perfect candidate for such an obstinate organisation was the twenty-sixth president, Theodore 'Teddy' Roosevelt (1858–1919).

Meetings of the club of course required the membership's strict observance of the calendar and depended on how many Fridays fell on the thirteenth of a month.

Captain William Fowler died peacefully in his bed following a stroke. He was found dead on the morning of 6 July 1897 but, until his demise, had enjoyed good health. In the 1920s the club sadly faded away, although there were similar enterprises such as vampire-and morgue-themed clubs that followed similar traditions. So let's give Captain Fowler a rousing thirteen cheers or a thirteen-gun salute. He must have been quite a character.

Franklin D. Roosevelt, despite his club membership, was a superstitious president. He strongly believed in a popular superstition which had developed after the Crimean War and WWI, that it was bad luck to light three cigarettes with one match. The belief was that when the first soldier lit his cigarette, a sniper could spot the light; with the second from the same match the sniper would take aim and, as the unfortunate third soldier lit his cigarette from the same match, he'd be the one to be shot. At the Roosevelt's home at Hyde Park, their children's tutor was severely castigated by the president for breaking the 'one match, three cigarette' rule. The tutor repeated the offence during lunch, and Roosevelt, not known for reprimanding people loudly in public, went ballistic and no doubt the tutor learned a salutary lesson.

Roosevelt was also subject to triskaidekaphobia and acutely fearful of the number thirteen. If a dinner party had been planned for thirteen guests, Roosevelt would invite a fourteenth, usually his secretary. When travel was planned for the thirteenth of any month, he would amend the proposed departure time for 11.50 p.m. on the twelfth or 12.10 a.m. on the fourteenth. When he passed away in April 1945, he just missed dying on Friday the 13th, expiring instead on Thursday 12 April.

President William McKinley (1843–1901) followed a pleasant enough personal superstition. For good luck, he always wore a red carnation in his lapel. Sometimes he felt like passing his luck on and would present someone with the flower. If someone petitioned him for something he couldn't provide, he'd present the carnation as a consolation. One story tells of two young boys being shown around the White House. McKinley removed his lapel carnation and gave it to one of the boys and, to equalise the distribution of luck, he took another from a vase and gave that to the second lad.

In 1901 McKinley was pressing the flesh at an exposition in Buffalo, New York. There was a young girl waiting to be greeted and McKinley removed his carnation and presented her with it. His lapel was now empty. Next in line was a young man with a bandaged hand. Hidden in the bandage was a pistol. It was then that Leon Czolgosz fired two shots and, eight days later, McKinley died from his wounds.

In Abraham Lincoln's White House, superstition played an important role. Ward Hill Lamon (1828–1893) was a personal friend and self-appointed bodyguard of President Lincoln. In Hill's book *Recollections of Abraham Lincoln, 1847–1865*, he described a dream Lincoln had experienced. Lincoln heard the faraway sound of crying. In an attempt to find the source of the mysterious sound, he wandered through the rooms of the White House. Upon arriving in the east room, he was confronted with the sight of a group of people crouched over a corpse covered with a shroud. The body's face was covered and could not be identified. Lincoln asks one of the guards standing by the cadaver who this was. 'The president!' cried the soldier, 'He was killed by an assassin!' And there the dream ended. On the night of 14 April 1865, when Lincoln was assassinated at Ford's Theatre, Ward was not present, having been sent by Lincoln to Richmond, Virginia.

Lincoln's wife, Mary Todd, experienced visions of their children who had died young, and held séances. Some of these had been attended by Lincoln; even though the president regarded mediums in general as charlatans, he respected Mary's attempts to communicate with the children. Despite his distrust of spiritualists, however, Abe still had faith in the portents and omens of his dreams. At a White House cabinet meeting, awaiting a report from General Sherman, the president told the gathering that he was confident that good news was imminent, because he had just had a recurring dream – always a good personal omen. Sadly, his dream about the corpse in the east room was anything but good. Soon afterwards, Lincoln was shot by John Wilkes Booth and that strange premonition was proved true.

Beating the bookies

LUCKY UNDERPANTS AND THE LOTTERY

It's hard to know what the bookies must have thought when HBO cancelled production of its high-profile TV horse-racing drama *Luck,* starring Dustin Hoffman and Nick Nolte, on 14 March 2012. Did anyone run a book on the show's survival?

During season one, two horses died on the set. Only partly into filming season two, a third horse died. This trio of tragedies finished the show off. The superstitious might ask what would they expect, naming a show *Luck* about a sport that is shot through with superstition. Maybe it would have helped if the HBO executives had worn some lucky underwear.

A survey in New Zealand in 2006 revealed that 21% of men involved in sporting activities owned a pair of what they called 'lucky' underpants. This fixation with underwear also has its adherents in the USA, and in the UK research carried out in 2014 by Mecca Bingo (blog.meccabingo.com/undies-lucky) revealed that owning lucky pants is a privilege enjoyed by one in ten gambling Britons. They usually keep their fortunate underwear for four years, but some hang onto it for ten years or more. Nineteen per cent of lucky pants owners have won money while wearing them. Mecca were keen to celebrate these statistics, so they designed and created lucky briefs for women and lucky underpants for men that could be bought for a charity donation of just £2.

Bingo is a relatively lightweight, pleasurable experience, enjoyed as much for its sociability as for the prospect of a big win. It is a game of luck and not wholly competitive, as some serious card games are. Picking fifteen balls for a full house out of ninety can mean that the odds of winning are probably slightly better than some wagers – depending on how many people are playing. But when it comes to the lottery, horse- or dog-racing cards and roulette, can superstition have any influence on the outcome? It seems doubtful, but, one thing's for sure, gamblers lead the field as the most superstitious people on earth.

Gambling is subject to numerous regular surveys to assess its impact on society, such as www.gamblingwatchuk.org, an on-going project led by

Professor Jim Orford at the University of Birmingham. What these various surveys reveal is that around 80% of gamblers believe that superstitions and lucky rituals might add to their confidence while gambling. As for the UK's national lottery, you'd need a whole truckload of good luck charms and a wardrobe full of lucky shirts and knickers. Originally, six numbers between one and forty-nine were drawn at random, and the chance of winning the jackpot was one in 13,983,816. In October 2015 more balls were introduced, making a win much harder. Matching six balls from fifty-nine lengthens the odds to one in 45,057,474, an increase of 3.2. Are you going to win? Of course not. You've as much chance as being next in line for the throne. As I write this, the current jackpot for the EuroMillions lottery alone stands at over £80 million and no one has won for a month. Yet even the non-superstitious are willing to have a regular go (including me).

Gamblers have so many levels and variations of luck. If there's a beginner at the table and he wins, that's immediately 'beginner's luck'. Some seasoned players might even choose to play alongside a beginner just in case some luck rubs off. Lucky charms, lucky clothes, regular rituals, even where the choice of where to sit and who with, all these are serious concerns for gamblers. Superstition can inadvertently affect the bookies themselves, those same, pragmatic calculating people who set out to fleece us at the tables.

There are only three Las Vegas resort properties which actually have a thirteenth floor. Many Las Vegas hotels not only re-name their thirteenth floor as the fourteenth but omit floor numbers that start with the number four. In various East Asian languages the number four is considered unlucky because it is a homonym for 'death'. So, for example, the Encore Hotel plays it very safe by starting its floor numbering at five, omitting floor numbers two, three, four, thirteen and forty to forty-nine. Presumably, some superstitious guests would even be unhappy in any of the first four floors.

The Rio Las Vegas Hotel claims it has fifty-one floors, but if you deduct the missing forty to forty-nine, it has forty-one.

Las Vegas hotels generally skip to the fourteenth, and those with more than forty floors skip floors forty through forty-nine due to Asian superstition. The Encore, Wynn and Palms Place hotels have no forty-numbered floors. The Encore also starts on the fifth floor and removes the thirteenth.

Some consider it unlucky to even enter a casino via the front door, so most of the buildings have a separate back entrance for access by the superstitious. As Disney discovered in Hong Kong, you need a world view to bring the punters in (see p. 15).

PLAYING BY NUMBERS

When it comes to gambling and the dreaded number thirteen as regarded by westerners, we have to wonder if they've ever examined their pack of cards carefully. There are fifty-two (4x13) cards in a deck of playing cards: thirteen each of hearts, clubs, spades and diamonds. Numbers figure largely in a gambler's hopes and dreams because it's only human for us to imagine that with some particular number we might possess some dominion over chaos.

Which numbers are significant enough to consider? If you're playing the lottery, you might go for the day, month and year you were born, your house number, your family's birthdays. It's a wide but easy choice; although you'll always regret the number you left out. In the casino, superstition is more complicated.

Leading the field is the number seven. Seven has biblical connotations, so if you've got God on your side in a game of poker, anything might happen. The Bible tells us there are seven levels of heaven, Revelation Chapters eight to eleven tell us of seven angels and seven trumpets, and let's not forget there are seven days of the week. Therefore, anything seven-fold could be regarded as planned by God. The seventh child is said to be lucky, and there's the old 'seven-year itch' some restless husbands and wives get. Can numbers control our fate?

The trouble is, of course, that the good old Bible is stuffed with all kinds of numbers. It even has a book of Numbers, relating the story of Israel's journey from Mount Sinai to the plains of Moab. Why not use the number five? There were five books of Moses (the Pentateuch). You could risk going further; there are other writings ascribed to Moses, the so-called Sixth and Seventh books of Moses, and there's magic there too, because these texts purport to explain how Moses won the biblical magic contest with the Egyptian priest-magicians, parted the Red Sea, and other miraculous feats. Magic . . . gamblers need it.

If you were feeling a little wicked, there's always the number of the beast, 666. Not feeling devilish? How about the four archangels, Gabriel, Michael, Raphael and Uriel, great to have around when you're sitting at a card table because this celestial quartet are invoked as guarding the four quarters or directions and their corresponding colours are associated with magical properties. Any one of these numbers could be regarded as sacred. Staying with four, there are the Gospels of Matthew, Mark, Luke and John. Yet in Chinese culture the number four is considered unlucky (it is pronounced similarly to the word for death).

If you're still feeling biblical and stopping short of that baker's dozen, what about twelve? There were twelve tribes of Israel. The choice is nigh on endless, but when you're picking up your winnings, taking them in fifties isn't too popular, as we shall now see.

THE BAD LUCK BILL

An American casino wouldn't pay out a gambler's winnings in $50 bills because that denomination is regarded as unlucky. Such has been the influence of gambling that this resulted for a time in a slump in the production of $50 bills. Some modern gamblers dismiss the idea of the bill's bad reputation, saying that if you think a $50 bill is unlucky, you shouldn't be in a casino in the first place. So how did this particular superstition get started?

It appears to have all kicked off with the owner of Las Vegas's Flamingo casino and hotel, Benjamin 'Bugsy' Siegal (1906–1947). Siegal was a mobster with some pretty heavy-duty associates, including Meyer Lansky and Lucky Luciano. He'd borrowed over $3 million from the mob to open the Flamingo. Its initial opening in December 1946 was a disaster, as half the construction work remained unfinished. He re-opened it a few months later, and by May 1947 it was turning a $300,000 profit. But the mob had lost patience. Siegal was shot on the night of 20 June 1947, nine times, through the window of his girlfriend Virginia Hill's house as he sat reading a newspaper. Legend has it that the only cash he had on him at his death was three $50 bills in his pocket (other versions claim a single $50 bill).

The crime remains officially unsolved, but there's a grisly aftermath to keep its memory alive. It is often claimed that one of the two shots Siegal took to the head was through his eye. It wasn't, although the bullet passing through his cheek and exiting from his neck had made his eyeball pop out. Mario Puzo's 1969 novel *The Godfather* (and the subsequent film) features a character based on Siegal called Moe Greene who is murdered with a bullet through the eye. The Cosa Nostra's love of style and establishing tradition decreed that future assassinations could be through the eye, and this messy spectacle became known as a 'Moe Greene special'. Other rumours suggest that victims of any mob killings since Siegal's have been found – often in the desert – with a $50 bill stuffed in their pocket. So, all in all, not perhaps the most comforting La Vegas thought as you cut the cards or spin the wheel.

Beginner's luck

If you're sitting next to a novice when you're playing the tables and you win, you may well imagine that the greenhorn next to you has brought you luck. If they win and not you, their good fortune is termed 'beginner's luck'. If you've never played competitively before or you're a newcomer to gambling, chances are – with or without any friendly guidance – you just might win. It often happens. Beginners don't feel the stress of regular, committed gamblers whose anxiety over winning or losing can affect their performance. A beginner's luck has also been attributed to a psychological phenomenon called confirmation bias. This in itself is a kind of superstition where the novice believes they could win purely because they're a beginner. And if you do win and become a gambler your confidence will be boosted because you'll only recall all the times you actually won, rather than when you ignominiously lost. This takes us back once again to Sir Francis Bacon (1561–1626), who said, long before we knew what psychology was, 'The root of all superstition is that men observe when a thing hits, but not when it misses.'

Popular gambling superstitions

Gambling superstitions have a lot in common with other types inasmuch as they are often quite peculiar. There was an American lady who travelled with a small urn of her former gambling partner's ashes because she believed that his portable remains brought her good luck. Many superstitions are similarly personal, characterised by inexplicable routines and rituals. Some are passed down through family generations.

After a game, depending on the resulting good or bad fortune, it's common for gamblers to go back carefully over everything they've done in an attempt to discover what may have been a good or bad luck move. Some devoted players have a routine that begins with the same breakfast they had on the day of a big win. There are lucky socks, medallions, belts and shirts. Were the cards held right? Were they distracted? Was there some small thing in the meticulous routine that was forgotten? Numbers, table etiquette and even colours are analysed to see if there was anything positive or negative, anything out of the ordinary which may have affected karma. As the table in a casino is the arena of battle, what goes on there is crucially important.

The grand mufti of Saudi Arabia, Sheikh Abdulaziz al Sheikh, has his own weekly TV show entitled *With His Eminence the Mufti*. All gambling in Islam is *haram* (forbidden by Allah), and when a viewer asked in 2013 about the game of chess, the mufti informed viewers, 'It is a waste of time and an opportunity to squander money, it causes enmity and hatred between people.' Of course, religion is nothing like chess. The mufti regards the game as un-Islamic, saying it contravenes the Qur'an. In Saudi Arabia, that's a recipe for trouble. The mufti's declaration has precedents.

Following the 1979 revolution in Iran, Ayatollah Khomeini banned the game. However, after nine chess-free years Khomeini had a re-think and allowed chess to return on condition that it did not interfere with daily prayers. He said it was 'good for the brain', but it must never be associated with gambling.

In 1996, the fun-loving Taliban included chess in their 'ban everything' doctrine in Afghanistan. Then, in 2001, as the Taliban were pushed out, chess returned. In Iraq, it was again declared *haram* by Grand Ayatollah Ali al Sistani, who informed chess enthusiasts that, even if you played the game online, it was still forbidden in the Qur'an. All this seems rather odd because during the period known as the Islamic golden age (c.786–1258), according to the notable book of the period, *One Thousand and One Nights* or *The Arabian Nights*, chess appears to have been very popular.

Chess has its roots in India, and after the sixth century it moved through Persia into the Middle East. When the Islamic armies conquered Spain, they brought the game with them. The rest of the world eagerly took chess up. Yet play it today in the Middle East and you'll cause 'enmity and hatred between people'. No wonder it's banned.

Table etiquette

In a poker game, good manners at the table are paramount. There are guidelines to follow. You display very bad taste if you ever count your money at the table – it's extremely unlucky. There's also a strange Chinese rule that dictates that books must never be mentioned and that there must be no touching of the shoulders.

While playing, you should never cross your legs because this will 'cross out your good luck'.

Don't offend the gods of gambling by singing or whistling at the table.

If you're about to throw dice and an attractive woman is nearby, you can transform her into Lady Luck by asking her to blow on your dice. Just be very careful how you make this request; there are still plenty of burial plots out there in the desert . . .

WINNING COLOURS

Asia's superstitious passion for the colour red was the subject of discontent with some Welsh football fans in 2015. The Malaysian owner of Cardiff City football club, Vincent Tan, was at odds with the fact that Cardiff's strip had always been blue. In fact, the team were known as the Bluebirds. Mr Tan, however, had a firm belief in the colour red and managed to upset thousands of angry Bluebirds fans by insisting they changed their gear to red, regarded as lucky back in his part of the world. Three years of angry protest and campaigning from fans followed, none of which provided a sign of good luck for Mr Tan. He had to relent and get rid of the red shirts. Now the blue shirts even have a bluebird logo. Mr Tan might also know that in China during the Shang Dynasty (1766–1122 BC) the lucky bluebird was the harbinger of happiness, as it is in other cultures around the globe. So Cardiff FC should get lucky soon.

Because red is so lucky to the Chinese, it's well known that when placing bets they wear all manner of red underwear in the casino. This includes the women, who'll don red lingerie or red bras, while their men wear red boxer shorts or Y-fronts.

THAILAND'S LUCKY PENIS

The 'honourable surrogate penis', worn as a necklace, local name *palad khik*, takes wacky superstition down below the belt. These wooden, bone, metal or plastic schlongs are very popular in Thailand and can be bought on any street stall, measuring just a few inches to several feet. They are usually worn around the waist under the trousers, reassuringly close to the real appendage. In order to show off, many, especially gamblers, wear a small one around their necks. The gamblers who wear these neck willies do so under the impression that such a thoroughly male amulet will not only make them a winner but irresistibly attractive to women.

Palad khik came from Cambodia to Thailand several centuries ago. They are Hindu in origin, relating to the god Shiva, who is usually represented by *shiva linga* (male genitalia). The Chinese have a similar concept. Yang is with the representation of Shiva in the form of male genitalia, often accompanied by Yoni (female genitalia). This combination symbolises unity and the powers of creation and destruction. But if your little wooden dick helps you win at roulette, who needs ancient philosophy?

Winning ways around the world

Perhaps they're too busy thinking about their routines and next moves, but regular gamblers, some prone to not shaving or wearing the same clothes, are often seen as a bit untidy or dishevelled. This reputation may be more compelling in India, where apparently the grooming habits of Indian gamblers sometimes leave a lot to be desired. They believe it unlucky to wash their hair on Thursdays, shave on Tuesdays or cut their nails on that day or on Saturdays. Perhaps if you add to these superstitions the fact that many gamblers stick to the clothes they've been wearing during a lucky streak and throw in some hot weather, placing your bets in India could be a bit of a ripe experience.

Gambling in South Africa gets truly primeval and certainly does nothing for the wild bird population. It was widely reported in 2010 that the vultures of the region were in rapid decline. Steve McKean, from KwaZulu-Natal Wildlife, studied the decline of vultures related to killing birds for a sinister practice called *muti* magic.

Mr McKean said, 'Our research suggests that killing of vultures for so-called "traditional" use could render the Cape vulture extinct in some parts of South Africa within half a century. In the worst case, the Cape vulture could be suffering population collapse within twelve years.' This is because South African gamblers believe smoking the dried brains of vultures will give them special winning powers. This voodoo practice has created a high demand for vulture brains, but beyond gambling, it gets much darker.

On 11 October 2013, Swaziland's second-largest hospital was accused of operating a black market in human body parts for use in *muti* spells. Apparently, this ominous trade at Raleigh Fitkin Memorial hospital in the central commercial hub of Manzini is an open secret. Traditional healers will buy their herbs at the Manzini market and then nip around to the mortuary. There seemed to be no shortage of customers for bones, hearts, brains, lungs, arms, jaws, fingers, genitals, tongues, ears, eyes, hands, legs and other human body parts for use in *muti* medicinal rituals. As for lucky underpants, it might seem safer in the region to wear a few pairs at once . . .

Some you win, some you lose

Perhaps it's the regular stories of successful gambling winners, many with well-known quirky superstitions, that keep the rest of the massive army of punters on the treadmill. There are gamers who eschew any hint of the supernatural in exchange for what they believe to be a scientific or mathematical winning technique. Very few of these have been successful, but those who did win were pretty impressive characters.

When the UK's national lottery was launched, the TV ad with the giant index finger, accompanied by the slogan, 'It could be you', certainly made people think. Buying a lottery ticket on Friday the 13th in October 2006, the same day a mirror fell from their wall and smashed, might have seemed like a waste of time for Irene and Ronald Jones, but they scooped a £9.3 million half-share of the triple-rollover Lotto jackpot.

The following year in Somerset, as 51-year-old Paul Hardacre and his son Matthew left their local snooker club, they looked up as a shooting star shot across the night sky. It seemed a good omen, so young Matthew made a plain wish – for a pint of beer. His dad had a better idea. He wished for a lottery win. That Saturday he won £4,986,272. Hopefully Matthew got a few pints after that.

WWII German generals, unlike their superiors, Hitler and Himmler, weren't all that superstitious. Erwin Rommel (1891–1944) once said, 'Don't fight a battle if you don't gain anything by winning.' Many gamblers firmly believe that their superstitions have had such positive outcomes that the idea of the random nature of luck has no meaning. There's another, supernatural force at work. If you do become a winner, then the uplift is even greater if you win big. It impresses everyone in the gambling fraternity and boosts your self-confidence.

At the 2005 World Series of poker, the final table was filled by colourful gambling legends like Scott Lazar, Mike 'the Mouth' Matusow, Andrew Black and Aaron Canter. Although the big winner was Australian Joe Hachem, pocketing $7,500,000, it was the man with the superstitions, Steve Dannenmann, who would be remembered that day. He refused to ride in a cab unless its registration ended in an even number, wore the same shirt and visor seven days in a row and used his lucky globe as a card protector. Seeing as he won just over $4.2 million, his superstitions appear to have paid off and he's been doing well since. Dannenmana certainly gained something by winning. Although $4.2 million is impressive, in April 2014 another superstitious gambler, ten-time World Series of poker title holder Phil Ivey, netted $9 million, and there have been similar wins with or without superstitions. We always have to remember that 'the house' i.e., the bookies, will always have the edge.

Number seventeen and 007's gold fingers

Sean Connery was arguably the quintessential James Bond. The character of 007 was no stranger to casino life, and you could see him winning big time in 1971's *Diamonds are Forever* (USA). But whatever gambling his alter ego got up to, Sean Connery could equal. For a working-class lad, ex-milkman and Royal Navy sailor, the casino held no fears. His father had been a gambler and Sean had grown up with the risks of betting. In 1963, basking in the success of the first Bond film, *Dr No*, with the follow-up, *From Russia with Love*, already in the can, eyebrows must have been raised when the super-smooth Connery entered the Casino de la Vallee in Saint-Vincent, Italy. That night he played roulette, betting on the number seventeen for three consecutive spins. He won 17 million lire, which was over £10,000 (around £163,000 today). After the third seventeen, Connery coolly picked up his winnings and made his exit. This memorable event started a new legend of luck around the number seventeen. For a long time after Connery's Saint-Vincent win, any roulette croupier, asked what the most popular number was, would always say it was seventeen.

To get a feel of how cool Connery must have seemed in Italy, you can watch Bond as he does a re-run in the fictional casino in *Diamonds are Forever*. For triskaidekaphobics, here's a final oddity from the same film. According to imdb. com, 'The final scene Sean Connery filmed as Bond (at least in the official movie series) was the one in which an unconscious Bond is loaded into a coffin at the funeral home. So, Connery's last ever day of playing James Bond for EON Productions was Friday the 13th of August 1971.'

GRANDDAD KNOWS BEST

It's often difficult for parents, even as their children reach adolescence, to imagine what they might become in their adult life. But back in 2000 Welsh grandfather Peter Edwards had an uncanny kind of premonition that his grandson, three-year-old Harry Wilson, might one day play football for the national team of Wales. Even before he was two years old, Harry liked knocking a ball around the carpet. So confident was his granddad that he placed a £50 bet with bookmakers William Hill in Wrexham that Harry would one day play for the Welsh national football team.

Sixteen-year-old Harry Wilson made his international debut on 15 October 2013 as a substitute against Belgium, becoming Wales' youngest-ever senior player. Back in 2000, his granddad had been offered odds of 2500:1. He collected his winnings of £125,000 and retired from his work as an electrical contractor a year early.

BETTING ON THE MOON

The bookies realise that betting on what happens out in the cosmos is probably following a loser, as London man Matthew Dumbrell proved to be when they gave him odds of 1,000,000 to one that the world would end before the end of the year 2000. We're all still here. However, one wonders if he'd thought it through; if the world had ended, where would he have gone to pick up his winnings?

Appearing only slightly more realistic in 1964 was David Threlfall of Preston, Lancashire, who placed a £10 bet at 1000:1 with bookies William Hill for 'a man, woman or child from any nation on earth being on the Moon or any other planet, star or heavenly body of comparable distance from the earth before January 1971.' He'd heard President Kennedy's speech in which the intention to go to the moon was revealed. In the summer of 1969 the bet paid off at £10,000 (the equivalent of £127,600 today), Threlfall collecting his cheque live on ITV's *Man on the Moon* special as Neil Armstrong stepped onto lunar soil. Threlfall then went out and bought himself an E-type Jaguar and gave his family a tenner apiece.

WHEN A $34 MILLION WIN TURNED TRAGIC

Las Vegas's Monte Carlo casino must be a tempting place to work, surrounded by all those big games and slot machines. On 26 January 2000 Cynthia Jay, a cocktail waitress, had a night off. Together with boyfriend Terry Brennan and her family, she went out for a night on the strip. This was a pleasant change for Cynthia from her regular casino role behind the bar.

Jay was attracted to the Megabucks slot machine. Any number of superstitious punters would park themselves at similar machines. They'd have their lucky teddy bears, lucky baseball caps and rabbit's feet, yet the machine Cynthia had eyes on hadn't appeared to be paying out for a while. It now had a lottery jackpot built up to just under $35 million – $34,959,458.56. After nine pulls on the machine, this staggering amount became hers. Two significant things would happen to her before April that year. The first would be her marriage to Terry Brennan, just two weeks after her mega-win. The second would be the most tragic reversal of gambling luck ever. A drunk driver, Clark Morse, with sixteen previous convictions, slammed into Cynthia's new Ford Camaro as she was stationary at a red light. In the car, her sister was killed and the accident would mean that Cynthia would never walk again. Morse was sent to prison for a minimum of 28 years and Cynthia was permanently paralysed from the chest down. She is now confined to a wheelchair, unable to comb her own hair or even feed herself. It's easy to understand why she said that she'd happily surrender all of that $35 million just to have her previous life back.

THE FULL MONTY AND THE BLACK SHROUD: THE MEN WHO BROKE THE BANK AT MONTE CARLO

There are three men who may warrant the title 'The man who broke the bank at Monte Carlo'. They were perhaps more analytical characters than superstitious, but in the field of gambling they remain legends. Composer Fred Gilbert was inspired by newspaper reports of their achievements to write the famous song, made popular by Charles Coburn, and there is still one school of thought which suggests that the phrase 'the full monty' originally applied to taking the Monte Carlo casino to the cleaners.

Suspect number one was Joseph Hobson Jagger (1830–1892), an engineer at Bottomley's Mill at Shelf in Yorkshire, not far from Bradford. In the 1870s, he became fascinated with the technicalities of the roulette wheel. On 7 July 1875 he placed his first bet in the casino and a week later had amassed around about a million pounds in winnings, a staggering sum back then. When someone 'breaks the bank', it doesn't mean the winner has wiped out every penny in the casino – it just means winning more chips than there are on the table. When that happens, in a bizarre – almost superstitious – routine that lasts until more chips are produced, a black shroud is thrown over the table. Seems there can be no worse corpse for some people than their departed money.

The second suspect is Kenneth MacKenzie Clark, father of famed TV art historian and member of the House of Lords, Baron Kenneth Clark (1903–1983). Clark senior, after phenomenal success in the casino, retired in 1909 at the age of 41 to become, according to his son, 'a member of the idle rich'.

However, Fred Gilbert later claimed that the man behind his famous song (sung to great echoing effect by Peter O'Toole in the film *Lawrence of Arabia* as he crosses the desert) was the amazing Charles Deville Wells (1841–1926). Wells was a colourful rogue posing as an inventor who borrowed money from banks to 'develop' his ideas, yet spent it gambling. He wanted to be rich and, for a while, he was. His closely guarded roulette winning secrets won him a million francs (about £328,000 today) and enabled him to break the bank twelve times. He seemed inexplicably to deny the laws of probability and challenge the winning statistics of casinos. He called his method 'high risk martingale', a strategy in which he doubled the stake to make up for losses. No one could crack Wells' method. He became a celebrity and a legend, the luckiest man in the world. Until it turned sour.

He broke the Monte Carlo bank on six more occasions but eventually lost every penny. His sham dealings with bank loans pushed him into fraud. Poor and struggling, he was arrested in France at Le Havre and extradited back to England. Found guilty of fraud and sentenced to eight years at the Old Bailey, he died penniless in Paris aged eighty-five in 1926. But the song he inspired lives on.

So how do you attract good luck? Lucky charms and numbers? Some may believe that their superstitions help. Yet Richard Wiseman, professor of psychology at England's University of Hertfordshire, who kindly provided us with the UK Survey of Superstitions earlier in this book, believes that people shouldn't look to numbers or the stars to bring them luck. In his fascinating 2004 book, *The Luck Factor* (Arrow, London), he believes that people can make their own luck. He tells us:

It is all a question of how you think and behave. Lucky people are good at spotting opportunities in their lives, they are optimistic and, perhaps most important of all, bounce back from any ill-fortune they encounter rather than let it drag them down.

When I'm driving in my car

As the motor vehicle was not around in medieval times, any superstitions surrounding our four-wheeled chariots will have developed since the start of the twentieth century. Some curious motoring rituals and beliefs have built up in that time.

For a number of years, 1976–1997, I was lucky enough to be in employment where a company car was part of the deal. One of the topics among car salesmen was red vehicles. I don't know if such a statistic ever existed, but it was commonly claimed that more accidents occurred with red cars than any others. Or was this superstition? A more recent study in New Zealand (published in the *British Medical Journal* in 2003) looked at the effect of car colour and the risk of injury in a crash and suggested that silver is the safest colour. A 1998 AA survey found that red and blue cars were the most popular target for thieves. Why would this be?

I had three red cars; a Volkswagen Passat, a Ford Sierra and my final company vehicle, a bright-red Ford Mondeo. Within six months of taking delivery of the Mondeo I had three accidents, the most serious when a green Vauxhall Cavalier slammed into my rear as I was stopped at a red light. Of course, the general consensus from the guys on the sales team was 'Yeah, well, what did you expect?'

Some drivers believe that a new car is in greater danger than a used car of being involved in an accident or a collision. This could be that its pristine quality just cries out for a few dents and scratches. To banish this state of brand-new perfection and stall fate, some drivers would make a little scratch somewhere on the vehicle, either outside or – the more popular choice – inside, behind the steering wheel.

Some driving rituals were peculiar, and one I adhered to came on the day before important sales pitches at which I would hope to clinch a deal. I always had my car washed and polished and thoroughly tidied inside. The effect seemed to suggest determination and organisation. At the very least, before setting off I'd wipe all the windows, even though they were already clean.

WEIRD DRIVING SUPERSTITIONS

1. Do you hold your breath while driving past graveyards?
2. Do you hold your breath while driving across county boundaries?

3. Do you make a wish when you see a tractor or the end of a tunnel?
4. Do you raise your feet while crossing bridges, streams or railway tracks?
5. Have you ever touched the ceiling of your car if you've driven through an amber traffic light?
6. Do you insist on always parking in the same place?

Unless you're the boss with your own company space, you can forget number six. As for four and five, they hardly seem like a safe idea if you're the driver, but if you're a superstitious passenger, they're worth a try.

According to one Japanese superstition, if you are walking or driving and a funeral car passes, you should hide your thumb to avoid bad luck. The Japanese also have their black cat superstitions when a sooty feline is seen crossing the street in front of their Toyota. They think it's bad luck, which it is if you brake harshly, and even worse for the moggy if you don't. To avoid such misfortune in some countries, drivers have been known to make an 'x' on the left side of the windscreen with their right hand, a desperate routine which doesn't seem conducive to good driving. The Japanese also believe that a snake will appear if you decide to start whistling in your car while driving at night.

There's an old custom called car-coining in New York and New Jersey, areas which have numerous toll roads. So when you've bought a new car in these areas, friends and family will often toss a handful of coins onto the vehicle's floor. It sounds quaint, but it's practical. If you're ever stuck at a toll booth and you've run out of coins, just ferret around on the floor and you'll find what you need to get through the barrier.

A few dumb superstitions we almost missed

When you're whittling away at the hoary old trunk of superstition, you end up ankle-deep in shavings and some of them are too quirky to throw away. Here are a few old ones from around the western world which, if nothing else, ought to raise a smile. The disrespectful responses are mine.

It's bad luck to enter a house through one door and go out through a different door. Well, not if you're a burglar or in the act of committing adultery . . .

If you start on a trip and forget something, it's bad luck to go back and get it. So, you'd still carry on to the airport knowing your passport was in a drawer back home? Come off it!

If you sneeze with food in your mouth, there will be a death in your family. Well, if that's the way you eat your dinner, it could be you.

If strange noises are heard in the house and you don't know what they are, it is a sign of death. Alternatively, you're being burgled, the cat's chasing a mouse, your dog's looking for his bone or you need a new boiler.

Deaths occur in series of three. Yes, of course they do, and they also come in sequences of four, five, fifty and historically in thousands. Everybody dies.

Always pick all the beans out of your garden. If any of the old beans come up the next year, someone will die. *What?* Are there any statistics for superstitious, dead, bean farmers?

You can hold up a piece of cloth and look toward the evening star and there will be some little stars around it. The number of stars indicates how many children you will have. If one of the stars disappears, one of the children will die. Well, give the poor mites time to be born first, and hope you get a cloudy night. What a crock of . . . rubbish.

When sharpening a straight razor, strap it three times on each side. If you don't do this, you'll cut yourself. Alternatively, get yourself a safety razor and stop scaring yourself witless.

If you find a pin on the floor, don't pick it up if the head is pointing toward you because there is trouble ahead. If the point is toward you, pick it up because trouble is behind you or you'll have sharp luck. This also means that (a) you're blessed with amazing eyesight and (b) you have far too much time on your hands.

Always get out of the same side of the bed as when you went to bed. If you don't do this, you'll have bad luck. Easy – just put your bed next to the wall. Problem solved.

It brings bad luck to take the ashes out of a stove on Friday. Really? Not if it's twenty below and you want to keep warm on Saturday.

If a woman comes to your house on New Year's Day, you will have bad luck. But if a man comes in first, he brings good luck. Unless the woman is bringing you your national lottery winner's cheque or she's agreed to meet you after friending you on Facebook.

A crowing hen and a whistling woman will come to some bad luck. Only if they're on the front row in your local cinema.

If you hang mistletoe over the door, the first unmarried person who walks under it will be the first to get married. Fine for Christmas, but what do you hang over the door the rest of the year?

Never rock a rocking chair unless you're sitting in it. If you do, it means bad luck. Unless you're trying it out to see if it works. Not much point to a rockless rocker.

If you've got a dog, clip the end hairs off his tail and bury them under your doorstep and he'll never leave home. He may well leave if you're not careful with the clippers, and you could get a hernia lifting the doorstep.

Always get married when the hands of the clock point up so the love will be in its cup. Yes, much better than at 6.30 p.m., when the registrar's already gone home for the day.

Part two

Origins

Out of the darkness

All of our knowledge has its origins in our perceptions.
Leonardo da Vinci (1452–1519)

Do superstitions have consequences? Historically, at least, it would appear so. People and animals alike have died because of them. Perhaps it is worth restating what a superstition is: a widely held but irrational belief in supernatural influences and the idea that practices based on this will lead to good or bad luck. This involves identifying significant days, omens, premonitions and rituals to avoid misfortune. And every time we hear of someone following this path (even if we don't ourselves like spilling salt or walking under ladders), we're likely to say, 'Oh, that's just old-fashioned superstition.' We like to think of ourselves as a sensible, scientifically savvy species with a limited regard for the mystical. It's all a bit of harmless fun. This may be the best way to treat superstitions. Yet it can be entertaining to give them a little forensic attention.

As science and technology widen our horizons, the veils draped around what were once strange mysteries have fallen away. One hundred and fifty years ago the idea of communicating via radio waves would have been regarded as superstitious. Anyone suggesting the idea of television or projected moving images would have been asking for a straitjacket. Even in the 1960s, despite Stanley Kubrick and Arthur C. Clarke, we could never have imagined that within four decades the cell-phone and the home computer would be commonplace. So with all this domestically available technical beneficence, wonderful though it is, we look back over our shoulder to simpler times. We invent misty, primeval scenarios for ourselves, imagining the past, what life was like when we still had folk beliefs, magic spells and precious little else. There is still mystery in the darkness, a potential threat in the shadows, a hint of something always lurking in silent woods, abandoned houses or empty valleys. It suits us to imagine that superstitions, omens and rituals are part of something deeper, something primeval that is always willing to step out of the ancient nightfall and make us pause for thought.

Today, we see the supernatural mainly as an adjunct of entertainment. There is a growing interest, especially among the younger generation, in films and TV shows dealing with subjects such as zombies, the afterlife, Frankenstein and his monster, vampires and ghosts. The less gullible among us realise that vampires can't possibly be real (although politicians and bankers come close), that you can't cobble together a living body from the offcuts of fresh corpses, and that ghosts and zombies remain figments of our imagination.

We are also greatly interested in the Middle Ages, approximately AD 500–1500, and those medieval sagas of kings, invasions, battles and sorcery, either through fantasy such as *Game of Thrones* or the bloody authentic histories of warring monarchies after the fall of the Roman empire. Those dark ages, before electricity, flushing toilets, gas and running water, appear to be the seedbed of superstition. Everyone back then, with a life expectancy of forty-five, had to have faith in something or other. So we can feel better about our modern rationale if we assume our persistent superstitions were all connected to spirits of the woodland, the sun, moon, pagan gods, rivers, the sea, stars, animals or even human sacrifice, until eventually Christianity and Islam began to level the field.

Some of us are more pragmatic, saddled with Benjamin Franklin's stark wisdom, 'In this world nothing can be said to be certain, except death and taxes.' We're worldlier, we know there is life and there is death and that thousands are born every hour, with thousands dying. Today's atheists, who would have been burned at the stake five centuries ago, believe there is no great creator and nothing after death but a void. Agnostics haven't made their minds up, and those with a strong faith in a particular religion eschew superstitions and live by their scriptures. For those people in faith's no man's land, non-churchgoers open to suggestion, if you're looking for omens, signs and comfort, there's another potentially superstitious option: spiritualism.

Divine will hunting

There are many uncertain side roads off superstition's main highway. Can mediums and spiritualists contact the dead? The growing ranks of the faithful seem to think so, and in the UK, according to the Spiritualist National Union, 'Spiritualism is a religion that embodies the main ideas of all religions: that there is a life after death, immortality and the existence of a God.'

The *Spiritualists' Lyceum Manual* expands on this, telling us, 'The aim of Spiritualism is to effect an at-one-ment [sic] and unison of Humanity with God until every action and thought of Humanity is in perfect harmony with the Divine Will.'

Members of the Spiritualist National Union are obviously sincere and dedicated believers in their faith. Yet, going back to the 'harmless fun' motif, we might look askance at a Catholic priest, an Anglican vicar or a rabbi if they took time out to sign up with a West End variety agent, have venues booked around the country and advertise that they could contact your deceased loved ones at £25 a ticket. If there is anything in showbusiness mediumship, why is this 'divine will' placed in the hands of often floridly dressed ex-hairdressers, New Age boutique managers and otherwise insignificant middle-aged ladies? They offer themselves as 'trance mediums' and 'psychic seers' and some tell us they have a 'gatekeeper' to the 'other side' who helps them to communicate with their paying customers. Those who don't fill theatres and leisure centres make a good income online where a reading will cost you anything from £40 to £150. These people know nothing about us, other than the dates we give them. We don't question their arcane methodology. Surely, with their charts, tarot cards and crystal balls they have hopefully invested years of their lives in honing their antediluvian 'science' to what they believe is perfection? Your money enhances their confidence to the point where they believe they occupy that land at the end of the rainbow, the place where all the pots of gold are stored.

Watching the live, showbiz mediums is bound to leave a rational sceptic gasping in incredulity as they indulge in floodlit, random guessing games with the repeated mantra to their hapless victims, 'Do you understand this?'

If you stalk around the stage, eyes closed, in front of predominantly female spectators and clutch your temples with thumb and forefinger long enough, eventually there will be a person in the audience with a recently deceased relative whose name begins with 'N'. Once that tearful contact with Norman (or Norma) has been made, all the medium has to do is say, 'He's telling me that he's very happy in the spirit world and he loves you very much'. The tears flow in row five, seat seventeen, to be followed up with that question, 'Do you understand this?'

Rarely, if ever, does the reply come, 'No, I don't.' No one in a packed, attentive audience wants to appear ignorant.

Yet mediums would probably not agree that their act was in any way pandering to superstition. They consider themselves to be privileged conduits of the heavenly host, where the dead, in séances, let us know of the hereafter by the less than convincing methods of knocking on tables, blowing out candles and levitating trumpets. One might think, with the modern facility of the internet and email, that there might be laptops in heaven and that the departed might type the odd message to their loved ones and bypass the well-heeled mediums altogether. What a great modern superstition that would make.

We can't pin superstitions down. They are ethereal, slippery eels, and although it's easy to knock on wood or regard black cats with vague joy or suspicion, to most people it hardly seems worth delving any further into these seemingly silly rituals because life's too busy for all that pointless research. But once you decide to dig below the compacted top soil, you'll find just how odd human behaviour can be due to these unquantifiable practices. Some are rooted in ritual, mythology, ancient forgotten cults. Others only appear so. They're blown around the world on a wind of antiquity, settling in the most unlikely places.

There are strange locations, any number of lucky charms, and many bizarre annual rituals and festivals which centuries of religious policing have failed to stamp out. So let's start with a nailed horseshoe above the door and examine where that odd custom might have originated.

The lucky horseshoe

There's something nice about a horseshoe. A cardboard version, encased in silver paper, was hung around my wife's trembling wrist at our wedding ceremony. Everyone agrees that it's a harbinger of good fortune. Like confetti, which we'll be examining later, the horseshoe has always been a sign of joy at weddings. A floral version has also been adapted in the USA at times to inspire good luck and a feeling of well-being at new business start-ups or new showbusiness ventures.

The horse was revered by the ancient Greeks and other civilisations. When horses first had iron shoes fitted, it was remarkable to anyone who studied the blacksmith's craft that this sensitive, beautiful animal could have nails driven into his hooves and not show signs of pain. This added an extra touch to equine sanctity. The fact that the iron had been forged in a kind of holy flame was also significant. If iron could stand fire then that horseshoe was a perfect talisman to ward off the evil eye.

The tradition is that the best and luckiest horseshoe is always one that you've found accidentally, preferably in the vicinity of an old smithy or on a road where horse-drawn traffic might have been regularly seen. Ideally, the horseshoe had to be made of iron and fall from a horse by natural means without human assistance. It you are lucky in this random way, you must take the horseshoe home and nail it above your door. You'll notice most old horseshoes have six nail holes, but if you find one with seven then you'll be *really* lucky.

How you hang your horseshoe is crucial. The favoured way is in the 'U' position, with the opening at the top. This is said to prevent the good luck from running out, which could be the case if it points downwards. If you're of a Christian frame of mind, you could hang your horseshoe in the 'C' position with the points facing right; this represents the 'C' in Christ. As with many such artefacts, there's a legend attached. It was a common belief that horses ward off witches. In order to prevent witches from entering their homes, horseshoes were placed over doorways.

The nineteenth of May is St Dunstan's Day. Dunstan (909–988), a very religious young man, was a talented craftsman who at one time worked as a blacksmith in Mayfield, Sussex. He would eventually become the archbishop of Canterbury. The legend goes that the devil visited his forge asking Dunstan to shoe his 'single hoof'. Dunstan wasn't fooled and recognised him as Satan straight away, securing him to the wall with ropes. He then began hammering nails into the devil's cloven hoof. Satan did not enjoy this at all and Dunstan made him promise upon release never to enter any dwelling where a horseshoe was nailed above the door. Of course, as ever, Old Nick proved to be a wily opponent.

On a second visit, he disguised himself as a sexy young damsel with the intention of inveigling the holy craftsman into a bit of sacrilegious nooky. But there was something odd about this girl; Dunstan spotted not a pair of delicate feet under her dress but a pair of cloven hooves. Pulling a pair of red-hot tongs from the fire, he snapped them onto Satan's nose. The devil was in pain and took to the air, flying off to Tunbridge Wells. He thrust his scorched proboscis into the local water, which turned red and evidently since has retained a whiff of sulphur. Apparently, in the convent in Mayfield (now a Catholic girls' school) the tongs used by Dunstan on the devil's nose can still be seen.

The game of pitching horseshoes remains very popular and, to increase your luck when throwing, it's recommended that you rub two together.

In the north of England another superstition suggests that if you're lucky enough to find a horseshoe, you should make a wish, spit on the horseshoe then chuck it over your left shoulder.

In some fishing fleets it was customary to keep storms at bay by nailing a horseshoe to the mast, and, surprisingly, even such a level-headed sailor as Admiral Lord Nelson ensured one was attached to the mast on the *Victory*. While we're on the subject of Nelson, and nothing to do with horseshoes, his name has been superstitiously adapted for use in two fields of sport. One is in a series of holds in wrestling – the quarter, half and full Nelson. In cricket scores, a 'Nelson' is usually the name given to the number 111. Originally, this came from an old but inaccurate saying about the great matelot, who in later life had 'One eye, one arm, one leg'. The first two are correct, but Nelson died with a full complement of legs. More realistic cricket umpires will tell you, however, that the authentic 111 saying is 'One eye, one arm and one arsehole.'

The prophet's thumbprint

There is much ancient lore surrounding horses, and one of the legends is still believed by some breeders and trainers today. It involves a horse having a certain groove on its neck, a feature which has become known as the prophet's thumbprint.

If you can place your thumb gently into this groove on the neck, then it has been suggested the horse's bloodline goes all the way back to the five sacred brood mares owned by the prophet Muhammad (pbuh). [Footnote: Despite the author's infidel status, it is understood that in Islam any mention of the prophet's name is usually followed by the salutation 'Peace be upon him'. As a gesture of respect I will adhere to this tradition, usually with the accepted abbreviated version 'pbuh'.] This makes your horse lucky, although there's always some historical doubting Thomas ready to extinguish this colourful myth, because some sceptics refer to it as the devil's thumbprint. Equine atheists take a more biological view by saying this physical feature is caused when a foetal hoof presses against the neck or shoulder of the foal in the womb.

Most avid horse-riders researching this are usually directed to a folk tale written by Manhattan-based writer and researcher into mythology, Dr Ilil Arbel, entitled 'The five mares of Muhammad' (pbuh). (See ililarbel.weebly.com). In this story the prophet is being tested in a religious ordeal which involves not drinking water. When his daughter Fatima brings him a jug of cold water, he tells her that once the test (which his unfortunate horses are also being put through) is over, he will drink. Fatima says she doesn't like the fact that the horses are also being denied water. Yet he tells her that this is the command of Allah and it will help the expansion of Islam, which will depend upon the loyalty and strength of his hundred horses. On the third day of the test Muhammad (pbuh) takes his battle horn and goes to the fenced-off horse enclosure. Nearby, within the thirsty animals' sight, is the oasis with its water hole. The horses look back at their master reproachfully as he opens the gate and then they gallop towards the water. Yet before they reach it, Muhammad (pbuh) blows his horn, the sound of which is a call to war. As the rest of the herd rush to the oasis, five of the mares stop and go to their master's side in complete obedience. In tears, the prophet then leads these five to the water, assured in the knowledge that (as the tale concludes) they 'would foal the finest of Arab horses, the only horses of pure blood, the horses that would help bring Islam to every corner of the earth.'

Avoiding that ladder

Not walking under a ladder is probably the best known of all superstitions. First of all, it's a very practical idea. If there's a ladder in use we can assume there's something going on at the top of it and loose components might be involved. In my younger days in the construction industry I often found walking under a ladder was unavoidable and the chances of a dollop of mortar down my shirt collar or, worse, a length of four-by-four or a house brick on my head were pretty high. But that's not supernatural. That's plain common sense.

There are various origins for this superstition. A century ago it was bad news if a single woman walked under a ladder, as this was seen as an omen that she would never marry. There's a more elaborate US version of this – if a black cat passes under the ladder, then woe betide the next person who climbs it. In parts of the Netherlands it's the rungs of the ladder which give concern; you shouldn't pass your hands through the rungs and walking beneath the ladder is more than bad luck – it could mean you'd end up hanged. No doubt this idea has its roots in the fact that ladders were used at gallows executions. However, as usual, religion rears its insistent head. Since the Crucifixion, the sight of the ladder has reminded more devout Christians over the centuries of the ladder placed against the Cross to enable the body of Christ to be brought down. Apparently, it would be very unwise to walk beneath the ladder as our old arch-villain the devil would find this a handy place to hide. If you forget, and inadvertently pass through Beelzebub's hiding place, there are a couple of antidotes available; either spit on your shoe or cross your fingers – keeping them crossed until you see a dog. How Fido got in on the act is another question, but there's a packed catalogue of canine superstition. For example, some cultures believe that a dog can 'absorb' evil from human victims and sense if you are ill, and it was always thought that a strange dog following you could mean good luck.

In recent years there has been another, more fanciful, interpretation. This is that a ladder leant against a wall forms a triangular shape and as such it represents the holy trinity. Walking through the father, son and holy ghost would be a massive act of disrespect. As the idea of the ladder used in the crucifixion already makes a claim for a religious provenance, this spurious elaboration sounds more than a little desperate. In the final analysis, the message is simple. Don't walk under a ladder or Satan will drop something on you.

Knocking on and touching wood

This one's certainly on a par with the ladder. In fact, if we passed under a wooden ladder, we could kill two birds with one stone. In Italy, the practice is different, as people 'touch iron' (*tocca ferro*) to prevent a comment they just made from tempting fate, or if they've seen an undertaker. Wood, however, is often closer to hand than iron. As for the aforementioned birds/stone phrase, that's not superstition – it's a cliché, according to James Rogers in his *Dictionary of Clichés* (Facts on File Publications, 1985). It dates back in English to 1656 when Thomas Hobbes used it in a work on liberty, writing: 'T. H. thinks to kill two birds with one stone and satisfy two arguments with one answer.' However, that diversion aside, we could have given a wooden ladder a knock.

These timbered superstitions are ubiquitous – with a few international cultural twists – yet there are separate proposed derivations for knocking and touching. The popular suggestion of the origin for knocking is a belief that wicked spirits lived in trees or timber. In pagan times, entering a forest, especially at dusk or in darkness, must have been a daunting prospect. If there were spirits living in those trees, perhaps they could hear your hopes and dreams. The best way to deal with this was to knock on the wood to drown out your thoughts and preserve your hopes and wishes. One knock woke the spirits up, a second knock was to thank them. This is an aspect of apotropaic magic, supposedly having the power to avert evil influences or bad luck.

As we've already seen in Germany, where knocking the *stammtisch* is a way of announcing one's arrival in the pub, that knock proves you aren't the devil. Contact with wood is also traditionally a way to avoid tempting fate. You may be bragging about something, telling people about a journey you're intending to make, even talking about your own mortality. Such situations are ultimately out of your control, so knocking on wood, or saying 'touch wood,' hopefully placates any wayward spirits bent on intervention. This seems to be a protective measure rather than a way of bringing good luck. There's an infrequent variation in which you touch wood and whistle, although ostentatiously combining the two might become embarrassing.

Christianity is never far behind when there's a folk tale to hijack. The cross Jesus died on was obviously made of wood and the more fanciful adherents of the New

Testament would have told you that touching wood means you are seeking the protection of God by touching the Cross of the Crucifixion. In Chaucer's time in the fourteenth century, for example, small slivers of wood purporting to be relics of the 'True Cross' were sold to pilgrims who kept them in their pockets for luck and protection (one could speculate that, with the vast number of chunks of the True Cross in circulation around Christendom, the original construction must have been several hundred feet tall). So far, so good. Wood has been around for millions of years. It's been used for everything and it still is; crosses, furniture, houses, coffins, ships. So any superstition attached to the sawn-off planks of a dead tree must be ancient.

Yet as the song says, 'It ain't necessarily so'. A busy forum on the *Guardian's* Notes and Queries page opened up in 2011 when a reader asked 'Where does the phrase "touch wood" come from?' A few readers went for the tree spirits, one said it was nautical, but a response from a Mr Clapham of Cobham in Surrey was intriguing:

> There is no evidence to suggest that this phrase is anything other than the legacy of a children's game (such as that known as tig or tag) . . . (or) used before the nineteenth century – which would suggest no earlier pagan or Christian origins.

It would be easy to think he was wrong. It's an ancient superstition, isn't it? Well, not according to the meticulous research of Steve Roud in *The Penguin Guide to the Superstitions of Britain and Ireland*. He dates it back to the early nineteenth century. It was also know as a children's game named tig-touch-wood, a chasing game where touching wood meant safety. Perhaps this is a correct assessment from a British historical standpoint, yet the superstition still seems to be scattered elsewhere in various forms throughout Europe and beyond.

THE SEMANTRON'S CONVOCATION

In the Eastern Orthodox tradition, knocking on wood takes on a different religious meaning. In Romania, for example, the basic superstition is practised but certain wooden items such as tables are not used. This is because of the church's call to prayer, or convocation, is traditionally made on a revered wooden plank called the semantron. This basic instrument has been traced back to the sixth century. Legend has it, for example, in the Syrian Orthodox Church, where the semantron enjoys great veneration, that the instrument was an invention of Noah himself. According to Reverend John O'Brien (1841–1879), writing in *A History of the Mass and its Ceremonies in the Eastern Church*, the Syrian Church says that God told Noah:

> Make for yourself a bell of box-wood, which is not liable to corruption, three cubits long and one-and-a-half wide and also a mallet from the same wood. Strike this instrument three separate times every day: once in the morning to summon the hands to the ark, once at midday to call them to dinner and once in the evening to invite them to rest.

The semantron is struck to herald the liturgy and to assemble the faithful for public prayer. O'Brien tells us that 'their tradition also links the sound of the wood to the wood of the Garden of Eden that caused Adam to fall when he plucked its fruit and to the nailing to the wood of the Cross of Jesus Christ, come to atone for Adam's transgression.'

Paul Hillier, in his eponymous book on the composer Arvo Pärt (OUP, 1997), explores Russian Orthodox views on music and minimalism. It is suggested that the semantron was a substitute for the trumpet, which had always been the call to prayer in the Egyptian and Palestinian monasteries, including Saint Catherine's in the Sinai; the struck wooden rhythms were reminders of earlier rhythmic blasts from trumpets and this was eventually translated into the sound of Russian bells.

Islam changes this tradition, as bells and even music itself are considered by some sects to be *haram* (forbidden by Allah; see www.myreligionislam.com). There have been serious incidents of violence against certain Christian sects whose churches have bells in Muslim communities. So there's more to wood knocking than meets the ear . . .

Around the world, additional acts often go along with simple wood knocking. In the eastern Mediterranean, where the evil eye remains a supernatural force to be reckoned with, wood superstitions vary. In Iran the act is called *bezænæm be tæchte*. When a person is speaking well about something or someone, they will knock on wood as they say '*bezan-am be takhteh, cheshm nakhoreh*', meaning that they are knocking on wood to prevent the subject of the conversation being jinxed or influenced by the evil eye.

In Indonesia, should you be speaking ill of someone or something, the person listening to you would knock on wood (or anything) as well as their forehead saying '*amit-amit*'.

In Iran, knocking on wood's essential if something good is being said, to prevent a jinx or the effects of the evil eye. In Egypt, it's slightly different. '*Emsek el khashab*' means 'hold the wood', when good luck is mentioned, in the hope that any luck you've had in the past will continue into the future. It is also said to prevent envy. In English folklore, knocking on wood occurs when speaking of secrets. There's a less known version that features Christian monks who wore wooden crosses which they would tap or knock to drive away evil.

In Bulgaria, knocking on wood protects against evil rather than for attracting good luck. Usually the practice is a reaction to real or imagined bad news. In most cases the nearest wooden object is used, although, in some areas, tables are exempt. If there's no wood available, the practice is to knock on one's head, followed by pulling one's earlobe with the same hand accompanied by saying 'God guard us or 'May the Devil not hear.'

Wood knocking is also practised in Serbia and Croatia for being positive about something or a person. The knock may be accompanied with '*Da ne ureknem*' ('I don't wish to jinx this') or '*Da pokucam u drvo*' ('I will knock on wood'). In Poland and Russia, the wood in question should be unpainted.

In Sweden they say 'Pepper, pepper, touch wood.' The Czechs take it a stage further by knocking on a piece of stone or metal, as they are fireproof. The Czechs also have another variation; knocking on teeth.

The Turks double the insurance by knocking on wood twice as well as pulling on an earlobe, saying, 'God save me from that thing.'

In the age of the muzzle-loader rifle, eighteenth-century Americans tapped on the rifle's wooden stock to make sure the gunpowder was settled for a clean shot. One correspondent to the *Guardian's* Notes and Queries displayed a remarkable memory, stating that in a US TV show called *The Rifleman*, broadcast in May 1962, a 'female Irish character' said that she knocked on wood to thank the Leprechauns for the good luck they provided . . . to be sure.

There have been other suggestions from rural Hertfordshire and Warwickshire in the UK that the superstition has a more sexual origin, meaning to playfully grab the nearest penis. One would imagine that such a non-PC process requires the prerequisite of an intimate relationship with the startled owner of said organ, otherwise some embarrassing litigation could result.

A further proposition has it that knocking on wood has its origin in the 1800s, when auctions were held, either in barns or auction houses. The sound of the auctioneer's wooden hammer hitting the block confirmed a lucky bid. Becalmed sailors knocking on the mast or the deck for a good wind could be another possibility. Lumberjacks are said to have given a tree a hug to ensure it fell harmlessly, and safety-conscious miners were known to have knocked on wooden pit props to check they weren't rotten.

The prominent suggestion may be that the practice originated in a British children's game, but this superstition remains fascinating because of its persistence all around the world. From Russia to the Caribbean and from India to the Far East, the practice of knocking on wood appears to have a place in every culture.

Strange days

There are certain saints to whom the faithful should pray in times of trouble. For example, if the land is suffering from a drought, direct your prayers at St Swithin, who was the Anglo-Saxon bishop of Winchester and subsequently patron saint of Winchester Cathedral's Benedictine monastery. Kept in an ornate reliquary, his bones became famous for their healing powers until the Reformation, when all traces of his shrine were obliterated. In the UK the superstition runs that if it rains on St Swithin's Day, 15 July, it will rain for the following forty days. Swithin himself asked for his body to be buried not within the church but outdoors, 'where it might be subject to the feet of passers-by and to the raindrops pouring from on high.' Swithin was bishop of Winchester from around 862 until his death in AD 865. The aptly named James Raine (1791–1858), clergyman, writer and librarian, suggested that the rain superstition came later, around 1315, when there was a tremendous downpour on St Swithin's Day.

Other countries have similar saint-derived wet-weather traditions. In Sweden on St Andrew's Day, 30 November, a rainy day can mean an icy Christmas. The French have an assortment of superstitions in the month before Swithin. They start on 8 June with St Medard, and if it rains on 19 June, St Gervase, St Protais (the patron saints of haymakers) and St Urban begin their influence on the weather in the same way as St Swithin. At least you can look out at the downpour as you enjoy a drink, because St Urban of Langres is the patron saint of winemakers.

Just over a week later, on 27 June, rain in southern Germany on *Siebenschläfertag*, Seven Sleepers' Day, which determines the summer weather of the next seven weeks, means you could be in for some rainy days. The day is a peculiarity dating back to early Christianity that also gets a mention in Islam in the Qur'an (Surah eighteen, verse 9–26), in which they are referred to as 'the people of the cave'. There's a touch of Rumpelstiltskin to the Christian version of this tale about a group of seven youths who in AD 250 hid in a cave outside the city of Ephesus to avoid religious persecution by the Roman emperor Trajan Decius (201–251). Decius, famous for building baths and repairing the Coliseum, had no time at all for Christians, insisting by decree that everyone in the empire should worship the ancestral gods. The seven youths were walled up in the cave until, years later – versions include 180 and three hundred years – a farmer opened it. The lads woke up, went into Ephesus to buy food and discovered to their relief that Christianity had triumphed. The story became a favourite among crusaders looking for some battlefield inspiration.

Bearing some similarity to Europe's weather omen days, the US Groundhog Day, 2 February, is when people await a groundhog emerging from his burrow. If the sun is out and the groundhog sees his own shadow when he appears, he'll scurry back into his hole and the omen is that there'll be an extra six weeks of winter. If the weather is cloudy, he's liable to stay out and there'll be an early spring. Groundhog Day is a big festival in some parts of America and chronicles are kept of the results. The largest event takes place at Punxsutawney, Pennsylvania, where up to 40,000 people turn up. They claim that their groundhogs are accurate 75–90 per cent of the time. This is a German custom dating back to the eighteenth century, although it no doubt goes back long before they settled in Pennsylvania.

In ancient European pagan weather lore – lacking groundhogs – bears or badgers may have been involved. On 2 February, the ancient Celtic festival known as Imbolc marked the start of the lambing season and the stirring of new life with the approach of spring. It was immensely popular in Ireland and Scotland, where it was known as *'feile brighde'*, the 'quickening of the year'. Imbolc honours Brigid, a pagan goddess so important to Celtic culture that she was eventually adopted by the Christian Church as St Bridget. The original word was Imbolg, translating as 'in the belly', and Imbolc also had its own well-regarded weather predictions.

All fools together

It may make you smile, but 1 April is superstitious. I was born on 1 April and that embarrassing fact has led me over the years into delving into the scattered lore of All Fools' Day while trying to spot in advance the bizarre 'jokes' which always crop up. I recall that in my native Yorkshire it was known also as 'legging-down' day, when thoughtless buffoons thought it hilarious to inflict potential injury by tripping you up. Oddly enough, for fun-loving Iranians, it coincides with the number thirteen. This day, known as *Sizeh Bedar* or *Sizdah Bedar*, takes place on the thirteenth day of the Persian new year and marks the end of the *Norouz* holiday, when everyone goes out and enjoys a picnic. In the Philippines the 'joke' is to daub your victims with yellow dye. The Scots know it as Hunt the Gowk Day – 'gowk' meaning 'foolish person'. For hearty Caledonians it's also a day all about your derrière and is also known as Taily Day, the side-splitting legacy of which is that sign hung on your back saying 'kick me'. Oh, such fun. Pranksters also abound on 1 April in Scandinavia, Poland and especially in French-speaking Canada, where the Gallic joviality includes sticking a cutout of a paper fish on people's backs. (Ooh, la-la, those gleeful French.) In modern France, 1 April is called *Poisson d'Avril* or 'April Fish'. As a young April fish is easily caught, French school kids tape paper fish to the victim's back. Upon the discovery of this, the hapless 'fool' has to exclaim 'poisson d'Avril!' Apparently it has something to do with Napoleon Bonaparte marrying Marie-Louise of Austria on 1 April 1810. The Portuguese throw flour at one another.

So where did this festival of dodgy 'humour' originate? No one really knows. One possibility takes us back to those sons of fun, the Romans. Their religious festival of Hilaria was a day of laughs to celebrate the Cybele-Attis cult and the Isis-Osiris cult, on 25 March and 3 November respectively. The cult of Attis and Cybele doesn't seem all that hilarious, as it notably included anorexia, bulimia, and self-castration – in which an upwardly mobile man, loved by the goddess Cybele, offered her the gift of his body sans gonads. The dictionary jury seems to be out on whether the word 'hilarious' stems from this weird festival, but the wacky goings-on during Hilaria are reminiscent of today's April Fools' Day, thankfully minus the castration. Chaucer's *The Canterbury Tales* (1392) contains a story about how a vain cock, Chauntecleer, is tricked by a fox on 1 April, so it seems like a bit of hocus-pocus on All Fool's Day goes back further than we think.

The darkest day: a history of Friday the 13th

There is much debate on whether Friday the 13th is bad luck or good luck, but most people in the west continue to regard it in a negative way. However, this remains one of the most persistent of all superstitions and each story attached to it is equally engrossing. There are some uncertain indications that it all started as a bad day in ancient Hindu philosophy. It does seem to have maintained this reputation in India to this day. Some Bible scholars maintain that it was on a Friday that Eve tempted Adam with the naughty apple. Significantly, it is believed that Abel was slain by Cain on Friday the 13th. In ancient Rome, witches reportedly gathered in groups of twelve and, should another hapless necromancer turn up, the thirteen participant was believed to be the devil. And therein lies thirteen's problem – it isn't the number twelve.

Numerologists have come to regard twelve as a 'complete' number. There are twelve months in a year, twelve signs of the zodiac, twelve gods of Olympus, twelve labours of Hercules, twelve tribes of Israel and twelve apostles of Jesus. Adding one interferes with this 'completeness'. This would certainly ring true with Christians who will point out that there were exactly thirteen people present at the last supper and, as we all know, in the potential role of number thirteen, Judas Iscariot, a man who enjoyed having a full wallet, betrayed Jesus for thirty pieces of silver. But we need to delve into an ancient, mythological world which existed long before Christianity.

Bloody Vikings!

If we go way back, a possible source for friggatriskaidekaphobia may exist in Norse mythology. The story goes that there were twelve gods whooping it up at a jovial dinner party in the Norse heaven, Valhalla. There's always a gatecrasher and, on this occasion, it was rascally shape-shifter Loki. Loki's reputation was mixed; sometimes he helped the gods, but equally he seemed to enjoy annoying them. Sadly, this uninvited thirteenth guest was in a mischievous mood. He incited the blind god of darkness, Hoder, to fire a fatal mistletoe-tipped arrow at the god of gladness and joy, Balder the Beautiful. Balder died, causing widespread grief and plunging the world into darkness. Since then, thirteen people at a dinner party, especially if one of them arrives with a bunch of mistletoe, has been regarded as bad luck. Even by the time those axe-swinging marauders, the Vikings, had colonised half of Britain, eventually to dabble with Christianity, thirteen remained a dodgy number.

Kabbalah, rooted in Judaic tradition and now popular with New Age followers, lists thirteen evil spirits and, in the book of Revelation, chapter thirteen deals with the antichrist and the beast. As we're obsessed with numbers, this is the same Bible segment which tells us in 13:18:

> Here is wisdom. Let him that hath understanding count the number of the beast: for it is the number of a man and his number [is] six hundred three-score [and] six.

However, new photographic evidence of an ancient fragment of papyrus from Revelation indeed indicates the number is 616, instead of 666. This must upset the apple cart for any number of black magic fans, but if we fancy being superstitiously pedantic, two sixes and a one? That's 13 again . . .

CAN WE MAKE IT TUESDAY?

In parts of South America such as Venezuela, Chile and Argentina, if the thirteen falls on a Tuesday, then this is the big bad luck day. Yes, this phobia has a name, too, *trezidavomartiofobia*. This is especially so in Spain and Greece. There's an old saying in Spain '*En martes, ni te cases, ni te embarques, ni de tu casa te apartes*' ('On Tuesday, don't get married, embark on a journey, or move away'). That's because Tuesday is said to be dominated by Ares, the Greek god of war, or, as we more generally know him, the Roman god Mars. So it's easy to see where the Spanish word for Tuesday originates – Martes. Mars is bad enough, but he looks even worse for bad luck when you consider his sons, Phobos (fear) and Deimos (terror), and even his sister who rides on his chariot, Enyo, is discord.

In Italy, the day of bad luck is traditionally Friday the seventeenth (the number thirteen is often considered to be lucky by Italians). Some believe that the origin of this fear of seventeen originates in the writing of number seventeen, which is XVII using Roman numbering. That initially seems meaningless, yet somewhere in history some pedantic doom merchant re-arranged XVII to form the Roman word VIXI, 'I have lived', which suggests you may be about to die, therefore a bad luck omen.

For the Greeks, Tuesday is generally considered an unlucky day. This goes back to Tuesday 29 May 1453, the day Ottoman forces pushed them from the place they called the queen of cities, Constantinople. It was taken after a forty-day siege in which the use of gunpowder to smash the walls was a new innovation. The week before the city fell there were omens and portents which troubled the Venetian, Genoese and Byzantine defenders. As they led a religious Christian procession, carrying an icon of the Virgin Mary, during an ominously heavy thunderstorm, the sacred statue of our lady fell from her podium. This signified the end of the city as a Christian centre. Oddly enough, on the 500th anniversary of this Greek tragedy in 1953, the US pop charts featured a jaunty record by the Four Lads entitled 'Istanbul (Not Constantinople)' which somewhat cheekily referred to the official renaming of the city of Constantinople to Istanbul in 1930. The Greeks may have hated it, but it certainly enlightened my generation with a little bit of historical pop geography.

Friday the 13th and the Knights Templar

As we've already discovered in part one, it seems that fear of Friday the 13th is a Victorian invention. However, the Middle Ages is a treasure chest of superstition and omens – along with the fact that the chronicles of the mysterious Knights Templar continue to inspire numerous books, films and even videogames – and taking a detour into this murky period is irresistible.

This is a long, complicated story. In history's romantic panoply of bizarre religious conspiracy theories and arcane symbolism, the Knights Templar occupy a special place. The holy grail, the ark of the covenant, the shroud of Turin, Dan Brown, Indiana Jones and the Freemasons all bear the hallmark of the Templars, and some even believe the order still survives. Of all the sources for the dread of Friday the 13th, the Knights Templar story has always been a favourite starting point. Yet the knotty history which surrounds it needs to be examined in order to comprehend the violent medieval world they lived in.

From 1285 to 1314 France was ruled by Philip IV (1268–1314). Son of king Philip III and Joan of Navarre, he's known historically as Philip the Fair, but that was down to his tall, blond good looks rather than his character, which was somewhat unpleasant and volatile. He was ruthlessly ambitious for the monarchy and this set him on a colli-sion course with the all-powerful Roman Catholic Church. Any careful examination of the papacy in the Middle Ages reveals a network of opposing factions and scheming families who would make the Corleones or Sopranos seem like the Teletubbies.

Philip IV would eventually have to face up to two awkward pontiffs. One was Bertrand de Gouth (1260–1314). Bertrand, born of a noble Gascon family, was destined to become Pope Clement V from 1305 to 1314. He studied the arts in Toulouse and law in Orleans and Bologna, becoming a canon at Bordeaux and then vicar-general to his brother the archbishop of Lyons (who in 1294 was created cardinal bishop of Albano). Bertrand was made a chaplain to Pope Boniface VIII, who in 1295 nominated de Gouth bishop of Cominges in the south of the Haute-Garonne region. He was later to become the archbishop of Bordeaux in 1299.

By all accounts, de Gouth's pontifical predecessor was a very odd, obdurate character. Pope Boniface VIII's real name was Benedetto Gaetani (1235–1303). He was born in Anagni, just over 30 miles south-east of Rome. As canon and later cardinal, Gaetani showed great skill as a papal diplomat. He travelled to England with Cardinal Ottobono Fieschi to suppress a rebellion by a group of barons against Henry III. On 5 July 1294, after two years of deadlock and electoral indecision following the death of Pope Nicholas IV in 1292, a devout Sicilian hermit monk, Peter Murrone (1215–1296), in his eighties and generally regarded as incompe-tent, was elected pope. As Pope Celestine V, the somewhat befuddled old man conferred privileges on anyone who requested them, issued contradictory edicts and, when his bungling behaviour stirred up controversy, he simply requested that everyone leave him alone to pray. He was not a happy man in his elevated role, and lasted a mere five months before he made the shock decision to resign. Prior to Celestine V, only two popes had resigned in the Church's history.

Those papal resignations happened some time before the foundation of the Knights Templar, but it's worth taking a brief diversionary look at their reasons, as this shows us a vastly different Church of Rome to the celibate, media-savvy organ-isation we know today. One of the popes, Benedict IX, occupied the role three times between 1032 and 1048 alongside four other papal incumbents – seven popes in 24 years. The Roman clergy, who appear in the Middle Ages as dubious wheeler-dealers forever involved in shady politics and questionable commerce, had drifted from the path of biblical study.

Many cardinals and priests were licentious and hypocritical and hardly living the life of the poor carpenter they were supposed to follow. Despite their love of the high life and their blatant hypocrisy, the pope stated, 'We declare, state, define and pronounce that for every human creature to be subject to the Roman pope is altogether necessary for salvation.' Rome taught that all who did not acknowledge the pope as God's representative on earth and the Roman Catholic Church as the only true church were damned. Those who disagreed could expect a heresy trial and perhaps excommunication. Excommunication meant the loss of one's soul. That may not sound much of a threat today, but a thousand years ago it was a horrifying prospect.

A pope opera 1032–1056: Benedict IX, Gregory VI, Clement II, Damasus II, Leo IX

During this disorderly period, to paraphrase Groucho Marx, there were more popes than you could shake a stick at. Pope Benedict IX (1012–1056), far from being a squeaky-clean pillar of the church, was reputedly bisexual with a reputation for licentious and wild living that has continued to horrify ecclesiastic historians. His extremely wayward and irreverent conduct provoked such insurrection in Rome that he had to leave the city. In January 1045, Bishop John of Sabina was elected to succeed him as Pope Sylvester III. Members of Benedict's family, the forceful Tusculani brothers, managed to oust Sylvester, who fled home to a quiet life as a bishop in the Sabine hills, according to some sources. Others suggest Sylvester was imprisoned as a false claimant as pope. Benedict returned, although later, in 1045, after ten turbulent years in and out of the job, he resigned in order to get married – and was paid by his godfather to do so with seven thousand gold florins and a promise of a pension to step down. Giovanni Graziano was a well-heeled Roman priest who wanted to replace his godson and became Pope Gregory VI in 1046.

Things went wrong for Benedict. It seems the woman he'd left his job for didn't want him after all and, as he was missing the thrilling and orgiastic life of popery, he made his way back to the Lateran palace, much to the consternation of his godfather. For a while there were two popes, a source of much confusion and anger for the cardinals and priests. They asked the emperor of the Holy Roman empire, Germany's Henry III, to invade Rome and sort the battling popes out. For his part

Henry treated Gregory VI as the rightful pope, although he was under a cloud with the clergy for bribing his way into the job.

A German bishop, Suidger, was then crowned as Pope Clement II, Gregory's successor. Clement II died in October 1047, and Benedict, ever the opportunist, returned the following month to seize the Lateran palace. Seven months later he was ejected by German troops. The former Bishop Poppo of Brixen was elected as Pope Damasus II. Poppo was accepted as the real pope, but his reign lasted only 23 days from 27 July 1048 until 9 August when Poppo died (possibly of malaria). He was replaced by another German, Bruno of Egisheim-Dagsburg (1002–1054), who became Pope Leo IX from 1049 to his death in 1054.

Still simmering with discontent, Pope Benedict IX, summoned in 1049 to appear on charges of simony (the act of selling church offices and roles), ignored the summons and was excommunicated. The last of the popes from the powerful Tusculani family, he probably died in his mid-40s in 1056, a penitent at the monastery of Grottaferrata, where he no doubt had some wildly entertaining tales to tell the curious yet cautious monks. Granted, this all took place before the fall of the Knights Templar, yet this period of pugnacious popery hopefully provides a window on an ecclesiastic mafia more interested in politics, power and pleasure than the saving of souls.

THE KNIGHTS TEMPLAR

Just over six decades after the death of Benedict IX, the 161st pope, Gelasius II, was ruling in Rome. Meanwhile, in the Jerusalem of 1118, Hugues de Payens – a French nobleman from the Champagne region – selected eight knights (all his relatives), including Godfrey de Saint-Omer, to establish the order of the Knights Templar. Their task was the protection of pilgrims visiting the holy land. King Baldwin II of Jerusalem allocated headquarters for the order on the Temple Mount. Disciplined men at arms, they proclaimed themselves as

> The fine vocation of the sword and lance,
> With the gross aims, and body-bending toil
> Of a poor brotherhood, who walk the earth
> Pitied.

The Templars inspired the foundation of similar organisations, such as the order of Saint John, known as the Hospitallers. Not to be left out, the Germans set up their own, the order of Brothers of the German House of Saint Mary in Jerusalem, who became known as the Teutonic Knights.

In the early years the Knights Templar soon became famous as determined, chivalric fighters and ascetics, although criticised by some clerics because they claimed to be holy men, yet wore swords. They may have declared themselves a 'poor brotherhood', but the Templars soon became adept at fundraising, and as the money they raised was promised for the protection of pilgrims and Jerusalem, they had no shortage of rich, land-owning pious donors, including numerous kings and noblemen.

In 1139 Pope Innocent II gave the order a boost when he issued the papal bull, *omne datum optimum* (a papal bull is a particular type of letters patent or charter issued by a pope. It is named after the lead seal (*bulla*) that was appended to the end in order to authenticate it). This would allow the Knights Templar to cross any border, owe no taxes and answer only to the authority of the pope. It seems possible that this remarkable and wide-ranging free passport may have been organised with the pontiff by Bernard of Clairvaux, patron of the Knights Templar. This generous papal approval of a rapidly expanding sect of religious men at arms could well be payback for Bernard, as the man who had done much to help Innocent II become pope.

Throughout western Europe, a long way from Jerusalem, the order continued to grow. New chapters were soon established in Spain, Portugal and France. The Templars also set up branches in England and Scotland, each year expanding their powerful influence while accumulating more land and greater wealth. Over the next century and a half the steady rise of the Templars as a wealthy, powerful, independent crusading order propelled them into formidable positions across Europe. During France's protracted war against the English king, Edward I, they acted as the French monarchy's financial agent.

By 1305, Clement V, the Gascon-born pope who had pleased Philip by transferring the Papal Curia (the administration centre) closer to Philip's realm from Rome to Avignon, was about to fall foul of Philip's erratic and unpredictable relationship with all things papal. The war with England was a massive drain on the treasury. Clement V's predecessor, Boniface VIII, had already enraged Philip by intervening in the English war with his big papal plans for a crusade. Aggressively stepping in between the French and the English to promote peace, Boniface infuriated the French king by his tactless meddling.

He did himself no favours when, in 1296, he issued the papal bull *Clericis Laicos*, prohibiting lay taxation of clergy without papal approval. This did not go down well with the two warring kings. Philip asserted his right to tax the clergy for the defence of the realm, making permanent a special tax permitted by the popes for support of crusades. Both Edward I and Philip regarded the pope's edict as an open threat to their treasuries and authority. The monarchy retaliated. Philip publicly burned the papal bull. The following year Boniface backed down, issuing a new proclamation that allowed clerical taxation for special circumstances, if the ruler attested its necessity, without the pope's permission.

Pope Boniface VIII was one of the most stubborn and arrogant pontiffs, but his truculence was well matched by Philip's wrathful responses. In 1301 the king arrested Bernard Saisset (1232–1314), bishop of Pamiers, in the county of Foix in the south of France, for showing no respect for Philip. He was now charged with high treason. Boniface demanded that Saisset should be tried in Rome. The pope stoked Philip's anger by issuing two further bulls denouncing the king, and called for a council at Rome in November 1302. Philip, in retaliation, summoned all the clergy, nobility and commons to gather for the first French states-general (1302–1303) to hear a justification of the pope's call. This political battle continued with Boniface issuing yet another bull, *Unam sanctam*, an extreme statement of his right to intervene in temporal and religious matters. Philip was now threatened with excommunication. Church or no church, for the king this was the last straw, so he had Boniface seized at Anagni. The pope was eventually freed, but – probably to Philip's relief – in 1303 Boniface died.

Enter pope number 194, Benedict XI. Benedict calmed things down, erased some of the various indignities piled upon Philip by his predecessor but, following a brief pontificate of eight months, Benedict died suddenly at Perugia – possibly by being poisoned (as ever, the Lord moved in mysterious ways . . .). Philip secured the election of Bertrand de Got (1264–1314) as pope 195, Clement V.

Archbishop of Bordeaux, Bertrand de Got had been a close friend of Philip IV since their youth but was actually a subject of the king of England. Despite this, he had remained faithful to Boniface VIII. Clement V annulled Boniface's bulls and it was then that he made the transfer of the Papal Curia to Avignon.

Always in desperate need of cash, Philip was in serious debt to various organisations who had acted as his bankers and advanced him the funds he needed for his wars. Of course, if you were an unprincipled monarch with a large, violent army, there was a way to write off your debts . . .

A few years earlier, in 1290, Jews living in England who had been crucial fundraisers had been expelled by King Edward I, many of them crossing the Channel. In France they operated for the king as tax collectors, but now Philip took a leaf out of Edward's book, and 100,000 Jews were arrested in July 1306, their property seized. Problem solved. Once expelled, any Jews found remaining in France risked death. Philip continued in true Gestapo style by expelling and expropriating their money-raising replacements, the Italian bankers, the Lombards. But there was one huge remaining raft of debt and a potential source of wealth Philip had his eyes on. It was time to deal with the mighty Knights Templar.

From 1307 Philip set about the destruction of the Knights Templar. The Templars acknowledged only one authority, the papal throne. In order to seize their assets the king used the old tried and trusted method of accusing them of heresy, with a raft of other sins and perversions thrown in for good measure. The man chosen to organise this frame-up was Philip's chancellor, Guillaume de Nogaret (1260–1313). Pope Clement arranged for a council to meet at Vienne, Dauphiné, to examine the case. To flex the ecclesiastic muscles, the first victims in the heresy firing line were the Spirituals, a sect of Franciscan extremists who observed absolute material poverty.

If Philip was to destroy the Templars, he would have to do so outside the council and he forced Clement to suppress them on his behalf. Clement was initially outraged by the order, but buried his distaste and did the king's bidding. What followed would be extremely unpleasant and damage the reputation of a monarch who had been incongruously called 'the most Christian king in Europe'. Secret plans were drawn up for the mass arrest of the order. At dawn on Friday the 13th of October, 1307, Philip's armed forces captured all Templars found in France. The hearings would begin six days later in Paris. According to Barbara Frale, an Italian paleographer at the Vatican Secret Archives and Templar expert, in *The Journal of Medieval History*, the charge of heresy – including the obligatory sodomy, always guaranteed to panic the pious – was colourfully embroidered with accusations such as:

when professing, the brothers were required to deny Christ, to spit on the Cross and to place three 'obscene kisses' on the lower spine, the navel and the mouth; they were obliged to indulge in carnal relations with other members of the order, if requested, and, finally, they wore a small belt which had been consecrated by touching a strange idol that looked like a human head with a long beard.

Almost a year later, in 1308, a florid catalogue of new charges was concocted, insisting that the Templars 'worshipped idols, specifically made of a cat and a head, the latter having three faces'. There was never any physical evidence of any such idols produced.

The misery and torture of the arrested Templars would last years. If the Third Reich had its SS, then the medieval Catholic Church had its own religious storm troopers, the Dominican order, known as *Ordo Praedicatorum*, 'the order of preachers'. In later history, they became known as the Black Friars and with religious pride as *Domini canes*, the 'hounds of God'. In his papal bull *Ad Extirpanda*, of 1252, Pope Innocent IV authorised the Dominicans' use of torture.

Spain's first grand inquisitor, Tomás de Torquemada, was a member of the Dominican order. The arrest of the Knights Templar would provide a fine training period for the Church's inquisitors. New methods to gain 'confessions' were always being devised. Naked, hands tied behind their back, heavy weights attached to the feet, 'heretics' would be hoisted up on a pulley, hung suspended by their arms, twisted out of their natural position. Then the rope would be slackened, suddenly halted before the sinner reached the ground, causing an agonising shock throughout the body.

Other techniques included basting a victim's legs with fat and sitting him close to a roaring fire so that his legs roasted. The iron heel was slowly tightened with a screw, resulting in excruciating pain. Or there was the more subtle, yet no less painful, treatment of placing sticks between fingers and compressing the hand until the finger bones snapped. Quick 'confessions' were often gained by burning men's feet or dislocating joints. The teeth of the Templars were occasionally drawn, all part of 'God's good works' in the Middle Ages.

After seven miserable years of trials, inquisition, torture and humiliation following that fateful Friday the 13th in 1307, hundreds of Templars had suffered, many died, and others were left to rot in dungeons. The 23rd and last grand master of the Knights Templar, Jacques de Molay (1243–1314), and the order's preceptor of Normandy, Geoffroi de Charney, were both burned to death in front of Notre Dame de Paris on an island in the river Seine, in March 1314. It is said that Molay, as he was burning, cried out that he would soon, 'see Philip and Clement before God!' Within a month, on 20 April, Pope Clement V died at Roquemaure. On 29 November at Fontainebleau, Molay's vicious oppressor, Philip IV of France, died.

Arguably, this remains the biggest 'black Friday' story. Were the Templars a bad lot? Historians are divided. Their heritage is shrouded in mystery, tied up with rumours of freemasonry, hints of black magic and all the other dark barnacles attached to their legacy by five centuries of myth, legend and conspiracy. In the final analysis, their ungodly demise was all about money, greed, religious jealousy and war.

In the few months Philip survived after destroying the Templars, did he get hold of their massive wealth? No. He had hoped that his crime would pay such a dividend as 'a profit of justice'. But the Templars' lands and wealth was redistributed to other orders, mainly the knights of St John (who had wisely steered clear of any dealings with kings and princes) and their new branch in Portugal, the Crusading Order of Christ. Many romantic souls still believe the bulk of the Templars' treasure lies buried somewhere. If it is, then perhaps it should stay so. As the great US lawyer Clarence Darrow (1857–1938) observed, 'History repeats itself and that's one of the things that's wrong with history.'

The ambassador's surprise

In the *Washington Post* of 13 November 1905, there appears a rather odd report concerning the Austrian ambassador, a certain Baron Ladislaus Hengelmuller, and the famous black educationalist, freed slave and leader of the African-American community, Professor Booker T. Washington. It was a coincidence that Washington and the ambassador should visit President Theodore Roosevelt at the White House on the same day and at the same hour. As the ornate media reportage of the time had it:

> The ambassador escaped first and, in the hurry for his craving for fresh air, took down Professor Washington's overcoat in mistake for his own. As he passed down the asphalt semi-circle, revelling in the peace and serenity of the surroundings, he reached for a pair of gloves and, after dragging the deep Charybdis of the pocket, came to the surface with a rabbit's foot. No gloves – just the left hind foot of a graveyard rabbit, killed in the dark of the moon.

As a 'Charybdis' is a ship-devouring whirlpool off the Sicilian coast, this seems to be quite an elastic metaphor, even for 1905. The baffled baron made it back into the White House and exchanged Washington's overcoat for his own, but not without a careful examination of the strange item in the pocket. The story concludes in the *Post*'s persistently flamboyant style:

> The Austrian ambassador recovers his overcoat and gloves, while the Hon. Booker Washington does not know – at least, until this moment – that he was ever in danger of losing his rabbit's foot . . . the cloud has passed and the orb of glory follows its bright pathway un-obscured by envy and contention.

Perhaps there's something in the old saying that 'you can take the boy out of the south, but you can't take the south out of the boy.' Booker T. Washington, born in 1856 and raised in South Virginia, was freed from slavery by the Thirteenth Amendment in 1865. Four decades on from emancipation and now a pioneering educationalist, confidant of presidents, campaigner and founding father of

Alabama's Tuskegee University, Booker T. still has need of one of those primeval antebellum amulets – that famous lucky charm, a rabbit's foot.

The rabbit's foot may not appear much in novelty shops in these days of animal rights, but you can still buy this relic of an ancient central African folk magic known as hoodoo.

With regard to the term 'voodoo', in many areas of the south, you'll not hear it mentioned. It is usually used as a subject in fiction by white authors. Separate to voodoo is African-American folk magic, which has its own terms, such as 'conjure', 'witchcraft', 'rootwork' and 'hoodoo'.

Before delving deeper into hoodoo, it's worth reminding ourselves that carrying a rabbit's foot around is only one example of the way many of us still cling on to archaic personal practices, beliefs and fetishes which we hope will be the catalysts of luck and good fortune. As we shall see, many sports stars, actors and artists have their own superstitions.

Going back to the bunny, some older people still exclaim 'White rabbits!' for luck on the first day of the month, yet it used to be considered extremely unlucky for a deep-sea fisherman to utter the word 'rabbit' before sailing, and if a miner saw a white rabbit on his way to the pit, this usually foretold a disaster.

Of course, it's one thing for us in the fat, affluent Europe of the twenty-first century to dabble in such quirky peccadilloes as lucky underpants or favourite lottery numbers. But African-Americans mired in the dire poverty of the interminable post-slavery period needed all the luck – and magic – they could get.

The bad news is that the poverty's still around – but the good news is that hoodoo is alive, well and available. The rabbit's foot is just one example of a hoodoo amulet. It features in many blues lyrics, can still be bought in specialist curio shops and apparently even from some vending machines in the south, and way back in the old minstrel shows it often cropped up in folk songs such as 'There'll Be a Hot Time in the Old Town Tonight', with the line 'And you've got a rabbit's foot to keep away de hoodoo'.

However, a good luck charm can't be any old rabbit's foot. It needs to be the left hind foot and the poor bunny must have been shot (preferably with a silver bullet!) or captured in a cemetery. There's even more authentic fine-tuning – the rabbit should have been taken in the full moon or the new moon and, if possible, on a rainy Friday the 13th.

So, what's so special about the fluffy, lovely bunny rabbit? Well, as we saw at the beginning of the book with the white rabbits, when it comes to prosperity and success, the rabbit's a prolific breeder. Rabbits provide for their offspring and construct burrows with a high level of intelligent creativity. Some researchers suggest that, as young rabbits are born with their eyes already open, perhaps they can recognise and see off any evil straight way from the moment they come into the world.

For Americans, the Easter rabbit is a good luck symbol. Small children are indulged in the legend that bunnies bring the Easter eggs. You can also hang a rabbit's foot over a baby's pram for protection, and some gardeners believe that using a rabbit's foot to transfer pollen has special benefits for fruit trees. Very few traditional poachers would step out at night without this charm in their pockets.

Hoodoo and the blues

On the outer edge of hoodoo, some suggest that the rabbit that loses its foot might well be a shape-shifting witch, and this would make the missing pinion a powerful substitute for a human body part. Another recurring, furry contributor to hoodoo is, of course, the cat. If you check out Muddy Waters' thrilling rendition of Willie Dixon's classic, 'Hoochie Coochie Man', you'll get a crash course in hoodoo when in one verse alone Muddy mentions a black-cat bone, a mojo hand and John the Conqueror root.

A black-cat bone is one of ancient witchcraft's staples – it has the potential to bring invisibility, to lure back a lost lover – the list of its powers goes on, and most of the old blues players from the Delta to Chicago would never be without their black-cat bone. As for the mojo hand, mojo has its origins in slavery and emanated from the Congo. Its nearest equivalent could be karma or life force. A mojo hand is often a small bag containing any kind of personal objects – maybe fingernail clippings, a small prayer on a slip of paper, lucky dice, herbs and so on. Those familiar with the lyrics of New Orleans musician Dr. John will have heard the term *gris-gris* (pronounced 'gree-gree'), from the Bantu language, which signifies the same thing. African-descended Haitians have their own name for it – wanga.

John the Conqueror root or 'conqueror root' takes its name from a legendary African prince who was sold into slavery yet never allowed his spirit to be broken. This root can be traced to the sweet potato or morning glory, both in the species known as *Ipomoea*. Also known in some regions as jalap or bindweed, as well as used in the mojo bag for various sexual spells (prudes look away now – you're supposed to rub it and it can resemble a pair of well-tanned testicles), it'll provide plenty of luck too if you're constipated. Taken internally, it's an effective laxative.

Down at the crossroads

Anyone drawn into the rich musical heritage of the blues, either as a fan or as a musician, will inevitably stumble upon the legend of Robert Johnson selling his soul to the devil at the crossroads in exchange for his remarkable skill on the guitar. The crossroads motif possesses an impressive African provenance in folklore, but the Robert Johnson story can be regarded as a good old superstitious musical folk tale. That said, according to the unrelated bluesman Tommy Johnson, he recommended taking your guitar to a crossroads before midnight where a phantom black man would arrive and tune it for you. Tommy said that's the way he learned to play.

The great British blues guitar player and singer Dave Kelly offered me a different angle on Johnson's fretboard prowess. Over his fifty years playing blues, Dave has worked with legends such as Howlin' Wolf, John Lee Hooker and country blues stars such as Mississippi Fred McDowell and Son House. The latter was one of Robert Johnson's mentors. The story of Johnson meeting the devil at the crossroads is often attributed to Son House. He told Dave that when he first came across Robert Johnson he wasn't very good as a guitar player, but he then vanished for a while and no one knew where he was. Legend has it that when he came back onto the scene, he was playing brilliantly. As House suggested wryly to Dave Kelly, 'Maybe he'd just gone away for a while and *practised!*'

As to whether this might work on a crossroads in the UK is highly debatable. After a few pints I once tried it one midnight on a crossroads between Grimsby and Scunthorpe, but the 'big black man' didn't appear, I was nearly run over by an Eddie Stobart truck and my playing became even more abysmal. This is not to deny that there certainly was a cultish obsession with the crossroads. This goes all the way back to ancient Greece, India and Japan.

There is even a deity – Legba, guardian of the crossroads and keeper of the gates. 'Papa' Legba (as he's known in New Orleans) has his roots with the Fon people of Dahomey in Africa. In folklore that includes Native American beliefs, the crossroads has sinister connections – a burial place for murderers and suicides and a popular rendezvous for witches. So perhaps it was Legba who provided Johnson with his legendary fretboard skills. Those who accept the idea of the

Legba cult think Robert Johnson's highly symbolic lyrics indicate he could have been initiated, as his peculiar imagery seems at odds with what must have been a more mundane existence in 1930s Mississippi.

After slavery, racism continued to spread like a cancer, as many white observers, writing from what they perceived to be the lofty moral heights of Christianity, began to catalogue the 'primitive' folk beliefs of their former goods and chattels. One such was Virginia's professional angler and fishing rod manufacturer, Thaddeus Norris. Norris and his ilk believed that slavery 'improved the negro – and improved his superstitions'. Here he is taking a swipe, complete with the requisite offensive Uncle Tom language, in 1870:

There is also the 'conjuring gourd' and the frog bones and pounded glass carefully hidden away by many an old negro man or woman who, by the dim light of a tallow candle or a pine torch, works imaginary spells on any one against whom he or she may have a grudge.

There are also queer beliefs . . . that the cat-bird carries sticks to the devil and that by its peculiar note – 'Snake, snake' – it can call snakes to its rescue and drive away those who would rob its nest. Another is, that every jaybird carries a grain of sand to the infernal regions once a year and that when the last grain of sand is so taken away from the earth the world will come to an end; all of which, of course, is at variance with Father Miller's calculations.

Then there is a belief in a certain affinity and secret communication between themselves and wild and domestic animals. Many persons have observed a negro's way of talking to his dog or to a horse. 'Aunt Bet' will say as she is milking, 'Stan' aroun' now, you hussy, you. You want to git you foot in de piggin, do you?' and the cow with careful tread and stepping high will assume a more favourable position.

Among the mythical animals of the woods is the moonack. It is generally supposed to live in a cave or hollow tree. The negro who meets with it in his solitary rambles is doomed. His reason is impaired until he becomes a madman or he is carried off by some lingering malady. The one who has the misfortune to encounter it never recovers from the blasting sight: he dares not speak of it, but old, knowing negroes will shake their heads despondingly and say, 'He's gwine to die: he's seed de moonack.'

Considering the cruelty and privations inflicted over three centuries upon captured Africans and their descendants throughout the Americas, requiring almost every trace of their original culture to be mercilessly exterminated, the survival of hoodoo, which today has such strength and vigour, is nigh on miraculous. The racial barriers erected between white Europeans and the so-called 'dark continent' have sometimes left us believing that our own pagan past, with its spells, mythical witches, wicca and vampire lore, is of no consequence after having been swept away by the arrogant, blood-stained juggernaut of 'Christian' self-confidence. But slip a Howlin' Wolf, John Lee Hooker or Muddy Waters CD into the slot and listen carefully. The drums were never silenced. Our mojos are intact – and they're still working.

The fantastic feline

In ancient times cats were worshipped as gods;
they have not forgotten this.

Terry Pratchett (1948–2015) *The Unadulterated Cat* (Pratchett and Gray
Joliffe, Gollancz, 2002)

When my daughter Sarah was diagnosed with cancer in 2011, the shockwaves
rippled through the family. During the months of treatment which followed –
MRI scans, PET scans, chemotherapy and radiotherapy – a regular visitor came to
her house. He was a black tom cat from further up the street, and she gave him a
name, Philippo Berio (after the brand of olive oil, Filippo Berio). The cat would
come to Sarah in the mornings and stay. As the lymphatic cancer spread through
her body, she eventually lost the use of her legs and 'Philip', as he became known,
would sit at her feet, sometimes in her lap for hours, always very affectionate. She
found him to be a great comfort, even though he hadn't been her pet originally and
had arrived uninvited. Philip, in feline years, was an ancient cat. According to
neighbours down the street, he was at least seventeen. He was very thin, slow,
with a good appetite and very loving. In Sarah's final weeks before her death on 23
December 2012, Philip spent many hours sitting with her. Then, following that
desolate Christmas, in early January 2013, Philippo Berio quietly died.

The reader may justifiably ask why I would include such a sad little personal
story in what is in the main a light-hearted text, but that thin, old black cat meant
so much to Sarah, and if there is any veracity in the many feline superstitions
which are still held throughout the world, then the way he comforted a dying
woman certainly comes close to persuading me that there may be something
strange going on. It seemed to us that Philip was performing a final act before his
own end. Even allowing for his age, it seemed very odd that he should expire just
days after Sarah left us.

In July 2007 the BBC reported a groundbreaking study by Dr John Church,
published in 2004, that claimed to prove in principle that dogs could detect

bladder cancer in urine. There is also anecdotal evidence of dogs scenting a wide range of cancers such as lung, breast and skin, ahead of conventional diagnosis. The report was triggered by the story of a cat in the USA. At the Steere House Nursing and Rehabilitation Centre in Rhode Island a cat called Oscar had begun showing regular affection to terminally ill patients and seemed to warn families that their loved ones had not long to go. Jacqueline Pritchard, an expert in animal behaviour in the UK, suggests the explanation is biochemical rather than psychic, surmising that in sensing and smelling the organs shutting down, it appears that the cat is aware of the symptoms that indicate death approaching. Humans change their behaviour when we know someone is dying, which animals pick up.

We watch hours of natural wildlife documentaries on TV, and while we find wild animals cute, entertaining, sometimes frightening, as humans we still adhere to the notion that our own interactions and general intelligence remain light years ahead of any other species. We should pause and consider, beyond our familiar cats and dogs, the behaviour of dolphins, whales, elephants, meercats, penguins, gorillas and a whole range of animals and birds that display a fascinating range of strange emotions and considerate social behaviour which at times can be truly moving.

Of all the animals associated with superstition, the cat reigns supreme. For this reason alone the domestic moggy deserves a sizeable section in this book. Search for comments and quotes about cats and you'll find many, including these: 'dogs have masters. Cats have servants.' 'Dogs come when they're called; cats take a message and get back to you later.' 'Dogs believe they are human. Cats believe they are God.' 'Cats are magical; the more you pet them the longer you both live.' Many great writers and musicians, from Mark Twain to Albert Schweizer, frequently waxed lyrical about man's feline companions.

That said, there is often a gulf between dog lovers and cat fanciers. I have friends who can't stand cats. Some are allergic, while others have a genuine anxiety in their presence called ailurophobia, a fear of these animals which can inspire genuine terror, panic and even illness. While the dog is a loving, trusty companion with much to recommend him, the cat can be a stubborn, mysterious being for which the term 'cupboard love' has real meaning. This derives from the way in which a cat will give the person who feeds it superficial 'love', normally exhibited when it wants to be fed. Cats are domestic organisers. They have timetables. They don't give a damn about your schedule – their breakfast comes first.

I grew up with dogs as family pets, usually very faithful, loving labradors, although we had cats as well. I gave up as a dog owner years ago. But as I write these words, one of our three cats, Flossie, sits sphinx-like on the desk next to this keyboard following my actions with inscrutable, silent curiosity. Looking at her, it's easy to see why, in the ancient world, cats occupied their own religious pedestal. I find it strange that we can usually remember the names and personalities of all the family dogs we had, but some cats often escape our memory. The cat is a truly enigmatic creature, always curious, forever the hunter, mostly self-reliant, incapable of being enslaved, its capacity for training limited to the litter tray. A cat shares love only on its own terms and usually finds its own abode.

But as will be seen, the story of this animal's unbelievably awful treatment over the past thousand years is tragic and puts humanity with all its superstitions in a truly bad light. For centuries the domestic cat, whose service in the control of vermin such as mice and rats was invaluable, has suffered from accusations of witchcraft, mistreatment, murder, suspicions of infanticide, and has been repeatedly subjected to murderous pogroms.

Black cat superstitions

The black cat is lucky in some cultures but unlucky in many. They have generated serious and strong emotions in humans throughout history. Because of this, black cats have fallen victim to all manner of religious and superstitious claptrap for centuries, the result being a massive persecution of countless innocent felines. That said, it must be remembered that towards the end of the Middle Ages all cats began to fall victim to human cruelty and there was a time when black cats had been all but exterminated, so the next in line, tabby, white, tortoiseshell, fulfilled the human desire for a bit of superstitious torture and painful annihilation. All this for an animal that was once considered godly.

Cats as gods

It is estimated that cats were domesticated as far back as 7,500 BC. They were held in high regard by the Greeks and Romans, whose favoured household pet for keeping vermin at bay was a weasel, yet the cat was admired for its sense of independence.

The ancient Greeks associated them with cleanliness. Greek mythology tells of how the goddess Hecate assumed the form of a cat in order to escape the monster Typhon. Following this event, she extended special treatment to all cats.

In ancient Egypt the feline deity Bastet was usually seen as a gentle protective goddess. She was one of the daughters of the sun god Ra. However, although often depicted with a cat's head, she sometimes appeared with the head of a lioness. This was to protect the pharaoh in battle. The Egyptians built a great temple in her honour at Bubastis in the Nile Delta. Bastet was the protector of women's secrets, guardian against evil spirits and keeper of hearth and home, as well as being a protector against disease and, of course, the goddess of cats.

Herodotus (484–425 BC) reported that when a cat died, 'All the inhabitants of a house shave their eyebrows as a sign of deep mourning. Cats which have died are taken to Bubastis where they are embalmed and buried in sacred receptacles.' Once your eyebrows had grown back you could stop mourning. At the battle of Pelusium (525 BC) the king of Persia, Cambyses II, defeated Pharaoh Psamtik III's armies in the campaign to conquer Egypt by using cats. Herodotus does not mention this, but there are other accounts that do.

Cambyses realised just how much the Egyptians thought of their felines so he sent his men out days before the battle to collect as many animals as possible, stipulating that cats dominate. The animals, thousands of them, were carried by frontline troops and, as the army approached the Egyptians, the animals were released. The Persians supplemented Cambyses's clever move by painting cats on their shields. The strategy worked a treat when the Egyptians, loath to kill a single cat (the penalty was death), lowered their bows and the demoralised troops surrendered, letting their country fall to the Persians. On his victory march into Pelusium, the callous Cambyses rubbed salt in the Egyptian's wounds by throwing cats at the crowd.

There is still an ancient superstition in China that you can tell the time of day by looking into a cat's eye. The Chinese *Book of Rites* tells of an extremely popular goddess called Li Shou who took the form of a cat to whom sacrifices and petitions were presented to help fertility and pest control. There was a widely held Chinese myth which told of the creation of the world by the gods who appointed cats as the newly created world's managers. Knowing them as we do today, this seems highly feasible. However, although the gods gave cats the power of speech to enable them in their administrative role, both gods and men became exasperated by the fact that all the cats seemed to want to do was snooze under the cherry trees and play with the falling blossoms. The gods came to earth on three occasions to check on their appointees, only to discover the feckless felines sleeping in the shade or playing with breeze-blown petals. So the cats, obviously disinterested in human affairs, had their power of speech removed and transferred to humans, but, as humans were incapable of understanding the language of gods, cats were left with the important task of keeping time and maintaining order. To some extent they continue to do so today – at least, when they're awake.

Poland has a big black cat spirit with fiery eyes, known rurally as Ovinnik, the spirit of agricultural buildings. Its name derives from the word *ovin* meaning 'threshing house'. This fearsome feline protects your barn from danger and is said to bark like a dog. It is unwise to neglect Ovinnik because he'll lose his temper and start devouring your livestock. He appears to have a connection to Bannik, the spirit of bath houses. Bannik is important at the outset of the new year when he predicts coming events. You summon him and he touches you. A cold, icy touch doesn't bode well, but a warm, loving touch promises fortune and luck. People make offerings to Bannik by chopping a rooster's head off and sprinkling the blood around the four corners of the house. Good luck for you, bad news for the chickens.

Japan has its famous image of the *maneki neko* figure, a cat with one raised paw known as the 'beckoning cat'. Legend has it that one day a Japanese emperor was passing by and a cat beckoned to him. The emperor went over to the animal, and was suddenly shocked as a bolt of lightning struck the ground where he had stood. The cat had saved his life and became a cultural favourite.

The lusty Vikings loved their cats. Farmers left offerings for the cats to ensure a good harvest. The Norse goddess of love, fertility, war, wealth, divination and magic, Freyja, was given a present by the god Thor. Why have your chariot pulled by horses? Thor presented Freyja with two giant, grey cats to do the job.

In England and Scotland black cats have been thought to portend good luck. As October turns to November, pagans from North America to Europe and beyond still observe the sacred time of Samhain, generally known as Halloween. Samhain is a festival of the dead, the end of the harvest and the start of the year's coldest months. The ancient Celts had a fairy cat named Sidhe who was suspected of soul-stealing. At Samhain, if you left Sidhe a bowl of milk your abode would be blessed as a kind house. Also known as the cat Sith, Sidhe resembled a large black cat with a white spot on its chest. Other legends suggest that Sidhe wasn't a cat but a witch who had nine opportunities to appear as a cat.

There was also a shape-shifting pre-Incan Peruvian deity named Ai-Apaec, said to have evolved from an ancient cat god and to be able to assume the form of a tom cat. Ai-Apaec was a god of the Mochica civilisation who sometimes appeared as an old, wrinkled man with cat-like whiskers and long fangs.

Mother of the famous bard Taliesin, the Welsh goddess of wisdom Ceridwen, had her own entourage of white cats who carried out her orders on earth.

The superstitious French had a black magical cat called Matagot. As a black cat it was considered devilish and evil. However, if you could get hold of your own matagot – with the right treatment and by following the rules – apparently it could bring you wealth and good fortune. To trap your matagot you had to tempt it with a chicken. You needed a secure box nearby to transport the captured cat, and while taking it home you had to ensure you never looked back. The next stage was getting your matagot settled in your house. The cat had to have the first helping of every single meal you ate. Do this and prosperity would be yours, but with one last caveat – you had to release the matagot before you become too old, otherwise you'd suffer an agonising death. The etymology of the word matagot has its root in the Spanish *matar* (to kill) and *gothos* (Goths). After settling in Spain, southern France and Italy, eventually the Germanic Goths converted to Christianity, so 'Goth' once referred to marauding tribes with pagan beliefs, and eventually to be a Goth meant you were more likely to be a Christian. Yet true to European Christian prejudice, a Matagot would be regarded as an evil spirit who kills Christians. Gothic Christianity is the earliest instance of the Christianisation of a Germanic people.

The Egyptian god Ra was variously pictured as a ram, beetle, phoenix, heron, serpent, bull or a lion. But due to Egyptian reverence for all things feline, he was often depicted as a cat. There is an Egyptian religious work dating from the New Kingdom known as *The Book of Gates* (also as *The Book of Pylons*). It describes the journey of a deceased soul through the underworld with reference to the journey of the sun god Ra during the night hours. Cats and the night were often regarded as synonymous and not too friendly; the practice of 'putting the cat out' at night still persists. The Egyptian underworld was divided into twelve hours by a series of gates. Each gate was guarded by a large serpent and two deities; in order to pass safely, the deceased was required to name them correctly.

Superstition and stereotyping have affected our love of animals. The dog is man's best friend. Lions are the kings of the beasts. Vultures are evil flesh-eaters. Monkeys are cheeky thieves. We love the chirpy little robin red-breast, the sparrow and the blue tit. Pigeons are either racing champions or flying vermin. Hedgehogs and squirrels are cute, and the badger, beloved of night-vision TV documentaries, is a rural entertainment. The equally 'cute' meercat, which in reality has some pretty unpleasant social habits, now speaks in a Russian accent and gets to go out on dates with Nicole Kidman, thanks to a long-running series of UK TV adverts. It goes on. We have imprecise views on everything from spiders and cockroaches to rats and field mice and superstitions about them all. But when it comes to dogs and cats, our affections are split three ways. Many of us love both species, while some have little time for dogs but love cats. For others, the common domestic cat is hated, feared and disliked.

If you wonder about the way cats behave towards humanity today – the way they decide whom they'll live with, how much affection they'll dole out and the methods they employ making their clever demands whilst 'managing' a household, then you must examine their history of abject persecution. It would be historically and culturally distasteful to use the term 'holocaust' in an animal context, since it has been associated with human brutality since WWII. Yet, next to homo sapiens, the aristocratic *Felis silvestris catus* has been one of the most persecuted species on the planet. What instigated this persecution and kept it chillingly active for a thousand years was superstition.

Perhaps the domestic cat's haughty, suspicious attitude first attracted the slow-burning revenge. There are other, subsidiary, human motivations for their suffering, which are often quite bizarre. They include misguided concerns about public health, inexplicable political and religious paranoia and, although people in the west might consider the canine cuisine of some eastern lands disgusting, the rest of the human world has eaten its fair share of marinated moggy – boiled, grilled or fried. So if you feel that cats regard us with inscrutable disdain and mistrust, there's a reason. If there's a folk memory in regard to humans among felines, then it will be bitter and joyless. Sadly, as ever, in the Middle Ages, the

Church and its inquisition has a lot to answer for, and when the monks fancied a break from human bonfires and torturing, there was always poor old Tiddles to throw into the flames.

CATS AND THE DEVIL

One of the more famous works by the poet Charles Kingsley (1819–1875), remembered for his books *The Water Babies* and *Westward Ho!*, is *The Saint's Tragedy*. This tells the sad tale of St Elizabeth of Hungary, born in 1207, daughter of the Hungarian King Andrew II. Married at fourteen to Louis, son of the *landgrave* of Thuringia, she was known for her compassion and charity work, helping her people during famine and plague and building hospitals. Unfortunately, her husband died on the way to the sixth crusade in 1227. The bane of this young woman's life became Konrad von Marburg (c. 1180–1233).

Marburg was a zealous, sadistic German nobleman and priest. He was more interested in his merciless 'religious' methodology than he was in God. He was commissioned by Pope Innocent III to root out heretics such as the Albigensians. He became confessor to Elizabeth of Hungary, inflicting upon her many acts of brutal physical discipline. In 1231 Elizabeth died and Pope Gregory IX (1170–1241) made Konrad the chief inquisitor in Germany. In his drive to exterminate heresy, he instigated mass atrocities and massacres. He denounced clerical marriage, and sought to reform monasteries. His reign was so bloody and terrifying that a deputation to Gregory by the German bishops sought his removal.

Marburg arrogantly excommunicated the Holy Roman emperor Frederick II for failing to join the sixth crusade. In 1233 he accused Count Henry II of Bendorf-Sayn of heresy and indulging in satanic orgies. In this Marburg's warped imagination was allowed free rein. Needless to say, whenever Beelzebub's followers appeared, cats were heavily involved and Pope Gregory IX happened to have a serious abhorrence of cats.

Count Henry's knightly friends soon had enough of Marburg's venomous campaigns and murdered him in an ambush. But with his zealous, fearsome Dominican and Franciscan legions, Marburg had set in motion an engine of oppressive religious terror that would serve as the template of inquisitions to come, reaching its agonising zenith with Torquemada's Spanish Inquisition in the fifteenth century. Pope Gregory IX (1134–1241, real name Ugolino di Conti) would set a precedent for the cruel persecution of cats.

There is much academic dispute over whether or not Gregory issued a papal bull entitled *Vox in Rama* ('a voice in Rama') between 1232 to 1234. The word 'Rama' should not be confused with the Sanskrit term, where Rama is the seventh avatar of the Hindu god Vishnu. The Catholic version probably comes from the Bible: 'Jeremiah said: "A voice was heard at Ramah, Rachel was weeping over her sons, because they were no more."' (Jeremiah, 31:15). However, it is claimed that this edict condemned a form of devil worship, a German heresy known as Luciferian. *Vox in Rama* describes in highly fanciful detail the licentious goings-on at Satanic get-togethers. How all this 'information' was gathered, seemingly as eyewitness reportage, is a mystery, yet all you needed if you were working for the pope back then was a vivid imagination. If his holiness expected it to be steamy and deviant, the scribes delivered. The following two extracts reveal just what convoluted bunkum you could get away with once Rome had given you high office. It's spiced up with all manner of sexual depravity, including man-on-man, bestiality and acts of incest, and then informs us:

> Afterwards, they sit down to a meal and when they have arisen from it, the certain statue – which is usual in a sect of this kind – a black cat descends backwards, with its tail erect. First the novice, next the master, then each one of the order who are worthy and perfect, kiss the cat on its buttocks. Then each to his place and, speaking certain responses, they incline their heads toward to cat. 'Forgive us!' says the master and the one next to him repeats this, a third responding, 'We know, master!' A fourth says, 'And we must obey.'

To the best of our knowledge, cats can't read, but if they did, they wouldn't like this continuation:

> . . . from a dark corner of the assembly a certain man comes, from the loins upward, shining like the sun. His lower part is shaggy like a cat.'

Once the gullible public had absorbed this kind of dark fantasy, the poor domestic cat was doomed. It would be killed wherever it was found, and black cats were particular targets throughout western Europe, right up until the nineteenth century, by which time almost all black cats had been slaughtered. The pope's zealous fantasist Konrad von Marburg may have been disposed of, but he'd 'confirmed' in his warped view that the domestic pussy was nothing less than the devil himself. Yet he wasn't satisfied with murdering moggies. Horses, dogs, toads, weasels and bats were all supposedly capable of being a witch's familiar. Even geese and goats, according to the Church, became evil vessels of Satan.

Throughout southern Germany people and thousands of cats were rounded up as witches and burned alive. For many years the mass murder of cats continued. It has been suggested that this may have led to the more serious disaster of the black plague because poor old Tiddles was no longer around to perform his public service of eliminating plague-carrying vermin such as rats. That was one outcome the inquisition hadn't bargained for, and in any case, such misfortune was all part of Lucifer's plans.

But the moggy as a plaything for sadists goes way back in folklore. Cats suffered terribly at the time of the summer solstice on 24 June, in the feast of St John the Baptist. It was a time of drunken madness with massive bonfires. Superstition suggested that if you threw things into the fire this would ensure good luck, and one of the favourite items to burn to a crisp was a live cat. They tossed them on in bags, or ceremoniously hanged them first. In the hope of good fortune for the coming years, crowds made bonfires, jumped over and through them, danced around them and threw into the flames objects they thought had magical power. Cats were first tied up in bags, suspended from ropes or burned in smaller fires at the stake.

Richard Darnton's *The Great Cat Massacre and Other Episodes in French Cultural History* (Basic Books, Perseus, 2009) reveals a truly horrible level of cruelty to cats in France in the 1730s which would have made Konrad Marburg and his pontiff boss proud. Parisians liked to incinerate cats by the sackful, while the *courimauds* (*cour à mioud*, or cat-chasers) of Saint Chamond in the Rhône-Alpes region in central France preferred to douse a moggy in something inflammable and chase the flaming feline through the streets.

A disgraceful episode was instigated by Parisian apprentice printers named Jerome and Levaille who were justifiably extremely embittered at their atrocious working conditions. They had to live on the print-shop premises in a squalid attic room, start work very early and finish – exhausted – late at night. On top of this, the food they received was, literally, bordering on garbage. Yet their master's wife kept a pet cat called *la grise* and the lads were angry as this Parisian pussy was pampered with the finest meat morsels and other delicacies. We have to remember that at this time cats were still lumbered with the grim superstition that tormentors like Marburg had initiated centuries earlier, so being cruel to a satanic cat did not seem to be outrageous. Levaille hatched a plan to redress the balance.

Every night for a week he crawled out of the apprentice's room onto the roof and made very convincing cat noises, howling and meowing to such an extent that everyone on the premises was kept awake. Eventually, their boss could stand no more and instructed the lads to somehow get rid of the cats that he now believed were plaguing his domestic peace. The apprentices eagerly obeyed and one of the first doomed felines among the many they rounded up was their mistress's beloved *la grise*, who was hanged by the neck. They gathered tools from the workshop and used them viciously in a carefully orchestrated cat massacre. The bludgeoned animals had mock trials, with named 'confessors', guards and a specially erected gallows. The merciless spectacle continued to peals of cruel laughter as cat after cat was beaten and hung. It's uncertain what improvement, if any, this made to their working conditions, but they had punished their master and his wife with their cowardly cruelty and bragged about it for months afterwards.

In Lorraine and Burgundy the locals enjoyed an inflammable maypole to which they tied a live cat then danced around it. In the Metz region one cat's agony was insufficient so they devised wicker baskets which held a dozen cats that would burn nicely on top of a bonfire. This pathetic ritual took place with great pageantry until it was abolished in 1765. The mayor and his administration would walk in a 'dignified' procession to the large funeral pyre at the Place du Grand-Saulcy and, as it was set ablaze, riflemen from the garrison encircled the screaming, burning cats as they fired off volleys to mass human joy and cheering.

The practice varied throughout Europe but the basic routine was repeated: a bonfire, mock witch-hunting plus incinerated cats and mass hilarity. This dark legacy can still be enjoyed today in Ypres, Belgium. One might think, with the town's dark WWI history, that the Belgians might have had enough of smashed bodies and cruelty. Not so; the *Kattenstoet* ('festival of the cats') has been held on the second Sunday of May since 1955. The forty-fourth outing was on 10 May 2015, with the next planned, at the time of writing for 13 May 2018. So what does such a jolly gathering celebrate? This civic tourist attraction celebrates Ypres in the Middle Ages, when cats were thrown from the belfry tower of the Cloth Hall to their painful death in the town square below. Today they throw stuffed kiddies' toy cats, but the echoes of animal cruelty must echo around the town.

For four centuries after the pope's *Vox in Rama*, the feline slaughter continued. Any excuse triggered another cat pogrom. It may have had more to do with misinformed public health scares in those later years, but cats still had that dark burden of superstition to carry. As time progressed, it wasn't only black cats that would suffer. All cats fell under the threat.

In Switzerland in the town of Berne in 1809, eight hundred cats were rounded up and killed. The French were still well into cat massacring in the mid-nineteenth century. Some members of what was left of the French nobility liked to think they were doing the community a service by rounding up a town's cats and letting their hunting hounds loose on them. A certain marquis liked to traverse Europe with his pack of hounds in tow, and, if they could find any feline victims en route, the dogs did their grisly business until, in one instance, a treasured cat was torn asunder by the canine horde. The important local woman to whom this cherished and much-loved moggy belonged made sure that its disfigured cadaver was served up on a plate to the vicious master of the hunt for dinner. As an angry statement by an animal lover it appears powerful. However, in a land where snails, small birds (such as the cruelly tortured little ortolan, a disgusting delicacy apparently making a comeback) and frogs made up the regular cuisine, the cat was always a good substitute for a fluffy roast bunny.

In the 1850s, cat-catchers in Paris, armed with a heavy club, a terrier dog and handy sack, would throw chunks of liver into the street at night. When the local cats got the scent of this morsel, they would gather around, only to be savaged by the dog or clubbed to death, thrown into the sack and sold to Paris's many *palaces d'cuisine* the next day. Then, still on the subject of French animal husbandry, came this report in the *British Veterinary Journal* in 1889:

A massacre of cats has been organised at Corbeil, not far from Paris. Two persons living in the town were bitten by a local 'tabby' which was declared rabid by a veterinary surgeon, whereupon the destruction of the town pussies en masse was decreed by the inhabitants. It is to be hoped, however, that the people who have organised the massacre will be brought to their senses before they pave the way for a plague of rats and mice – a contingency to which their present wild and extraordinary conduct would seem to point.

Religiously inspired cruelty was often the mainstay of the cycles of carnivals throughout the year, and none was more important than blowing off steam at the celebration of Lent. Lent was a period of abstinence and the carnival was an excuse, especially among apprentices and other youth, to stage a *charivari*. The term is defined by the *Oxford English Dictionary* as 'A cacophonous mock serenade, typically performed by a group of people in derision of an unpopular person or in celebration of a marriage.' For example, the *charivari* gave you the chance to take the mickey out of the cukolded husband who would be mocked to loud, coarse music. Other victims were husbands who had allowed their wives to beat them, older brides who had married younger men, in fact any hapless local who was deemed to behave outside the traditional norm. Were cats involved? Oh, yes. In Burgundy, while mocking your hapless victim, a live cat was passed around between the baying youths, each one taking a turn to tear some of the poor animal's fur out to make it howl, the louder the better. They had a nice name for this torture; *faire le chat*. The Germans seemed to have enjoyed the howling of cats to the point where they called their *charivaris Katzenmusik* (cat music). All this sadistic jollity culminated on Mardi Gras, Shrove Tuesday, with the ritual trial and execution of a straw mannequin, known as King Carnival or *Caramantran*.

Why did the poor cat have to suffer so much, and what sense of 'humour' did Europeans possess to find such heartless malice so side-splitting? Perhaps that superstitious Beelzebub brand remained as a valid passport to pussy persecution.

Most animals, including us, have a patron saint. Dogs have been well served by St Roch (1295–1327), but the cat had to wait a little longer. St Gertrude of Nivelles (626–659) founded Belgium's Benedictine monastery of Nivelles with her mother Itta. Although she was never formally canonised, in 1677 Pope Clement XII declared her universal feast day to be 17 March. Gertrude has recently been honoured as the patron saint of the cat due to her reputation for dealing with mice and rats, although the first mention of her as patron of the cats is in a 1981 catalogue issued by New York's Metropolitan Museum of Art. But if we add cats to her other duties as a patron saint of travellers, gardeners and mental illness, then it's pleasant to know the feline belatedly fares well in the Catholic canon.

It would be almost a century and a half after the Corbeil cat massacre before brutality towards innocent animals such as cats was curbed legally. Here's what a famous twentieth-century law decreed about such heartless torture:

Section I #1 (1) It is forbidden to unnecessarily torment or roughly mishandle an animal.

(2) One torments an animal when one repeatedly or continuously causes appreciable pain or suffering; the torment is unnecessary in so far as it does not serve any rational, justifiable purpose. One mishandles an animal when one causes it appreciable pain; mishandling is rough when it corresponds to an unfeeling state of mind.

. . .

Section IV Provisions for Punishment #9 (1) Whoever unnecessarily torments or roughly mishandles an animal will be punished by up to two years in prison, with a fine, or with both these penalties.

At last! Humanity had woken up to the sublime innocence of the animal kingdom. Sadly, at the same time, regard for humanity was going into reverse, because the above quoted act was passed into law in Berlin on 24 November 1933 and enthusiastically signed by a superstitious but dedicated animal lover, Adolf Hitler.

Worse things happen at sea

There is one knows not what sweet mystery about this sea, whose gently awful stirrings seem to speak of some hidden soul beneath.

Herman Melville, _Moby-Dick_, 1851

I was a merchant seaman for seven years, with a few breaks ashore, and, coming from a family of mariners, I already knew how superstitious many sailors were. I say 'were' because many of these sea-going superstitions have slowly sunk out of use over recent decades. This is probably the result of both engineering and scientific progress and the more accommodating social world we now live in.

In the days of wooden sailing ships, the voyages of which could take years, the sea, which covers seven-tenths of the earth's surface, was as wild, mysterious and unpredictable as outer space is proving to be today. The voyage of a whaling ship out of Nantucket or New Bedford in the first half of the nineteenth century could easily last four years and circle the globe. Many parts of the seven seas remained unexplored and in such an environment good luck was at a premium. When strange things happened, there was usually a superstition to blame.

One of the oldest superstitions held by sailors was that of the ill luck expected by having a woman on board. Even when I was at sea, the thought of a female navigation officer was unheard of and the nautical school I attended, Trinity House, was an all-male establishment in 1959, with the exception of the headmaster's secretary. There were probably female operatives in Soviet Russia's shipping fleets, just as there were ashore digging roads and driving trams, and on the big UK passenger liners there were stewardesses, but that was it.

Today, the navigation of huge container ships is often shared by women and my old school happily accommodates female students. Women were a distraction, causing intemperate seas to take their revenge out on the ship, unless they were naked, in which case they were welcome because naked women were thought to calm the sea. This is why many vessels had a figurehead of a topless woman perched on the bow of the ship. Her bare breasts would shame the stormy seas into calm while her open eyes guided the seamen to safety.

Before the naked lady made her welcome appearance in the nineteenth century (always a nice painting job for an imaginative sailor), a figurehead could be a war hero, the vessel's owner or – on warships – a proud beast such as a lion. The tradition may have come from the ancient Egyptians who painted eyes on the bow to help the ship find its way and as a protection against evil. This ancient practice is still in vogue in many Mediterranean fishing fleets.

As for real, live naked women on board, it was definitely against regulations. When I sailed the coast of New Zealand in the early 1960s, the more experienced senior crewmen would smuggle girls on board in Auckland or Wellington and hide them in their cabins, dropping them ashore at the next convenient port. I was too inexperienced at seventeen to get such pleasure for myself, but the sight of a naked off-duty Auckland hospital nurse in the showers one morning is burned into my memory.

I grew up in Hull, Yorkshire, the UK's third-busiest port for the merchant service. Its main oceanic trade was deep-sea fishing. As with the country's mining industry, Hull's fishing prowess is today a thing of the past, the once bustling St Andrew's fish dock, finally closed in 1975, is a silted-up swamp of dereliction.

In deep-sea fishing's heyday, which lasted just over a century, trawler crews and their families had so many of their own peculiar beliefs. Many of those odd superstitions were left over from a previous golden age from the early eighteenth to the mid-nineteenth century, when Hull was one of the whaling capitals of the world. Massive stocks of cod and haddock began to be plundered in the North Sea in an area which became known as the silver pit, and Hull exchanged whaling for another kind of fishing. From then on fish became an immensely profitable industry and fish and chip shops spread throughout the UK. Yet the man who discovered the silver pit is said to have died penniless in a Hull workhouse.

By 1962 some fisherman superstitions were facing steady extinction while many of those held by their wives, families and relatives still hung on. It was that year that Jeremy Tunstall wrote one of the best books on Britain's trawler fleets, *The Fishermen* (Granada Publishing). Tunstall discovered that deep-sea trawler men were indeed a breed apart, and after attending a service at the Fishermen's Bethel in Hull, with a congregation of 150, he noted that the congregation were 'mostly middle-aged couples with a sprinkling of children and ugly girls' (hailing from Hull, I take exception at the 'ugly girls' bit). He reached his own, but accurate, conclusions as to what made these men different. Tunstall said, 'Life at sea is so harsh, the talk so obscene, the values enshrined in formal religion so despised, that the religious fisherman is an eccentric.'

I can certainly vouch for the extreme verbal obscenity of the fishermen I knew, some being members of our family. It went beyond the confines of the lexicon of sexual expletives, yet oddly enough there was still a residue of respect for God. So although after a few pints a fisherman on shore might call you (brace yourself) something like a 'bastard, jam-strangling, cross-eyed f**k-pig,' you'd rarely if ever hear him say 'Jesus Christ' or 'bloody hell'.

Tunstall tells the rather uncouth yet amusing story of a trawler's galley boy who had looked up at the bridge when the nets were being pulled in, seemingly packed with cod. But as the promising harvest broke the surface, it was clear that the net had split and all the fish were falling back into the sea. The incandescent skipper yelled, 'God – if there is a God – I hope you catch the pox from the Virgin Mary!'

Living on Hessle Road, the heart of the fishing community in the 1950s, the first superstition I recall took the form of a regular warning issued by parents. 'If you don't behave, one of these nights Harry-off-Dock will get you.' The said Harry was obviously a local substitute for the ubiquitous bogeyman. This chimerical figure was a distillation of everything the more straight-laced West Hull residents hated about trawler crews. They were seen as loud, roaring drunken wastrels with a penchant for brawling and consequently, to some, an embarrassment to the city. The superstitious myth of 'Harry-off-Dock' among us kids conjured up a wild-haired rubicund wiry man who walked with a roll and dressed in the fisherman's shore rig, a bell-bottomed powder blue suit with a Spanish waistband and white shirt opened to the waist, the whole package smelling strongly of rum, Hull Brewery beer and stale Woodbines. There were many such characters around on winter nights and each one we saw could well have been the real horrible Harry.

Considering the deadly rigour of their occupation, their on-shore lifestyle was hardly surprising. Three weeks at sea, often in bitter, dangerous Arctic conditions in mountainous seas, would only be rewarded by three days ashore before setting off again. Basic wages for a deckhand in the 1950s were around £8 per week, although with a share of the catch money he could double that, and with beer at just over a shilling (5p) a pint, you could have a good pub crawl for a pound. Safely ashore, if they'd had a good trip, they were nicknamed the 'three-day millionaires', travelling everywhere from pub to pub by taxi. Up in Aberdeen, trawler men tended to be more religious. Not in Hull. Even though the crew mess in every trawler carried a pristine copy of the *New Testament,* it was rarely if ever taken from the shelf. Many of the city's older fishermen were indeed superstitious, but the younger breed did not always follow suit. However, when fishermen were criticising other fishermen, perhaps those of the rival fleet in Grimsby, they might dub them 'stupid and superstitious'. Yet there were odd words, inexplicably never to be mentioned on board, such as 'rabbit', 'drowned', 'pig' or any reference to elephants and monkeys. Saying 'goodbye' or even 'good luck' was often frowned upon. There was a bad luck superstition about the colour green, associated with jealousy and envy. This always seemed odd because the vessels of Hull's most successful cargo fleet, Ellerman's Wilson Line, were mostly painted grass green.

On sailing days, fishermen's wives would not wash their clothes in case doing so might lead to their men being drowned. It was regarded as 'washing your man away'. It was bad luck for a ship to sail on Fridays. Keen internet surfers should not be taken in by the myth that the Royal Navy attempted to nail superstitions once and for all by launching a vessel called HMS *Friday*. The legend goes that she was launched on a Friday and a Captain James Friday placed in command. Then the doomed boat mysteriously disappeared. Julian Thomas at Portsmouth's Royal Navy museum will tell you that HMS *Friday* never existed. He told the BBC that the story regularly arose, particularly around Friday the 13th.

In ancient times Thursdays were said to be bad sailing days because that was Thor's day and he was considered to be the god of thunder and storms. Also avoided in earlier times was the first Monday in April, believed to be the day Cain slew Abel and – still on a biblical theme – the second Monday in August, allegedly the day the kingdoms of Sodom and Gomorrah were destroyed. Later, the religious references faded, to be replaced with superstitions including one that said a man sleeping in his bunk on his stomach represented a bad omen; the ship might sink. The same applied to cutting bread and then turning the loaf upside down, or upturning a hatch cover. Most sailors, especially in Nelson's time, couldn't even swim, so going into the briny for a dip would have been pushing the sea gods just too far. There were instances where, if a man fell overboard, he might not even be thrown a rope, because superstition could have dictated that his death was preordained. In ancient times, a sailor suffering such a fate might even have been considered to be a sacrifice to Neptune or Poseidon.

Whistling on board has been frowned on since the days of sail as it could encourage a storm. The religious version has its root in a legend that as Christ was being nailed to the Cross a woman stood by and whistled. One has to wonder what tune she used back in old Judea.

In the unlikely instance of your fiancée bringing you a bouquet to see you off, she'd discover that flowers were unwelcome on a ship due to their association with funerals. They were quickly thrown overboard. Although they didn't throw the vicar overboard, clergymen weren't welcomed either because of their own connection with funerals.

You would not stir tea on board with a knife or fork, cross knives on the galley table or lay a broom on top of the nets. In some fishing fleets, as the fishing season commenced, the nets were 'salted in' to bring good luck with a blessing by sprinkling them with salt.

Long before the mechanisation of trawling for fish became synonymous with shareholders' profits, fishing on every day of the week was considered greedy and unlucky. It expressed your dissatisfaction with what the oceanic gods had provided.

Sharks following a ship were thought to be an omen of death. In the days before adequate refrigeration, if somebody did die aboard ship, it was considered bad luck to keep their corpse on board, and the body received the ceremony for burial at sea as soon as possible. A ship's carpenter would not keep an empty coffin on board as that signified that one of the crew was about to expire. Sail-makers would make a canvas shroud to sew a dead sailor in, making the last stitch through the victim's nose. That last stitch ensured the man was truly dead – had there still been a spark of life there, then he would certainly have cried out in pain.

Variations of all these superstitions and more emanated from all the fishing ports, such as Fleetwood, Brixham, Lowestoft, Grimsby and Aberdeen. To avoid bad luck, you'd never kill a dolphin or a seagull. Were some of these beliefs still current in recent times? To answer this, in 1962 the intrepid journalist Jeremy Tunstall took a trip on a Hull trawler and decided to test out the old superstitions. He wore a green shirt and no one commented. A few days out at sea, he noticed to his surprise that the wheelman was casually whistling on the bridge. When Tunstall mentioned this to him, the reply was, 'Are you superstitious or something?'

Blame the Ancient Mariner

'Ah! well a-day! What evil looks
Had I from old and young!
Instead of the cross, the albatross
About my neck was hung.'

Samuel Taylor Coleridge, *The Rime of the Ancient Mariner*, 1798

One of the strangest maritime prohibitions – known even by landlubbers – is that it's fatal to kill an albatross. Samuel Taylor Coleridge (1772–1834) had been told of a dream by a friend called John Cruikshank in which a phantom, decaying ship was manned by a crew of skeletal ghosts. The idea stuck with Coleridge, who conceived his weird and haunting poem 'The Rime of the Ancient Mariner' after he'd been out walking with his friend William Wordsworth and Wordsworth's sister. The ramble took place at the port of Watchet on the banks of the Bristol Channel. Wordsworth apparently contributed a few lines to the poem on the walk, referring to the central character as the 'old navigator' and planting the idea that he might kill an albatross as the ship rounded Cape Horn and be attended by that location's traditional 'tutelary spirits'. The poem is peculiar for many reasons, but it always seems puzzling that a poor hapless bridegroom en route to his nuptials has to listen to the batty old sailor's awful yarn, hardly the kind of thing you'd want to put up with on your wedding day.

Penalties for killing birds of any kind loom large in superstitions – to kill, for example, a blackbird or a robin is tantamount to signing your death warrant. The albatross, however, has much wider implications for the crew of a ship as a whole. I was told by seagoing relatives long before I sailed that spotting an albatross was a sign of bad weather to come and that old seamen used to believe the albatross was the spirit of a dead sailor giving warnings. When I did get out to sea I learned that dolphins swimming with the ship were seen as a good sign (and sharks following us weren't) but no one mentioned anything about albatrosses and I saw plenty of big, magnificent specimens. I once mentioned the possibility that some fool might want to kill one and I was told that the only time this might happen was in a lifeboat, adrift and full of starving sailors, and then only for food. If your survival depended on it, then perhaps the albatross would, if anything, be a good-luck bird.

As with Friday the 13th, the dread of which is a Victorian invention, I'm grateful once again for the erudition of Steve Roud in his *Pocket Guide to Superstitions of the British Isles,* for confirming my belief that before Coleridge wrote his sinister, doomy poem, the albatross superstition did not exist.

THE CURSE OF THE CALPEAN STAR

As original superstitions go, Coleridge's albatross worked well down the centuries, as was demonstrated by the story of Liverpool vessel the *Calpean Star.* According to a report in Ohio newspaper the *Toledo Blade*, the ship was originally launched as the *Highland Chieftain* in 1928 and belonged to a fleet of cruise ships which carried passengers and cargo. At 14,000 tons, the *Highland Chieftain* measured 163 meters in length and sailed between Europe and South America with 150 first-class passengers, seventy second-class and 500 in jam-packed third class. During WWII she was a troop carrier and suffered heavy bomb damage. She did not return to service until 1948. In 1959 the *Highland Chieftain* was bought by the Calpe shipping company, completely re-furbished and re-named *Calpean Star.* And that's when the trouble started – even changing a ship's name can be a bad omen.

In June 1959 she took on board a cargo of assorted animals and birds, including a caged albatross, which were bound for a zoo in Germany. One of the crew charged with feeding the menagerie gave the albatross the wrong food and it died. Apparently some sailors were already distressed by the bird being in a cage, regarding the albatross as the mariner's friend. Now they'd killed one. The frustrated Canadian skipper, Captain Philip Everett Price, later said 'I had to have courage bringing that thing on board . . .'

When the ship arrived in Liverpool, her 62-man crew were now convinced that the ship was cursed. They demanded to be paid off and refused to sail to her next port, Oslo. The men were replaced and the vessel left for Norway. The generators broke down several times. Oil leaked into the ship's water supply. A break in the main engine compressor left the vessel adrift without power for days. Eventually, after several repairs, by which time she was bound for South America, her rudder was fractured and a tug had to tow her into Montevideo for more repairs.

As the *Calpean Star* left Montevideo, her engine room was wrecked with a massive explosion followed by a fire. Some crew drowned as the ship was abandoned and thoughts of the albatross naturally occupied those in the lifeboats. The *Calpean Star* partially sank beneath the waves, her mast remaining above the surface before she was finally broken up in the 1960s. The company decided to repatriate the surviving crew by air but the plane's landing gear broke down as it touched down in Rio de Janeiro. Only when the surviving crew finally made it home did they feel secure in claiming that the curse of the dead albatross was at an end.

Mother Carey's chickens

Thanks to Coleridge and his Ancient Mariner, the stately albatross may have become the figurehead of avian maritime superstition, but there is another seabird that was suspiciously regarded by sailors long before Coleridge picked up his pen. Storm petrels became known as Mother Carey's chickens. Dark in colour, they are the smallest of seabirds, and their hovering, bat-like fluttering must have been quite unnerving for superstitious seamen. They give the impression of walking across the water's surface in a peculiar manner. Storm petrels making their appearance in the vicinity of a vessel were considered the harbingers of seriously bad weather, hence their name, which inevitably has religious connotations. 'Petrel' is connected to St Peter because the word is a diminutive form of his name. So who was Mother Carey?

Among most English-speaking sailors of the eighteenth and nineteenth centuries she personified the cruel and threatening sea. She shared a reputation in this respect with Davy Jones, and many mariners considered her to be his wife. The name Mother Carey appears to have originated in the Latin for 'precious mother' – '*Mater cara*' – yet another title of the Virgin Mary. In his collection from 1902, *Salt Water Ballads*, that great sea poet John Masefield (1878–1967) included the poem 'Mother Carey (as told to me by the bo'sun)' in which he links Davy Jones and Mother Carey as an irresponsible couple plotting shipwrecks and storms.

In France and the UK this superstitious reputation has earned the bird names such as '*satanique*', 'water-witch', '*satanite*', and '*oiseau du diable*'. Marine superstitions in Brittany have a touch of the *Flying Dutchman* about them, as Breton sailors see the storm petrel as the embodiment of the lost souls of drowned sailors or captains who were cruel to their crews. Davy Jones and Mother Carey were believed to occupy a seabed wonderland called Fiddler's Green, a place where the fiddler plays continuously, the dancing never stops and the beer flows free. No one could accuse old-time sailors of lacking imagination.

The storm petrel also inspired the revolutionary Russian poet Maxim Gorky. The bird appears in an approximate translation as the name of the lead character in 'Song of the Stormy Petrel', Gorky's 1901 poem describing Russian society's attitudes to the coming revolution. This poem became known as the battle anthem of the revolution and Gorky earned the title of the 'storm petrel of the revolution'. Some armed groups in the Spanish civil war went under the name Stormy Petrel, and it was also the title of publications by several anarchist groups both in Russia and the UK. The legendary Spanish civil war anarchist leader José Buenaventura Durruti (1896–1936) was described in 1936 by the American socialist writer Emma Goldman as 'this stormy petrel of the anarchist and revolutionary movement'. So, forget the poor old albatross; seems like Mother Carey's chickens rule the roost.

A SON OF A GUN, TOUCHING THE BUN

Contrary to all the superstitions about women on board, such an embargo appears to have been frequently broken in the Royal Navy because numerous births occurred on board. Male children were referred to as a 'son of a gun', the gun deck being the most convenient place to give birth. A male child on board was a sign of good luck.

Of course, if a crew were strict in never having women on board, they would still need some female good luck to see them on their way. Many sailors in all branches of seafaring followed a practice well into the twentieth century of 'touching the bun' before setting off for the docks. It simply means cupping your hand over your wife or girlfriend's pudenda to ensure good fortune on your voyage and a safe return. Risqué lot, those salacious sailors . . .

Superstitious ink

There are other oddities to a sailor's life, one of which spilled into mainstream culture like a Texas Gulf oil slick. Seamen and some soldiers used to get tattoos at each port, using their skin to tell their story. Like a logbook, their body revealed the important moments in their lives. My father, who spent twenty years in India with the army, was the original illustrated man. He had the flags of the British empire on his back, lions and tigers on his chest, a crucifix, and in the 1930s was told by a tattooist in Rawalpindi that the 'lucky' snakes which encircled his arms, their forked tongues emerging onto his wrists, were a permanent protection against 'the evil eye'. Perhaps they protected him in India, but he certainly wasn't lucky for the rest of his life in the UK and died of cancer.

One drunken night in 1959 in Valetta, Malta, I sat in the tattooist's chair ready to have a Popeye-style anchor inked on my forearm. In the chair next to me sat a bulky US Navy sailor, stripped to the waist ready to have the one square inch of his torso still vacant inked in. His crassly daubed body seemed so repulsive to me that I sobered up and left. I'm glad I made that decision. But if you're a recent convert to the dubious 'art' of the inky needle, you may want to skip this section.

Today, especially in the grimly stained nation of the UK, tattoos as a fashion accessory seem to have crept across acres of once pristine British skin into what appears to me like a dirty, grey-green ingrained fungus which in my opinion will forever identify their owners in their sad, wrinkled days to come as coming from the 'Look at me – I'm from the "windswept and interesting" generation of the early twenty-first century.' Great athletic bodies have been ruined by this inky blight – would any sensible man, given the gift of a body like that of David Beckham, choose to turn it into a facsimile of a graffiti-disfigured urban underpass wall? Yet they do. This tragedy is compounded by the ruination of countless female limbs, too. Even the prime minister's wife, Samantha Cameron, has a tattoo. Why? Thousands of already less-than-attractive people have added to their ugliness in the hope of adding a touch of the exotic to their waddling physique. Yet how many of the inked masses will live to regret their sorry Celtic swirls, skulls, badly translated Chinese graphics, greengrocer's apostrophes and deficiently placed rosebuds? How few realise what real tattoos once meant?

Seafarers would usually tattoo a nautical star on their bodies as the North Star represented a signal that they were nearing home. It was a sign of luck. Bad luck was to have the name of your lover as a tattoo. Even today many tattooists will not recommend this, because the superstition persists that once your relationship becomes an inking, you'd be doomed to part. It is also considered unlucky to be tattooed with your own zodiac sign.

Religious tattoos from any denomination are replete with superstition, especially in countries like China. It is considered bad luck and disrespectful to get a tattoo of a deity, especially on your back where you would be 'resting on them'. The Chinese consider a back inking as being 'stabbed in the back', resulting in bad karma.

The Chinese take the saying 'the eyes are the windows to the soul' literally. They believe when you dot or fill in the eyes, the creature, thus completed, comes to life. If it isn't brought to life by this completion it brings bad luck and imbalance. Superstitious tattooists undertaking Japanese and other oriental animals and creatures won't highlight or fill in the eyes until the piece is almost complete. Similarly, the lion dance of the Chinese New Year is started by 'dotting of the eyes' of the lion with incense, thereby waking up the creature to start the dance that wards off evil.

Although tattooing is forbidden in most prisons, it still happens in secret, with any tools which come to hand. Ink can come from melted rubber from the sole of a shoe, soot or ash, and sterilisation is achieved with urine. Large criminal organisations such as the Russian or Mexican mafia now use tattoos widely. Each image has a meaning, including gang membership and certain achievements, and they are often only understood by fellow criminals. For example, the seven onion domes of a Russian cathedral across your shoulder blades may indicate seven years in prison. Other mafia tattoos are often enforced on those who have betrayed them or committed some crime they find disagreeable, such as child molestation. You're likely to have your guilt brutally engraved across your forehead for all time.

In equatorial Africa, tattooing and mutilating of the bodies of family members among some tribes indicates that one of their loved ones has met the grim reaper.

Those who seek a real artistic experience with extensive body inking are inevitably drawn to Japan, and reading Jill 'Horiyuki' Mandelbaum's *Studying Horiyoshi III: A Westerner's Journey into Japanese Tattoo* (Schiffer, 2008) is essential for inkers and inked alike. Japan has an ancient tattoo culture, but the practice is also associated with the Yakuza criminal gangs, who go in for full-body inking. Establishments such as hot springs (*onsen*), beaches, water parks, swimming pools and theme parks still ban tattoos entirely, and where a ban exists you will see prominent warning signs. Just as many UK employers are still wary of taking on staff with visible tattoos; and the mayor of Osaka launched a controversial campaign in 2012 to force employees of the city to declare their tattoos.

Whether or not tattoos are taboo with Christians is still debated. Some American ministers affirm that as long as an inking said 'Jesus' or was of a 'Christian' nature that would be permissible. However, Leviticus 19:28 says explicitly, 'You shall not make any cuts in your body for the dead nor make any tattoo marks on yourselves: I am the Lord.' Born-again evangelists would argue that this command was invalid as it comes from the Old Testament rather than the new. So the controversy rumbles on. In the end, despite all the superstitions, tattoos are a matter of personal choice, like clothing or hairstyles. The only difference being that you can change your hairstyle and when your flared trousers wear out you throw them away. Like a dog at Christmas, a tattoo is for ever – not just the current fashion season.

Subject over – tattoo fans can start reading again.

On-board oddities

Back to the ocean – a pierced earlobe on a sailor used to mean that he had crossed the equator and sailed around the world. The pirate look has remained popular, thanks to the likes of Johnny Depp in *Pirates of the Caribbean* (2003, USA) – superstitious sailors wore gold hoop earrings to bring good fortune. It was thought that gold possessed magical healing powers and was considered as a protective talisman that would prevent the wearer from drowning. Another was the odd belief that it would improve a sailor's eyesight. Not to forget that gold earrings provided back-up funds when needed. If you ended up blind drunk and penniless in some foreign port you could buy your way out of trouble, and, if you were to die, your aural bling would cover the cost of a coffin and funeral. So earrings served other purposes than making you look exotic and vaguely interesting.

In ancient times, gold coins placed on the eyes of a corpse were used to pay the boatman, Charon, for the voyage across the river Styx. Perhaps it was the slump in the world economy in later centuries which resulted in gold coins being replaced by pennies.

The catalogue of marine superstitions is a long one. 'Red sky in the morning, sailor take warning, red sky at night, sailor's delight.' This is undoubtedly the best-known English weather prediction, possessing some basis in fact. Britain's weather conditions emanate from the ocean to the west. If the air is clear, sunset will be tinted red. In the morning, red light will be reflected by clouds to the west, signifying moisture in the air and possible storms.

Sailors also used to say 'Rain at seven means fine by eleven.' There is also a ring of truth here. Rainy days are usually made up of sporadic showers, rarely lasting for over four hours.

Another sign of rain was a ring around the moon, formed by ice crystals in the upper atmosphere that meant a possibility of rain.

Cutting your nails, hair or trimming one's beard on board were considered to be bad omens by old-time buccaneers.

In later times, you would never encourage foul weather on a ship by bringing an umbrella on board, and no one ever got a round of applause because the clapping of hands was thought to invite thunder. Nor would you throw stones into the sea because that might create a heavy swell or a storm.

There was also the thorny question of a sailor being expected to 'pay his dues'. Seamen who avoided settling their debts could be blamed for storms and any other catastrophe experienced at sea.

Then there's that humble and tasty snack – the banana. US Army crews had regarded the apricot as a definite no-no in tanks since WWII, and on a ship the fruit in question was the banana. They may be the stock-in-trade for slapstick comedy, yet they were thought to bring bad luck – which was unfortunate if you signed on a banana boat when trade was at its height between Spain and the Caribbean in the sixteenth century. Before refrigeration, bananas spoiled rapidly without a cool hold and ships and crews were pushed mercilessly to shorten the length of the voyage. With the sun beating down on a sealed ship's hold, over-ripe bananas also ferment quickly, the result being toxic fumes. In addition, I knew Hull dockers who often reported encountering some hideously large venomous spiders when unloading cargoes of bananas. As Harry Belafonte's 'Banana Boat Song' had it: 'I see deadly black tarantula . . .' There are many grim yarns about bananas but they all seem over-exaggerated, and I recall eating plenty of the yellow delights with custard in the mess room.

What's in a Name?

People often wonder why sailors always refer to their vessels as 'she'. This may have originated in the word for 'ship' in most Mediterranean tongues being feminine. So even if your ship had a butch name like *Hector* or *Achilles*, it would still be a 'she'. Ships were associated nostalgically with the wives, girlfriends and mothers the sailors had left ashore. This was hardly surprising. In the old whaling days, crews could be away for years and would spend more time with their boat than they'd ever spend with the ladies back home. In Melville's *Moby-Dick*, Captain Ahab tells Starbuck 'For forty years has Ahab forsaken the peaceful land, for forty years to make war on the horrors of the deep! Aye and yes, Starbuck, out of those forty years I have not spent three ashore.' He regards his living wife as a 'widow'. In an all-male crew, the ship takes on feminine aspects and is often regarded as a woman with her distinct personality and in the ways she prefers to be handled. Oddly enough, though, the feminine seems to have been side-lined with the term 'man of war'.

Traditionally, launching and naming a ship was a special ceremony accompanied by a ritual to bring good fortune and safety to all who sailed in her. The ceremony dates back thousands of years. There is evidence that the Babylonians celebrated ship launching in the third millennium BC, and the Egyptians, Romans and Greeks called upon their gods to protect new ships. It appears that the Vikings, living up to their violent reputation, enjoyed spilling blood during a longboat launch. Legend has it that they tied prisoners or worn-out slaves to the skids, the new boat crushing their bodies as it slid into the water. Oh, those playful Norsemen, always ready for a laugh or two . . . The supposedly civilised Greeks were also believed to have greased the skids with blood. Eventually, a touch of humanity intervened and blood was replaced with a few deftly placed symbolic red ribbons. Another substitute was wine and more recently champagne. Today, women launch vessels, whereas historically it would have been local male dignitaries or priests. When a ship was fitted out, a coin would be placed under the base of the mast for good luck. If the mast was ever replaced, an additional coin would be put there.

Changing the name of a ship is weighed down with portents and omens. It was thought to make the vessel very unlucky and superstition demanded yet more ritualistic behaviour to send a vessel off with a new name. Maritime mythology has it that the Roman god of the sea, Neptune, keeps a ledger of the deep in which he logs the name of every vessel ever launched. If you don't wish to anger the gods of the ocean you must seek to obliterate every vestige of a ship's previous existence from land and sea and thereby from Neptune's memory. A de-naming ceremony used to be vital. This was carried out by writing the vessel's original name on a piece of paper which was folded up and placed in a small wooden box. The box was then burned and the carefully preserved ashes cast into the sea.

It has been said that it was bad luck to give a ship a name ending with the letter 'a'. The *Lusitania* and HMS *Britannia* were sunk in WWI and the *Laconia* was torpedoed in WWII. More recently, a vessel with two potentially doomed parts of its name – *Costa Concordia* – went down off the coast of Italy. Yet, no doubt, you could find examples of numerous similar tragedies with every letter of the alphabet. Sir Ernest Shackleton (1874–1922) was on the Antarctic exploration ship originally called the *Aurora*. The great man had a family motto, 'Through endurance we conquer', and changed the name to *Endurance*. Knowing as we do now what befell the *Endurance*, we could say that superstition prevailed. Shackleton, however, was a remarkable leader, and following the loss of the *Endurance* in 1915, he guided his 28-man crew on a gruelling journey to Elephant Island. He then made a bitterly punishing sixteen-day crossing of more than eight hundred miles in an open lifeboat to reach South Georgia and trekked across the island to a whaling station to seek help. The suffering men left on Elephant Island were rescued when Shackleton returned in August 1916. Not one member of the expedition died.

If sailors ever did find their ship's name ending in an 'a' to be disturbing, how worried might the crew of the US Navy's first aircraft carrier, the *Saratoga*, have been? She served well in WWII but was unlucky enough to be targeted by Japanese kamikaze pilots, yet she stayed afloat. Her sad end wasn't the result of bad luck, however. When they began testing the atomic bomb at Bikini Atoll in the Pacific in 1946, the *Saratoga* was sunk as part of the test process. In recent years her wreck has been a firm favourite for adventurous diving clubs.

Finally, let's not forget the Jonah. A Jonah was a crewman who brought bad luck. The superstition has its origin in the Bible, where the prophet Jonah is sent by God to the sinful city of Nineveh to knock some sense into the citizens there.

Jonah 1: 'The word of the Lord came to Jonah son of Amittai.

2: 'Go to the great city of Nineveh and preach against it because its wicked-ness has come up before me.'

3: But Jonah ran away from the Lord and headed for Tarshish. He went down to Joppa where he found a ship bound for that port. After paying the fare, he went aboard and sailed for Tarshish to flee from the Lord.'

So the cowardly Jonah shouldn't have been at sea at all. A series of violent storms threatened his ship, and when the crew became disgusted with Jonah, he was chucked overboard and he was swallowed by a 'great fish', which has come to mean a whale. Of course, the whale spat him out and he fulfilled his mission in Ninevah.

Was there ever such a man at sea you could call a Jonah? Well, in 1961 while I was on an old tramp steamer, we picked up a spare engine-room fireman, an Egyptian called Abdul, and he brought with him a definite doomy ambience. We shunned him; he predicted a hurricane a few days out from Panama and we got one – a real force-twelve humdinger. He knew he was unpopular and went ashore in Colon and we never saw him again (or another hurricane).

Superstition? Why not . . . it just might be true . . .

Saints of superstition

Saint, n. A dead sinner revised and edited.

Ambrose Bierce (1842–c. 1914), *The Devil's Dictionary* (1911)

Saints should always be judged guilty until they are proved innocent.

George Orwell (1903–1950), 'Reflections on Gandhi' (1949)

Most saints and holy people have specially designated feast days on which they are remembered by the faithful in some special way. Because of the spread of Christianity, especially through the Catholic Church over two millennia, just about every day of the year is a saint's day. Inevitably, these amalgams of myth and legend, preserved to inspire devotion and holiness, become engulfed by superstition and ritual. When the faithful under pressure utter 'saints preserve us!' arguably they are performing the same act as knocking on wood or avoiding ladders. The fascist dictator Benito Mussolini once commented that 'the history of saints is mainly the history of insane people'. It seems just as odd that, even without the involvement of any church, many people of questionable intelligence considered Il Duce to be a kind of secular saint, along with fellow tyrants such as Hitler, Stalin or Chairman Mao.

The history of saints is complex and colourful and the way they figure in our superstitious ways is varied. However, to examine even a single month of saints' days would be a book in itself, so I have chosen to examine the antiquity of three in particular who still loom large in our lives.

VALENTINE'S DAY

In January the tills have briefly stopped ringing and you've cut up the credit cards now that Christmas and New Year are out of the way. But the corporate world is still busy gorging itself on our long-held superstitions with massive marketing and product waiting in warehouses, with 14 February, Valentine's Day, coming up. Flowers! Wine! Cards! Chocolate! In Russia, 8 March is Women's Day. The event is similar to Valentine's Day: Russian men give gifts to their special ladies as well as take care of any household chores that need to be done. But for the rest of us, 14 February is the romantic staging-post between Yule and Easter.

It was the cocky over-confidence of the French against Henry V's 8000 archers at the Battle of Agincourt six hundred years ago that lost them the battle. It gave us a great Shakespeare play and coloured our anti-French arrogance for all time. It may also have given us the Valentine, card. Charles, Duke of Orleans, one of the French nobles captured at Agincourt would spend twenty-four years in England as a prisoner of war. He used his incarceration to develop his reputation as a poet, beginning with a poignant letter to his wife which read 'I am already sick with love, my very gentle Valentine . . .' The earliest known English Valentine may have been sent in 1477 in Norfolk, a letter from Margery Brews to John Paston, whom she described as 'My right well-beloved Valentine'. By the time Victoria was on the throne, so many cards were being sent that postmen were being paid overtime. This is the day on which an estimated one billion cards are sent each year, running second only to Christmas. But who was this lovers' champion? We need to go way back to establish how this fantasy character has survived over the centuries to become the patron saint of hearts and flowers.

The first question we need to ask is how many St Valentines were there? Was he a martyr called Valentinus, executed in the third century AD on 14 February? Was he the bishop in a city called Terni in the southern portion of the region of Umbria in central Italy, known in ancient times as Interamna, also killed on 14 February. Or was he yet another Valentine, expiring on the same day in the Roman province of Africa with his companions, about whom nothing else is known. In fact, there are about a dozen other saints named Valentine including a woman, a virgin named Valentina, said to have been martyred in Palestine in AD 308. Another Valentine was pope of Rome for about forty days in 827, but little is known about his life.

Most of the other saints don't connect to the modern favourite day of sweethearts. The Catholic Church's 'official' St Valentine of Rome is a widely recognised third-century Roman saint commemorated on 14 February. There is also a more recent Valentine, beatified by Pope John Paul II in 1988, a Spanish Dominican named St Valentine Berrio-Ochoa. He went to Vietnam as a bishop and was beheaded in 1861.

Of course, if you're a lover and you're going to take passionate advantage of this romantic day, none of this need concern you. In any event, in 1969 the Catholic Church, not knowing much about Valentine, removed his name from the general Roman calendar, leaving us to celebrate him in our own fashion. However, the history behind this quest for romance is intriguing.

Before we knew it as Valentine's Day, there was a similar festival of fertility and love in Athens in ancient Greece which was a celebration of the marriage of the deities Zeus and Hera. The Romans enjoyed a comparable ancient festival called *Lupercalia* that aimed to banish evil spirits and purify the city as well as encouraging fertility and good health. This commenced on 13 February and lasted for two days. Before it was known as *Lupercalia*, there appears to have been an earlier, similar festival at the same time called *Februa*, a ritual purification based on washing or cleaning that gave us the name of the month, *Februarius* (February). Here's what the good old Brewer's *Dictionary of Phrase and Fable* (1894) tells us about the cave in Rome called *Lupercal*:

> The place where Romulus and Remus were suckled by the wolf (*lupus*). A yearly festival was held on 15 February each year on this spot in honour of Lupercus, the god of fertility. On one of these festivals Antony thrice offered to Julius Caesar a kingly crown, but seeing the people were only half-hearted, Caesar put it aside, saying, 'Jupiter alone is king of Rome.'

The *Lupercus* priests drank lots of wine and slaughtered goats as part of a purification ritual to honour the god Lupercus, after which they ran along the streets of Rome with the skins of the goats, touching anyone they met. This inspired lots of young women to come out and be touched by the skin-carrying priests in the hope that conception would be easy, along with a stress-free childbirth.

The first official St Valentine's Day was declared on 14 February in the year AD 496 by Pope Galasius I for a third-century martyred priest who is actually commemorated on 23 July. His name was Valentinus. It is generally thought that he was the most religiously respected candidate, buried at a cemetery in the north of the city on the Via Flaminia, close to the Milvian bridge. However, the day could well have been for either of two other Valentines; we're not sure.

The amorous aspects of the 'official' St Valentine's Day have their roots in early Christianity in the Roman empire. In the year AD 270 the Roman emperor Claudius came to the odd conclusion that if a young man got married he'd not perform well as a soldier. Therefore Claudius banned all marriages between young people. Valentine defied this decree. As a bishop who believed that marriage was sanctified by God for the good of the world, he still carried out clandestine marriages, tying the knot in secret ceremonies for many young couples, some apparently as young as twelve, providing they were seen to be genuinely in love. Now it gets really romantic. Bishop Valentine's covert match-making was discovered by the authorities. He was arrested, imprisoned, and condemned to be stoned, beaten with clubs and beheaded (Romans loved a touch of variety). However, while in jail he fell in love with the warder's daughter. Legend has it that the night before his execution she received a written note from him bearing the words 'From your Valentine'. Valentine's Day as we know it was born. Or was it?

It has been suggested that a poem by Geoffrey Chaucer (1342–1400) entitled 'Parliament of Foules' (or 'Parliament of Fowls'), written sometime after 1370, may be responsible for today's passionate goings-on. There are few if any references of amorous celebrations on 14 February before that mid-fourteenth-century work. Chaucer's might be the first St Valentine's Day poem ever written. Brewer suggests that it was begun in May of 1382 and was completed by 14 February 1383. It alludes to a favourite English tradition, that of courtly love, alongside his mention of the St Valentine's Feast Day. He makes some peculiar suggestions about this day, writing:

> For this was on Seynt Valentynes day,
> Whan every foul cometh ther to chese his make.

In other words, this was a special day when all the birds (fowls) and men and women came together to choose their mates.

Several verses go on to list just about every bird there is. What makes this connection seem more viable is the inclusion in Philippa Waring's *Dictionary of Omens and Superstitions* (Souvenir Press, 1978) of a list of birds a girl could see on Valentine's Day that would indicate the kind of lover she might expect. Excluded from this list is the woodpecker, because seeing old Woody meant she'd stay single. Of the most common birds more likely to be spotted, owing to the fact that Valentine's day falls at the end of winter, are a blackbird (clergyman or priest), robin (sailor), sparrow (farmer), bluebird (happy man) and crossbill (argumentative man). Whereas any yellow bird such as a goldfinch suggested marriage to a rich man, predictably, a dove implied she would end up with a good man.

So, was it the ingenious English talent of Geoffrey Chaucer that paved the way for the greeting cards, flowers and chocolates?

Romance knows no borders and Valentine's Day is celebrated in eastern style in Korea, China and Japan. It's a special day in Japan and Korea for industrial employees, when special chocolates known as *giri-choco* are presented to male workmates by women (not the other way around as you might expect). On 14 March, White Day, those men who received chocolates return the compliment to the women by presenting either marshmallows or white chocolate. Squeezing the last drop of romance from it all, the Koreans even have a third day on 14 April, Black Day. This occasion is for all the poor blokes who didn't get any Valentine's goodies. They overcome their sad neglect by getting together to eat a meal called *Jajangmyun*, black noodles in a black sauce.

Valentine remains the go-to saint to watch over the lives of engaged couples, happy marriages and lovers. Valentine is also the patron saint of beekeeping and epilepsy, with sidelines in travel and fainting as well as helping out with the plague. In the early nineteenth century excavations of Roman catacombs revealed what was thought to be Valentine's skeleton. You'll find what's left of him in Italy, namely his skull, on show in Cosmedin, Rome, at the basilica of Santa Maria. As for the rest of his bones, they're in churches in Dublin, Prague, Vienna, Glasgow and Birmingham and a few other places.

There's also a St Valentine of Viterbo's Day on 3 November. You can also celebrate St Valentine of Raetia on 7 January or the female St Valentine (Valentina) of Palestine on 25 July. There are two Eastern Orthodox Church St Valentine's days: 6 July and 30 July.

St Christopher – still hanging on in there

From ship's captains to truckers and taxi drivers, perhaps the most ubiquitous lucky charm is the image of St Christopher.

A St Christopher medal on a silver chain was given to me by my mother on my sixteenth birthday, the day I first went to sea, and it stayed with me for the next seven years. My wedding ring has a St Christopher cameo. Has St Christopher protected me? Well, I'm still here, despite the odd hurricane, car crash and the perils of the Atlantic in winter.

St Christopher, popularly depicted carrying travellers across a river, is the saint most valued in Christianity as a demonstration of charity. The legend goes that eventually he was blessed with the privilege of carrying Christ himself across the turbulent river. That's a good story, but is it any more than just a religious cult, another myth or fable?

He is also the protector of fruit dealers and even surfers, and, like Valentine, he's also on the side of epileptics. To most people even with a slight leaning towards superstition, this staple of Catholic gift shops remains an inspiring talisman. One doesn't need to be a Christian to seek his blessing for safety, either. Many members of other faiths, Buddhists for example, are quite happy to have him around. He also travels regularly with the military. Many soldiers in recent wars such as Iraq and Afghanistan have sought his lucky company. But is he really a saint and did he exist? It has been suggested that because of his dubious provenance, the holy fathers of Rome may have downgraded his saintly status. However, on closer examination this does not appear to be the case.

St Christopher's feast day was 25 July. He did indeed lose his rating in the Catholic calendar due in part to his scant historical prestige. Yet he was never de-sanctified. Being busted down the ranks was more the result of Vatican archive de-cluttering. The Church has a universal calendar which, by the 1960s, was bursting at the seams with saints. As with Valentine, St Christopher was dropped off the calendar in 1969, but it remained at the discretion of any church or parish to celebrate his special day, and many still do so.

Recorded as being martyred in the fourth century, his existence is now regarded more as a legend. The myth of Christopher comes from the Middle Ages. Medieval legend has him as a rather unsavoury giant of a man who liked the idea of serving a strong master. He was supposed to have died after converting 40,000 pagans to Christ after carrying Jesus in the form of a child across a dangerous river. If he did exist, then who was he?

One suggestion has been made by David Woods, professor of Ancient Classics at Ireland's Cork University College. He believes Christopher was perhaps genuine, but more likely an early Egyptian martyr called St Menas, a convert to Christianity serving in the Roman army. When his legion arrived in Phrygia, a kingdom in the west-central part of what is now Turkey, Menas was very upset at the various violent edicts the emperors Diocletian and Maximian had issued against the Christians. In dismay, he left the army and went to live alone in the mountains where he prayed and fasted.

He came out of solitude when a huge festival was in progress and, surrounded by pagan celebrations, he made a loud public proclamation of his Christian faith. He was arrested, tortured and finally beheaded, possibly in the year AD 308. Professor Woods has gathered from early Greek and Latin texts that his body was taken back to his native land. In the fourth century his Egyptian burial place had become the focus of a Menas cult based around a soldier who had become a martyr in a place far from his own country. The city of Antioch was a chief centre of early Christianity and it was there in later years that the Church attempted to gather what scant information there was about this legendary martyr whose name, by this time, had been forgotten. Because of this he was simply referred to by a general title given to the virtuous, Christopher, which translates as 'bearer of Christ'. Professor Woods suggests that the cults of St Menas and of St Christopher both developed independently in different areas of the Middle East but are centred on the same historical person. So the meaning of the name comes from the late Greek 'Christophoros' meaning 'bearing Christ', derived from 'Christos' combined with 'phero', which means to bear or to carry. Early Christians used it as a metaphorical name to express that they carried Christ in their hearts. Today, we carry St Christopher everywhere in the hope that he'll carry us safely home.

'Ho, ho, ho!' It must be Santa

Father Gerardo Cioffari is the director of the Centro Studi Nicolaiani, Basilica San Nicola, at Bari in Italy. On the centre's website he provides us with the following information:

On the evening of 9 May, the feast of the translation of St Nicholas from Myra-Turkey to Bari-Italy in 1087, the stone sarcophagus is opened. In the crowded crypt, the archbishop of Bari extracts one or two glasses of water formed during the year around the Saint's bones. It is the so-called manna that the Greeks call *myron* and the Russians *myro*. A father of the Dominican community pours this manna into large containers of blessed water, making a large quantity to fill small bottles in order to satisfy the requests of sick people and pilgrims. Sometimes the rector gives extremely small bottles of pure manna as relics, but only after official requests of the Orthodox or Catholic hierarchy.

Father Ciofarri's information appears to reveal the very essence of the man, the myth and the legend of the universally loved Santa Claus, a.k.a. Kris Kringle, Père Nöel, Sinterklaas or Father Christmas, the rotund, jolly and benevolent spirit of yuletides past, present and future. His prominence today as the modern image of Santa may only go back a couple of centuries but certainly does not belong to the Coca-Cola Company of Atlanta, Georgia, USA.

St Nicholas was a bishop in Myra in Asia Minor, today's Turkey, in the fourth century AD. The story goes that he came from a rich family and his parents died early, leaving Nicholas a hefty fortune. Unlike many billionaires, Nicholas liked to spread his wealth around and had a soft spot for the poor in society. Our modern tradition of hanging our stockings up on Christmas Eve is based on a rather attractive old legend of Nicholas knowing of a very poor man who had three daughters. The oldest daughter wished to marry but had to have a sum of cash – a dowry – before tying the knot. It seems outrageous now, but this wealth was transferred from the bride's family to the groom by the bride's parents, but her family were stony broke. Nicholas stepped in by clambering onto the poor man's roof and dropping a bag of gold down the chimney that landed (as unlikely as it seems) in a stocking which had been hung by the fire to dry. The daughter was successfully married and kindly bishop Nicholas carried out the same covert operation for the other girls.

Their puzzled father sat by the fireplace determined to discover where the cash was coming from and eventually caught the benefactor. The two men agreed that his identity should not be revealed, but somehow the news got out and before long anyone who received a clandestine gift began to associate their good fortune with Nicholas. It was this reputation for kindness which eventually earned him his sainthood. Other positive tales arose.

Nicholas is also the patron saint of sailors, having calmed a storm on board an endangered ship off the Turkish coast and saving the terrified crew's lives. One might think that with a good man like him around, everyone would be happy to leave him in peace, but enter the villains of the period, the Romans. The emperor Diocletian stepped in and St Nicholas was exiled from Myra, imprisoned and persecuted. The date of his death is uncertain, but is thought to be on 6 December in 345 or 352. Centuries later, Italian sailors stole his bones from Turkey and in the year 1087 took them to the Italian port of Bari where they now rest in the Basilica San Nicola. Each 6 December, the feast day of St Nicholas, Bari's mariners still carry his statue from the cathedral down to the sea so he can bless the ocean for the year to come and give them safe passage.

Nicholas also features as the patron saint of bankers, merchants, archers, repentant thieves, children, brewers, travellers and pawnbrokers. The three gold balls outside the pawnbroker's shop are said to refer to the dowry gifts of the poor man's three daughters, and, more touchingly, those of us brought up in harder times will remember them as spherical stocking fillers – oranges or other fruits.

As saints' stories go, that of Nicholas proved hugely popular, and by the sixteenth century many embroidered tales about his kindness were in circulation. The powerful presence of other deities and ancient pagan figures appears to have blended in with old St Nick to form the composite character we now know as Father Christmas.

In northern Europe, and especially in Britain, we already had our own Father Christmas who had little or no connection to St Nicholas. His antecedents were somewhat ominous. In the pagan midwinter festivals the master of ceremonies was always known as the Lord of Misrule or the Father of the Feast. You certainly wouldn't let your kids anywhere near *this* Father Christmas. His existence is still celebrated today in various mummers' plays around the UK. In pagan times his task was to ensure there was plenty of sexual jiggery-pokery and copious amounts of food and alcohol to please the dark gods. This pre-Christian Santa could have been associated with the original pagan horned god, Cernunnos, and there are elements of the pagan fertility figure the Green Man, a nature spirit, who has been found for centuries carved in wood or stone in churches, chapels, abbeys and cathedrals. Charles Dickens, writing in *A Christmas Carol*, has his spirit of Christmas present dressed in a green robe and wearing a headdress of greenery. All across Europe the Green Man appears in Christian church architecture, and as far away as Cyprus you'll find the Seven Green Men of Nicosia dating from the thirteenth century, carved in the facade of the former St Nicholas Church in Nicosia, which today doubles as a *bedestan* or covered market, as well as a mosque.

It was Dutch sailors visiting Turkey who took the legend of St Nicholas or Sinterklaas over to the USA. Back then he was a bearded old man on a white horse. The jolly fat man in white-trimmed outfit bearing his sack of toys was the invention of German-born American artist Thomas Nast (1840–1902), who in 1881 gave us the image we all recognise as Santa, smoking a pipe. It was another American artist, Haddon Sundblom (1899–1976), who gave the world the classic Coca-Cola Santa in 1931, replacing Thomas Nast's politically incorrect pipe with a bottle of the 'real thing'. Sundblom, who although a commercial artist has been compared to more respected contemporary Norman Rockwell (1894–1918), carried on painting Santa for Coke for the next thirty-three years, and he's also remembered for the head-and-shoulders portrait of the jolly gentleman on the Quaker Oats box (posed by fellow Coke artist Harold W. McCauley), which appeared in 1957.

The famous poem 'A Visit from St Nicholas, or 'T'was the Night before Christmas', was published anonymously in the *Troy (NY) Sentinel* on 23 December 1823. The author, Dr Clement Clarke Moore (1779–1863), claimed to have written it for his children. In this he features eight reindeer and, just in case you're struggling, they were: Dasher, Dancer, Prancer, Vixen, Comet, Cupid, Donner and Blitzen. A ninth reindeer came later in 1939 when 'Rudolph the Red-Nosed Reindeer' was created in song by Robert Lewis May. The original eight reindeer, however, hint that there may well be a Scandinavian mythological element to the Father Christmas story.

The God Odin rode through the winter night skies on his white eight-legged horse, Sleipnir. A fearsome fiery steed with eight legs might have been a bit creepy for kids, but eight cuddly reindeer? That worked. Moore was a highly educated man in the field of religion and mythology and he was no doubt aware that the bearded Odin also wore a fur-trimmed robe. There is also a suggestion that Santa's Christmas Eve ride around the world could be connected to the Wild Hunt of Odin. He was accompanied by two black ravens, Huginn and Muninn, who would listen at a house chimney to gather information about the good behaviour (or otherwise) of the occupants.

The black ravens may be represented in today's controversial Dutch traditions of Santa Claus, where he is accompanied by a helper known as Black Pete or *Zwarte*

Piet, who appears – Al Jolson-style – in black-face because he is supposedly a Moor from Spain. As many people in the Low Countries have challenged this tradition as racist, the counter argument is that Black Pete's face is that way because he has to climb down sooty chimneys delivering gifts for Sinterklaas. But *Zwarte Piet* remains very popular and, according to a survey in 2013, over 90 per cent of the Dutch public denied the sooty-faced helper was a racist caricature and remain totally opposed to changing the way he looks.

In the French Santa tradition, St Nicholas is accompanied by St Fouettard, a hideous warty creature armed with the tools of flagellation, whips and sticks. The original purpose of Fouettard was to give naughty children a thrashing.

Around parts of Europe, Santa has other dubious 'helpers' with bizarre names such as Hans Muff, Rumpelklas, Krampus and, in Russia, Little Babushka. Some European countries celebrate St Nicholas' Day on 6 December, when children leave something for Santa's reindeers or his horse, along with their clogs or shoes, hopefully to be filled with presents.

Odds and ends: umbrellas

It's one of the common superstitions; an umbrella should never be open indoors or you will bring bad luck on everyone under the roof. The possibility is that this belief has its roots in the Middle East or especially any country where shading from the hot sun is desirable, such as in ancient Egypt where the sun was regarded as one of the gods. Then the purpose of the umbrella was to act as a sunshade. If opened indoors, the action may be construed as a direct insult to the sun. So the following restrictions have stayed with us:

It is bad luck to give an umbrella as a gift.

If you drop an umbrella, do not pick it up. Instead, have someone else do it for you or you'll have bad luck.

If a single woman drops an umbrella, she will never marry.

If an umbrella is opened outside when it is not needed, rain and other bad weather will follow.

Part three

The Danger Zone

Religion or superstition?

To one who has faith, no explanation is necessary.
To one without faith, no explanation is possible.

Thomas Aquinas (1225–1274)

The instruction in Proverbs 14:7 is: 'Leave the presence of a fool, for there you do not meet words of knowledge.' So if you possess a strong religious faith, stop reading now. What follows is not intended as disrespect but inquiry and curiosity. If your faith teaches tolerance, consider Jude 1:22: 'and have mercy on those who doubt'.

Few areas of human behaviour are so burdened with superstitious ritual, myth and fable as religion. It would appear that superstitious beliefs and pagan rituals were adopted to decorate some religions in order to attract the multitude. Despite the incontrovertible daily revelations of physics, science and biology, the idea that everything is down to a supreme being whose ancient books, saints, priests, scribes and prophets should be continually worshipped stubbornly endures.

Is religion a good idea? Those with a strong faith believe it to be. I am not a card-carrying atheist and I have close spiritual friends including devoted Christians, Muslims and at least one Buddhist. The selfless work their faith inspires them to do is admirable. If your belief in your chosen scriptures inspires you to help the less fortunate, to enhance the society in which you live and put some heart into your community, that's a laudable extension of your worship. It was great to see, for example, in Yorkshire and other parts of northern England during the terrible floods of 2015–16, not only local Christian churches organising food and relief, but the Muslim community matching that help to all, regardless of their god.

When the Church speaks out against poverty and inequality, when the faithful dedicate their spare time to worthwhile charitable causes, then that's religion in splendid action. As an agnostic I'm quite happy to regularly attend events organised by religious friends and colleagues, support their charitable works and, thankfully – excepting the dogged persistence of Jehovah's Witnesses – they rarely try to recruit me to their flock. I already have a faith; and although it takes a severe battering at times, it's a faith in mutual human respect and common sense. What differentiates it from others is that I have no desire to ostracise, persecute, maim or kill anyone who doesn't think like me. I hope that even without a bible and a prayer book I can be seen as a peace-loving, decent person with natural compassion. What a forlorn hope *that* is.

I often read the wise words included on a Catholic website, patheos.com. I was impressed by an article on 25 June 2013 by Father Dwight Longenecker entitled 'Mercy or Tolerance?' In this he says:

> It struck me that mercy is so much bigger than mere tolerance. We may be tolerant of others but what real good is that? It is really little more than an absence of bigotry and malice. Indeed, it is little more than indifference. 'Can't we all just get along?'

Apparently not, for these are the comments he received in return: 'We can show all the tolerance and mercy we like, but in return, we should not expect anything other than martyrdom,' and 'Would you accept Satan? Would you tolerate him? Would you show him mercy? Does evil exist on earth? If so, are we to show it tolerance and mercy?'

So it is with great sadness and apprehension that there was no other option in the current social climate than to call this part of the book the Danger Zone. Ostensibly, examining the subject of superstitions could be regarded as a light-hearted diversion. Unfortunately, as so many superstitions, rituals and omens have religious roots and cultural implications, then any overtly glib attempts to comment in this tricky area is like staggering blindfolded through a minefield. When a religion exhausts its stock of love and compassion then intolerance and hatred take over.

There are those who believe that the world should be dominated by just one religion and then all will be well and God will be happy. This will never happen simply because humanity is a discerning, questioning species steered by social history into various political mindsets. That's why we have conservatism, liberalism, socialism and a number of other 'isms'. Depending on the group your mental faculty places you in, you will always fail to comprehend the others and be in opposition.

As a writer lacking an academic background or training, in research I am bound in many instances to utilise the works of serious historians and yet it is often amazing how many of these who possess a strong religious faith approach their subject with that faith set aside, intact. They will examine primary and secondary sources in their chosen area of study meticulously, yet if that history conflicts with the fables and scriptures of their faith, cognitive dissonance comes into play. This suggests that we have an inner drive to hold all our attitudes and beliefs in harmony and avoid disharmony. So an accredited, often famous, historian might write extensively about, say, the crusades or the Conquistadores, but if he's a devout Catholic or Protestant he'll avoid attitudes that question the dogma of those faiths. The same, of course, applies to politics. One historian's glorious revolution is another's social Armageddon. Beyond this there are American historians with doctorates who are total Christian evangelists or creationists who will actually be prepared to launch expensive expeditions to show us where and how Moses parted the Red Sea, discover the remains of Noah's Ark, or spend a whole career looking for the garden of Eden or the ark of the covenant with the generous financial support of a major TV channel.

Once you lift the lid on the superstitious ritualism of religion, you're peering into an abyss devoid of reason or logic. The more rigid and demanding a faith or its holy scriptures may be, the more humanity recedes and the gulf between rationality and unreason grows ever wider. Those of us who see it this way will inevitably be regarded as infidels – irreligious non-spiritual beings bound for hell, unworthy of any mercy or sympathy.

Part of my Catholic childhood was spent in Sunday school sessions where we studied the catechism almost parrot-fashion under the watchful eyes of spiteful, knuckle-rapping nuns armed with heavy wooden rulers. That 'sisters of mercy' image may seem like a cliché – it's even included in *The Simpsons* – but I can vouch for its veracity. After a few months of this, Matthew 19:14, 'suffer little children and forbid them not to come unto me,' lost most of its meaning.

If there is a God and if he or she is indeed, as the faithful keep repeating, 'merciful', it is to be hoped that the supreme being's existence can be proved to me in a form of forgiveness for this expression of personal opinions and observations. They are simply influenced by what I have seen and experienced in life to date. In other words, if there is a heaven, I hope they'll let me in.

'GOD TOLD ME TO DO IT'

'God told me to do it' is a recurring plea in numerous murder cases. Similar heavenly instructions to murderers in recent years, especially in the USA, have been issued by the archangel Michael, Jesus and Mary, and, just occasionally, Satan gets a look in.

However convincing 'God told me to do it' may sound in a courtroom, it will not get you off, and 'the devil told me to do it' will only get you a psychiatrist. In contrast to this, one has to ask a corporate question – if the court doesn't accept God as the instigator of murder, how come insurance companies still quote 'acts of God' when they don't want to pay out?

One has to wonder how ancient phobias, prejudices, lapsed arcane rituals and superstitions became stuck between the pages of holy books to congeal over centuries and to end up hanging like millstones around our modern necks. Many of the examples included here represent the more orthodox attitudes to various religions. When scribes and prophets laid down laws as mentally instructed by their particular God, such utterances were made in historical times when the idea of being secular was itself profane. In their time, many prophets would have been considered by the authorities or even their next-door neighbours in the same way as many people today regard the 'azure messiah', David Icke. It is surprising how these prophecies, omens and elaborated superstitions became woven into the tapestry of priestly performance. Selecting those convenient holy laws which advanced their power, emperors and kings used their priests and bishops to convince their impressionable subjects that there was only one legislature and that was God's. The message was profound and effective, especially for the poor, as in Matthew 6:19–21:

> 19: Lay not up for yourselves treasures upon earth, where moth and rust doth corrupt and where thieves break through and steal.
> 20: But lay up for yourselves treasures in heaven, where neither moth nor rust doth corrupt and where thieves do not break through nor steal.
> 21: For where your treasure is, there will your heart be also.

It was OK if you'd already been lucky enough to convince the masses to work themselves to near fatal exhaustion to help you to 'lay up' your own worldly treasures (a modicum of wealth not, presumably, corrupted by 'moth nor rust'). The gullible multitudes would receive their share when they got to heaven. Meanwhile, there were serious manmade religious rules and regulations to observe, usually on pain of death.

THE SUPERSTITIOUS CONVERT

American writer and neuroscientist Samuel Benjamin Harris (born 1967) is the co-founder and chief executive of Project Reason, a non-profit organisation that promotes science and secularism. He enrages the religious faithful with comments like this:

> If you wake up tomorrow morning thinking that saying a few Latin words over your pancakes will turn them into the body of Elvis Presley, you've lost your mind, but if you think more or less the same thing about a cracker and the body of Jesus, you're just a Catholic.

It may be crude and direct, yet there is a question contained in his utterance which goes back to the establishment of Christianity. Where, why and how did all the colourful holy rituals begin? Albert Einstein, in his essay 'Religion and Science', in the *New York Times* magazine on 9 November 1930, gave his view about religion's beginnings:

> With primitive man it is above all fear that evokes religious notions – fear of hunger, wild beasts, sickness, death. Since at this stage of existence understanding of causal connections is usually poorly developed, the human mind creates illusory beings more or less analogous to itself on whose wills and actions these fearful happenings depend. Thus one tries to secure the favour of these beings by carrying out actions and offering sacrifices which, according to the tradition handed down from generation to generation, propitiate them or make them well disposed toward a mortal. In this sense, I am speaking of a religion of fear. This, though not created, is in an important degree stabilised by the formation of a special priestly caste which sets itself up as a mediator between the people and the beings they fear and erects a hegemony

on this basis. In many cases, a leader or ruler or a privileged class whose position rests on other factors combines priestly functions with its secular authority in order to make the latter more secure; or the political rulers and the priestly caste make common cause in their own interests.

The first three centuries of Christianity proved to be a tough, dangerous time for the faithful. Any and every persecution going was inflicted upon these simple adherents of what was a very basic new religion. Christians then were simple, determined people who lived by the words of Christ, loved their enemy and turned the other cheek. For that they were seen as superstitious heretics who denied the great gods of Rome and as a result were punished.

Then along came the emperor Constantine (AD 272–337), also known as Constantine the Great or St Constantine. He is revered in Christian history as a convert to the faith, yet how far he converted to the faith may be debatable. His edict of Milan in 313 made Christianity legal and it seemed possible that the religion might be unifying, especially as the Roman empire, with all its many different gods, was beginning to fall apart.

Constantine realised that the unwieldy size of the crumbling empire, stretching across the Mediterranean and Europe, wasn't meekly going to accept Christianity overnight. The old gods, festivals and rituals were still powerful, widespread and rigorously worshipped, and even Constantine didn't abandon his pagan beliefs entirely. His 'Christian' church was a convenience, mixing the old Roman paganism with Christ's teachings.

In 325, Constantine called the council of Nicea in an attempt to unify this new religion. The pick-and-mix result, a blend of Jesus's teaching and the adapted pre-Christian pagan rituals, myths and fables, is still with us today. Worshipping a single god while accepting that other deities exist is called henotheism, and in Rome most people, from the emperor down, were henotheists. They had a 'top' god, Jupiter (different occupations chose their own god – there were plenty on offer, including gods of peace, love and wisdom etc.). Sailors worshipped Neptune. Soldiers followed Mars. Henotheism was well established and Constantine knew that Christianity, simple and straightforward though it was, did not have the immediate power to sweep all this accrued superstition away. It was more pragmatic to 'Christianise' the existing pagan system.

A good place to start was with the widely popular Egyptian mother goddess, Isis. Described in the *Egyptian Book of the Dead* as 'She who gives birth to heaven and earth, knows the orphan, knows the widow, seeks justice for the poor and shelter for the weak,' she was also known as 'mother of God' and 'queen of heaven'. Isis was the perfect template for the Virgin Mary. Origen of Alexandria (AD 185–254) wrote about the early worship of Mary, Alexandria being the centre for the Isis cult, and the 'divine maternity of Mary' was proclaimed as a dogma of the Church in the Council of Ephesus in 431. Today, Mariology, the cult of the Virgin Mary (who seems a very different woman to the mother of Christ in the Bible), dominates the Catholic Church and is even adhered to by many Protestants.

During the first five centuries of the Roman empire, the popular religion, especially among Roman soldiers, was Mithraism. Mithraism's 'seven sacraments' appear to be similar to those of the Roman Catholic Church and there are some remarkable similarities elsewhere in Mithraism. It was a sun cult centred on Rome. It was male-only. Their rituals were led by a person with the title *Pater* (Latin for 'Father'). Above this level stood another, that of the *Pater-Patratus* or 'pope'. The lower initiates were referred to as 'brothers'. The priests wore cross amulets and black costumes. Mithraism had a trinity: Mithras, Rashnu and Vohuh Mahnah, regarded as three beings yet one. The sun was known as *Mithras Solis Invictus*, and had a special day of the week which was holy and sacred and was known as 'sun day'. On this day all were expected to rest under the Roman edict known as the Blue Laws. Blue Laws are still in operation today in many parts of the USA and in parts of Europe. Constantine ruled that all officials, artisans or merchants should not engage in any work on 'sun day' and spend the day praising Mithras. The twenty-fifth of December was observed as *Natalis Invictus*, or Mithras's birthday.

One of the rituals of Mithraism was the sacred meal of sacrifice. This practice in religion is known as theophagy, 'eating your god', and it refers to the ritual of eating what the follower believes to be the flesh of their deity. Roman followers of Mithraism ate the flesh of a bull and drank a cup of its blood. Transubstantiation – the belief in many branches of Christianity that the bread and wine given at communion become the body and blood of Jesus Christ – depends upon a literal interpretation of Luke 22:17-19: 'And he took bread and gave thanks and brake it and gave unto them, saying, "This is my body which is given for you: this do in remembrance of me."' It is also in Matthew 26:26-28 and Mark 14:22-24.

As Christianisation progressed down the centuries, the pantheon of sacred gods was slowly replaced by saints. Pagan beliefs were given new, Christian identities. As Rome had always been the central hub of the empire, it was natural that bishops would be based there. A whole range of ornamental and symbolic equipment was developed, pagan temples with their altars became churches and the higher clergy in their dress took on the splendour of the old Roman emperors. Once the Roman empire finally collapsed, the popes assumed the title that had previously belonged to the Roman emperors – *Pontifex Maximus*, 'supreme priest'.

Rituals developed slowly, beginning with the washing of hands and the reading of Psalm 25: 'Unto thee, O Lord, do I lift up my soul'. Kneeling or standing for prayer and such ceremonies as the kiss of peace, were all inherited from the Jews. The Romanisation of the Lord's supper completed the transition to a sacrificial consumption of Jesus Christ, which would become known as the Catholic mass.

By the seventh century, popes were so self-important that they demanded their feet should be kissed. Pope Eugenius II, who died in 827, was the first who made it the law to kiss the papal foot. From that time it was necessary to kneel before the popes. Gregory VII ordered all princes to submit to this practice. This all seems a long way from the simple life of a humble Judean carpenter and his compassionate common sense.

By the eleventh century, Christianity had become a complicated and belligerent field of study. Rituals and saints proliferated. Most Roman cities in the empire had their own specific god, so the Catholic Church replaced these with 'patron saints'.

As in all empires, rivalry, jealousy and ambition, alien to the teachings of Christ, caused political, ecclesiastical and geographical splits down the centuries. Simple arguments such as whether or not leavened or unleavened bread should be used at the eucharist (a word which may refer not only to the rite but also to the consecrated foods) led to the east–west schism which began in 1054 and has never been healed, leaving us with the Eastern Orthodox Church, with its Greek and Russian versions.

At about the time the popes were considering having their feet kissed, about 3,500 miles away in the Arabian peninsula, the biggest challenge to Constantine's project was about to arise in the city of Mecca. Tradition suggests that the prophet Muhammad (peace be upon him, or pbuh) was born around the year 570. He belonged to a powerful merchant tribe, the Quraysh, who controlled Mecca. The tradition in Islam is that the Quraysh were descended from Abraham's first son, Ishmael.

At the age of forty, Muhammad (pbuh) began to receive revelations from the angel Gabriel. These collected disclosures would eventually become the holy Qur'an. Gabriel instructed the prophet to establish a strict monotheistic faith. The angel also told him that he should spread the news of the impending judgement day and that Muhammad (pbuh) was to challenge the corruption and social injustice within the city of Mecca. The city's establishment vigorously opposed the prophet but he enjoyed the protection of a powerful man, his paternal uncle Abu Talib, who was also the father of Ali, the fourth caliph and Muhammad's (pbuh) son-in-law. At first the prophet had only a few supporters, and when his uncle Abu Talib died, Muhammad (pbuh) left Mecca for the city of Yathrib (today's Medina). His growing band of followers went with him. Today's generations of Muslims regard this time as the *hijra*, the beginning of the Islamic era.

In Medina, Muhammad (pbuh) became an arbitrator between the various communities and in the year 622 laid down the forty-seven clauses of a remarkable human rights document which would be the foundation of an Islamic society based on the Qur'an, the Constitution of Medina. This sets out the rights and responsibilities of Muslims, Jews and other groups in Medina during the war between that city and its neighbours. The charter describes the formation of a sovereign nation-state with a common citizenship for all communities. It protects fundamental human rights for all citizens, including equality, cooperation, freedom of conscience and freedom of religion. Considering the way modern history has unfolded in the Middle East, today some of the original clauses seem truly remarkable, such as:

15: The security of God is equal for all groups.

25: Non-Muslim members will have the same political and cultural rights as Muslims. They will have autonomy and freedom of religion.

37: Non-Muslims will take up arms against the enemy of the nation and share the cost of war. There is to be no treachery between the two.

45: Non-Muslims will not be obliged to take part in religious wars of the Muslims.

The Constitution of Medina is claimed to be the first document in history to establish religious freedom as a fundamental constitutional right. The Qur'an's verses provided guidance on matters of law and religious observance. Sadly, wars raged between the prophet's enemies in Mecca and assorted Jewish tribes, but Muhammad (pbuh) eventually took control of Mecca. Later he achieved various allegiances throughout the peninsula and many accepted his status as a prophet and were happy to financially support his new government, which by the time of his death in 632 had its own army, deputies and a public treasury. Thus the first Islamic state was formed and was soon to become a major religious challenge to the Church of Rome and its allies. Judaism and Christianity were about to be confronted with something very powerful, equally zealous and very different to what had gone before.

Islam was a major military state which had sprung from the heavenly advice of the angel Gabriel as interpreted by the prophet, but in retrospect it seems, in its pristine genesis, a model social and political construct. Yet as with Christianity, human bitterness and arrogance would seek to override the rule of God and carve their own places in Islam's proud edifice.

Following the death of Muhammad (pbuh), the religious group now known as Sunnis chose Abu Bakr, the prophet's adviser, to become the first successor or caliph to lead the Muslim state. The opposing religious group, the Shiites, favoured Ali, Muhammad's (pbuh) cousin and son-in-law. Ali and his successors are called imams, who not only led the Shiites but were considered to be descendants of Muhammad (pbuh).

Today, although they grew from the same root, these sects differ in doctrine, ritual, law, theology and religious organisation. Conflicts have raged in Lebanon, Syria, Iraq, throughout north Africa and in Pakistan. Of the world's 1.5 billion Muslims, the majority are Sunnis – estimates suggest the figure is somewhere between 85 and 90 per cent. In the Middle East, Sunnis make up 90 per cent or more of the populations of Egypt, Jordan and Saudi Arabia. And so, a 1400-year-old argument rumbles on, making a mockery of Muhammad's (pbuh) original, boldly progressive constitution.

Whilst writing this, a phone-in discussion has been in progress on BBC Radio 2's *Jeremy Vine Show* of 4 January 2016. This followed the execution of the popular Shiite cleric Sheikh Nimr al Nimr and forty-six other prisoners. Executioners have been in demand in the kingdom of Saudi Arabia. Beheading is a civil service job, and in 2015 eight new beheaders were needed to keep up with the increasing number of death sentences being handed down by Saudi judges. The advert stated that the job required 'no special qualifications' and would include the task of amputating limbs for lesser offences. The successful candidate would be regarded as a 'religious functionary'. So, that's OK, then. God's involved.

The subject of the phone-in was the differing prominent Muslim cultures of Iran (Shiite) and Saudi Arabia (Sunni). One English contributor, who had spent time in both countries as a construction worker, told the sorry tale of his time living in the foreign compound in Saudi Arabia. Beyond the fence, Saudi religion dictated that the contributor's wife could not drive or move freely without a man. When she gave birth to twins, one of the little boys died. Because they were not Muslims, the authorities would not allow the child's burial. The father had to sneak out into the desert, secretly cremate his child and smuggle the boy's ashes back into the UK in a metal container used for welding equipment.

The caller also spoke of a nearby Muslim girl's school in Mecca in which a fire broke out on 11 March 2002. This killed fifteen people, all young girls, who, because they were not wearing 'correct Islamic dress', were forced back into the burning building by the *mutaween*, Saudi Arabia's 'religious police' (known as the Committee for the Promotion of Virtue and the Prevention of Vice), who hindered rescue workers.

How utterly amazing is it that, in the twenty-first century, innocent children had to burn to death because 'religious policemen' did not want physical contact to take place between the girls and the civil defence forces 'for fear of sexual entice-ment'? As if such crazed desires could surface while you're rescuing a victim of any age or gender who is burning to death!

Unfortunately, since 9/11 and the US-UK's disgraceful and illegal Iraq war, the polarisation between what many like to think of melodramatically as the 'crusader west' and the 'saracen east' has developed into a looming, malevolent threat of biblical proportions. Many Muslims in the Middle East now regard the rest of the world in those age-old superstitious terms; Europe and America have become the 'great Satan'.

To counter the staggering brutality and primeval cruelty of organisations such as Islamic State – Daesh/Isis – it is easy for the barking mad, extremist, self-proclaimed 'Christian' fringes to delve into the Qur'an and 'prove' the unforgiving nature of Islam with examples such as Surahs 5:33 and 8:12, neither of which I shall risk expanding on here. Most of the Muslims I've met and know seem pretty balanced, decent people, and I'm sure they wouldn't wish to follow those grim commands. In any event, when it comes to blood, suffering and sacrifice, the Bible can match the holy Qur'an chapter and verse. And let's never forget that those jolly, lynch-happy rednecks so handy with a rope and a burning cross, the Ku Klux Klan, are proud to call themselves a 'Christian' organisation. It seems that with all super-stition-driven faith, this sanctimonious rejection of humanity and compassion runs like scar tissue through many religions.

The superstitions these beliefs are founded upon split humanity itself into many opposing camps, even male against female. The religions of the book – Judaism, Christianity and Islam and others – are patriarchal, with women forever pushed aside into docile subservience. For example, in parts of India a superstition dictates that pregnant women should stay indoors during an eclipse because the Sun has been consumed by a demon. This will ensure their babies are not born with any deformities. Thankfully, eclipses don't happen too often, but, when they do, pregnant Indian women can't chop vegetables or do any sewing. Some families during an eclipse avoid cooking and eating altogether. Yet superstition has always had a firm grip when it comes to female biology.

ONLY WOMEN BLEED

In numerous cultures, superstition decrees that menstruating women are consid-ered impure and unclean. She must be kept out of the kitchen because she *must not* cook. She must stay away from temples, mosques and all religious spots in the house itself. Needless to say, the 'holy books' make it official:

> Leviticus 15:19: And if a woman have an issue and her issue in her flesh be blood, she shall be put apart seven days and whosoever toucheth her shall be unclean until the even.

This irrational paranoia goes on for another seven verses, advising men to wash their clothes, etc., culminating in the following bizarre requirements, which probably explains why the UK government still levies tax on women's sanitary products:

29: And on the eighth day she shall take unto her two turtles or two young pigeons and bring them unto the priest, to the door of the tabernacle of the congregation.

30: And the priest shall offer the one for a sin offering and the other for a burnt offering and the priest shall make an atonement for her before the Lord for the issue of her uncleanness.

There's no let-up in Islam, either:

Qur'an Surah 2:222-223: They ask you about menstruation: say, it is harmful; you shall avoid sexual intercourse with the women during menstruation; do not approach them until they are rid of it. Once they are rid of it, you may have intercourse with them in the manner designed by God. God loves those who are clean. Your women are the bearers of your seed. Thus, you may enjoy this privilege however you like, so long as you maintain righteousness. You shall observe God and know that you will meet Him. Give good news to the believers.

Note how these grandiloquent commands read as if emanating from a male perspective to a male recipient, speaking of women in the third person almost as if they were another species.

Neither does Judaism have any sympathy for natural female physiology. *Niddah* is the Talmud word used to denote the menstruating woman and her period of 'uncleanness'. The Old Testament specifies that a woman is unclean during menstruation, but the Talmud stipulates that her period of uncleanness lasts for an additional week after menstruation has ended. The *niddah* supposedly defiles everyone and everything she touches. She may not have sexual intercourse with her husband. If she does, he could be subject to arrest and perhaps, in centuries past, the death penalty. It was said that some *niddah* laws applied to 'gentile' (non-Jewish) women, too. Even the *British Medical Journal* in 1878 published an article which suggested that in the presence of menstruating women, 'bacon could putrefy'. That would rule out a job in Sainsbury's for a start!

In the Eastern Orthodox Church women having their periods are not to receive communion, and in eastern Europe they must not bake bread or churn butter while 'unclean'.

It can be argued that these religious superstitions were created by men, not gods, to subordinate the position of women in society. Only Guru Nanak of the Sikh faith condemned this attitude to menstruating women. When preparing this chapter I asked a Sikh shopkeeper what superstitions he followed and he told me he was disappointed that I should ask such a question, saying; 'Sikhs do not believe in superstition. There are no good days or bad days, good or bad moments, good numbers or bad numbers. Some Hindus say Tuesday is a sacred day and those of them who eat meat avoid it on Tuesdays. The month of Ramadan is sacred to Muslims. All the days of the week and all numbers are the same to us, none is better than the other. I've heard Christians say 666 is a wicked number of the devil but that 777 is a good number. Sikhism believes none of this rubbish. We don't fast, we don't sacrifice animals, torture ourselves or go on pilgrimages. Sikhs don't need superstitions to receive God's love. If a black cat crosses my path, he's as welcome as a brown cat or a white one. Superstitions are made by men and such ridiculous beliefs and silly rituals waste the valuable time we have on earth.'

THERE WILL BE BLOOD

In general, a high percentage of humanity tends to be carnivorous, and in all the world's ancient religions, cruel animal sacrifice rituals have always been used as a short cut to desired godliness. In India, the goddess Kali likes a goat with its throat cut or any other animal which heightens the holiness. Killing animals for religious purposes is done supposedly to relieve negative emotions such as fear, anger and jealousy. One could also argue that in a modern, supposedly enlightened age, it actually creates those emotions.

For Muslims, the rules for the slaughter of animals are based on Islamic law. The Arabic word *halal* means 'permissible'. Only a Muslim using the appropriate ritual is allowed to kill the animal, which must be healthy and alive, and the animal's throat must be cut by a sharp knife severing the carotid artery, jugular vein and windpipe in a single swipe. Blood must be drained out of the carcass. The situation is similar in Judaism, where the practice of animal slaughter is known as *shechita*:

Deuteronomy 12:21: If the place which the Lord thy God hath chosen to put His name there be too far from thee, then thou shalt kill of thy herd and of thy flock which the Lord hath given thee, as I have commanded thee and thou shalt eat in thy gates whatsoever thy soul lusteth after.

The Lord instructs that sheep and cattle should be killed 'as I have commanded thee' but none of the slaughtering practices are described anywhere in the five books of Moses. Instead, they have been handed down orally in Judaism's traditional oral Torah and codified in *Halakha*, the collective body of Jewish religious laws derived from the written and oral Torah.

As for eating the pig, both Muslims and Jews are commanded not to eat pork. This restriction may well have applied to Christians at one time.

Deuteronomy 14:8: And the swine because it divideth the hoof, yet cheweth not the cud, it is unclean unto you: ye shall not eat of their flesh, nor touch their dead carcase.

In the Qur'an, in verses 2:173, 5:3, 6:145 and 16:115 the command is clear:

He has only forbidden you dead meat, and blood, and the flesh of swine and any (food) over which the name of other than Allah has been invoked. But if one is forced by necessity, without wilful disobedience, nor transgressing due limits, then Allah is oft-forgiving, most merciful.

Buddhists, Jains and Hindus usually avoid eating any kind of meat, and many eastern traditions discourage the eating of pork. The *Confucian Book of Rites* says, 'A gentleman does not eat the flesh of pigs and dogs,' although pork today plays a big part in Chinese cuisine and, as for Fido and Rover, maybe the Koreans haven't read Confucius lately.

Unless you are a dedicated vegan, the distaste I express here for the ritual treatment of animals can be fairly viewed as hypocrisy. In Europe and the USA we are daily bombarded with commercial exhortations to gobble up as many hamburgers, sausages, portions of pulled pork and 'finger-lickin' chicken as we can stuff into our faces, and rarely do we concern ourselves with the cruel existence the meat-providing animals experience prior to their undignified death. At least a million chickens in the UK alone will be slaughtered today, every day, and even after they've been crispy-coated and deep-fried, several tons of them will end up dumped in waste bins.

The death of animals for our culinary pleasure is a massive, continuous and unseen production line of cattle, pigs and poultry often reared and bred in the most disgustingly inhumane industrial manner. Vegetarianism is a difficult option but surprisingly the most food wasted weekly in the UK (a country which tops the European charts for throwing away good food) is not meat but vegetables, fruit and bread products. But all food, and especially meat, is tainted with superstition.

Below the Mason-Dixon line in some southern states in the USA you would find superstitions narrowed down to one particular day – in this case New Year's Day.

New year superstitions and Hoppin' John

You'll have bad luck if you eat lobster or crab on New Year's Day. Why? Because they move sideways. If you wish to avoid the destiny of becoming a 'scratcher in the dirt' you'd avoid chicken or turkey, because they scratch backward for food.

Stay away from catfish, because they're 'bottom feeders', and eating one on New Year's Day means you could end up feeding on the bottom. Other fish swim in a forward motion and you can get them in the pan, no trouble.

Stay away from beef on that day because the cow remains stationary while eating, and the last thing you want is to stand still in the coming year.

The big food to start your southern year has to be black-eyed peas. But the animals aren't off the hook, because the south's good ole' boys regard the humble pig as a very 'lucky' animal. Porky likes to forage for food rooting in a forward motion and that's supposed to be good.

Therefore, superstition dictates that the best meal you can eat on the first day of the year is a dish called Hoppin' John – black-eyed peas, rice and pork. Don't forget the collard greens, kale, spinach and cabbage, because they're green and signify money, as do lentils. One last move to bring you luck is to throw a coin in your Hoppin' John pot. The lucky diner who cracks a tooth on it gets an extra helping.

Thicker than water

Religion is very touchy about that fluid around which are many superstitions, blood, yet as we're seeing currently in certain parts of the world, the righteous have no qualms about spilling it. And here's another question – why don't Jehovah's Witnesses accept blood transfusions? And here's the official answer:

> This is a religious issue rather than a medical one. Both the Old and New Testaments clearly command us to abstain from blood (Genesis 9:4; Leviticus 17:10; Deuteronomy 12:23; Acts 15:28, 29). Also, God views blood as representing life (Leviticus 17:14). So we avoid taking blood not only in obedience to God but also out of respect for him as the giver of life.
> www.jw.org

If God 'views blood as representing life' then why can it not be used to preserve life? All those scriptures quoted; who wrote them? What authority did those self-appointed scribes have to deny medical progress and condemn generations hundreds of years hence? What kind of a god thinks like this?

Primitive people regarded blood as the flowing liquid of the soul, the life essence. In losing blood a person lost their spirit, to say nothing of their health. If the loss was heavy, then death resulted because it was seen that your soul had drained away in the lost blood. Thus did blood equal liquid power and as such could be used for ritual and religious rites.

Such beliefs and their accompanying customs mingled in with religion and inevitably superstitions arose. If innocent blood was spilled, it was said that the perpetrator was cursed. Blood-stained floorboards resulting from a murder would always bear signs of the stain, no matter how well scrubbed. The blood had the power to remind witnesses that evil was done in that place. Some killers, haunted by their deed, themselves believed that they could never clean the bloodstains from the weapon they'd used.

Some people believed that, if a dead body was touched again by the person who had committed the murder, then the corpse would bleed again.

Innocent blood was at a premium in medieval times for those who suffered from leprosy. Superstition dictated that the blood of a virgin or an innocent child could produce a remarkable cure. To begin with, a leprous individual might be treated by an alchemist with an unusual potion containing gold and symbolising purity and richness. The poor leper, thinking that by quaffing this mixture the gold would restore and cleanse them, hoped for a cure. Another method was to cut into a vein at a place on the leprous body where the sores were at their worst in the hope that the disease would exit with the blood that issued forth. As we now realise, that was sheer futility. The medieval practice of spilling sacrificial innocent blood sometimes led to another possible cure with the leper sitting in a bath medicated with the blood of an infant or a virgin. The afflicted hoped it might act like a transfusion: drawing the diseased blood out of the body as the innocent, untainted blood replaced it. No doubt you would have had to have been a fairly rich leper to try that treatment.

But blood was flowing in the darker ages for all manner of odd reasons. It was said that if you drew the blood of a witch this would diminish her power. This belief persisted to 1822 in the case of elderly Ann Burge in Wiveliscombe, near Taunton, Devon. She was accused by neighbour Elizabeth Bryant of 'bewitching' two of her three daughters. Taking the advice of a local sage called Baker that the witch's spell could be broken if they drew the woman's blood, the three women set about Ann Burge with large iron nails, tearing at her arms. She certainly bled that night. At the subsequent court case on 26 November the would-be bloodletters each got four months' imprisonment.

Beware the blood moon

On 15 April 2014, there was a total lunar eclipse which was the first of four consecutive total eclipses in a series, known as a tetrad; a second one took place on 8 October, the third on 4 April 2015 and another on 27 September. It is one of eight tetrads to take place during this century.

During the 15 April eclipse the moon appeared to be red through the same effect that causes sunsets to appear red, the cause being a scattering of sunlight through the earth's atmosphere. Needless to say, such 'blood moons' – and especially four in a row – throw the apocalyptic doom-merchants of the Bible belt into full tilt. Ancient portents and prophecies are attached to this spectacular astronomical pleasure. The idea of a blood moon is said to be the omen of the 'end times'. It features in the book of Joel:

> 2:31: The sun will turn into darkness, and the moon into blood, before the great and terrible day of the Lord comes.

Just to hammer home the promise of terrible times, the message is repeated in Acts 2:20 and the blood moon also appears in the book of Revelation, chapter six, verses eleven-thirteen:

> Revelation 6:12: And I beheld when he had opened the sixth seal and, lo, there was a great earthquake and the sun became black as sack-cloth of hair and the moon became as blood.

Blood is very important if you're going to South Korea. There people think that your blood type is representative of your personality, your mood swings and even your compatibility when it comes to romance or making friends. This belief is reminiscent of the way many people in the west rely on horoscopes and astrology. South Koreans are more likely to ask what your blood type is than your star sign.

This obsession with blood has a dark past. Both the imperial Japanese and Germany's Nazis were convinced before WWII that there was superior blood in some races which would eventually triumph over what they believed to be inferior blood. Today, thanks to a Japanese writer named Masahiko Nomi (1925–1981), writing in the 1970s, the more objectionable aspects of the blood theory have been toned down, but in effect this can be traced back to 'scientific' racism.

There is still a Japanese blood type chart which, like the zodiac, purports to tell you what personality and prospects you have depending on your blood group. There's also a very simplistic heading for each blood group:

Blood type A – farmers
Blood type B – nomads
Blood type AB – humanists
Blood type O – warriors.

Of course, even after several surveys and tests, there is no scientific evidence to back up this superstition. Yet, thanks to Masahiko Nomi, you'd probably be hard-pressed to find anyone from Japan to Taiwan and South Korea who doesn't know their blood type.

Creationism

Why, in the face of all the scientific evidence collected, the radiocarbon dating and geological research, do over 40 per cent of Americans believe in creationism, according to a Gallup poll from May 2014? Forty-two per cent of Americans hold the creationist belief that God created humanity as it currently exists less than a mere 10,000 years ago. Such obstinate faith puts science in conflict with religion and yet it was science which made the USA great; it put man on the moon, gave the world atomic power, Apple and Microsoft. So is science doomed to be religion's enemy?

Princeton economist Roland Bénabou, with co-authors Davide Ticchi and Andrea Vindigni, unveiled a surprising finding in a paper on this subject in 2015 Titled 'Religion and Innovation', it bolsters the idea of conflict between science and religiosity. It appears that across countries and some US states, higher levels of religiosity are related to lower levels of general innovation. Said Bénabou, 'Places with higher levels of religiosity have lower rates of scientific and technical innovation, as measured by patents per capita. Patents will include technological inovations but also industrial and commercial ones.'

Bénabou, Ticchi and Vindigni used an economic model to explore how scientific innovation, religiosity and the power of the state interact to form different 'regimes'. They identified three kinds of regimes:

(1) A US-style regime in which religion and science both thrive, with the state supporting science and religions (mostly) trying to accommodate themselves to its findings.
(2) A secular, European-style regime in which religion has very little policy influence and science garners great support.
(3) A repressive, theocratic regime in which the state and religion merge to suppress science.

In certain parts of the world, once could argue that (3) is on the rise. If you have no religion, you may find the ancient earthy belief system of the Australian aborigine ridiculous, just as an atheist would find all faiths to be. Those in the northern hemisphere with a strong faith will regard the aboriginal's almost magical belief in the spirits of the earth, trees, animals and fire to be quaint but unacceptably pagan, yet that same Bible reader may well deny evolution and believe in angels and miracles and accept that a man turned water into wine, fed the multitude with a couple of loaves and fishes, gave the blind man his sight back, walked on water and came back from the dead.

Tacitus (AD 56–117), senator and a historian of the Roman empire, surrounded by his own panoply of invented gods, called Christianity a 'pernicious superstition'. Constantine (AD 272–337) called paganism superstition. The Roman Catholic Church venerated bones, artefacts, saintly relics and images, and Protestants began regarding all that as 'ungodly' and idolatrous superstition.

As the armies of Christ and Islam continued their conquests, the religion of each new country's population was seen as some kind of infantile paganism ripe for rectification. The ancient beliefs of indigenous peoples of the Americas, as well as the Hindu and Buddhist practices of the east, were all thought of as superstitious by Christianity. The contradictions rumble on.

Each branch of faith vies for some kind of proof of its intellectual superiority. The peripheral beliefs of religion are limpet-like superstitions which have accumulated down the centuries. One person's religion can often be seen as another one's superstition. If a devout Christian caught you checking your horoscope in the daily paper he might sneer at you in outraged disgust. He would regard astrology the same way as the fictional fantasy world of *Harry Potter*; irreligiously evil. Yet when he seeks guidance he'll let his Bible fall open at any page and whatever verse appears will make his day. Here's an experiment. I will now leave the keyboard, take down the Bible from the shelf and open it at random.

I'm back. The book, the Authorised King James version published by the Bible society of Swindon, falls open at page 537, the book of Isaiah. My random gaze falls on verse six, chapter thirty-four:

The sword of the Lord is filled with blood, it is made fat with fatness, and with the blood of lambs and goats, with the fat of the kidneys of rams; for the Lord hath a sacrifice in Bozrah and a great slaughter in the land of Idumea.

Here we go again: slaughter and blood; such comfort. No doubt a dedicated Bible student will make sense of a 'fat sword' and I'm sure many a religious butcher or abattoir worker will find some solace in the rest, and I notice that in verse thirty-five that follows, unicorns make an appearance. *Unicorns?* In the *holy Bible?* Isn't that a superstitious mythical beast, or is it a mistranslation of the Re'em, an ancient ox?

Anyone belonging to one of the faiths 'of the book' – Judaism, Christianity and Islam – will be prepared to believe that a very long time ago God spoke to various prophets. The prophets then wrote down God's words and commands which must be obeyed. Doing so makes readers 'one of the faithful' through belief. On what evidence do you base that belief? How can anyone ever know that God spoke to him? Even more, how can anyone be *certain* that God spoke to any person? Whose god – which god? Some Baptist churches in the USA have been known to display a sign reading 'Reason is the greatest enemy that faith has'. To display such an obdurate proclamation to a congregation in a modern world seems totally abnormal. What is the definition of 'reason'? The *Oxford English Dictionary* tells us it is 'the power of the mind to think, understand, and form judgements logically: what is right, practical, or possible; common sense.' That Baptist sign is the equivalent of saying black is white, dogs have ten legs and an octopus can tap-dance while singing opera. And there's another thing. That glib comment I've just made was conceived tongue-in-cheek, with humour. But don't try having a laugh with the godly, those followers of the religions of the book, because humour has no place with them. They seem obsessed with sin, punishment, blood, terror and the *fear* of God. A good person can be praised as 'God-fearing'. What kind of deity is it that wants its followers to live in constant fear?

The superstitious state

In the west, where secularism still occupies some ground, we've been joking about religion for decades. When Monty Python's *Life of Brian* came out in 1979, a simple, very funny film about a man mistaken for the messiah, the po-faced hydra of Christianity raised its many heads in humourless horror.

In the Middle East, in Iraq and Syria, with their suicide bombings, beheadings, civil war and daily cruelty in the name of God, one might think that no one would have the necessary courage to find any humour in the situation. Yet in Iraq, in September 2014, Al Iraqiya TV aired a promo announcing an anti-Isis satirical series called *The Superstitious State* – its title in Arabic being a play on the words *khilafa* (caliphate) and *khirafa* (superstition). The show featured an assortment of colourful characters, including a red-clad devil with a pitchfork, whose union with a Jewish woman wearing a large star of David begets an 'Isisling' in the form of Isis front-man Abu Bakr Al Baghdadi, hatched from an egg in the desert. Other characters included the Joker from *Batman*, Dracula, a green-clad lady based on sheikha Mozah, wife of the former Emir of Qatar, a gun-toting, booze-swigging American cowboy and a character based on Stalin. The promo was broadcast on the Iraqi TV channel and was shown several times a day, although some of the cast were justifiably in fear of their lives. All the Monty Python team had to face was a miffed archbishop and a befuddled, outraged pundit – Malcolm Muggeridge. With Iraqi TV's *The Superstitious State* being broadcast just miles from the advancing legions of darkness this seemed like bravery above and beyond the call of satire.

It is truly astonishing that in the twenty-first century, any slight whiff of disrespect for someone's chosen deity can result in, at least, very threatening excoriation, and even, in some cases, your violent mutilation or death.

DEATH OF A PROUD OLD MAN

When they arrested the proud old man in that hot, dusty ancient corner of his beloved country, they took him to their field headquarters for more than a rigorous month of painful interrogation. He steadfastly refused to answer their questions.

Outside, in the blazing sun, the ancient columns and magnificent edifices stood proudly as they had done for over 2000 years. Somewhere, in a hidden location only the old man might be able to reveal, were some of the treasures of that ancient civilisation, treasures he had studied for decades, treasures he had stored and secured for the benefit of human knowledge and shared understanding. He suspected that his violent jailers in their black hoods (do hoods hide shame or cowardice – or both?), although professing zealous religious reasons for their torturous enquiries, were more interested in thievery than in the work of any god. So in the name of that god whom they served, the old man's captors took him out into the sunshine, placed a hood on his head and decapitated him with a sword. They hung his headless corpse high on an ancient column, with signs claiming he had served idolatry and 'attended infidel conferences'. Using high explosives, they destroyed the precious sites of antiquity he had devoted fifty years of his life to preserving for all to enjoy. Such is the unforgiving power of religion and superstition.

Now there are two men in Syria whose similar names will not be forgotten. One is the fifty-year-old president, Bashir al Assad. The other is the 83-year-old Khaled al Asaad, scholar of antiquities, born in Palmyra, Syria, in 1932. He was married with five daughters and six sons. Khaled was ritually murdered in his cherished Palmyra on 18 August 2015, a victim of the highly organised vindictiveness of Isis militants. What was his crime? He loved history. Yet that simple fact was regarded as idolatrous and the antiquities he cared for seen as pagan and sacrilegious under a merciless puritanical interpretation of Islam.

Syrian state antiquities chief Maamoun Abdulkarim said, 'The continued presence of these criminals in this city is a curse and bad omen.' Curses and bad omens seem to be the lingua franca of some religions. In many such commitments, superstition is the grape which makes the heady wine of blind faith. Although it appears to possess no rational substance, those who follow superstition often imply that they have certain superior knowledge or evidence for their philosophical, scientific, or religious convictions, which is never revealed.

The twenty-first century-world is gasping for breath at the rate of technological change. As rapidly moving science fact challenges age-old superstitious beliefs, huge swathes of humanity hang onto their well-thumbed holy books and scriptures, intent on slipping back into some vague medieval mindset. They are oblivious to the contradiction that the iPhones and the internet that are obviously the artefacts of Satan are also their own tools of self-promotion. The International Space Station circles the earth at 17,500 mph, medical students labour in training for eight years to become skilled surgeons dedicated to preserving life and we search for a cure for cancer while the mysterious layers of the onion of the universe are peeled away by precise research. At the same time, religious fundamentalism is proving with renewed vigour that any doubt in the existence of a 'merciful God' warrants only one response; torture and a barbaric death.

In 1930 Joseph Wheless published his book *Forgery in Christianity* (reissued by FQ Classics, 2007). In this he wrote:

Faith hates facts; they are forever divorced on grounds of congenital incompatibility. The church, true church and Protestant, has screamed and reviled at every truth of science which was ever discovered; with high priestly anathema, the curse of God, with prison, rack, and stake, it has sought to suppress and kill every thought of the human mind, every bold thinker, whose truths for the benefit of mankind have contradicted and ridiculed it and its holy dogmas.

Though raised a Southern Methodist, when he qualified as a lawyer Wheless went on to defend free-thinking and atheist organisations. At the time Wheless was writing, he displayed a penchant for communism, which he fondly believed was the answer to continued superstition and religious dogma. Yet as Stalin was proving, Uncle Joe's eventual demolition of Lenin and Trotsky's foundations resulted in a new form of obsessed political superstition, in which anyone daring to stand beyond the party line became the new agents of Lucifer. Later in the century, the files of the Stasi in east Berlin were to be crammed with paranoid chronicles of twentieth-century demonology. So why do people always have to die for thinking aloud in the wrong places?

When it comes to Islam, Abu Abdullah Al Qurtubi (1214–1275) was a Sunni Muslim scholar who wrote the *Tafsir al Qurtubi*, a classic mainstream exegesis of the Qur'an. At 2:217, Qurtubi says this:

Scholars disagree about whether or not apostates are asked to repent. One group say that they are asked to repent and, if they do not, they are killed.

Some say they are given an hour and others a month. Others say that they are asked to repent three times and that is the view of Malik. Al Hasan said they are asked a hundred times. It is also said that they are killed without being asked to repent.

It's notable that there seems to be little chance of *not* losing your life and, depending upon which band of zealots you're captured by, your potential survival for an extra hour or two depends on which version of the holy book is in vogue.

Most religions, somewhere in their literature, will talk about a merciful God, peace, love and a tolerance for other beliefs inherent in their creed. Sadly, in reality this professed magnanimity rarely includes live and let live, and turning the other cheek only invites yet more blows. So it is with some trepidation that, wearing my hobnailed agnostic boots, I tread over these potentially explosive eggshells.

Allah in the aubergine

For the faithful, God moves in mysterious ways, reminding us of his presence by turning up in the most unexpected places. He likes to send messages. Way back in 2003, as reported in the *Metro*, he decided to make an appearance in our comestibles, a channel which has become an old favourite down the years.

Naila Khan of St Mary's, Southampton, had visited her brother in law Ikram Khan's grocery store. It was the holy month of Ramadan and she planned to make a vegetable curry. Back home, she sliced open an aubergine, only to discover the Arabic word for Allah in the flesh. Stunned as she was, she was even more amazed when she saw the other segment, because that displayed 'Ya Allah' or 'Oh, God'. Two messages from God in one aubergine.

Mrs Khan's daughter, Maria, said: 'When I saw the aubergine I thought it was amazing and that it must have meant good luck.' Claiming an omen of fortune contradicted a faith which sternly claims to have eradicated all superstition, yet local religious leaders were summoned and decided this was a miracle. Her brother immersed the slices in holy water then stored them in reverence in the freezer.

Then in October 2011 came the miracle tomato of 52 Willow Street in Bradford. It was bought in the Tahrir grocery store by Shabana Hussain, who said, 'It was the first tomato I picked out from the bag. As I was slicing it in two I said, "Bismillah," which means, "In the name of Allah." I glanced at one of the halves and there was that very word.' The other half of the tomato revealed a phrase from the Qur'an – 'There is no God but Allah'. Shabana had been examining tomatoes for two years following the 2009 discovery by Shaista Javed in Huddersfield of a miracle tomato bearing the Qur'anic scripture, 'There is no God but Allah' and 'Muhammad (pbuh) is the messenger.' Hindus, too, have found the sacred symbol 'Om' in their various foodstuffs.

There have been similar reports since. According to the dictionary, such visual surprises are a simulacrum, a representation or imitation of a person or thing.

In September 2007 the monkey tree phenomenon broke out in Singapore, when someone spotted a callus on a tree which looked like a monkey. This instigated a social mania as people, believing the growth on the tree to be of divine origin, became keen to worship a monkey God and flocked to the site to pray. Those of a more rational scientific outlook believe this to be an effect of pareidolia, in which random stimuli are perceived as meaningful.

Our lady of the cheese

A further example of supernatural divinity is a ten-year-old, carefully preserved grilled cheese sandwich bearing the image of the Virgin Mary that was sold on eBay to internet casino GoldenPalace.com for $28,000. The woman who made the sandwich, jewellery designer Diana Duyser, spotted Our Lady of the Cheese staring back at her as she took a bite. She has since claimed that the sandwich has brought her luck over the years and is truly convinced that the image is divine and represents the Virgin Mary, mother of God. Diana said 'People ask me if I have had blessings since she has been in my home. I do feel I have. I have won $70,000 on different occasions at the casino near my house.'

The Catholic Church loves a good simulacrum, and over many decades they've had some dazzlers in this department. Yet beyond messages in vegetables, holy cloud formations and slices of toast, this insistent branch of heaven often despatches a visible messenger. Over the past 2,000 years there's been no shortage of signs and wonders.

Ave Maria

The Virgin Mary frequently pays a visit, and in 1858 she appeared to a 14-year-old peasant girl, Bernadette Soubirous, in the grotto of Massabielle, near Lourdes, France. Mary had plenty to say to Bernadette because she appeared to her on no fewer than eighteen occasions, identifying herself as the Immaculate Conception. She gave Bernadette a message to impart to humanity: 'Pray and do penance for the conversion of the world.' It took the Church four years of deliberation before approving devotion to Our Lady of Lourdes. Since then, this shrine has attracted more than a million pilgrims each year.

In 1941, in the dark days of WWII, the event was novelised by Franz Werfel in *The Song of Bernadette* and spent more than a year on the *New York Times* bestseller list, enjoying thirteen weeks at No. 1. Whereas Allah in an aubergine might not float

Hollywood's boat, a spectral Mary appearing to children was just the ticket for a message of wartime hope. After becoming a Broadway play that opened at the Belasco theatre in March 1943, Hollywood director Henry King took on the challenge of filming Werfels' novel. As usual in Tinseltown, historical accuracy took a back seat. For example, French prosecutor Vital Dutour (played as an anti-religious character by an excellently sinister Vincent Price) merely thinks Bernadette suffers from hallucinations. In reality, Dutour was a devout Catholic. The 1943 film *Song of Bernadette* won four Oscars and was nominated for more. Even Igor Stravinsky was on board to write the soundtrack, until the job and the musical Oscar eventually went to Alfred Newman. Perhaps the film's runaway success was due to its positive spiritual message at a time when the world was at war and many were suffering abject grief and misery.

In the immediate aftermath of the war, screenwriters were poised for a profitable follow-up. A miracle which occurred fifty-nine years after Lourdes would inspire Hollywood to continue in this supernatural vein.

Three young Portuguese children, Lucia dos Santos, Jacinta Marto and Francisco Marto, reported the apparition of Our Lady of Fátima in 1917. At first the local authorities arrested the children, jailed them and made the somewhat irreligious threat to boil them one by one in a pot of oil, obviously as a demonstration of the love of innocents. The kids stuck to their story, and today Fátima is a place of pilgrimage. After the children's release, the visions at Fátima gathered widespread respect.

In October 1930 the bishop of Leiria-Fátima declared the visions 'worthy of belief'. Whether or not such events are regarded in ecclesiastic circles as superstition, it is notable that no fewer than five popes – Pius XII, John XXIII, Paul VI, John Paul II and Benedict XVI accepted the supernatural origin of the Fátima events. In fact, John Paul II said that it was the same Portuguese Virgin Mary who saved his life in 1981 when some deranged gunman aimed a potshot at him on the feast of Our Lady of Fátima.

John Paul donated the bullet to the Catholic sanctuary at Fátima and today it is placed in the crown of the Virgin's statue. Three films came out of this miracle; *The Miracle of Our Lady of Fátima* (USA, 1952) is the best known, *Apparitions at Fátima* (1992) claimed to be more authentic, and recently the very arty *The 13th Day* (UK, 2009) can be viewed at *www.the13thday.com*. Omens and apparitions appear to be very inspirational, and, handled correctly, make for good box office receipts. As the Bible had it in Timothy 4:3:

3: For the time will come when they will not endure sound doctrine but after their own lusts shall they heap to themselves teachers, having itching ears. 4: And they shall turn away their ears from the truth and shall be turned unto fables.

Astronomy vs astrology

In the 1980s it was always confusing having two senior politicians in the White House with similar names. One was, of course, President Ronald Reagan and the other was White House chief of staff Donald Regan. Ronald and Donald . . . it sounds one step away from a hamburger. In May 1988, a book by Donald Regan came out entitled *For the Record*. Mr Regan revealed one of the odder aspects of his duties up on the hill; making sure the president's schedule fitted in with that of Reagan's astrologer, Joan Quigley.

Quigley's access to the presidency was through first lady Nancy Reagan. The two women had met initially on the Merv Griffin TV talk show in 1973. It was an auspicious event. There was said to have been something of a 'curse' on the White House for 148 years, inasmuch as presidents elected every twenty years from 1840 to 1860, 1880, 1900, 1920, 1940 and 1960 – had died in office. Nancy would always be grateful to Quigley for breaking this unfortunate chain and helping her husband get through to the end of his second term. Beyond this achievement, the horoscope, as utilised by Quigley, would be seen as highly influential at crucial stages in Ronnie's career.

When two of the president's protégés for appointment to the US Supreme Court were blocked by Congress, Quigley used her star charts to come up with a precise time – namely, 11:32:25 a.m. – when she said the president should nominate his third candidate, Anthony Kennedy. Remarkably, Kennedy was confirmed 97–0 on 11 November 1987.

At one time, Nancy asked Joan Quigley if she would waive her fee, to which she responded in true stargazing style, 'People tend not to value advice they don't have to pay for.'

During a less attentive astrological period for the president, John Warnock Hinckley Jr (b. 1955) attempted to assassinate Ronald Reagan in a misguided effort to impress his idol, actress Jodie Foster, on 30 March 1981. Following this debacle, Quigley reminded Nancy that if she had been hired to study Ronnie's chart she could have predicted the shooting.

While Christianity generally appears to lead the field in purloining ancient superstitions from our pagan past to suit scriptures, the Bible has little time for astrology. As Deuteronomy 4:19 states:

And beware lest you raise your eyes to heaven and when you see the sun and the moon and the stars, all the host of heaven, you be drawn away and bow down to them and serve them, things that the Lord your God has allotted to all the peoples under the whole heaven.

Superstition is definitely perceived as the work of Satan, and Peter 5:8 warns us:

Be sober-minded; be watchful. Your adversary the devil prowls around like a roaring lion, seeking someone to devour.

However, few can resist a quick glance at their stars in the press. For example, as I write this on a dull winter's day, I am both uplifted and slightly nervous as my daily email horoscope tells me:

Today an average exchange of ideas will generate a sublime experience in your life, so be open to talking to anyone at any time. During an everyday email, text message or voicemail you should try to get a little bit more creative – add a dash or two of your special brand of wit and you will inspire other people to do the same. Express yourself honestly and show everyone you encounter today just how unique you are. Don't be afraid to raise a few eyebrows.

Well, thanks for that, Aries. We'll give it a try. Yet as for 'raising a few eyebrows', the godly will regard this as evil superstition. Here's what Christiananswers.net has to say: 'Astrology should not even be consulted for amusement. It is connected with the forces of evil and can lead to other occult practices and bondage to sin.'

Christians believe that astrology, a superstition, can't be tested against reality because such a test will fail. At the point of your birth the position of heavenly bodies is supposed to give you your future personality traits under your astrological sign. If that's the case, why don't twins have absolutely identical lives? As outlined by Rebekah giving birth to Jacob and Esau in Genesis 25: 19–34:

25: And the first came out red all over like a hairy garment and they called his name Esau.

26: And after that came his brother out and his hand took hold on Esau's heel and his name was called Jacob. And Isaac was threescore years old when she bore them.

27: And the boys grew and Esau was a cunning hunter, a man of the field and Jacob was a plain man, dwelling in tents.

28: And Isaac loved Esau because he did eat of his venison but Rebekah loved Jacob.

As a tool of debate for the faithful, the Bible comes into its own.

Another reason given for astrology's invalidity is that today's star signs are incorrect. Astrology is based approximately on the positions of stars as they were 3000 years ago. Each year, the error in dating the zodiac signs grows greater.

If it is the gravity of the stars and planets that affects world events and individuals, then – due to the astronomical distances these bodies are from the earth – such traces of gravity as might exist are negligible.

Aries personalities (21 March to 19 April) are impatient and apparently like to be the first in the queue. Although I'm an Aries and frequently impatient, I'm reluctant to cause a ruckus if there's a long queue in the post office.

It seems remarkable that astrology – seen by many, both religious and secular, as simple superstition of itself – even has extra built-in superstitions regarding the characteristics of individuals. The following examples will no doubt be contradicted by the many astrological websites and numerous publications, but this very condensed list gives a flavour of what personal traits stargazers believe their sign dictates.

Aries (21 March to 19 April): impatient, likes to get things over and done with.

Taurus (20 April to 20 May): enjoys luxury and sensuality.

Gemini (21 May to 20 June): it is bad luck for a Gemini not to be talking or communicating. They like making plans.

Cancer (21 June to 22 July): likes collecting and saving things; bad luck might follow if they dispose of any item saved from earlier times.

Leo (23 July to 22 August): likes you to know who they are; they'll also remember your name and you should definitely remember theirs.

Virgo (23 August to 22 September): are supposed to be obsessively superstitious with fastidious routines from which any deviation will bring bad luck.

Libra (23 September to 22 October): placid, harmonious and only happy when you're happy.

Scorpio (23 October to 21 November): another superstitious person who believes in omens and signs.

Sagittarius (22 November to 21 December): are also superstitious, following all sorts of arcane rules, careful about what they wear and always having one eye on luck.

Capricorn (22 December to 19 January): apparently avoid superstitions, but astrologers claim most of them marry Pisces, who can be stubbornly spiritual.

Aquarius (20 January to 18 February): queue-jumpers who tend not to follow rules.

Pisces (19 February to 20 March): are superstitious about the weather and rigidly follow other popular superstitions.

If we look dispassionately at the personal traits above, no doubt we'll all find something we agree with. As an Aries, I recognise my exasperations. Yet my wife is also an Aries and she's the exact opposite; she has mastered every sensible procrastination and will only do things when she's good and ready.

Shakespeare says, 'The fault is not in our stars but in ourselves.' Astrologers will tell us, 'The stars impel; they do not compel.' St Thomas Aquinas says, 'The planets influence the more elemental part of man than passions.'

If we accept that astronomy is a science and that astrology is a pseudo-science, it may be wise to keep them apart. Astronomy is concerned with the measurements of distances, the movement, birth and death of stars, and much more. However, we have to remind ourselves that all the resulting calculations are made in relation to planet earth. The study of astronomy from the surface of a distant planet in the Crab Nebula would produce very different results.

As for astrology, what kind of a zodiac would inhabitants of Jupiter or Neptune consult? Modern astronomy seeks to solve the unanswered questions regarding the origin of man and the final, possible end of his existence. Astronomers regularly reveal new knowledge of the universe and the galaxies, which must put immense pressure on religions to re-evaluate their age-old superstitions and beliefs regarding the creation of life. Yet these two areas of study have close-linked historical roots.

Over the past century, some psychologists and psychiatrists have come to recognise that there may well be more to the human mind than the hardcore materialists have been ready to accept. Quantum physics and the experiments at the CERN Large Hadron Collider (LHC) seek to reveal a parallel dimension to the one we live in; if they are successful, a completely new universe will be revealed. Scientists at the LHC suggest that gravity from our own universe may 'leak' into this parallel universe. Such a revelation would require a total re-write of physics books and even philosophy. Even the world-weary scepticism espoused in this present book could be blown away.

Psychologist Carl Jung (1875–1961) used to cast the horoscopes of his patients. He made an astrological analysis of about five hundred marriages, discovering that the findings of the Greek mathematician, astronomer and geographer Ptolemy (AD 90–168), on which modern western astrology is based, were still valid. Favourable aspects between the sun and the moon of the different partners seemed to produce a happy marriage.

Although he originally held a negative view of astrology, French psychologist Michel Gauquelin (1928–1991) made a survey of about 20,000 horoscopic analyses and found to his surprise that the personality traits of those studied coincided with characterisations produced by modern psychology. Although most of his published work was highly critical of traditional astrology, many thought Gauquelin was advocating an uncritical return to its old-fashioned form. His research produced something called the Mars effect, a purported statistical correlation between successful athletic ability and the position of the planet Mars relative to the horizon at the time and place of an athlete's birth. Unsurprisingly, he had many serious critics, and subsequent experiments to repeat his results have failed.

We have a choice. We can regard astrology as what it often appears to be, a collection of superstitions based on ancient calculations, or we can take it as a bit of harmless fun in a less romantic modern world. As for astronomy, we can take the platonic view on board, that it compels the soul to look upwards and leads us from this world to another. If we persist in failing to distinguish between science and pseudo-science, then perhaps the words of Voltaire (1694–1778) succinctly sum up the problem; 'Superstition is to religion what astrology is to astronomy; the mad daughter of a wise mother. These daughters have too long dominated the earth.'

Myths, gods and legends: don't shoot the messenger

Superstition and religion go together like salt and pepper, fish and chips or Laurel and Hardy. The following paragraphs are here for a purpose and they do not necessarily represent all of this writer's beliefs. Rather, they are an attempt to look behind the turbulent drama of 'big religion', at the dusty, backstage scenery, the first-draft scenarios that time has conveniently forgotten.

Throughout history, our constant search for reason and understanding, for something beyond our short biological life – the divine – has led mankind to latch onto the utterances of all manner of spiritual leaders, many convincing enough to inspire whole nations to sanctify their pronouncements. Some of these characters were real, others mythical. Fervent atheists and hard-nosed sceptics will make strenuous efforts to deconstruct the very foundations of Christianity by outlining all the ancient mythology which preceded it and then compare this to what Catholics and Protestants believe today.

As for Jesus Christ, the man, inveterate atheists like to think they have a loaded gun in the fact that Christ's historicity is, to say the least, opaque. Christ's story in the Bible was written more than six decades after his crucifixion, and the other source, Flavius Josephus (AD 37–c. 100), is generally regarded as unreliable, meaning that atheism's argument with the faithful is unending. Those who accept the gospels as authentic justification of their faith will sometimes quote a letter describing Jesus and his fate written by Pontius Pilate to Seneca in Rome. In this, Pilate, the governor of Judea AD 26–36, describes Jesus very sympathetically, in terms which could back up anything in the New Testament. However, the main source for the letters of Pilate is William Percival Crozier (1879–1944). He was a British journalist and editor of the *Manchester Guardian* from 1932. His 1928 book *Letters of Pontius Pilate: Written during his Governorship of Judea to his Friend Seneca in Rome* is an interesting read (available at: members.tripod.com/~owen_eir/pilate.html).

Crozier is described as the scholarly editor of Pilate's letters. So, Pilate wrote some letters about Jesus. Did he? Believe that if you must, but this book was

Crozier's first *novel*, a fictionalised account of what he *thought* Pilate would have written. The letters therefore appear to be fiction. But as in all ecclesiastic debates, there's always back-up. If Crozier was fiction, Christian scholars can examine *The Annals* by Roman historian and senator Tacitus. This is a history of the Roman empire AD 14–68, from Tiberius to Nero. In this he writes of the Christians:

> Nero fastened the guilt and inflicted the most exquisite tortures on a class hated for their abominations, called Christians by the populace. Christus, from whom the name had its origin, suffered the extreme penalty during the reign of Tiberius at the hands of one of our procurators, Pontius Pilatus, and a most mischievous superstition, thus checked for the moment, again broke out not only in Judea, the first source of the evil, but even in Rome, where all things hideous and shameful from every part of the world find their centre and become popular.
>
> Tacitus, Annals, 15:44

Note that Tacitus calls this 'mischievous superstition'. The view of historically minded, secular bystanders is that new dogmas ride piggy-back on old beliefs and superstitions in all religions. The creeds grow like an evergreen privet hedge, constantly pruned and clipped into an acceptable profile while in the adjacent garden other branches grow, each one determined to strangle the other. Professing a love and respect for mankind, Christianity, Buddhism, Islam, the Sikhs and Hindus all sprang from a sturdy, well-meaning root which proceeded to generate numerous contorted branches.

ARTICLES OF FAITH VS SUPERSTITION

The articles of faith for the three 'religions of the book', Islam, Christianity and Judaism (the latter being 'fundamental principles' rather than 'articles'), are interesting even if you're a non-believer. If you're searching in them for superstitious elements, evidence of the fantastic and supernatural, you'll probably settle on some examples. But just remind yourself – if US soldiers believe that having apricots in their tanks is a bad omen, and if a lone crow on your lawn gives you the shudders, then, religious or not, we're all in this together.

The term 'credendum' comes from the Latin: a thing to be believed, from *crēdere* to believe. Many people around the world would claim they do not 'believe' superstitions, yet they will still, in some small way, allow them to influence their behaviour. In religion, what is *essential* to belief comes under articles of faith. For example, Christianity is a monotheistic system of beliefs and practices based on the Old Testament and the teachings of Jesus as embodied in the New Testament, emphasising the role of Jesus as saviour. Allied to this is dogma or tenet – a religious doctrine that is proclaimed as true *without proof*.

CHRISTIANITY

An article of faith can be seen as an unshakeable belief in something without need for proof or evidence. How many articles of faith there are differs from faith to faith. For example, the Church of Latter Day Saints (Mormons) profess thirteen articles of faith, while the Roman Catholics have twelve; these are;

1: I believe in God, the father almighty, creator of heaven and earth.

2: And in Jesus Christ, his only son, our Lord.

3: Who was conceived by the power of the holy spirit and born of the Virgin Mary.

4: He suffered under Pontius Pilate, was crucified, died and was buried.

5: He descended into hell. The third day he arose again from the dead.

6: He ascended into heaven and is seated at the right hand of God the father almighty.

7: He will come again to judge the living and the dead.

8: I believe in the holy spirit, This part reminds the believer that God exists in three persons, the holy trinity: God the father, God the son, and God the holy spirit.

9: The holy Catholic Church, the communion of saints, is an essential institution.

10: The forgiveness of sins, Christ came to save the world from sin.

11: Belief in the resurrection of the body and

12: in life everlasting. As Christ our saviour died, so, too, must mere mortals. As he rose, so shall all human beings.

The Anglican Church has thirty-nine articles of faith, some coinciding with Catholicism. Many that date back to the sixteenth century are not taken down from the shelf too often. According to their 'ask an Anglican' website at conciliaranglican.com, the seventeenth-century Irish Anglican archbishop, John Bramhall, puts it this way:

> We do not suffer any man 'to reject' the thirty-nine articles of the Church of England 'at his pleasure'; yet neither do we look upon them as essentials of saving faith or 'legacies of Christ and of his apostles'; [. . .] as pious opinions fitted for the preservation of unity. Neither do we oblige any man to believe them, but only not to contradict them.

ISLAM

The prophet (peace be upon him) made it clear that in Islam there was no such thing as ill omens. Such a belief was regarded as leading to polytheism and therefore goes under the term 'shirk'. Regarding superstitions, for example he stated that the cry of a bird or the way it flew could not be interpreted as ill omens. He advised that unusual objects and events be interpreted in a positive way. He also mentioned that casting spells or carrying amulets would harm the belief in *tawhid* (the unity of God).

Before Islam, the people in the Arabian peninsula used to worship heavenly bodies, in particular the sun and the moon, and had regard for spiritual creatures such as angels, genies or demons. Moreover, they held superstitious beliefs about them. For example, they believed that rain fell from the stars. The prophet indicated that these beliefs stemmed from the period of ignorance before Islam. Arabs thought that the sun was an angel and demons were housed in idols. They interpreted the shooting or falling of a star as signifying the birth or death of an important person or the coming of a disaster to that region. The prophet stated that these beliefs were superstitious. One night, while the prophet was sitting together with his companions, a falling star lit up the surrounding area. He asked his companions what they would have said about this event in the period of ignorance.

They replied, 'We would have said an important man had been born or had died tonight.'

Then the prophet told them, 'A star does not fall for a man's death or for his birth.'

When Islam came to Arabia, spells such as calling on demons, the tying of knots, using arrows for fortune-telling and stargazing were very common in addition to the idolatry the people practised. Islam was wholly opposed to these rituals. The prophet cited the casting of spells as one of the greatest sins; once he had mentioned it as coming after polytheism, superstition became the greatest sin. He stated that a person who casts spells would lose their faith in Allah. Special punishment could be implemented for sorcerers, namely beheading.

In the important task of conveying Islam, the prophet's conversations with people who came to Medina a decade after the *hijrah* (migration) were significant in his fight against superstitions. The prophet tried to demolish the enduring folk beliefs and practices. When members of the Asad tribe asked about a verdict on soothsaying practices such as making birds fly, interpreting the names of the birds, their cries, their manner of flying or making interpretations using stones, the prophet prohibited all of these superstitious activities.

A Muslim believes in the following six articles of faith:

1: Oneness of God. A Muslim believes in one God, supreme and eternal, infinite and mighty, merciful and compassionate, creator and provider. God has no father or mother, no son or daughter. None is equal to Him. He is God of all humankind, not of a special tribe or race.

2: Messengers and prophets of God. A Muslim believes in all the messengers and prophets of God without any discrimination. All messengers were mortals, human beings, endowed with divine revelations and appointed by God to teach mankind.

3: Revelations and the Qur'an. A Muslim believes in all scriptures and revelations of God as they were complete and in their original versions. The Qur'an is the unaltered and direct words of God, revealed through the angel Gabriel, to the final prophet, Muhammad, peace be upon him (pbuh), some 1400 years ago.

4: Angels are a creation of God. They are purely spiritual, spend their time worshipping God, being splendid beings that require no food or drink or sleep. Angels cannot be seen by the naked eye.

5: Day of judgement. A Muslim believes in the day of the judgement. This world as we know it will come to an end and the dead will rise to stand for their final and fair trial. Good people will enter paradise, bad people hell.

6: Predestination. A Muslim believes in the ultimate knowledge and power of God to plan and execute His plans. Humans should think, plan and make sound choices and then put their trust in God. If things happen as they want they should praise God. If things do not happen as they want they should still praise God, recognising that He knows best what is good for the affairs of mankind.

On the face of it, these six articles of Islam seem concise and easy enough to follow for the faithful. The claim is frequently made (as it is with most faiths) that this is a religion of peace, and we often hear the phrase 'Allah is merciful'. And then we're faced with Islamic State – Isis. Islam claims to have eradicated superstitions. However, here's a short selection of those which may have slipped through the net in recent times:

1: It's bad luck to cut your nails or sweep the house after the *maghrib* (just after sunset, the fourth of five daily prayers).

2: Superstitions about certain numbers such as 92, 786, 666 and 999. This is no longer allowed in Islam.

3: A belief that the Qur'an should not be touched if you are wearing shoes (also, not leaving your shoes upside down to avoid bad luck).

4: Eating three of anything – fish, apples, bread rolls etc. – at the same meal will render women infertile. Eating onions at night is unlawful.

5: Peacock feathers bring sadness.

6: If you repeat specific attributes of Allah for a number of times, you will receive rewards.

7: Women should wear the *hijab* all the time, even alone at home.

8: Men should not wear fragrances or perfumes as this attracts female devils.

9: You should not get your hair cut on a Wednesday, and don't cut your nails on a Saturday.

10: Moles in a garden are good fortune but removing them brings bad luck. Owls represent misfortune but turtles represent good fortune.

No. 7 is based on a misconception. In the Qur'an, Allah orders women to wear the *hijab* or cover themselves, hide their beauty and guard their modesty. However, there are apparently no rulings that women must wear a *hijab* when she is on her own in the house or with her husband and other *mahram* men (those who can't be married, such as father, brother or son, etc.).

> And tell the believing women to reduce some of their vision and guard their private parts and not expose their adornment except only that which (necessarily) appears thereof and to wrap their head covers over their chests and not expose their adornment (i.e., beauty).

> Qur'an, Surah An Nur 24:31

JUDAISM

Unlike the Christians and Muslims, the Jews do not have articles of faith, yet their thirteen principles serve a similar function. It is the custom of many congregations to recite these, prefacing them with the words '*Ani Maamin*' ('I believe') after the synagogue's morning prayers.

Rabbi Moshe ben Maimon (1136–1204 a.k.a. 'Maimonides' or the 'Rambam'), was the great codifier of Torah law and Jewish philosophy. He compiled the 'Thirteen Fundamental Principles', referring to them as the *Shloshah Asar Ikkarim*. Maimonides refers to these thirteen principles of faith as 'the fundamental truths of our religion and its very foundations.'

The thirteen principles are as follows:

1: Belief in the existence of the creator, who is perfect in every manner of existence and is the primary cause of all that exists.
2: The belief in God's absolute and unparalleled unity.
3: The belief in God's non-corporeality and that He will be unaffected by any physical occurrences, such as movement or rest or dwelling.
4: The belief in God's eternity.
5: The imperative to worship God exclusively and no foreign false gods.
6: The belief that God communicates with man through prophecy.

7: The belief in the primacy of the prophecy of Moses our teacher.

8: The belief in the divine origin of the Torah.

9: The belief in the immutability of the Torah.

10: The belief in God's omniscience and providence.

11: The belief in divine reward and retribution.

12: The belief in the arrival of the messiah and the messianic era.

13: The belief in the resurrection of the dead.

As we're considering faith, what to believe or otherwise here, it's worth mentioning two statements by Maimonides: 'Do not consider it proof just because it is written in books, for a liar who will deceive with his tongue will not hesitate to do the same with his pen.' And, 'The risk of a wrong decision is preferable to the terror of indecision. Teach thy tongue to say "I do not know," and thou shalt progress.' Wise words indeed.

HINDUISM

For many Hindus it's more what you do than what you believe when it comes to religion. It's all about practice and practice makes perfect. Hindus believe in Brahman, a universal soul or god who takes on many forms that some Hindus worship as gods or goddesses in their own right. Hindus believe that there is a part of Brahman in everyone, and this is called the *atman*. They believe that the soul is eternal and lives many lifetimes in one body after another. Sometimes you're born as a human being, others as an animal, and you can even be a plant. Hindus also believe that all forms of life contain a soul and all souls have the chance to experience life in different forms.

For many Hindus there are four goals in human life (*purusharthas*):

1: *Moksha.* The release of the soul (*atman*) from the cycle of rebirth. The individual soul unites with Brahman the universal soul. There are different ways to *moksha.* This involves acquiring spiritual knowledge through yoga and meditation and devotion to God as well as working selflessly for the good of society.

2: *Dharma.* The code for leading one's life. Respect for elders is considered important and many consider marriage to be a son's religious duty.

3: *Artha*. The pursuit of material gain by lawful means.

4: *Karma*. Through pure acts, knowledge and devotion, you can reincarnate to a higher level. The opposite achieves the contrary result. *Samsara* means going through the cycle of repeated births and deaths – reincarnation. Hindus believe that existence of this cycle is governed by *karma*. How a person is reincarnated is determined by *karma*.

BUDDHISM

In Buddhism there is no god as the other religions understand it. Buddha was a man. According to Buddhism, for a man to be perfect he should develop two qualities simultaneously: compassion (*karuna*) and wisdom (*panna*). Buddhist compassion represents love, charity, kindness, tolerance and other such noble qualities on the emotional side – or qualities of the heart – while wisdom represents the intellectual side or the qualities of the mind. So to be perfect one has to develop these qualities equally. That is the aim of the Buddhist way of life: the linking of wisdom and compassion. To achieve this a Buddhist follows the noble eightfold path, which requires:

1: Right understanding (*samma ditthi*).
2: Right thought (*samma sankappa*).
3: Right speech (*samma vaca*).
4: Right action (*samma kammanta*).
5: Right livelihood (*samma ajiva*).
6: Right effort (*samma vayama*).
7: Right mindfulness (*samma sati*).
8: Right concentration (*samma samadhi*).

It all sounds fairly simple and straightforward, but, like Christianity, Islam and Judaism, even in this seemingly simple faith there are sects and subdivisions, often at odds with one another. There is Theravada, the 'Way of the Elders', Mahayana, the 'Greater Vehicle', and Vajrayana, the 'Diamond Vehicle'. Theravada and Mahayana Buddhism went their separate ways in the first century AD. Mahayana then subdivided into several diverse schools, such as Zen, Pure Land and Nichiren, many of which flourish today in East Asia. The Vajrayana Buddhist tradition is an esoteric sect that is predominant in Tibet and Nepal.

With regard to superstition, Buddha did not believe in luck, fate or chance. He taught that whatever happens does so because of a cause or causes. However, this seems overlooked by many Buddhists today. Many visit 'holy people' for blessings, to be touched on their heads, believing that this will stabilise their lives in some way. Items such as statuettes and other artefacts are blessed by priests and are then regarded as imbued with some power. I was told by one Buddhist busy polishing her brass Buddha statue that the act was regarded as producing 'good karma'.

Around their necks many Buddhists will wear something special, even more so if it has been 'blessed', hoping it will protect them from any danger. They attend long-life ceremonies thinking that this will prolong their existence, even though they do not change their lifestyle or follow any required practice such as meditation. In Tibetan culture, which we most associate with Buddhism, starting a journey on Saturdays is bad luck. So people pack their luggage on Friday and leave the house, pretending to have started their trip. But in fact they only take their bags to a friend or a relative's house and then return home. On Saturday they leave home and collect their bag and then start their journey. This way they believe they have tricked the superstition.

Out with the old, in with the new?

When disbelievers and agnostics take up the challenge to 'expose' the borrowed foundations of a faith, they too have no idea what superstitious embroidery may have been added to the armoury of legends they'll utilise in their quest to debunk. All that can be relied upon is the feasible notion that superstitious beliefs and rituals were adopted to decorate a religion in order to attract the multitude.

Scholarship advances and expands over the decades, but back in the 1970s the National Geographic Society's book *Great Religions of the World* would have undoubtedly caused uproar in its assessment of the cult of the deity known as Mithras. We have already touched on Mithraism in the conversion of Constantine and the foundation of the Roman Church, yet there are still remaining elements too fascinating to overlook.

This secretive religion which some claim predates Christianity by several centuries was built round the following familiar beliefs, namely that, when Mithras was born on 25 December (considered to be the winter solstice in the ancient world), he was visited as an infant 'saviour' by three wise men from Persia. They brought him gifts of gold, frankincense and myrrh. He performed miracles, lived in celibacy, died on the cross, and enjoyed his last supper with twelve followers who are thought to have represented the signs of the zodiac. His body was laid in a stone tomb. He rose again then ascended to heaven during the spring equinox. This religion was avidly taken up by the Romans and, as Christianity gained ground, Mithraism faded away.

Such is the awkward mythos passed down the centuries, but modern Christian scholars will strongly argue that this is all balderdash. The most comprehensive dismissals of Mithraism can be found in publications such as *Catholic Answers* magazine, where ecclesiastical scholars will go to great lengths to persuade us that Mithraism's rites are not parallel to Christianity.

As ever, it's an ecclesiastical case of 'our myth is better than your myth'.

So, Mithras aside, what are we to make of Attis? Our first mention of Attis comes from the Greek historian Herodotus, writing that Attis was a shepherd from Phrygia and the son of King Croesus of Lydia, a country in western Asia Minor (corresponding to modern-day Turkey). As with Mithras, Attis was born of a virgin called Nana on 25 December. He too was thought of as a saviour who would give his life for mankind. Those who came to worship Attis after his death, like modern Christians, ate his body symbolically in the form of bread. Regarded as the divine son and the father, he was crucified on a tree, on 'black Friday'. The blood from his wounds seeped into the earth to redeem it. He was resurrected after three days (see www.theoi.com).

The further one goes back into ancient Egypt, the more superstitious it becomes, but even there we can find familiar legends of virgin births and saviours. Although Horus was a mythical deity rather than a human being, the ancient Egyptians claimed that he too was born of a virgin. The Egyptians used to carry a manger containing a child through their city streets around the time of their winter solstice, approximately today's 21 December. Horus was regarded as the son of the god Osiris. As with the story of cruel King Herod threatening Judea's babies, Horus was threatened with death as a baby.

The life of Zoroaster, or Zarathustra, also regarded as a saviour, has many similarities to other stories of the immaculate conception. Baptised in a river, he was tempted in the wilderness by the devil, making a great impression on his elders with his wisdom and knowledge, and is said to have begun his ministry at the age of thirty. He is reputed to have performed miracles, including giving a blind man his sight back. His followers promise a second coming as a saviour.

These and other myths proliferate throughout the ancient world. What makes Christ different is the rapid spread and acceptance of his ministry throughout a world which had so many powerful pagan gods and deities.

Islam's equally swift rise was made possible despite the foundations of Judaism, the teachings of the Bible and of the New Testament. Large sections of the population remained unconvinced by these other faiths, even though they were living in the very part of the world where the chronicles were promulgated. They found themselves in a world of war, greed and corruption. They were ready and willing to put their own plan into action.

All of these faiths have basic human values at heart but they appear to be buried by dogma. In November 2014 the *Huffington Post* launched its excellent thread of religious debate, Beyond Belief. This opened with the results of a HuffPost/Survation poll of 2004 people on attitudes to religion. Fifty-six per cent of those surveyed claimed to be Christians, 2.5 per cent Muslims and 1 per cent Jewish. The remaining

31.5 per cent were of some other faith or had none at all. More than half the UK residents polled thought religion was more harmful than beneficial (saying that atheists are just as likely to be moral people as religious people) while a quarter believed in a positive force. Even among those declaring a faith, 60 per cent said they weren't religious whilst only 8 per cent claimed to be 'very' religious. One unexpected result of the survey was that young people are actually more likely to have a positive view of religion. Around 30 per cent of 18–24-year-olds believed that religion does more good than harm, compared to just 19 per cent of 55–64-year-olds.

Andrew Copson, chief executive of the British Humanist Association, said, 'This survey just confirms what we know is the common sense of people in Britain today – that whether you are religious or not has very little to do with your morality.'

Phil Zuckerman spent a year in Denmark and Sweden researching his book *Society Without God: What the Least Religious Nations can tell us about Contentment* (NYU Press, 2008). In this work he discovered that the populations of these two countries, generally regarded as two of the happiest places to live, had little time for organised religion and were all the happier for it. His research concluded that the least religious societies also tend to be the most peaceful, prosperous and equitable. They have always been welcoming, open-door societies. Sadly, since then, the massive refugee problem caused by the Syrian civil war, worsened by the appalling harassment of women by some men presumed by the media to be Muslims from the Middle East in Cologne and Belgium on New Year's Eve 2015, has meant that even the Danes and the Swedes are erecting cultural fences.

Several thousand years of superstition distilled into thousands of diverse religions around the globe have resulted in a situation in which many people are firmly anchored in the pagan past, bound by rituals, incantations, ancient books and the constant fear of damnation and punishment. Religion promotes tribalism. If you're not one of the chosen tribe then you're a heathen, a heretic or an infidel. The priests demand that we 'trust and obey' if we are to accept that faith is a virtue. We are led to believe that without God we are helpless.

Scandals such as priestly child abuse are uncovered, God 'instructs' horrors such as suicide bombing and terror, and women are degraded and subjugated, yet many of the faithful prefer to look away. By doing so they believe that, unlike the rest of us, they will see heaven while we burn in hell.

Much of the aggression the religions of the book generate today in the cradle of their creation is the result of political and corporate meddling by people who will always proclaim that 'God' is on their side. Little wonder that nihilistic young men and women choose martyrdom in a suicide vest when high-tech death rains down daily from indiscriminate drone strikes. Immorality breeds immorality. Almost every political leader has perpetuated the age-old traditions of conquest, invasion and interference in other nations, always under the banner of some 'god' or other. America chose this path over two centuries ago when George Washington stated:

> Let us with caution indulge the supposition that morality can be maintained without religion. Reason and experience both forbid us to expect that national morality can prevail in exclusion of religious principle.

This part of this work has strayed away from the comparative fun of superstition, so the time has come to pull out of this dark valley and find a little sociable sunshine. Hopefully, that's a place where compassion, tolerance and understanding still have some currency. In the words of Albert Einstein:

> I cannot imagine a God who rewards and punishes the objects of his creation, whose purposes are modelled after our own – a God, in short, who is but a reflection of human frailty. Neither can I believe that the individual survives the death of his body, although feeble souls harbour such thoughts through fear or ridiculous egotisms.

> (Albert Einstein, quoted in the *New York Times* obituary of 19 April 1955)

Irrational relics

On 19 September each year the people of Naples, Italy, celebrate the anniversary of the martyrdom of their patron saint Januarius, known as San Gennaro, who died c. 305. At this event a 'miracle' takes place; the saint's dried blood becomes liquefied. The miracle occurs several more times throughout the year. Science has questioned the phenomenon, but that makes little difference. The religious world denies any research into the shroud of Turin, which the faithful insist against any evidence has an image of Jesus on cloth, and the celebration of holy relics, no matter how dubious their provenance, will continue.

San Gennaro's blood is said to protect the town that has Mount Vesuvius nearby. What legitimises the belief historically is the fact that in years when the blood failed to liquefy things went badly wrong, including the plague of 1527 and an earthquake in 1980. The failure to liquefy has also been blamed for the defeat of Napoli's football team.

The Russians and Greeks kiss their icons. In the Sioni cathedral in Tbilisi, Georgia, you can find the grapevine cross. Legend has it that a Cappadocian woman, St Nino (296–340), was a fervent preacher of Christianity in fourth-century Georgia and the Virgin Mary herself presented Nino with a cross with peculiar drooping arms. Since then, the grapevine cross has travelled from country to country before finding its home in Tbilisi where it is now displayed and adored.

In Islam, relics are regarded as idolatrous and have no official sanction, but their presence for some Muslims is too much to resist. Take, for example, Muhammad's (pbuh) beard. It was said that the prophet's whiskers were removed after his death by his favourite barber. You can see the beard today in the Topkapi Palace museum in Istanbul, Turkey. While you're there, you may like to see other items associated with Muhammad (pbuh). Some Muslims claim that his left foot made an impression in the earth wherever he roamed. As well as the footprint on display in Istanbul, you'll find others which have been collected throughout the Middle East on display in various museums and mosques.

In Damascus at the Umayyad mosque you can see John the Baptist's head on display. However, he must have had more than one because there's another Baptist's head in Rome's church of San Silvestro in Capite, while among the faithful the belief is that the real head is buried in the south of France or some-where in Turkey.

If you're a Buddhist, there's a Sri Lankan legend which tells of the survival of just one of the Buddha's teeth which remained after his cremation. The tooth, his left canine, took on mystical qualities to the point where anyone possessing it thought they could rule the country and the faithful. Considering the professed peaceful nature of Buddhism, historically quite a few nasty battles took place for its possession. Today it has its own resting place, the Temple of the Tooth in Kandy, Sri Lanka. It enjoys daily rituals, and on Wednesdays the tooth is symbolically bathed in scented herb-infused water with fragrant flowers. This brew is said to have healing powers and is distributed to the congregation.

Just before the Virgin Mary ascended to heaven she gave Thomas the Apostle a gift. It was her hand-woven, camel-hair belt. In the fourteenth century the belt, known as the Sacra Cintola, turned up in Prato, Italy. You can see it displayed five times a year – at Christmas, Easter, 1 May, 15 August and on Mary's birthday, 8 September. However, Mary divested herself of something else before going to heaven.

At the splendid gothic Chartres cathedral in France pilgrims flock each year to see the Sancta Camisia. This is the tunic the Virgin Mary wore during the birth of Christ. It was given to the church in 876. In 1194 it was thought to have perished in a fire. But it was found intact in the treasury three days later. The bishop wasted no time in proclaiming that Mary herself had given Chartres a sign that a new cathedral should be built.

When the apostle Peter was thrown into a Jerusalem jail for preaching about Jesus he was bound in an iron chain. But the angels intervened. He was visited by an angel and released from his shackles the night before his trial and soon found himself being led from the jail. At the San Pietro in Vincoli ('St Peter in chains') basilica in Rome the chains now have a special reliquary beneath the altar. When Pope Leo I (400–461) was presented with the chains by the Empress Eudoxia (422–462) he placed them next to the chains from Peter's first impris-onment in the Mamertime prison at the foot of the Capitoline Hill in Rome. This was the same jail which held the resolute Goth Jugurtha and the invincible Gaul Vercingetorix. When Leo placed the two chains together, they miracu-lously fused into one.

Saints vs superstition

It may not seem overtly superstitious, but the way in which religion branches out in all manner of bizarre directions to keep the faithful on message is, to say the least, bizarre. As the saying goes, 'You couldn't make this up,' but apparently, in the name of the Lord, the Church can make up anything it likes.

Nowhere is this more obvious than with the beatification of vague and sometimes mythical characters who become saints. Myths, legends, gossip and rumours handed down the ages are cobbled together to make icons of sanctity. No doubt in most cases in which a saint is proved to have existed, it would appear that they were – by the measure of the times they lived in – decent people. Perhaps for every walk of life, from humble ditch-digging to banking, having their own religious patron is a clever device to encourage a sense of classless inclusivity. The banker who I may never meet is blessed, but so is my sewage trench, which he may never smell. Praise the Lord. As we've already seen with St Christopher, the object of your inspired devotion is not always, when examined in detail, connected to many (or any) historical facts.

There are notable exceptions, such as Irish-born St Fiacre (d. 670) who, among other commitments, is patron saint of sexually transmitted diseases. He's also the saint for gardeners and taxi drivers, particularly in Paris. French cabs were referred to as '*fiacres*' because the first establishment in seventeenth-century Paris to admit coaches on hire was in the Rue Saint-Martin, near the hotel Saint-Fiacre.

He built a hospice for travellers in what is now Saint-Fiacre, Seine-et-Marne in France, and he's also the patron saint of haemorrhoid sufferers. His feast day is 1 September. Yet the subjects of these stories occupy the faithful, sending the more devout among them into a state of worshipful bliss. All you need to do is believe. Here are some of the more unusual saints.

St Isidore (560–636)

In 1997, Pope John Paul II declared Isidore of Seville to be the patron saint of the internet. Considering Isidore logged off in the year 636, quite a while before the first web connection in 1969, he's been granted this Silicon Valley status probably because the Church likes to keep pace with popular culture. In Isidore's case, at least we know something about him.

He was bishop of Seville in sixth-century Spain. Two of his brothers, Leander and Fulgentius, and one of his sisters, Florentina, also achieved sainthood. Leander and Fulgentius served as bishops and Florentina as an abbess. So why is he patron saint of the internet? Because he tried to record everything ever known in an encyclopaedia, a twenty-book production called *Etymologies*, also known as the *Origins*, which was published after his death. It was a kind of Wikipedia, and for a thousand years it was considered to be the ultimate wellspring of human knowledge. His feast day is 4 April. St Isidore of Seville shouldn't be confused with St Isidore the patron saint of farmers and labourers.

St Columbanus (543–615)

The patron saint of motorcyclists is not official, as his position was only suggested by an Anglican bishop, John Oliver, who happens to be a biker. Columbanus was a well-educated Irishman and, by all accounts, handsome. As a free-wheeling young man he apparently liked the ladies a little too much, and one day one of them gave him some stern advice to mend his ways. Much against his family's wishes, he decided to become a monk at Bangor Abbey in County Down to save his soul.

His image as a biker seems a little tenuous. Aged 42, Columbanus left Ireland and began travelling Europe as a missionary with a dozen other monks to the pagan tribes in Gaul, who were probably closer to being the Hells' Angels of their day. Over thirty years the brotherhood founded monasteries and finally settled at Bobbio in northern Italy, where he re-built a neglected church. That's where the biker's bones remain today. His feast day is 23 November.

St Drogo (1105–1186)

It is not quite clear why St Drogo is the patron saint of coffee-shop owners. Had he been somewhere where coffee has a history, for example Ethiopia, there might have been a coffee link.

Drogo, also known as Droun, was a Flemish orphan who became a hermit. He visited shrines on penitential pilgrimages and for a while was a shepherd at

Sebourg, France. Apparently, he suffered a terrible illness which left him disfigured. So he stayed in his hermit's hut for forty years. He is also patron saint of shepherds, unattractive and repulsive people, bodily ills, hernias, broken bones, cattle, deaf people, dumbness, gall stones and insanity. That's the great thing about saints – no one is forgotten. You could say he'd need a few cups of coffee with those responsibilities. His history reveals that he spent the last forty years of his life in seclusion, 'surviving only on barley, water and the holy eucharist'. His feast day is 16 April.

St Bibiana

Here's one for Christian homophobes; birth and death unknown, the fourth-century St Bibiana, patron saint of hangovers, has her feast day on 2 December. She had a tough time fighting off a determined lesbian named Rufina, a woman whose methods of seduction descended into violence. Bibiana was a good Christian virgin and was having none of this. So, deprived of a promise of girl-on-girl action, the perverted governor of Rome, Apronianus, ordered Bibiana to be tortured and beaten with scourges that were loaded with lead plummets until she died. Bibiana died with a smile on her face, and although her body was thrown out for the wild animals, none of them touched it. Around her grave so-called 'magical and mysterious' herbs were said to grow. It remains unclear what these were, but apparently they could cure a hangover.

The catalogue of saints is long and complex, and most of them have weird and wonderful stories that never cease to amaze the casual browser into religion's ambiguous history. For recreation value alone, here's a selection of some other wacky saints, minus their birth and death dates or feast dates. If you're keen to know more, they're all out there, waiting to entertain and convert you.

St Vitus: patron saint of oversleeping.
St Arnulf of Metz: patron saint of beer.
St Giles: patron saint of the fear of breastfeeding.
St Apollonia: patron saint of dentists.
St Matthew: patron saint of accountants and tax collectors.
St Ivo of Kermartin: patron saint of lawyers.

St Bernard of Menthon: patron saint of mountaineers and skiers.

St Ambrose: patron saint of beekeepers.

St Cajetan: patron saint of gamblers and the unemployed.

St Genesius of Rome: patron saint of stand-up comedy, plumbers, actors, clowns and torture victims.

St Gummarus: patron saint of lumberjacks and separated spouses.

St Honoratus (Honorius) of Amiens: patron saint of bakers.

St Saint Lidwina: patron saint of ice-skaters.

St Malo: patron saint of pig keepers.

St Barbara: patron saint of firemen and people who work with explosives.

ANYONE FOR FENG SHUI?

If religions are underpinned by superstition, what are we to make of ancient oriental practices such as feng shui (pronounced 'fong shway')? It has been claimed that it has nothing to do with religion or meditation and is not a New Age cult. *Feng* means wind and *shui* means water. In Chinese culture wind and water are connected to good health. Feng shui represents over 3000 years of accrued knowledge that claims to help us to balance the energies of any given space to assure health and good fortune for the people inhabiting it. It is a Taoist vision and understanding of nature, suggesting that the land is alive and filled with chi or energy. It has been in practice at least since the Tang dynasty (618–907), which employed feng shui masters to select auspicious sites, and feng shui texts were required reading for imperial exams. Therefore, it's ancient, mysterious and harmless, lurking in the grey area between cultural superstition and vague science. That's good enough to make it popular today and, used to full effect, it can make you a lot of money.

The direction your building faces, its proximity to water, the dimensions of a room, even the way furniture and ornaments are positioned all have positive or negative meanings. There is even a kind of feng shui 'map' or guide, the *bagua*, which you can study at luckypath-fengshui.com. This shows you how to place everything, from your sofas and tables to ornaments, in order to achieve chi harmony. It does seem very popular with rich people. The *bagua* is placed over the floor-plan of your room or your house to reveal nine main areas of energy that, apparently, are in every house; fame, wealth, family, helpful people and travel, children and creativity, romance and relationships, and self-development.

The most surprising adherent to this peculiar art is Donald Trump, who claims he doesn't 'have to believe' in feng shui – it just 'makes me money'. He may have used Polish labour to build Trump Tower, but The Donald used Chinese philosophy when deciding its aspect, facing New York's Central Park for the prosperity and positive chi this might bring. Apparently the globe in front of the building is a feng shui device to 'negate' the 'killing energy' of the street. If Trump ever gets to build his proposed border wall between the USA and Mexico, no doubt the feng shui masters will make a killing. As to whether he utilises the philosophy for his peculiar comb-over hairdo is unclear.

Other feng shui furniture-shifters are reported to include Eric Clapton, Bill Gates, Steven Spielberg, Bill Clinton, Oprah Winfrey, Gillian Anderson, George Clooney and a couple of names you'd expect on a list of similar exoticisms – Cher and Madonna. When you're as loaded as Bill Gates, feng shui principles can be used to full effect. So when Mr Microsoft was planning his home, he chose an ideal point in the hills with a mountain behind for support and protection, and there's a dragon and tiger on each side of the home to give the house energy. The watery expanse of Lake Washington in front of it completes the balance of the chi energy.

As for those of us at the other end of the income scale, it's hard to find any instances, for example, in British working-class history, when something vaguely approaching feng shui may have mattered. Yet I do recall the superstition that you should never, ever put your boots or shoes on the table. Was that some kind of early Yorkshire feng shui? When a miner died in a colliery accident his boots were placed on the table as a sign of respect.

Something similar to feng shui in Europe was the practice of taking a gift to someone in a new house. That still remains popular and has its origins in the belief that whatever spirits lived in the plot of land would also occupy the new house, so you were pleasing these mysterious entities.

To my absolute dismay, while researching this subject by walking around the house with a compass to see just how unfortunately placed just about every piece of furniture is, I discovered that having your bed facing north brings disease and facing west dulls the brain. I've been sleeping facing north for thirty years. No wonder I'm a mess. I need some feng shui for the body.

Looking at the healing hints of the ancient oracles recorded on various forums and websites online, I discovered that healthy sleep requires the following: never lie on one side for long. Keep changing. Never sleep with the top of your head pointing to the north and feet pointing to the south. The result will be terrible dreams and disturbed sleep. You will develop irritability, frustration and emotional instability and feel miserable. You will lose 50 per cent of your will power, and your soul power will not increase while you sleep.

So, oracles of ancient wisdom, what must we do?

For auspicious benefits, sleep with your head to the east. The same goes for sleeping with your head facing south, feet pointing north. Don't eat anything after 7 p.m. and don't sleep in the daytime.

So what are you waiting for? If you're seeking improved health, or more income or a successful career, then with feng shui you, too, could be Donald Trump. Meanwhile, the rest of us will have to make do with moving our beds around.

Sex, superstition and religion

Sex isn't often mentioned in conversation about superstitions, but there are certain areas of humanity's most pleasurable pastime that are lumbered with just as many prohibitive myths as the poor old black cat. Prominent among these historically are the terrors resulting from masturbation. It all goes back to Genesis 38:9 as the King James Bible tells us:

> And Onan knew that the seed should not be his and it came to pass, when he went in unto his brother's wife, that he spilled it on the ground, lest that he should give seed to his brother.

In previous centuries, those young men and women whose hand hovered over their codpiece or slipped beneath their bodice might find, if they'd been paying attention to the priest or the local monk, that the disgrace of Onan popped into their mind. As an example of avoiding sin, 'good people' – e.g. nuns, monks, priests and saints – ostensibly avoided self-pleasure and fostered the idea that they deprived themselves of the 'full Monty' when it came to human coupling. They were betrothed to God and had no need of 'that kind of thing'. Or did they? There's an old joke that goes, 'You can kiss a nun once, you can kiss a nun twice, but you mustn't get into the habit'.

Christian D. Knudsen, in his well-researched and highly informative thesis *Naughty Nuns and Promiscuous Monks* (University of Toronto, 2012), reveals all manner of wayward wanderings under the wimple and quite a lot of covert cassock-lifting. According to Knudsen, cloistered sexual misconduct in late medieval England was rife.

Humanist scholar and diplomat Sir Richard Morison (1513–1556) was a protégé of Thomas Cromwell, a propagandist for Henry VIII and then ambassador to the German court of Charles V for Edward VI. When Morison surveyed England's religious centres for Henry he came back with accusations of 'sexual incontinence' and 'great stolen wealth', of priests and monks regularly having it away with married women, colourfully described as 'sowing seed in other men's furrows', all of which drove him to total support of the dissolution as the 'putting away of maintained lechery, buggery and hypocrisy'.

Sodomy seems to have been a favourite pastime, with numerous cases of priests and bishops making young local lads' eyes water. As for nuns, being female, they had always been the vulnerable objects of sexual desire. In the ninth century, while many monasteries were attractive to homosexuals, so numerous convents were regarded as brothels. Should babies result, they would generally be killed.

St Ivo of Chartres (1040–1115), bishop of Chartres, France, from 1090 until his death and an important canonist, tells of whole convents with inmates who were nuns only in name. They had often been abandoned by their families and were really prostitutes. Every few years there would be a new purge of these centres by the righteous squads, usually sent out from Rome. A few trials, witch-hunts, floggings, excommunications and public burnings would dampen the fires of lust.

There was always that superstitious solo sin you could indulge in in the dark hours beneath the blankets, the act that Woody Allen would describe as 'sex with someone I love', requiring just the novice and his or her vivid imagination. Masturbation was said to be the hideous work of Satan. Onan's curse developed into a widespread fear. By the sixteenth and seventeenth centuries this was believed to be a sin by those who had never (as they would probably claim) laid hands on their own erogenous zones, namely doctors of theology and medicine. They said it led to nausea, indigestion, mental and general health illnesses, pimples, vomiting, epilepsy, blindness, cancer and insanity – with syphilis thrown in for good measure. And let us not forget the horror of hairs growing on the palms of one's hands.

By the time Queen Victoria was on the throne, you might hold one thing in a hairy hand but the other would hold a clutch of superstitions which promised just about every hellish curse in Beelzebub's Argos catalogue. Apart from the dissipated Onan, where else does the Bible condemn this self-pleasure? Could it be Matthew 5:27-30, which deals with 'adultery in the heart'?

27: You shall not commit adultery.

28: But I say to you that whoever looks at a woman to lust for her has already committed adultery with her in his heart.

29: If your right eye causes you to sin, pluck it out and cast it from you for it is more profitable for you that one of your members perish than for your whole body to be cast into hell.

30: And if your *right hand* causes you to sin, cut it off and cast it from you, for it is more profitable for you that one of your members perish than for your whole body to be cast into hell.

The usual heart-warming, cheery stuff. Could one of those perishing members be the clue? Or could it be that 'right hand'? What if you're a southpaw? And how does any man or woman, upon seeing someone they find at least physically attractive, commit adultery simply by surreptitiously thinking, Phwoar! Why were we given brains and minds at all – or indeed erogenous zones?

To find an explanation for this religiously driven paranoid ignorance, we need to understand the social, medical and cultural factors. Prior to the eighteenth century physicians believed that the human body was made up of just four fluids which had to be in balance: phlegm, blood, black bile and yellow bile. Vaginal fluid and semen were regarded by the good doctors as being related to the volume of our blood. It was their belief that a single ejaculation could cost you half a pint of blood. Polishing your rocket every day could be fatal. This superstition provided fertile ground for the moralists – let the repression commence.

The paragons of piety soon used their ethical creativity to devise all manner of bizarre methods and devices to prevent the young from fiddling with themselves. Young boys would be made to wear two or three pair of pants in bed and often a pair of heavy mittens. Penile devices of increasingly mechanical sophistication were devised to prevent Satan's snake from rising. Even as late as the 1930s in some parts of the western world, backwoods folk thought it a good idea to burn a girl's clitoris, and ritual female genital mutilation remains a prominent problem with some cultures. Even today, there are lads who still believe that ten minutes with Madame Palm will end with them having to learn to read braille.

Attitudes to male circumcision, another one of those inexplicable 'God told us to do it' peculiarities of the religions of the book, have changed, according to www.intactamerica.org. The circumcision rate in the USA is down from 81 per cent in 1981 to about 55 per cent today (and much lower in some regions). This means that nearly half of all baby boys leave hospital intact as more parents realise that circumcision is often medically unnecessary. The foreskin is a natural, functional part of the body. It's there for protection, pleasure and getting snagged on your zip.

The Catholic Church still regards masturbation as 'an intrinsically and gravely disordered practice' and, as for sex outside marriage, one worthy, doom-laden Jesuit comments:

> We could look at sexual pleasure outside of marriage as a root cause of the disintegration of once civilised nations who are literally committing sexual suicide. We could analyse the reasons behind this suicidal mania that our holy father identifies as the culture of death which pervades so much of modern society.

Suicide! The end of civilisation! How odd, then, that unmarried rumpy-pumpy has been in full swing without holy permission since long before the Bible. It's a wonder we ever had civilisation at all. The 'holy father' thinks it's a 'culture of death'? Yet I found the name of the American Jesuit priest who wrote the above words, listed as a 'servant of God', just too comically appropriate to resist. Under 'you can't make this stuff up', here it is: Father John A. Hardon, S. J. (1914–2000). This writer and theologian goes into more fire and brimstone on the subject in *Sexual Pleasure Outside of Marriage* at www.therealpresence.org. Due to the humour bypass most religious tub-thumpers seem to have had, poor Father John probably never came across the term 'hard-on' as his pen glided over the manuscript. Hopefully, his palms were not hairy.

In Islam, masturbation (for both men and women) is *haram* (forbidden by Allah), based on several *surahs* in the Qur'an, such as twenty-four, 30–31:

> Tell the believing men to lower their gaze (from looking at forbidden things) and protect their private parts (from illegal sexual acts, etc.). That is purer for them. Verily, Allah is all-aware of what they do. And tell the believing women to lower their gaze (from looking at forbidden things) and protect their private parts (from illegal sexual acts, etc.).

Each branch of Islam considers the practice to be a sin. However, it might be permissible if you're desperately trying to resist the even greater sin of fornication (*zina*), but if you succumb to this self-pleasure, you must then ask Allah for forgiveness.

The superstitious religious boundaries around this fraught subject remain impenetrable but our fearful forefathers might be surprised to learn that this sin is not only a big, wide world of fun but it can even save lives through preventing prostate cancer. Currently, there are 40,000 new cases and 10,000 deaths each year from this disease. From 1994–1998 an Australian team led by Professor Graham Giles, head of cancer epidemiology at the Cancer Council, Victoria, questioned more than 2000 men on their sexual habits as part of a prostate cancer study. It examined a thousand male prostate cancer sufferers below the age of seventy. These were compared to another thousand men of the same age who were fit and healthy. The survey reach a startling conclusion; the more men aged twenty to forty ejaculate, the less their chances of developing prostate cancer (www. theage.com.au/articles).

A US study, published as *The Social Organization of Sexuality: Sexual Practices in the United States* by Edward O. Laumann and John H. Gagnon (University of Chicago Library, 1994), conducted in 1994, revealed other equally startling results. This time it concerns both men and women. This survey shows that people who engage in solitary pleasures at least once a week would experience orgasms during almost every episode of sexual intercourse. Apparently, the more educated and intellectual people were, the more they masturbated. So the next time you call students 'a bunch of wankers', think on. But of course, this is all science, and as the Nobel Prize-winning physicist Richard Feynman (1918–1988) pointed out, 'Religion is a culture of faith; science is a culture of doubt.' No wonder Father Hardon got his cassock in a twist.

As we've strayed this far in the region of bad taste, you can find over five hundred eye-opening terms for the practice of masturbation at www.mantality.co.za/blog/wanking-euphemism, including spanking the monkey, bashing the bishop, teasing the trouser snake, jerkin' the gherkin, choking the chicken and stroking the sausage. And there's a selection of female versions such as petting the kitty, the two-finger tango and corralling the tadpole.

Sex superstitions around the world

German folklore warns against averting your eyes when toasting someone. The punishment, a bit like the broken-mirror curse, is seven years of bad sex. (Surely, some of it will be OK?)

Pagans have always been very relaxed about sex. In ancient times pagan belief linked sex with fertility and it became part of ritual. There had to be a good harvest for survival through the winters, so the believers gathered around the field for what can only be called the pagan circle-jerk. To appease the gods of fertility, they practised large-scale group masturbation.

Some Christian peoples in the Philippines regard Good Friday as one of the holiest days on the ecumenical calendar and believe that if you have sexual intercourse on that day then you're committing a profane act and you'll become 'stuck' to your partner for at least twenty-four hours.

In ancient Egypt masturbating was regarded as creative. You'd never get someone in a royal family doing it these days, but to protect against drought, pharaohs were required to masturbate into the Nile and the god Atum was said to have created the universe when he masturbated to ejaculation. Furthermore, the very flow of the Nile itself was said to be connected to the frequency of his ejaculations. It was one way of ensuring plenty of water for crops but a bit embarrassing, to say the least.

There's another old German superstition which was supposed to prevent parents from bringing up a rowdy, uncontrollable child. Only have sex on nice, sunny days. It was believed that if you conceived in dry weather, you'd have a boy. If you'd succumbed to the urge in a storm, you'd have a girl. There's a similar superstition in Korea which tells that a storm-conceived child will be a problem child. Best to keep an eye on the weather forecast then.

Some tribes in west Africa believe no one should ever have sex during the daylight hours. If you break this rule, you could have an albino baby. Anyone unfortunate enough to have twins faces bad luck, and triplets are a disaster.

Thailand is popular with sex tourists, but one thing the Thais will not have is a mirror in the bedroom. They believe that seeing yourself in the sack can cause an obsession with sex.

The ruling by many sports managers that their teams should avoid losing their edge by having sex before a match could have its roots in Africa. In Uganda, it was believed that intercourse before battle would result in defeat because warriors would be weakened on the battlefield.

Tibet's Lepcha people, 'beloved children of the Róng and of God', are among the indigenous peoples of Sikkim. They rule out any sex for three months in advance of going out to trap a bear. Similarly, the Cuna indigenous people of Panama who love a turtle hunt forbid any sex once one is under way. What this seems to indicate is that a bit of how's-your-father could mean an empty larder.

Dancing with the devil

Can there be superstition in classical music? We may have thought musical beliefs were restricted to the venerable blues and godless jazz of the deep south USA. Well, that isn't the case. The old tub-thumpers of the Middle Ages and the later Baroque Church would have told you so, as would composers into the twentieth century. Camille Saint-Saëns caused a few goosebumps with his *Danse Macabre*, and when I first heard Gustav Holst's 'Mars' from *The Planets Suite* as a child I was terrified. But those were later works, not subject to the ear trumpets of paranoid priests and bishops.

The word 'baroque' comes from the Portuguese word *barroco*, meaning 'misshapen pearl'. Can music be irreligiously 'misshapen'? When it comes to calling the tune, Beelzebub likes to present a few ill-tempered chords (bluesmen call them flattened fifths) for our listening pleasure wherever he can.

The explanation, if you are not a musician, can seem technical. To understand it you really need to hear it. I asked an old friend, a piano tuner and pianist who has on occasions played the mighty organ of Lincoln Cathedral, to spell out what's now called the devil's interval. So, for serious music scholars only:

A regular interval of a fourth covers six semi-tones (C-C#-D-D#-E-F). An augmented fourth adds the next semi-tone to go to F#. Playing the C and the F# together makes a disconcerting, dissonant sound that you hope will soon resolve. The augmented fourth, or tritone, is known as the devil's interval.

This is what medieval musicians, steeped in Christianity, believed as they laboured to develop the basics of sound. In his exhaustive work on musical theory, Austrian music researcher Johann Joseph Fux (1660–1741) called the tritone *'diabolus in musica'* ('the devil in music'). Other eighteenth-century theorists agreed with him over this feared tonal interval. With his 1725 dissertation *Gradus ad Parnassum* ('Steps to Parnassus'), Fux was regarded as a master of counterpoint who influenced many composers, including Haydn and the young Beethoven. Mozart had his own annotated copy. It is still used today for instruction in musical theory and composition. The baroque period of music began to fade away in 1750 and what we now regard as the 'classical' period began and would occupy much of the ensuing century.

Johann Sebastian Bach (1685–1750) knew all about the tonal problem. Some pitches on the early organs he played, when sounded together, gave the organ a 'howling' sound. Before 1770 organs were so difficult to tune that such noises were to become known as 'wolf tones'. Over time, tuning systems were gradually evened out and improved, hence the title of Bach's series of compositions begun in 1722, the *Well-Tempered Clavier*.

We have to think back to a time before electricity, radios, recording; music was not a continuous soundtrack to life as it is today. The great majority of the peasantry and working people might go through life without hearing the sound of an orchestra. Orchestras were for kings and emperors, and the great cathedrals had their choirs and organs. The hoi polloi made do with the occasional wooden whistle and a fiddle or, if they were lucky, a hurdy-gurdy, some pipes and a skilled lute player. Much of the grand, commissioned, formal music was liturgical and the province of the rich and titled.

Until the start of the classical period composers steered well clear of the devilish tritone. Having grown up in a period where witches were still being hunted and persecuted, the last thing a musician needed was some keen-eared bishop spotting a smidgeon of satanic dissonance in your latest piece of work. Then composers such as the impish Franz Liszt (1811–1886) deliberately used the tritone to conjure up Old Nick in various compositions, for example works such as the piano sonata which became known as the 'Dante Sonata'. Liszt's choice of Dante, a man possessed by hell's inferno, isn't surprising. The sonata's full title, 'Après une Lecture de Dante: Fantasia quasi Sonata' ('After a Reading of Dante'), must have raised a few eyebrows.

Soon everyone was using the devil's interlude as the old medieval fear evaporated, and it continues to be popular in music today. Leonard Bernstein (1918–1990) was proud to include the tritone throughout the classic musical *West Side Story*. Just listen to the opening phrases of the song 'Maria' or the show's opening number, *Cool Boy*. All through the score the tritone can be heard to great effect. It's even in the opening notes of the theme music for the TV series *The Simpsons*.

Of course, if we're talking Satan in popular music then the champions of rock'n'roll tritonic misbehaviour are heavy metal monsters Black Sabbath. The devil's there in guitar-man Tony Iommi's diabolic notes for the opening riffs of the song 'Black Sabbath'. Three hundred years ago the band would have been burned alive.

So does all this superstitious musical hogwash still worry many Christians today? Perhaps not, but the devil's interlude still features as a concern for some, and there are famous cases of religious fundamentalists finding satanic messages hidden in rock music – the band Judas Priest had a lot of explaining to do. You can hear what the god-fearing make of the tritone on YouTube and at www.cbyondmu-sic.org, where Dr Ken Read of the Worship University, in association with Cincinnati Christian University music, teaches 'the theory for worship' with a short lecture on the devil's interlude.

So can music actually scare people? Even without the devil's interlude, today, accompanied by the right cinematic image, an orchestra can give us a jolt. Think of the shower scene in *Psycho*, the threatening, underwater double-bass riffs from *Jaws* or the odd combination of *The Exorcist* with *Tubular Bells*. Beethoven and Mozart would have loved it all.

New ages, new cults

New Age religions represent a kind of cherry-picking of existing faiths and philosophies. Most of them began in the post-hippie era of the 1970s. They are generally referred to as NRMs (New Religious Movements), a comprehensive term used to identify religious, ethical, spiritual groups and communities of relatively modern origins.

They are usually regarded somewhat whimsically as slightly dotty, but it is worth considering that the cynical way many of us may regard these often cultish conglomerates is exactly the way the Romans would have regarded the arrival of Christianity and subsequently Catholic Rome's puzzlement at Muslims or Protestants. If we're prepared to believe in burning bushes, the parting of the Red Sea or Lot's wife turning into a pillar of salt, then arguably anyone can start a religion and base it on just about anything.

The author L. Ron Hubbard's science-fiction epics have led to the immensely rich and, to non-believers, unorthodox church of Scientology, supported by movie stars such as Tom Cruise and John Travolta. Yet most of the older religions are built on a foundation of what non-believers consider to be superstitions and myths, and one has to wonder how powerful Scientology might be five hundred years from now.

We can have a little fun here. In fact, if you can use astrology, Tarot cards, superstitions and fragments of ancient texts to create a following, there may be another religion already gestating in the shadows which is tailor-made for fans of *The X-Files*, vampires, horror, death metal music and pagan offshoots. It's also based on man-made superstitions, deities and legends. Let's call it the Cult of Cthulthu or 'The Old Ones'.

A grimoire is a textbook of magic. There are many ancient books outlining spells and magic and reporting on the methods of witches and wizards. One such book is known as the *Necronomicon*, a work containing an account of the 'old ones', the hideous alien creatures pre-dating humanity and charting their history and the means for summoning them. Lots of people think the book is real. But although some entrepreneurial publishers have cobbled a version of it together, the *Necronomicon*, purportedly penned by the 'Mad Arab' Abdul Alhazred, is purely the invention of horror writer H. P. Lovecraft (1890–1937) in his 1924 short story *The

Hound. Lovecraft was happy for other writers to big up his *Necronomicon*, saying it helped to create 'a background of evil verisimilitude'. So if you're thinking of becoming a disciple of the hideous Cthulthu, or the equally scary Yog-Sothoth, consider Lovecraft's take on it all in a letter he wrote to Willis Conover on 29 July 1936 (see www.hplovecraft.com/creation/necron/letters):

> Now about the 'terrible and forbidden books' – I am forced to say that most of them are purely imaginary. There never was any Abdul Alhazred or *Necronomicon*, for I invented these names myself. As for seriously written books on dark, occult, and supernatural themes, in all truth they don't amount to much. That is why it's more fun to invent mythical works like the *Necronomicon* and *Book of Eibon*.

What an incongruous image that conjures up – such a darkly morose, unpleasant yet admittedly brilliant writer of sheer horror having 'fun'!

Part four

The Comfort Zone

Knitting with fog

Factual information alone isn't sufficient to guide you through life's labyrinthine tests. You need and deserve regular deliveries of uncanny revelation. One of your inalienable rights as a human being should therefore be to receive a mysteriously useful omen every day of your life.

Rob Brezsny, American writer

Omen, n. A sign that something will happen if nothing happens.

Ambrose Bierce (1842–c. 1914), *The Devil's Dictionary* (1911)

The father of nuclear physics, Ernest Rutherford (1871–1937), once quipped, 'All science is either physics or stamp-collecting.' As it wouldn't be fair to physics to call the pursuit of superstition a 'science', it therefore seems even-handed to regard this book as an exotic stamp album.

People who collect bus timetables and locomotive numbers are known as 'gricers', 'festoons' and 'bashers'. They appear as a covert society bound by unfathomable codes of conduct, but I regularly encounter them on the platform of Chesterfield station with their Thermos flasks (usually tartan), notebooks and cameras. They seem to be everywhere – train-spotters.

As with locomotive numbers and philately, no matter how many superstitions you collect, there's always one more hidden heap of the damned things lurking in some forgotten siding or cultural bone-yard. Yet beyond the arcane fascination they inspire, superstitions could be regarded as surplus to requirements in a modern age. Attempting to pin some sagacity onto this subject reminds me of an old saying I'd heard in the Merchant Navy when talking on a night-watch with a chief mate about ghost ships. He said, 'Trying to make sense of these things is like trying to knit with fog.'

Having lived for thirty years in Mansfield, Nottinghamshire, close to the historical heart of Sherwood Forest, I once did some research for a now defunct magazine, Uri Geller's *Encounters*, on the subject of Robin Hood. Like another superstitious subject in this work, St Christopher, the jury remains out as to whether the great outlaw ever existed. If he was anything like the actors who portrayed him such as Errol Flynn, Kevin Costner or Russell Crowe, then that's just as well.

During my research I discovered the remains of King John's hunting lodge, stood by the Major Oak in Sherwood Forest, tracked down Will Scarlet's supposed grave beneath an ancient yew tree in a Blidworth churchyard and found a couple of churches where Friar Tuck was supposed to have preached. I was even amazed to find Little John's grave at Hathersage in Derbyshire and had a superstitious experience as a black cat walked across the tombstone.

Just a ten-minute drive from Mansfield is the historic village of Edwinstowe, named after King Edwin of Northumbria who was killed in the Battle of Hatfield (AD 633). In Edwinstowe's attractive and ancient St Mary's Church, legend has it that Robin Hood was married under the arch of the doorway to Marian. Perhaps Robin inspired a touch of rebellion in the village because in 1334 the vicar of Edwinstowe was convicted of trespassing in Sherwood Forest and killing the king's deer.

While my 'prince of thieves' research was far from conclusive, there was a bonus at this ancient church which has served me well ever since. In St Mary's church-yard I discovered the grave of Dr E. Cobham Brewer (1810–1897), author of the *Dictionary of Phrase and Fable*, a hefty and indispensable tome any writer needs on his or her bookshelves. I'd had my own 1324-page Wordsworth edition on my shelf for years, yet rarely took it down. Today I frequently dip into it at random and its contents never fail to impress. Between the initials 'A.B.C.' on page one which Brewer reveals is the 'Aerated Bread Company' and the final entry, 'Zulfa'gar Ali's sword (See sword),' you'll find all manner of fascinating information, much of it useful, some of it forlorn in today's world, yet all of it entertaining evidence of a buzzing, open and inquiring mind.

Brewer preceded this masterpiece with his *Guide to Science*, and the reason I'm mentioning him here is because his methodology in that earlier work has partly mirrored mine in preparing this. In his youth Brewer developed a habit of entering in an exercise book all questions on matters (particularly scientific) that he could not explain for himself. He'd leave a large space that he would fill in once he'd found an answer. Eventually, after some years, this became a substantial, thick manuscript. When Brewer asked a scientist what he should do with this completed work, the response he was given was, 'Burn it.' Thankfully, he didn't. The *Guide to Science* became the most widely known of Brewer's works. A French translation, requested by Emperor Napoleon III, was published, as well as others in several other European languages. In 1857 a Greek version was published at Smyrna.

The presence of Brewer's remains within a few miles of my desk serves as a reminder that the odd world of superstition, omens and fables sits on all our doorsteps, particularly in the UK.

This final section is called The Comfort Zone because it's a collection of other superstitions and practices that may not have provenances of such an objectionable nature as those with religious roots. Births, marriages and deaths occupy the atheist just as much as they do the faithful, and as for subjects animal, vegetable and mineral, these too are connected to us all as human beings.

Animal, vegetable and mineral

Every animal, everything we eat, even the rocks in the ground are encrusted with superstition, myth and fable. Space dictates that it is not possible to include an overview of everything in these categories, so the examples illustrated in the following selection are by necessity the barely visible tip of a very large iceberg of superstition. To even the score with the earlier sad story of the domestic cat (see p. 127), here the dog has his day. Birds and the trees they live in are also included. I propose that, after examining the grisly adventures of man's cruel pogroms against some animals, it is worthwhile to take a brief look at the way we human carnivores eat them. Tenuously connected to superstition, it also isn't a pretty story, but, then again, we're not altogether a pretty species ourselves.

MAN'S BEST FRIEND

> But the poor dog, in life the firmest friend,
> The first to welcome, foremost to defend,
> Whose honest heart is still his master's own,
> Who labours, fights, lives, breathes for him alone,
> Unhonoured falls, unnoticed all his worth,
> Denied in heaven the soul he held on earth –
> While man, vain insect! Hopes to be forgiven,
> And claims himself a sole exclusive heaven.
> Lord Byron (1788–1824) 'Epitaph to a Dog'

A dog will always be happier to see you than any person ever will, and our canine comrades can appear to be overshadowed by the domestic cat when it comes to exotic, colourful superstitions. As we've already seen, the cat has paid dearly for any supernatural association attached to it by injudicious humanity. Yet consider the old saying 'It's a dog's life' and the plight of this most faithful of animals comes into clear focus.

Their age-old supposed ability to see illness, spirits and ghosts is one of many superstitious beliefs about dogs, and they can be truly remarkable in the way they show deep concern when faced with the approaching death of their owners. When it comes to overt expressions of love for their masters, dogs lead the field, and yet they have suffered neglect and cruelty down the ages. At least cats have learned more than a few cautionary things about what they might expect from the two-legged brigade. Cats may seem affectionate, but they'll never fully trust us, and with good reason. A good dog, however, is always seeking affection, and he'll faithfully reward it tenfold.

Unlike a cat, a dog can be trained to perform all manner of useful services. He'll obey your commands, guide the blind, sniff out bombs and drugs, be happy when you are, and if necessary he'll fight to defend you. Together with his mates he'll trek for hundreds of miles pulling a sleigh across sub-zero, snowbound territory. Try putting half a dozen cats in a harness and you'd go absolutely nowhere.

Both cats and dogs are very intelligent but, unlike the inscrutable moggy, a dog's love, friendship and willingness to help are apparent as soon as you've formed a bond. Dogs are, like many animals, very insightful concerning the human condition. For example, the Lakota Sioux in South Dakota believed that if a member of the tribe had become sick they could lie with a dog and the sickness would transfer from the sick person into the dog. The ancient Greeks thought dogs could foresee evil, and there may be something in the superstition that if a dog does not like a man it is likely that the man has a bad character.

The Catholic Church recognises the early fourteenth-century St Roch (1295–1327, a.k.a. St Rocco), who lived in France, as the patron saint of dogs. He was known for miraculously curing plague victims either by touch or using the sign of the cross. It is said that he caught the plague while doing charitable work and went into the forest, expecting to die. But he was befriended by a dog that visited him every day and brought him bread. The dog licked his sores and eventually, unlike many plague victims, he was able to recover. This has echoes in the story told by Jesus of the poor man Lazarus whose sores were licked by street dogs.

The feast day of St Roch, 16 August, is celebrated in Bolivia as the birthday of all dogs. There's a church in Venice, San Rocco, dedicated to him, and he's also the patron saint of those who suffer from plague, cholera and skin rashes. Needless to say, St Roch earned his canonisation, but what about the poor dog that saved him?

In medieval times, very few people kept an animal as a pet. Life was hard enough without having to feed an animal which did nothing, so any domestic service or work, such as chasing vermin, shepherding or acting as a guard, made life a little easier. Yet these animals were not always regarded as innocent. Sometimes they took on what were believed to be human characteristics. In France in 1457 when a five-year-old boy named Jehan Martin was killed, a pig was arrested for the crime, subjected to a trial, found guilty and duly executed. Such odd – human – behaviour took centuries to die out. In the early nineteenth century during the Napoleonic wars, the people of Hartlepool hanged a shipwrecked monkey, believing him to be a French spy. 'Who hanged the monkey?' is a question to avoid in Hartlepool where, albeit affectionately, the locals have been known as 'monkey-hangers' ever since. So if hanging pigs and monkeys seems bizarre, could a greyhound become a localised saint? Of course. That's what's happened to St Roch's canine saviour.

Let's not forget another doggy saint, St Hubert (656–727), patron saint of mad dogs. He was revered in the Middle Ages and there were several military orders named in his honour. His father was Bertrand, duke of Aquitaine, making Hubert grandson of Charibert, the king of Toulouse. Hubert was passionately devoted to hunting so he serves also as a saint for hunters. Before becoming a priest, he was hunting a stag one Good Friday morning and had a vision of a crucifix between its antlers. Soon after this incident, his wife died so he gave up all his worldly possessions, titles and wealth and entered the priesthood. His passion and prowess as a hunter led to his patronage of furriers and trappers and he's the saint you now raise against bad behaviour and rabies, primarily in hunting dogs.

DIAMOND DOG

The legend of St Roch's wound-licking dog is a superstitious gem. According to the writings of a Dominican friar, Etienne de Bourbon (1180–1261), known as Stephen of Bourbon, we know what became of the remarkable animal who saved St Roch.

The friar had passed through the Dombes region of France, near Lyon, when he heard about Roch's compassionate dog. From Stephen's writings we know that the dog was a greyhound named Guinefort. After Roch died, Guinefort was taken in by a titled family that lived close to a village called Neuville. One day this noble young couple left their infant child in the house in the care of a nurse who failed to pay sufficient attention. A snake, described by Stephen as 'a large serpent', got into the house and made its way to the cradle, tipping it over, and the child landed on the floor. Guinefort was on the case immediately and entered into a bloody battle with the serpent that culminated in the snake being ripped to pieces. When the parents arrived home they found Guinefort wounded and covered in blood, but faithfully standing by the cradle as the family nurse stood screaming that the dog had 'eaten the child'. Thinking this to be the case, the master drew his sword and killed poor Guinefort. It was then that he discovered the baby was not dead, but out of sight near the upturned cradle. The faithful greyhound had simply been keeping guard until they returned. In a fit of remorse, the young lord had the dog's body placed in a well that was built up with stonework and surrounded by specially planted trees. It became, according to Stephen of Bourbon, a superstitious shrine.

A brave dog saving a baby was just the kind of mystical inspiration local peasants needed. Soon they were bringing their sick children to the site and making offers such as salt to the local woodland spirits and hanging baby clothes on the trees to subdue any evil influences. However, being a religious man, Stephen described their ritual attempts at healing – such as passing their babies nine times between the trunks of trees – as more devilish than Christian. Once women began leaving their children at the well, surrounded by flickering candles, sanctimonious Stephen had had enough. The body of Guinefort was removed, the trees chopped down and a local law passed to prevent this behaviour by the locals. The penalty for visiting the well to seek Guinefort's help was seizure of possessions. So this little avenue of superstition was finally blocked off. Or so it seemed. Despite criticism of the cult by Protestants, centuries later locals were still known to visit what had become known as St Guinefort's Wood. The dog may not have been canonised by the pope but he was a local saint and that was good enough.

Published in 1983 by Cambridge University Press, *The Holy Greyhound* by Jean-Claude Schmitt examines this story in forensic detail. A previous folklorist named A. Vayssière had written about the cult of Guinefort in 1879, as included in *Dialogues of Ancient History* (University of Franche-Comté, 1983). Schmitt was surprised that the veneration was still going in the early twentieth century. You'll not find it in the Catholic Church's saintly calendar, but St Guinefort's feast day is 22 August, not to be confused with St Gunifort on the same day, who was either British or Irish and martyred while on pilgrimage.

The story behind the holy greyhound is echoed in those of other faithful historical dogs such as Gelert, the thirteenth-century pooch who defended a baby from a wolf and is supposed to be buried in Wales in the village of Beddgelert.

Superstitions about canines

For thousands of years man and dog have shared a close bond. Many superstitions were derived from mythology and world religions. There are more than we might expect, yet, like the poor cat, dogs certainly have their own unfair burden of doomy, deathly folklore.

In Chinese astrology the dog is one of the twelve honoured animals. On what is considered to be the birthday of all dogs, the second day of the Chinese new year, the Chinese are expected to treat their dogs with loving care and acts of kindness. Yet one wonders if, when pungent oriental wind is broken during the feasting, the Chinese culprits do what the rest of the world does – blame the dog.

Good dog

Being followed home by a strange dog might indicate good luck.

It means good luck if dogs come to your house (especially dalmatians). A strange dog coming to the house means a new friendship.

If you're on your way to a business appointment, meeting a spotted or black and white dog is lucky.

It's good luck to encounter a greyhound with a white spot on its forehead.

Three white dogs seen together are considered lucky.

Treat the following two with caution: if you are sick, touch a piece of bread to your lips and then give it to your dog. You can detect how serious your condition is depending on whether the dog eats it or not. If you allow your new-born baby to be licked by a dog, the child will get better quickly when it's ill.

Bad dog

Black dogs are unlucky if they cross a traveller's path or follow someone and refuse to go away. Being followed by any strange dog – especially a black one – means bad luck.

A dog walking between a courting couple means an argument is imminent.

Howling dogs are said to have summoned death, heralding the taking of the spirits of the dead.

A dog howling at night is a sign of bad luck.

A dog howling for no reason is aware of invisible spirits.

In ancient Greece, dogs howling at a crossroads meant the goddess Hecate (goddess of magic, witchcraft, the night, moon, ghosts and necromancy) was near.

If a dog howls outside the house of someone who is ill, and particularly if the animal is driven away yet returns to howl again, this means death for the sick person.

A dog howling four times beneath a porch or entrance is a prediction of death.

If a dog howls three times, that means a death has occurred.

A dog eating grass suggests the dog needs a better diet – alternatively, it means it's going to rain. It's also a sign of rain if the dog lies on its back or crosses its front paws.

More death: howling at the moon or howling at night means someone, possibly a friend, is dead or dying.

Fishermen used not to take a dog to sea on a boat as they considered the animal unlucky, and even the word 'dog' would not be spoken on board.

Weird dog

When a dog is staring intently, at nothing, for no apparent reason, look between the dog's ears and you'll see a ghost.

A dog with seven toes can see ghosts (actually, this one's an invention by the creator of *The Simpsons*, Matt Groening).

If you scratch a dog before you go job hunting, you'll get a good result.

Beware the spectral black dog, the barguest, a phantom harbinger of death, particularly in Yorkshire and throughout the north of England. It's a legendary monstrous black dog with huge teeth and claws and can only mean bad news. It was the inspiration for Sir Arthur Conan Doyle's *The Hound of the Baskervilles*.

Traditionally, if you have a sick child you can take some of its hair and feed it to a dog between slices of bread and butter. The superstitious theory was that the illness would be transferred to the animal, enabling the child to be healed. Not recommended.

Odd dog

There are some odd sayings featuring dogs, such as, 'The dog in the manger,' a metaphor meaning someone who keeps something they don't want simply to prevent someone else getting it. This has its origins in Greek fable and appears as the 102nd saying of the apocryphal Gospel of Thomas. This is early Christian and non-canonical, and in which Jesus refers to oxen:

> Woe to the Pharisees, for they are like a dog sleeping in the manger of oxen,
> for neither does he eat nor does he let the oxen eat.

In the classical world, Cerberus was the three-faced guard dog of the underworld and dogs were closely associated with the goddess of magic and witchcraft, Hecate. Dogs were sacred to Artemis, the goddess of chastity, virginity, the hunt, the moon and the natural environment, and to Ares, the god of war.

A drink to settle a hangover is called, 'The hair of the dog that bit me' and comes from the old belief that the bite of a rabid dog could be cured by a potion containing some of the dog's hair. Science has yet to prove the efficacy of either of these analgesics.

Like many English sayings, we can attribute 'the dogs of war' to William Shakespeare. In *Julius Caesar*, act three, scene three, 'Cry "Havoc!" and let slip the dogs of war'.

The *Book of Tobit* is part of what is considered the apocrypha or deuterocanonical scripture. This was included in the Old Testament of Catholic bibles but not Protestant ones. In this, Tobias, son of Tobit, and the angel Raphael are faithfully accompanied by a dog on their journeys.

In ancient Egypt, dogs were associated with Anubis, the jackal-headed god of the underworld. The catacombs at Saqqara feature the buried remains of many dogs, animals that must have been quite revered by the pharaohs. They had a sacred role as an important symbol in religious iconography. The same situation existed in central Mexico, where the Aztecs appear to have attached much symbolism to the dog. Several ancient dog burial sites have been discovered.

Dogs appear everywhere in religion. For example, the Catholic Church reveres the man known as the 'hound of the hounds', St Dominic de Guzman (1170–1221).

Legend has it that his pregnant mother had a dream that a dog appeared from her womb with a flaming torch in its mouth. The order he would eventually establish, the Dominicans, was famous for its inquisitorial doggedness in forcing heretics to confess through its ever-inventive methods of torture, for, as the noble saint said, 'It is better to be the hammer than the anvil.' Although their official name was the Friars Preachers (*Ordus Praedicatorum* or 'order of preachers'), they became known by the Latin *Domini canes*, meaning the dogs or the hounds of the Lord. A black-and-white dog is sometimes used as their informal symbol.

According to superstition, a hound of the Lord could even be a werewolf. In 1692 an elderly German known as Thiess of Kaltenbrun openly proclaimed himself to be a 'hound of God' and a werewolf who acted as God's 'attack dog' when he ventured into hell three times a year with other werewolves to fight the devil and his witches. He was declared anti-Christian, got a good flogging and was exiled.

Among many Hindus, the common belief exists that caring for dogs paves the way to heaven. Hindus worship dogs in parts of Nepal and India, North Bengal and Sikkim during the Tihar festival, lasting five days every November. Hindus believe that dogs guard the doors of heaven and hell. The female dog of the gods, Sarama, is described as the mother of all dogs.

This is in stark contrast to the Islamic view of canines. There are several traditions concerning Muhammad's (pbuh) views about dogs. He said that dogs were only for hunting, herding and protecting the home, and anything more detracted from a Muslim's good deeds, although he did recommend kindness to animals. It is unlikely to find a Muslim family with a pet dog, as the majority of both Sunni and Shia Muslim jurists consider dogs to be ritually unclean because they are viewed as scavengers. Among some Islamic communities in Europe there have been active anti-dog campaigns, such as those led by a city councillor in the Hague, Hasan Küçük, and protests by Muslims in Lérida, Spain. The presence of canines was unwelcome in certain neighbourhoods and seen as a violation of religious freedom. Numerous cases of dog poisoning were reported in Lérida, although a connection has never been established.

In the UK, police sniffer dogs in sensitive areas such as a mosque are required to wear leather booties.

There are positive stories related about the prophet and his attitudes to this beleaguered animal. A much quoted *hadith* (collections of reports claiming to quote Muhammad, pbuh) is by Abu Huraira, from volume three, book forty, no. 551:

> While a man was walking he felt thirsty and went down a well and drank water from it. On coming out of it, he saw a dog panting and eating mud because of excessive thirst. The man said, 'This [dog] is suffering from the same problem as that of mine.' So he [went down the well] filled his shoe with water, caught hold of it with his teeth and climbed up and watered the dog. Allah thanked him for his [good] deed and forgave him. The people asked 'O Allah's apostle! Is there a reward for us in serving [the] animals?' He replied, 'Yes, there is a reward for serving any animate [living being].'
>
> Quoted at www.answering-christianity.com

In Judaism, keeping a pet, dogs included, is not prohibited under Jewish law. In fact, Jews are required to feed any animals they own before feeding themselves and, in advance of acquiring any animal, arrangements for feeding it should be made.

In other ancient cultures and religions the dog fares better. For example, in Mesopotamia there was a temple dedicated to the goddess Ninisia at Isin, the translation of which is the 'dog house'. It seems obvious that dogs were revered because when the area was excavated sculptures and drawings of dogs were found along with nearly forty ceremonial dog burials. In many other cultures in Asia and the Far East, the dog is respected, yet in some he'll end up on a plate. In Europe and the USA, life without dogs seems unimaginable. The cat and the dog go together to spice up our domesticity like pepper and salt. Long may it remain this way.

You are what you eat

We've seen how old traditions can have fairly cruel roots, as with cats, for example. Yet there is a practice – regarded as seriously illegal today, yet suspected to be still current in some parts of France – that must have at its forgotten source an almost satanic touch of covert cruelty. Let's examine the plight of a small bird – take out your handkerchief and prepare for a tragedy based upon a gourmet's greed, the plight of the ortolan.

In 1996, former French president François Mitterrand's last meal included this specially prepared bird. The ortolan bunting (*Emberiza hortulana*) is a bird in the bunting family, commonly known in Europe as the gardener bird. Despite the hunting of this bird being banned in 1999, its population decreased by 30 per cent before the law was tightened up in 2007. You may not find this 'delicacy' in a Parisian restaurant today, yet this golden goal remains for dedicated gourmets. If you're rich enough, you'll search it out. Even chef Anthony Bourdain describes the following recipe and the way it is devoured in his 2010 book *Medium Raw*. It's a small, cute and pretty bird. And apparently, if you leave your conscience at home, it tastes great.

The recipe for ortolan is as follows: capture the bird in the wild, poke it in the eyes to blind it, imprison it in a very small cage so it can't move, give it a forced diet of figs, millet and grapes until it swells up to four times its normal size. Then it will be put out of its misery by being drowned in armagnac (this part of the torture is important, as apparently the ingested armagnac enhances the flavour). The little bird can then be roasted for six to eight minutes before being plucked. Holding the bird's crispy head, the gourmand puts the bird feet first into their mouth and munches it whole, spitting out any bones and letting the severed head drop onto their plate.

As undoubtedly God will be watching, if you're going to wolf this little delicacy down you need some way of concealing your shame. This method is often attributed to the undisputed French saint of gastronomy, Jean Anthelme Brillat-Savarin (1755–1826). There is even a cheese named after him and he is regarded as the first epicure to recognise the causes of obesity – sugar and white flour. Some lax commentators on the sad plight of the ortolan refer to Brillat-Savarin as a priest.

He may have that status among epicures but he appears to have been a lawyer and politician and a famous gastronome, remembered for his holy utterance, 'Tell me what you eat and I will tell you what you are.' If you eat ortolan, there aren't enough expletives.

The traditional way to consume the bird is to cover your head and face with a large napkin or towel. The purpose of this is debated. Some claim it is to absorb the rich aroma and flavour of the armagnac-soaked corpse as it is chomped in one mouthful, while others have stated it hides the unsightly spitting out of bones. Perhaps you cover your head to hide the shame of this dish from God. The latter seems likely, and it was begun by a priest, a friend of Brillat-Savarin, rather than the man himself.

What, you may ask, does this nasty dish have to do with superstition? Apart from the strange tradition of hiding your sin from God, it connects to that historical evaporation of compassion that accompanies superstition and animals due to the interpretation of holy writ. To rejoice, laugh and celebrate as animals are tortured, sacrificed and hunted would seem to reveal that dark corner of the human psyche in which superstition is eagerly absorbed and stored.

Bird myths and superstitions

American playwright and director Robert Wilson (b. 1941) asked, 'If you see the sunset, does it have to mean something? If you hear the birds singing does it have to have a message?' The answer for many people is 'Yes.' This will not be an examination of every superstition about each and every bird – there's too many of them – but an inevitably small selection.

Steve Roud, in his *Penguin Guide to Superstitions of Britain and Ireland*, reminds us that as humans we should be careful never to let any birds get hold of our discarded hair as they might weave it into their nests and we'll get headaches. If a bird poops on us, as most of us know, that's good luck, but in addition, having birds' eggs in the house causes the opposite effect.

Birds put on some of the most fascinating and beautiful free shows nature has to offer. If they have a message for humanity, it is one of freedom. The world is theirs, all of it. They know no borders or boundaries. Consider the Arctic tern (*Sterna paradisaea*). In its long-distance migrations between the north and south poles in search of perpetual summer it makes the equivalent of three round trips to the moon, a return trip of around 44,000 miles each year. It flies between the breeding grounds in Greenland in the north and the Weddell Sea on the shores of Antarctica in the far south. In Iceland they call this bird the *kria*, a name that matches its banshee-like call. The terns appoint lookouts that fly high and sound a piercing alarm call on spotting incoming predators. Then they take turns (no pun intended) in lining up and dive-bombing the enemy.

Birds are amazing creatures. We know some of them are cute, like the sparrows, tits and buntings, and we know that, although the robin is pretty, it has some unpleasant behavioural traits. Robins puff out their red breast as a sign of masculinity and are aggressively territorial. Only one bird will occupy a small garden, attacking any other male robin that enters their space. Male robins are even known to attack their own reflections, imagining they are interlopers.

Yet the song of the birds is part of the soundtrack to human life. It greets us in the morning and it lulls us into a mood of reflection as the sun goes down on summer nights. Like all animals, these airborne adventurers display a wide range of conduct, some of it unbecoming, yet always engrossing. At one end of the scale we quietly admire the eccentric blackbird digging up worms, while at the other extreme we shudder at the sight of flesh-ripping vultures or become startled in the dark at the eerie cry of a barn owl.

Birds have been traditionally regarded as messengers between the world of spirit and our material world. Naturally, they fly on wings of superstition. A lot of these involve both good and bad luck. One of the most common superstitions, still accepted by some, is that a bird flying into your house signifies an impending message. If that bird flying into your house happens to be white, then you can expect a death.

Before street lighting and urban development, the night belonged to the devil and demonic spirits. A bird which flew and cried in the darkness of night would be regarded as a disturbing omen. The owl, being nocturnal, was widely associated with witches and magic. Seeing one flying around your dwelling in the dead of night portended a family death.

The wide staring eyes of the owl give them a wise appearance, and their ability to swivel their head around adds to their mystery. The feathery tufts on an owl's head made some people think of them as horned devils.

In ancient Greece the owl was regarded as a wise bird and was associated with the goddess of wisdom Athena, the deity of the city of Athens. The owl became the symbol of Athens. It appeared on coins as early as 520 BC. The coins were called *glaukes* – after *glaux*, the ancient Greek for owl. Athena was famed for her gift to the city, the olive tree, much appreciated for its culinary benefits, particularly oil, and for its wonderful wood. Images of Athena show her with an owl perched on her head. The species of owl associated with the goddess was the little owl. It also became known as the 'owl of Minerva'. Little owls were highly respected and lived protected, honourable lives in the Acropolis of Athens. The theme of wisdom and the owl even inspired the idea in philosophy that we only understand the implications and meanings of an era when it is coming to an end. The great German philosopher Georg Wilhelm Friedrich Hegel (1770–1831) wrote in 1820: 'The owl of Minerva spreads its wings only with the falling of the dusk.' Hardly surprising, then, that the following superstitions apply to this remarkable bird.

The death of a newborn child would be the result of an owl hooting or screeching at night. Even if the baby lived, it would have an unhappy life and might even become a witch. If the owl screeched during cold weather, this presaged a storm. If the noisy owl perched on your roof, this was another warning of death.

It was believed that owls were once the only creatures that could live with ghosts. Therefore if you found one nesting in a derelict house, it was obvious the place would be haunted.

Travellers on land or sea, should they reveal they had dreamed about an owl, would be warned that this signified they may be robbed or shipwrecked.

It used to be believed, incorrectly, that an owl could completely turn its head around in a continuous swivel. Superstitious country folk believed that if you walked all the way around a tree on which an owl was perched, its eyes would follow you, causing the poor bird to wring its own neck. In reality, an owl cannot turn its head around completely.

To counter all the owlish doom, in Afghanistan a legend stated that it was the owl that gave flint and iron to the human race and this gift allowed us to make fire. In exchange, humans presented owls with their feathers.

In Brittany, if you saw an owl on your way to the annual harvest this promised a good yield.

Australian aborigines believe owls are sacred because they are the spirits of women.

The Inuit people of Greenland rely on the owl for help and guidance, while the Indonesians listen to the owl's different calls very carefully because they regard the bird as very wise and the way it sounds determines whether or not they will travel that day.

Owls played a part in traditional medicine. Owl broth was thought to relieve the symptoms of whooping cough, while eating owl eggs was supposed to improve eyesight, prevent epileptic fits, and even sober you up after a heavy booze-up.

Dickiebird of doom: the raven

The poor old raven has always been regarded as a bird of ill-omen. See one flying around your chimney stack or perched on your gate? Well, there's guaranteed doom if you're superstitious.

It has been suggested that as ravens have a very acute sense of smell they can sniff out decay from far away.

Native Americans have traditionally referred to the raven as the 'messenger of death' and, if he decided to croak in the vicinity of your home, yet again, death was imminent for someone or other. There is evidence of this even in the collective noun for ravens. We may refer to a 'flock' of other birds but a flight of ravens is lumbered with 'a conspiracy' or 'an unkindness of ravens'. Yet they can still find supporters. The ravens at the Tower of London are popular attractions, mainly due to the old superstition that if they decide to leave then the monarchy will fall and England will face disaster. It seems unfair and risky to mess with fate, but the Tower's ravens don't leave because they've had their wings clipped. They have their own Ravenmaster, one of the red-uniformed Beefeaters. The birds are fed and supported by the UK government. For up to two months the Ravenmaster cares for the fledglings, and once they've grown up he'll see them installed close to the Wakefield Tower.

Today, the Tower ravens sleep in pairs in their cages because urban foxes in the vicinity of the Tower have been known to kill the birds. However, Britain almost lost its Tower ravens during WWII because they didn't cope well with the shock of Nazi bombs falling around them and many of the poor birds died. The tough survivors were a bird by the name of Grip and his partner Mabel. Grip was also the name given to Charles Dickens's pet raven, the bird featuring in his novel *Barnaby Rudge* some seventy or more years earlier. When Dickens toured the USA he met with Edgar Allan Poe and – although there's no proof – many believe it was the original Grip who inspired Poe's poem 'The Raven'. Dickens's original Grip was stuffed and mounted and bought at auction by an American Poe enthusiast and can still be seen today at the Free library in Philadelphia. When the first Grip died (apparently from eating paint), Dickens replaced him with an eagle and another raven that he also called Grip.

Our attitude towards ravens seems to be influenced purely by superstition, yet these quirky birds are talented, often acquiring a substantial vocabulary and, despite their dominant beak and black plumage, they can be very entertaining and likeable. Although the sight of ravens flying towards one another has been a warning of war, they're not always harbingers of death. In Scotland, deer hunters have traditionally welcomed hearing a raven's croak when the hunt sets out, as it signifies success, and you can expect warm sunny weather if you see them flying towards a cloudy sun.

Robins and other feathered friends

A robin red-breast in a cage
Puts all heaven in a rage.

William Blake (1757–1827), 'Auguries of Innocence' (1863)

Star of a billion Christmas cards, the cheery, red-breasted robin is also a bird lumbered with superstition. It used to be said that anyone stupid enough to cage a robin or indeed kill one would find whichever hand used in the act would permanently shake. In Ireland, they believed the hand would develop an ugly lump. Killing robins is one of the unluckiest of all actions, and, should you break a robin's eggs, the superstition dictates something precious to you will soon be broken.

His red breast is said to come from the blood of the saviour that splashed onto his feathers when the robin attempted to pull thorns from the head of Jesus at the crucifixion. Another religious myth suggests that the kindly robin got his red plumage after taking much-needed water to thirsty sinners in the fires of hell.

Single women should be aware that if the robin is the first bird you spot on Valentine's Day then you'll be marrying a sailor. As with most bird omens, death looms large – a robin pecking at your window or, worse still, flying into your home means an imminent family death. But there's good luck to be had too, particularly when you see the first robin of the year and you make a wish. If the little bird is seen singing in open spaces, this promises good weather, but if he's singing whilst sheltering in a tree then rain is on the way.

SPARROWS

In contrast to the robin's noble reputation with the crucifixion and flights into hell, the humble sparrow gets a bad press. He was supposed to have also attended the crucifixion with less noble motives, namely to encourage the Roman guards to torture Jesus because his repetitive call sounded like, 'He's alive! He's alive!' The fact that he doesn't run around like most birds but hops along is said to be his punishment, his little legs bound together by invisible cords as holy retribution for his lack of mercy. Sparrows are also said to carry the souls of the dead, quite a responsibility for such a small bird.

Yet it's bad luck to kill a sparrow or put one in a cage. If he's chirping rapidly and continuously that's a sign of rain.

BLACKBIRDS

The sky's sweetest singers, blackbirds are known to stake out their territory, and if that happens to be your garden or somewhere close to your house, it's a sign of good luck throughout the coming year.

In some cultures blackbirds are messengers of people who have died. It's also good luck to see two male blackbirds perched next to each other.

Whatever myths are attached to them, these birds are fascinating to watch, oddly entertaining and, as Paul McCartney proved, their song is as romantic as birdsong gets.

PIGEONS

Superstitions, especially about birds, can often be seen as the empty, archaic myths that they are derived from the evidence around us. Take the pigeon, for example. I feed our garden birds every day and the greediest scavenger of them all is the pigeon. Superstition tells that a group of pigeons gathered together on your roof indicates that a storm is coming. If that's the case, I'd be living in a permanent hurricane as these feathered eating-machines seem to spend most of their day on our roof. Another omen of death in the family is a lone white pigeon perched on your chimney. Seeing as our favourite pigeon, Whitey, spends every day up on our chimney, it's a wonder the whole street isn't dead by now.

When my time comes, I might test this one; in some parts of England an old belief suggested a dying person could prolong their life by having a pillow stuffed with pigeon feathers for a head-rest. Of course, first you need enough feathers, and getting them would be bad luck for the pigeons.

PELICANS

Although we don't see many in Britain, pelicans are another bird weighed down with religious myth and legend. They symbolise the love of parents for children because of their apparent acts of self-sacrifice. It was imagined that the food a pelican stored in its pouch to feed its chicks was actually flesh and blood from the pelican's own chest. Religion, as so often in mythology, plays a part in the story of the pelican in that the medieval idea of the bird feeding its offspring with its own blood was a powerful allegory of Christ's suffering, especially from the wound that he received when the lance pierced his side.

Thomas Aquinas (1225–1274) mentioned pelicans in his 'Adoro te Devote'. This hymn was translated by Gerard Manley Hopkins (1844–1889):

> Deign, O Jesus, pelican of heaven,
> Me, a sinner, in thy blood to lave,
> To a single drop of which is given
> All the world from all its sin to save.

Thanks in part to David Attenborough's work in educating us about the natural world, another superstition about pelicans can be utterly disproved. In the Middle Ages it was thought that pelicans only ate just enough food to keep themselves alive, and this 'fact' was used as an inspiration for religious fasting. If you've ever seen a pelican enjoying his dinner, you'll know that's way off the mark.

SATAN'S BLACK-AND-WHITE HELPER

> One for sorrow, two for joy,
> Three for a girl, four for a boy,
> Five for silver, six for gold,
> Seven for a secret never to be told.
> (trad.)

Magpies, like the unfortunate ravens, are also tainted with an association with Lucifer. Everyone knows the saying 'one for sorrow, two for joy' but, historically, the magpies used to be regarded as the devil in disguise. The Scots continue the verse with 'Eight for heaven, nine for hell, and ten for the Devil's own self.'

There was a myth that when Jesus died on the Cross all the birds cried in sorrow, except the magpie, and the magpie's black-and-white plumage indicated that these disrespectful birds refused to wear full mourning at the crucifixion.

There is also the often repeated biblical yarn in Genesis that the magpies refused to roost in Noah's Ark and sat out the flood on the roof, chatting about the foul weather. Trying to nail this down in the Bible is difficult because of different versions of the book and the fact that the ravens and crows also get a blasting from Noah, so you need to read between the biblical lines. For these irreligious transgressions the magpie was never forgiven.

Magpies are great fans of garbage and shiny human rubbish, and they are also great imitators. They can duplicate the sounds of songbirds, and some in captivity have been known to copy human speech and develop vocabularies similar to those of parrots. On rare occasions you might hear a bird sing or a cat meow yet look around to realise it is only a magpie in a nearby tree. The collective noun for a group of magpies also reveals the way the bird is darkly viewed; a group of magpies is known as a 'tiding'.

A lone magpie loitering in the vicinity of your home meant that the devil was afoot and stirring up trouble. In Somerset, to avoid any bother from Beelzebub it helped if you carried an onion around with you. Elsewhere, to let the devil know that you recognised him, you would say 'Good morning, Mr Magpie, how is your wife today?' and hopefully, he'd desist from mischief. Or you could try spitting three times over your right shoulder accompanied by the words 'Devil, devil I defy thee!' while crossing your fingers and doffing your hat.

In Scotland, it was thought that magpies were evil enough to conceal a drop of Satan's blood under their tongue.

The Chinese regard the magpie as one of the most popular of birds, a messenger of good news and fortune. Its name in Chinese means 'bird of joy'. The magpie is the Korean national bird and is a bringer of good luck.

DOVES

Doves are beautiful birds and always signify peace. One medieval superstition stated that on hearing the first dove of spring, you should get a lock of cat's hair, bury it and dance on your heels around it three times. If you didn't do this (here it comes again), there would be a death in your family.

The Romans regarded the dove as a messenger of Venus, of the goddess of love.

In India, killing a dove is very unlucky because the bird is said the contain the soul of a lover.

Back in the Bible, again, apparently Noah sent two birds off from the ark to find dry land. One was a dove, and the other a kingfisher. The latter flew so high in the sky that its orange plumage was a result of the sun, and its vivid blue reflected the sky. As doves are said to mate for life and remain devoted to each other, they have become associated with lovers.

Doves are also steeped in religious symbolism. A dove is the one bird Satan can't turn himself into. The dove, being the Christian symbol for the holy spirit, cannot be affected by the devil's curses. Little wonder that these lovely birds are released at weddings and have become symbols of something increasingly elusive – international peace.

Despite these lovey-dovey associations, there's the usual doom and gloom in superstitions about the bird. For example, if there's someone sick in a house and a dove flies around the building or pecks at the sick-room window, you may as well stay in bed because you're not getting up again.

Coal miners were often wary of seeing a dove near the pit as it was thought to suggest danger below ground.

Peacocks

As with the pelican, we don't see too many peacocks around in Britain.

As well as promising bad luck should you bring them into the house, peacock feathers are an anathema in the theatrical world. We're back to the ancient evil eye curse again, because the oval eye-shape on the bird's feathers promises misfortune. Peacock feathers on the stage in any theatre are a bad omen, whether part of the scenery, prop or costume. Technical failures and general chaos can result in any production.

A favoured decoration in the east, peacock feathers were once linked to the Mongol hordes who terrified Europe and by 1242 had got as far as Hungary. It was only the death of Ögedei Khan (successor of Genghis and possibly no theatre-goer, given his successes) that halted the advance into Austria and the rest of Europe.

Vegetable

Vegetables . . . superstitions . . . surely not? The term 'vegetable' is used loosely here as a heading, and, although I'm including trees in this category, I fully realise that there's a horticultural gap between a bunch of carrots and an ancient oak.

However, the humble carrot has its place in folklore and more recent history. It's always pleasant to hear a child answer the question, 'What will you leave for Santa's reindeers?' As well as the obligatory mince pie and milk, the choices include carrots. In the past, carrots were used in the preparation of aphrodisiacs and they do certainly have some medicinal qualities. For example, they are said to contain certain elements which relieve bronchial constriction, helping some asthma sufferers.

Yet the most common superstition about the pointy orange wonder is that it improves eyesight and allows us to see in the dark. The argument used to go, 'You never see a rabbit wearing glasses'. This old chestnut (and more on chestnuts later) has its root in WWII. Propaganda stories about RAF pilots being fed a special diet of carrots were believed by the Luftwaffe. What the Germans didn't realise was that this was all a ruse to hide the development of radar.

As well as the carrot, who would imagine that the broad bean had such a dark reputation? Their shape has been thought in the past to represent a receptacle to hold dead souls. Farm workers believed that when broad bean plants were in flower all manner of accidents might happen. At New Year's Eve, beans were traditionally thrown around the house accompanied by the proclamation, 'With these beans I redeem me and mine.' Kidney beans had their special lore, too. They had to be specifically planted on 3 May because sowing them on any other day was only asking for bad luck.

Planting days are also important for the potato. Any day will do except Good Friday when they'll refuse to grow. There is also a peculiar and persisting superstition about the humble spud curing rheumatism when you carried a dried-out, blackened, new potato in your trouser pocket. A cheap palliative, no prescription necessary.

We don't associate parsley too often today with superstitions, but in England's past it was the centre of some strange beliefs. One was that a girl with an unwanted pregnancy could remove the 'problem' by eating enough. This tasty garnish is also a reminder of the gentle, traditional old folk song, 'Scarborough Fair' which mentions four herbs: thyme, sage, parsley and rosemary. In the past these herbs were said by some to be closely associated with death, but if they were all combined they could be a charm against the evil eye. Sir Walter Scott suggested that young women en route to Scarborough Fair carried these herbs for protection.

When Paul Simon learned 'Scarborough Fair' from English folk hero Martin Carthy in 1965, before Simon and Garfunkel released it as the hit 'Scarborough Fair/Canticle', one has to wonder how much of the song's significance was understood by the two American musical magpies. There was a real agricultural medieval Scarborough fair which had its roots in the thirteenth century. It lasted for forty-five days, was packed with various forms of entertainment and food stalls, and all manner of traders, craft workers and merchants flocked to the event from across Europe and from as far away as Turkey. The words 'parsley, sage, rosemary and thyme' weren't included in the ancient song simply because they flowed nicely in the lyric.

Parsley (*Petroselinum crispum*) was an aid to digestion, and eating it was regarded as a way to improve your health. Indeed, anyone following the recent, medically researched SIRT diet, will find themselves daily consuming a great deal of the stuff. In the Middle Ages, the herbalist recommended it for stomach ailments as a cure for bitterness, but it had another, important spiritual meaning in emotional terms; parsley had the power to reduce sourness between lovers.

We may think of sage (*Salvia officinalis*) today as a stuffing component at Christmas, but it was even more important in northern Europe both as a medicine and as a spiritual source of wisdom and strength. It had recognised antiseptic constituents. Herbalists were the GPs of their time and knew that sage could help in healing wounds, be effective against animal bites and even relieve a chesty cough.

Sweetly fragrant rosemary (*Rosmarinius officinalis*), like sage and parsley, is still part of any good chef's armoury, but in addition it has its own romantic superstitions. It was used by medieval brides as part of their bouquet because it was a symbol of faithfulness and love; the fragrance would always remind the couple of that special day, and in some churches it was scattered along the aisle at weddings. In the old song, the herb is mentioned perhaps to remind lovers of the importance of fidelity.

The fourth plant in this historic quartet, thyme (*Thymus vulgaris*), is also part of our kitchen life, but it too has antiseptic qualities and was very useful in healing wounds. In ancient Greece thyme was regarded almost as the Prozac of its day, as the Greek physicians believed it could dispel despondency. However, beyond being a 'happy plant' it also had a spiritual function in inspiring courage, and it was popular in the courtly age of battling knights for their ladies to weave thyme into the embroidered champion's shirt or cloak. So in 'Scarborough Fair' we have a plea for just about every bit of good behaviour possible; love, fidelity, courage, wisdom and strength. That's a lot to ask from four humble herbs and something to think about when we fire up the stove for that next big dinner.

Onions have a fabled history. Hanging one up in your home was at one time thought to prevent disease. A stranger, even more odorous, superstition for wannabe lovers was to sleep with an onion under their pillow so that the possible romantic partner might appear in a dream. No doubt he'd have a keen sense of smell. Finding a four-leafed clover is supposed to bring luck, and if you come across one of these rare bits of wild greenery this is also an indicator of romance. The same superstitions apply to Ireland's shamrock. There's an old rhyme that spells out clover's potential:

> One leaf for fame, one leaf for wealth,
> One for a faithful lover,
> One leaf to bring your health
> Are all in the four-leaf clover.

Peas in the pod are the centre of a couple of ancient benefits, too. If you open a pod and find nine peas, you can make a wish while throwing one of the peas over your shoulder. If you're looking for good fortune, then you need to find just one lone pea.

In the UK we have the horse chestnut, but in the eastern and southern USA it's known as the buckeye. Chestnuts have been thought of as a regular preventative of rheumatism, arthritis and headaches. This belief was also common in northern Europe. Some optimists in Missouri believe the buckeye enhances your sexual power. As in Europe, African-Americans like to follow the superstition of keeping a chestnut in the pocket in the hope that its luck potential might double their money. It's a popular talisman for gamblers. The Japanese believed that dried chestnuts were emblems of success, victory and conquest.

Keep calm and carry garlic

It is only perhaps during the past half-century in British culture that garlic (*Allium sativum*) has achieved senior herb status in our kitchens. The fact that it had been a popular culinary and medicinal staple elsewhere for over 7000 years didn't stop our parents referring to anyone south of Dover as 'foreigners smelling of garlic'.

I was luckier than other teenagers in the late 1950s and early 1960s because I spent the years between leaving school and getting married travelling the world in the Merchant Navy. Our on-board cooks only used garlic for the more sophisticated passengers' menu, but when we went ashore in the Mediterranean ports and ordered food with our beer, we soon got used to garlic and olives.

Back home in England, along came Chinese, Indian and Italian restaurants and that rich odour took on a new and exotic dimension. Even so, when an Italian café, the 'Gondola', in Hull opened in 1963, specialising in the new culinary delight of pizza, I recall people quietly complaining in that 'mustn't grumble' English way about the 'pong' of garlic, and many an otherwise empty plate went back to the kitchen with all the discarded black olives picked from the pizza. The garlic thing left me wondering if the place was frequented by vampires. Prior to this new dawn of cuisine what we knew about garlic was laid out in Bram Stoker's *Dracula*, in which he describes Van Helsing's routine to protect Lucy, one of the Count's victims:

> The professor's actions were certainly odd and not to be found in any pharmacopeia that I ever heard of. First he fastened up the windows and latched them securely. Next, taking a handful of the flowers, he rubbed them all over the sashes, as though to ensure that every whiff of air that might get in would be laden with the garlic smell. Then with the wisp he rubbed all over the jamb of the door, above, below, and at each side and round the fireplace in the same way.

Yet if you believe in such superstitions (surprisingly many people do) then you'll have your own thoughts about protecting yourself. At www.vampirewebsite.net real vampires are the order of the day. The online vampires' argument used to prove their existence is:

The 'headache paradox': it is scientifically impossible to have a headache, seeing that there are no pain receptors in the brain. Yet we continue to search for answers to what causes a headache because we all know that headaches do exist.

Therefore vampires exist, according to the internet. Garlic has been repelling vampires long before Bram Stoker (1847–1912) published his classic horror tale in 1897. I've always had my doubts about waving the crucifix about when one of the undead turns up. What if he's a Jewish vampire or even a Muslim? In any case, as vampires are supposed to go back well into pagan times, the sign of the cross would seem to be simply a fictional weapon. But garlic; why should it ward off vampires specifically?

The age-old vampire myth seems to be connected to the scourge of disease, in particular rabies and the plague. British TV star and stand-up Paul O'Grady (a.k.a. Lily Savage) had this to say about garlic, 'I make a wonderful cure-all called "four thieves", just like my mum did. This is cider vinegar, thirty-six cloves of garlic and four herbs, representing four looters of plague victims' homes in 1665 who had their sentences reduced from burning at the stake to hanging for explaining the recipe that kept them from catching the plague.'

There are a few old wives' remedies for someone who has been bitten by a rabid dog, including a compress of lavender applied to the wound, and two ground-up teaspoons of cumin seeds and twenty black peppercorns added to water and applied to the dog bite. Those who caught rabies were said to be fixated on the actual odour of garlic. The plant itself has antibiotic properties which might treat the after-effects of a rabid dog bite. A few cloves of garlic three times daily will possibly assist in wound healing. That said, if you're bitten by a rabid dog, for heaven's sake call the emergency services. We don't all live in Transylvania.

In folklore, garlic is known as a natural repellent of mosquitoes. Mosquitoes are genuine little vampires in their own right and love sucking blood, as do fleas. The classic post-vampire attack symptoms – anaemia, exhaustion and fever – are well known to the *Twilight* and *Dracula* fraternity. If garlic put the buzzy, airborne bloodsucker off, the theory ran, it had to work when the vein-draining, bat version was around.

Garlic's mysterious power has been used for all manner of reasons – as a magical amulet, a medicinal cure-all and, when it comes to cuisine, it remains at the centre of any great feast.

There is one eastern meal that includes garlic as medicine and encompasses myth and superstition. A *haft-seen* table setting in Tehran, Iran, makes the UK's pancake day seem like a stale motorway sandwich. This meal is a broad and meticulous display of symbolism – a table arrangement of seven symbolic items traditionally displayed at Nowruz, the Persian new year. The *haft-seen* table consists of the following items that all start with the letter *sīn* in the Persian alphabet.

1. *Sabzeh*: wheat, barley, mung bean or lentil sprouts growing in a dish and symbolising rebirth.
2. *Samanu*: sweet pudding made from wheat germ to symbolise affluence.
3. *Senjed*: dried oleaster (wild olive fruit) that symbolises love.
4. *Seer*: garlic for medicine and health.
5. *Seeb*: apple for beauty.
6. *Somāq*: sumac fruit that symbolises sunrise.
7. *Serkeh*: vinegar – symbolising old age and patience.

There will be clay figures on view, whitewashed representations of domestic animals such as cows, donkeys, sheep, camel, nightingales and peacocks, and household objects such as bowls or a three-legged stool. These are said to bear witness to the triumphant works of creation. Other items include a mirror, a low brazier full of fire, sprays of cypress or pine, pomegranates, sprouts from seven different kinds of seeds, a goldfish in a bowl (this represents life and the end of the astral year), a lamp and some painted eggs.

A similar tradition exists in Afghanistan and central Asian countries such as Tajikistan and Uzbekistan.

However, in Islam, apparently the prophet himself disliked eating garlic and it is frowned upon to eat it before attending the mosque for prayers as the smell could put off other Muslims while praying.

Jainism is an ancient religion from India that teaches that the way to liberation and bliss is to live a life of harmlessness and renunciation. The aim of Jain life is to achieve liberation of the soul, but they tend to avoid onions and garlic.

In some branches of Hinduism it is believed that garlic enhances your desire while stimulating and warming the body. Yet some devout Hindus as a rule will avoid using onions or garlic in cooking whereas the less devout will only stick to the rule during religious events.

Many Buddhists regard garlic – along with other pungent spices such as chilli – as stimulants to sexual and aggressive behaviour that may affect meditation practice. Nuns and monks in Mahayana Buddhism avoid garlic and chilli as they are regarded as 'earthly pleasures'.

Back to vampires and werewolves. In eastern Europe, garlic could be hung in windows, worn around your neck or, as Stoker observed, rubbed on chimneys and keyholes to keep the evil spirits at bay.

There is a French tradition of roasting garlic bulbs on midsummer eve, again to protect against evil and create good fortune, and in some religious ceremonies in the Far East there has even been a belief that garlic had the power to bring back and save lost souls.

So the next time we tuck into a lamb biryani or a nice slice of pizza, it's good to know that we're connecting with something truly mystical, as well as making the existence of werewolves and vampires just that little bit more smelly and difficult.

Knots and branches: the wonder of trees

Poems are made by fools like me,
But only God can make a tree.

Joyce Kilmer (1886–1918), 'Trees' (1913)

The American poet Alfred Joyce Kilmer, known to us as Joyce Kilmer, will always be remembered for the poem 'Trees' (1913), the opening lines of which, 'I think that I shall never see/A poem lovely as a tree,' almost everyone knows.

Kilmer's poem became popular as a song in 1922, arranged by American pianist and composer Oscar Rasbach, who also set works by Tennyson, Rossetti and John Masefield to music. Many of us older folk can still sing it today. Kilmer died at the age of thirty-one from a sniper's bullet on the battlefield near Muercy Farm, beside the Ourcq river near the village of Seringes-et-Nesles, France, on 30 July 1918. When I stand in awe of trees I often think of him.

If we ignore fables and discard the supernatural, their longevity and ecology alone make trees the most overlooked source of amazement, usually standing as silent witnesses within a few yards of our homes. I live in the heart of Mansfield in Nottinghamshire and less than two minutes from my house in Westgate an oak tree grows. Beneath is a steel plaque that proclaims, 'This tree marks the location of the ancient heart of Sherwood Forest'. Great ships were built of wood, and even early aeroplanes. Trees make our doors, floors, roofs, windows, the chairs we sit on, the tables we dine at. We burn them when we're cold, we cook with their charcoal on our barbecues. A tree is a friend which offers shelter in its shade, a home for wildlife, and forests enrich the planet's atmosphere. No wonder trees are rich in magical tradition.

Tree myths and superstitions are legion. As Christianity spread across Europe, what were once pagan superstitions and fables were slowly converted into Bible stories. Every species has its share, and these vary in every country and sometimes from forest to forest.

The elegant poplar (*populus*), also known as the aspen or cottonwood, has a nice portfolio of yarns. If you were ill you could attach a lock of your hair to the tree and chant magic words to be cured. Leonardo da Vinci painted the *Mona Lisa* on a poplar wood panel. It's also good wood for making musical instruments such as violins and lutes. The poplar sometimes gives the impression in a light wind of quivering. Early Christians believed that this was the tree whose wood the Romans used for the crucifixion of Christ, so this shivering is the tree supposedly remembering the tragedy.

Or was the elder tree the guilty party that made the Cross? Other Christians think so, and many believe that Judas Iscariot, after his betrayal of Jesus at the last supper, hanged himself from an elder tree. This myth gave rise to a mean little slice of anti-Semitism based around a fungus, *Auricularia auricula-judae*, that grows on living or dead elder wood. In 1880, a mycologist named Joseph Schroter (1837– 1894) started calling this 'Judas's ear'. It soon got shortened to 'Jew's ear'. A less offensive term is 'jelly ear'. This brown fungus has a distinctly ear-like appearance, is quite a delicacy – particularly in Chinese cuisine – and was said by the imaginative faithful to be the last bit of Judas, hanging on as a grim reminder. Another species of tree is actually called the Judas tree, a common name for the flowering *Cercis siliquastrum*. Is this Judas's real tree? That's the beauty of myth and fable – there's so much choice. In the Bible, Matthew 27:3–8 tells us specifically how Judas died – by hanging. Then again, Acts 1:16–19 merely tells us that he fell headlong and his bowels gushed out. Maybe he fell off the tree.

In Ireland, where the elder is also known as the 'bore tree', it was unlucky for just about anything, and particularly bad luck to drive an animal or hit one with a stick of its wood. The same superstition applies to a willow stick.

Elder trees were favoured as a gathering place for witches, and it was deemed dangerous to approach them in the hours of darkness.

Despite the Bible's regular reference to forestry, many Christians were suspicious of the persistence of tree worship. After all, Adam and Eve didn't do too well with the Garden of Eden's tree of knowledge and many regarded tree worship as a form of idolatry.

In Islam trees also have problems. For example, some Muslims living in northern Europe and the UK have sought advice from their religious leaders asking if it is OK to have a Christmas tree with lights. They saw the modern Christmas as a secular, commercial event. The responses were negative, as the tree was regarded as *haram* and deemed to be the practice of the *Kafir*, a derogatory term for those not of Islamic faith.

The good old willow tree, beneath whose weeping shade we can relax, brought good luck if you presented friends or relatives with some of its branches in the month of May, although for some reason the gift had to be given in the morning. There was an opposing tradition with the willow that brought bad luck if it was used for firewood.

In the days of the great plagues, the juniper tree came into its own as a possible barrier to the killer disease. As the plague raged across Europe, people would burn juniper wood because it was believed that the smoke from the fire was the very thing which the devils causing the plague would retreat from. Sadly, it seems not to have worked. There were also superstitions concerning dreams that featured juniper berries. One suggested their appearance in a dream warned of bad luck. Another interpretation was that the berries signified the birth of a male child.

The oak, ash and thorn were all sacred trees to the druids. The oak was the most sacred of all, and in ancient times there were massive forests of oak stretching across Europe for thousands of miles. The druids were known for their legendary 'sacred groves' of worshipped trees.

The oak is extensively featured in Sir James George Frazer's magisterial study of magic and religion, *The Golden Bough*. The sturdy, generous oak was used for everything – it was not without reason that it became regarded by the European druids as the 'tree of life'. The name 'oak' comes from the Anglo-Saxon, 'ac'. In Irish this is 'daur', while the Welsh used the words 'derw' and 'dar'. There was also a word with an Indo-European root, 'wid', which meant to have knowledge or to know. It may be a contentious suggestion, but combining 'derw' and 'wid' it seems possible that the word we now know as 'druid' referred to those people who had a special knowledge of the oak tree. Not everyone will agree, but there's a further word from Sanskrit, 'duir'. This was another reference to oak, and over time it was transformed into the word 'door'. So perhaps the druids regarded themselves as guardians at some arcane door of knowledge.

As symbols of military power and conquest, crowns of oak leaves were worn by victorious Roman military leaders on parades, and oak leaves continue to this present day to be emblems on modern military uniforms, particularly in Germany.

As the oak was the most magical tree in European pagan mythology it was natural for them to be replete with superstition. For example, they were regarded as almost human and said to wail and cry if they ever fell or had branches removed. If you had toothache you could hammer a nail into the trunk. If you wanted to stop aging, you carried an acorn in your pocket. When lightning struck the oak it offered protection, and it was believed that a lightning bolt hitting an oak created the sacred mistletoe which often grew on the tree.

Generally regarded as a symbol of male virility and power, the oak was associated with the powerful pagan male gods of storms and lightning, Zeus and Thor, and, long before knocking on wood, it was common to stroke the tree gently and request its spirit to heal your illness or bless you.

Oak trees live long and prosper in legend and mythology. Sherwood Forest is a 450-acre country park in which the much-loved veteran Major Oak still stands. It is said to be between eight hundred and a thousand years old. Legend has it that the ancient oak sheltered Robin Hood and was the place where he and his merry men slept. Other famous oaks include the one at Boscobel House in Staffordshire, where the future King Charles II hid from Cromwell in 1651 after the battle of Worcester. There is an ancient oak at Hatfield House known locally as the Queen Elizabeth Oak, a name based on the legend that Elizabeth I first heard about the death of her sister Queen Mary as she stood beneath the tree.

Each year on 29 May, King Charles II's birthday and the day the monarchy was restored in 1660, a national holiday known as Oak and Apple Day was celebrated. The Victorians abolished the festival in 1859. Until then, monarchists sported a sprig of oak leaves or an oak apple. Some even covered their oak leaves with gold leaf. All the old pagan jollities banned by the Puritans came back – dancing round the maypole, wild feasting, drinking and Morris dancing. Failure to decorate yourself with oak leaves rendered you liable to being pinched, slapped with stinging nettles or receiving a good kicking.

Then there's the solid oak legend of Herne the Hunter, whom some folklorists identify with the old pagan god Cernunnos. In act four, scene four, of Shakespeare's *The Merry Wives of Windsor*, Mistress Page says:

> There is an old tale goes that Herne the hunter,
> Sometime a keeper here in Windsor forest,
> Doth all the winter-time, at still midnight,
> Walk round about an oak, with great ragg'd horns.

King Richard II (who reigned 1377–1399) had a favourite gamekeeper called Herne. He was a superbly skilled tracker and hunter and was always required at the king's side. Hunting with Herne guaranteed success. On one trip a stag turned on the party and charged Richard, killing his horse. Herne jumped between the stag and the king, otherwise Richard himself might also have died. But Herne had made one sacrifice too many, as he was brutally gored by the stag. The king offered a generous reward to any person who could save Herne. Yet his fellow gamekeepers, jealous of his closeness to Richard, were happy to have Herne dead and gone. And here's where the story turns weird.

A black horse ridden by a stranger approached. He alighted, chopped the stag's antlers from its head and tied them onto the head of the injured Herne. Within weeks he recovered, only to find his skills as a tracker and hunter had gone. Kings being the way they were, Richard sacked him. Herne, still wearing the antlers, disappeared into the forest, and the next time he was seen he was hanging from the branch of an oak tree. Before his body could be removed, it disappeared. And so began the spooky legend of Herne's ghostly 'wild hunt'. Those who witness it claim the vision is a portent of disaster, not only for them but for the country at large. There is today an oak tree called Herne's Oak which was planted in 1906, after the original was chopped down in 1796. There have been reports as late as the 1970s of sightings of the ghostly hunt.

As for the lovely ash tree, it has almost as many superstitions as it has branches. Bundles of ash wood bound by green twigs would be burned on Christmas Eve, and as it crackled away on the hearth you made a wish as soon as the bundle fell apart. This superstitious routine was especially popular with single girls. The girls would choose their own bundle, and if theirs was the first to fall apart in the fire, they would be the first in the house to marry.

An agricultural superstition applied to the ash if you had lame farm animals. First you had to hack a convenient hole or compartment in the ash tree's trunk. Into this you placed a live shrew. Then, somewhat cruelly, the hole was sealed with the poor shrew imprisoned. When the shrew died, the injury to the tree was supposedly healed and, miraculously, courtesy of the kind ash's spirit, the lame animal would be back in full working order.

If you had a child suffering from a common ailment such as a hernia or rickets, there was an elaborate routine with the ash to provide a cure. There had to be a wide split in the tree's trunk, and, before sunrise, the poorly child had to be passed naked through this gap. Then the father would bind the trunk back together and repair it with clay. The healing process of the tree was thought to run simultaneously with the child's recovery. The pagan world must have been a pretty weird place.

In Norse myths, Yggdrasil the world tree was a mighty ash whose roots and branches stretched everywhere, both into the sky and the bowels of the earth. It was on a branch of the ash that Odin sacrificed himself as the ravens pecked his eye out. Yggdrasil represented everything that the Norse heaven needed; this mighty ash even had a goat that nibbled the grass around its trunk, and the goat was milked to provide a special honey mead. After all the raids, murder and pillage, those Vikings certainly had a fine old afterlife lined up.

There is also the mountain ash, known in the UK as the rowan tree. It was regarded as yet another protector against witchcraft and evil spirits. It also protected livestock. Milkmaids, in order to ensure their milk would not sour, attached rowan twigs to their milking pails. Pigs would wear rowan 'necklaces', and rowan berries were fed to horses and cattle while they were giving birth to ensure a healthy calf or foal, as well as easing the mother's labour pains.

Seeing the white blossom of the hawthorn burst into view after a cold winter is always an uplifting experience. When dancing around the maypole was common, the pole was usually made of wood from the hawthorn. The hawthorn has been affectionately known down the ages as the may tree, representing love, passion, fertility and marriage. It was involved in summer time with the mysterious tradition of the Green Man, who wore a garland of hawthorn as his crown. Of course, all its exotic sexy paganism was swept aside with the arrival of Christianity. Because the month of May was dedicated to the Virgin Mary, the white hawthorn flowers would be denied their earthy heritage and would now be proclaimed to represent the 'purity' of Mary. But the blossom had a down side, as its fragrance was said to remind people of the smell prevalent in London during the black death. This does have some scientific basis, as the blossoms contain a compound, trimethylamine, a chemical with a strong fishy odour in low concentrations and an ammonia-like smell at higher concentrations, apparently reminiscent of decomposing flesh. Tradition also has it that the crown of thorns that was placed on Jesus' head was made from hawthorn wood.

The mystery of the Glastonbury thorn

There is one hawthorn tree in England that combines all the Christian superstition and mythology that a true follower of the Cross could ever want. Conversely, that same Christian may regard it as a pagan abomination. Sometime during the night of 8 December 2010, some religious vandal took a chainsaw to what was known as the holy thorn tree of Glastonbury in Somerset and cut it down. The Glastonbury thorn (*Crataegus monogyna* '*Biflora*') is a variety of hawthorn that flowers twice a year in winter and spring or, when conditions allow, at Christmas and Easter. According to superstition and legend, at some time in the first century AD Joseph of Arimathea planted the tree somewhat magically, by sticking his staff into the soil of Wearyall Hill near Glastonbury. The story of Joseph, a wealthy man who came from Arimathea in Judea, is told in all four gospels. Matthew 27:57–60 tells us:

> When it was evening, there came a rich man from Arimathea, named Joseph, who was also a disciple of Jesus. He went to Pilate and asked for the body of Jesus; then Pilate ordered it to be given to him. So Joseph took the body and wrapped it in a clean linen cloth and laid it in his own new tomb which he had hewn in the rock. He then rolled a great stone to the door of the tomb and went away.

We all know what happened next. But Joseph's connection to Glastonbury and the thorn tree has fascinated followers of myth, fable and superstition over many years, inspiring William Blake (1757–1827) to write the poem that would be set to music as 'Jerusalem':

> And did those feet in ancient time
> Walk upon England's mountains green?
> And was the holy Lamb of God
> On England's pleasant pastures seen?

The legend is fairly well known that Joseph was supposed to have visited England with the teenaged Jesus. As well as Glastonbury, the holy duo were said to have visited St Just in Roseland, Cornwall, and St Michael's Mount. He was Mary's uncle and thus Jesus' great-uncle and, as a merchant, he'd come to Britain to buy tin in Cornwall. Sent by St Philip (mentioned as one of the Apostles in the lists of Matthew, Mark and Luke, and in Acts), he returned with other disciples after the death of Jesus to bring Christianity to Britain, bringing with him two vials containing the blood and sweat of Jesus. It is also claimed that he built Britain's first church. Then the story becomes really fantastic, suggesting that Joseph brought the Holy Grail to England and hid it in a well at Glastonbury, now called the Chalice Well. Obviously, there was more to Glastonbury than the age of the rock festival, although the tree itself wasn't associated with Joseph of Arimathea until the seventeenth century.

So which rotten swine would want to chop down such a harmless, innocent and legendary tree? Apparently, it has happened before – British spiritual history has no shortage of killjoys. The tree was first written about in 1502, and what was believed to be the original holy thorn was felled in the 1640s during the English civil war. It was burned by Cromwell's misery-mongers, the Puritans, who regarded it as a superstitious icon. Sprigs and cuttings were secretly kept and re-planted.

In 1951 the local council planted a replacement. Following the tree's hacking in 2010, what was left of the savaged tree began to show signs of new growth that mysteriously 'vanish' every now and again. Someone really hates that tree. The despair continues: a sapling grafted from a descendant of the pre-1951 tree was planted and consecrated by the landowners and Glastonbury Conservation Society on 1 April 2012, but just two weeks later the anti-tree surgeons struck again and snapped it in twain. The present sacred thorn stands in the grounds of the Church of St John and was grown from a local cutting, of which there are numerous examples in the neighbourhood. By custom, a budded branch of the Glastonbury thorn is sent to the Queen at Christmas.

Glastonbury has become a strange place. These days it attracts more pagans than Christians. The high-street shops cover every kind of shamanism, magic, myth and legend going. The huge rock festival only occupies a week or so of the year. For the rest of the time, this is the domain of would-be necromancers, serious witches and trainee Gandalfs. It's all a lot of colourful, harmless fun, and one has to question the dark, superstitious mindset of persons unknown, hell-bent on destroying a simple bit of the UK's natural arboreal myth and legend, simply because, for some arcane and perverse lack of reason, it fails to fit into their odd religious view of the world. You don't need to be religious to take pity on a tree, so let's hear it for a much-persecuted example. After the nasty savaging it got in 2010, fans were sad and bewildered and someone wrote on Facebook, 'Blessed be the holy thorn – may it have as many fruit as the tears that have been shed.'

It was thought unlucky to have hawthorn in your house as decoration, but at the same time it could be helpful if you were haunted by ghosts or suffered storm damage or the occasional cursing witch. You could ask someone who was not a family member to place branches of hawthorn across the rafters of your house as spiritual protection. If there was a problem in the dairy and the cows weren't giving enough milk, you hung bundles of hawthorn twigs on the cowshed doors.

The yew tree is the Methuselah of the forest. Some are known to live for a thousand years or more. Many of the UK's old churchyards have their own ancient specimens that are believed to protect against storms. It is known to be fatally poisonous if you are dumb enough to ingest too much, and its fabulous longevity has prompted many superstitions. The pagans grew sacred yew groves and early Christians chose the same places to build their churches. There was something about the yew's magical power of regeneration that becomes evident when the branches of a yew stoop so low as to reach the ground. They appear to take root again and form a new growth, and ancient yew trees often appear to have many trunks. This appearance of 'rebirth' by the yew inspired many mourners to lay yew branches on the graves of the departed to enable the resurrection of the soul. As with other trees, the yew shares the dark distinction of being a suspect for the source of the wood used for the crucifixion.

In November 2015 the BBC reported on a remarkable Scottish yew, the oldest in Europe, at Fortingall, a small village in the heart of Perthshire at the entrance to Glen Lyon, not far from Loch Tay. The yew is reputed to be up to 5000 years old, although more conservative estimates put it between 2000 and 3000 years. According to local legend, Roman prefect Pontius Pilate was born in its shadow. If this isn't remarkable enough, for some odd reason this venerable tree has decided to change sex. The Fortingall yew has started sprouting berries on one of its upper branches – something only female trees do. Dr Max Coleman of the Royal Botanic Garden in Edinburgh discovered the berries on the tree and explained, 'Odd as it may seem, yews and many other conifers that have separate sexes, have been observed to switch sex. It's not fully understood – normally the switch occurs on part of the crown rather than the entire tree changing sex.' It has also been suggested by archaeologists that the tree may have been the focal point for some pagan cult in the Iron Age.

Finally, it's worth remembering that the weapon that played such a significant part in British history, the longbow, was traditionally made of yew wood. And if you thought the bow vanished with the arrival of the musket, you'd be wrong. The last recorded use of the longbow in war was by British lieutenant colonel John Malcolm 'Mad Jack' Churchill (1906–1996), who used it to kill a German soldier in WWII. He also captured forty-two German soldiers armed only with his claybeg sword – a smaller version of a claymore. He roused his men for battle by playing his bagpipes, and once said, 'In my opinion, any officer who goes into action without his sword is improperly dressed.' They don't make 'em like that anymore . . .

Plants of displeasure

Between 1982 and 1984 the Folklore Society carried out an interesting nationwide survey of plants that were traditionally considered to bring bad luck if thoughtlessly picked or, worse, brought into the house. The survey received 524 responses involving ninety species of plants from around the UK. This fascinating information now rests in the society's archive and you can find an engrossing summary of the outcome presented in Roy Vickery's *Unlucky Plants – A Folklore Survey* (Folklore Society, 1985). You can also see a selection of the results at www.plant-lore.com, and they make for intriguing reading.

Among the plants never to be picked to avoid misfortune were altar lily (also unpopular in hospitals), also known as arum lily and Easter lily and associated in Ireland with the 1916 Easter Rising. The flower represents republicans killed or executed and is featured on a mural commemorating the 1981 hunger strikers in the Maze prison, County Down.

Blackberries (a.k.a. brambles in the north of England and Scotland) shouldn't be picked after the end of September and certainly not after the old Michaelmas Day, 11 October. Why? Satan – again. Apparently, he fell into a bramble bush and the thorns injured him. The French in some instances would never eat brambles because they believed Lucifer had spat upon them, but the Folklore Society's Welsh correspondent gives a more earthy reason: it was said that the devil had peed on them by October.

Clover, colt's foot and cow parsley were never to be picked. Picking colt's foot would cause you to wet the bed, and the same embarrassment was attached to the dandelion. According to a Yorkshire superstition, picking cow parsley meant that your mother would die. Cow parsley was also known in some regions as 'Break your mother's heart'.

The list of plants, branches and flowers that superstition dictates you should never bring into the house is long and portentous. There's the fennel-like flower of a member of the carrot family, *apiaceae* (the celery, carrot or parsley collection), that grows alongside weeds and smells as if cats have been around. In parts of Lancashire it had the grim title 'mother-die'. Blackthorn indoors was an omen of death. Any kind of May blossom, particularly hawthorn, promised bad luck and was believed in some places to be detrimental to a mother's milk when breastfeeding. Other forbidden indoor plants included bluebells and a plant known as Queen Anne's lace or 'wild carrot'. This got its name either from Queen Anne or her great-grandmother Anne of Denmark, and it does resemble lace. It has a red central flower that is thought to represent a drop of blood that emerged when Queen Anne, making lace, pricked herself with a needle. Some people regard having honeysuckle indoors to be an omen of death. Having a bunch of lilac indoors is certainly a harbinger of doom, although in some regions this only applies to white lilac, not the mauve or other shades. Meadowsweet, water mint and vervain were sacred herbs to the druids. Aromatic, astringent, diuretic and sub-tonic meadowsweet with its fernlike foliage and creamy-white, delicate flowers blossoms from June to almost September. It is also not popular in Ireland as a house plant. This seems unfair, as in the fourteenth century it was known as the mead or honey wine herb, medwort, or meadwort. In 'The Knight's Tale', Chaucer mentions it as one of fifty ingredients in a drink referred to as Save, and meadowsweet flowers were often mixed with wine and beer. Some herb beers still include it today. The lovely snowdrop also gets a bad press as an indoor decoration, but, like many of these flowers accompanied by doom-laden stories, they are often irresistibly reliable for brightening up your sideboard.

You should never make a display of red and white flowers. This is redolent of blood and bandages and foretells death. Evidence from the recent past, within the last fifty years, shows that some NHS matrons would not allow a bunch of red and white flowers in wards.

This colour combination also provides a convenient point for a small diversion; the red-and-white barber's pole. Today we go to the barber for a haircut, but historically the man with the adjustable chair was known as a 'barber-surgeon'. He was skilled with a sharp knife, the go-to man when you needed a boil lanced, a rotten tooth removed or to re-set fractured bones. Yet his most popular service in medieval times was bloodletting. Folk believed that the state of your blood was a result of what you ate and drank. Draining blood from people was a major medical practice, but most qualified doctors were too aloof to get the scalpel out and would send patients to the barber-surgeon.

You sat in the chair and would grip on a pole to increase the tension and pressure in your arm. This helped prepare for a successful incision by making the veins bulge out. Bowls of blood were collected and almost regarded as a commercial trophy. Barber-surgeons would display the grisly basins in their shop windows as a reminder that you, haplessly window-shopping, might be in need of losing some over-indulged, fatty, alcoholic blood.

By 1307 the sight of buckets of blood along the high streets of London became a little too much to stomach and a law was passed to prevent its display. So, like everything else medievally repugnant (other than human poo and pee, which were commercial gold), the contents of the city's opened veins got dumped in the Thames. The barbers, bereft of their blood-basin window displays, opted for the gripping pole, painted in stripes and erected above their door as a handy symbol of their skill and trade. The pole was topped off with a brass ball, representing the forbidden basin of blood. Red and white symbolised the arm bound in bloody bandages. Once bandages had been washed for reuse (there was still a lot to learn about hygiene) they were often hung out on the pole to dry. No doubt the flies loved them.

There was a confusing period in the sixteenth century when the law required surgeons to have red-and-white-striped poles and barbers blue-and-white. Today you'll see red-and-white poles in the UK, while patriotic American barbers opt for the colours of the flag – red, white and blue. More affluent barbers who invest in an electric revolving pole sign need to remember that the red stripes are required to move downwards as it revolves, as blood does in the body's arteries.

The holly and the ivy

There is a commonly held superstition that holly, like May blossom, should never be brought indoors, although at Christmas these days we even have artificial holly. The fear was that holly brought bad luck, and if people took the risk, it was never to be hung over a mirror. It was perfect, however, for a display on the front door as a way of blessing the house and protecting the occupants and visitors from any misfortune. As with some other superstitions, transgressing these 'rules' could leave you with a death in the family.

Holly is considered to have protective powers against lightning and witches. The plant derives its name from the word 'holy' and its red berries represent the blood of the crucifixion.

Holly has been used for centuries as a symbol of good fortune and immortality. It was commonly presented to newlyweds to bless them with a happy and fertile married life.

An old cure for chilblains was to have your feet thrashed with holly as this was thought to bring out the cold blood. It probably rendered you immobile for a week, too.

As a weather predictor, the holly bush, when weighed with an excess of berries, signified that the winter ahead was going to be a tough one.

As holly is an evergreen, its shiny, sturdy leaves symbolise eternal life. The leaves are sharp and prickly and provide a defence against evil spirits. If the less prickly strain of holly is used for decoration, then the wife in the house will be in charge for the coming year. If it's the prickly stuff, then the husband will be the boss. So the best solution is to have both smooth and prickly holly and presumably there'll be domestic harmony.

An old holly superstition required young, unmarried girls to scratch the initials of their favourite male admirer on the leaves of holly. The leaves would be placed under the girl's pillow or in her nightdress. The desired result, of course, was a dream in which they'd see their future husband. To help the process along, some girls would borrow a wedding ring and wear it on the appropriate finger while they slept.

Ivy grows with the aid of other plants and trees and in some cultures it can be regarded as sinister, especially in the way it can soon dominate and shroud an abandoned derelict building. However, there's a good side to this because if it clads your house it is seen as a protective barrier against the devil and bad luck.

In the old days it was common to find ivy hanging outside many English inns and pubs to encourage good fortune. This was hardly surprising as ivy is closely associated the Roman god of booze and having a good time, Bacchus.

In ancient times ivy, like holly, symbolised marriage and fidelity. It is still used for some wedding decorations, usually in the form of wreaths, crowns or garlands. It is considered bad luck only to use ivy for the decorations.

Ivy and holly leaves share similar superstitions, a favourite of which, for a change, doesn't involve young maidens. If a man could pluck ten ivy leaves on Halloween, throw one away and put the remaining nine under his pillow then he'd see his future missus in a pleasant dream.

An ancient New Year's Eve ritual involved placing an ivy leaf in a bowl of water where it would remain until the eve of twelfth night, 6 January. Providing the leaf stayed green and healthy during those six days, you'd expect a good year. If it withered and black spots appeared, you'd prepare for the worst and call the doctor.

Mistletoe: the passionate parasite and dubious druids

———

We usually remember the Christmases of our childhood with a touch of joy, but I recall the Christmas of 1953 as a darker, more primitive affair. I was ten years old and we were living in a rented stone cottage on the moors above the town of Mytholmroyd in Yorkshire. There was no electricity or gas and, as far as we knew, central heating hadn't been invented yet. I remember that yuletide because it was the year we had no Christmas tree. Our father had been unable to heave one up the steep hill and, after talking to the well-established locals, he came up with a traditional alternative which he referred to as a 'mistletoe'. I have since discovered that the device he constructed, with two wooden hoops forming a kind of heliocentric display – one set inside the other at right angles – was actually a traditional kissing bough that predates the intro-duction of the Christmas tree, having been a popular decoration in medieval times.

In the past it was a garland of greenery, shaped like a double-hooped May garland or crown which was hung from the middle of the ceiling in the main room of the house. It could be decorated with candles and coloured paper, red apples hanging from the hoops and a bunch of mistletoe suspended from the centre. You were supposed to light the candles on Christmas Eve and every night throughout the twelve days of Christmas, although in our case the fear of burning a house rented from a Scrooge-like agricultural landlord with a penchant for evictions precluded any festive illumination. It was a cold, miserable bleak house of a Christmas best forgotten, apart from the fact that poor old Dad did his best with his Christmas tree substitute.

Mistletoe is a parasitic plant that grows in curious spherical clumps on various trees. It likes attaching itself to an apple tree and, traditionally, is particularly venerated when found on an oak. It was said to be unlucky to bring mistletoe into the house before Christmas Eve. All decorations had to be removed before old Christmas Day (or Twelfth Night) as one old saying went: 'It must come down before old Christmas Day or the devil will dance on every spray.' The name comes from the Old English *misteltān* and, of course, most people love the plant because it gets us a free snog beneath its leaves and berries every Christmas.

There is a lot of unfounded myth and fable about mistletoe involving the druids. An example concerns the winter solstice, known to the druids as *Alban Arthan*. You might have read that on the sixth night of the new moon the chief druid would cut the sacred mistletoe from the oak with a golden sickle. Well, it sounds suitably mystical and pagan. But what we think we know about the druids, according to Ronald Hutton's informative *Blood and Mistletoe: the History of the Druids in Britain* (Yale, 2009), is mostly made-up waffle. What we do know for a fact is that mistletoe was held as sacred – and that's about it.

The legends led us to believe that the chief druid instructed other members of the order to hold a cloth below the tree to catch the falling mistletoe sprigs, because touching the ground would be a profanity. The branches would be split up and handed out among the gathering to hang over the doors of their dwellings to protect them against thunder, lightning and all manner of evil spirits.

If you're wondering where they got the druidic plot for that excellent movie *The Wicker Man*, you can blame Julius Caesar. He wrote that the druids loved human sacrifices burned alive in large human-shaped figures built of twig and bracken.

Lots of early reports of pagan activity fall into the FOAF category – as told to the writer by 'a friend of a friend'. The Greeks, as well as the Romans, cobbled together other examples of ersatz British and Gaulish druid history, none of it from first-hand experience. Sixteenth-century physician John Caius suggested that it was the highly knowledgeable druids who founded Cambridge University.

Today, those seemingly deluded modern 'pagans', in their Celtic bling and M&S white robes, the devotees who argue about who has the right to act out a simulated midsummer Stonehenge ceremonial melodrama straight out of Hammer Films, are no more genuine druids than the ones conjured up by Julius Caesar or indeed Welsh poet Edward 'Glamorgan Eddie' Williams (1747–1826), better known as Iolo Morganwg. It was Eddie who invented *Alban Arthan*, Welsh for the 'light of winter'.

As for the 'golden sickle', the antiquarian John Aubrey (1626–1697) initiated the popular myth that Avebury and Stonehenge were druid temples. He was presented with an instrument with a curved blade used, particularly by ancient Greeks and Romans, to scrape sweat and dirt from the skin in a hot-air bath. It is known by archaeologists as a strigil. However, to Aubrey, it was no such thing – he immediately proclaimed it to be a druid's sickle for cutting mistletoe and the great 'bardic tradition' was soon under way.

This illicit kissing connection is said to go back to the ancient Greeks. At some time in the mythical past the plant in some way offended the gods and as punishment was to spend eternity having to look down at girls and women being kissed beneath it. Quite how a plant offended ancient gods is unclear, but mistletoe was certainly in trouble in Norse mythology.

The Norse deity Balder was seen as the god of purity, light, love, peace, forgiveness and justice. His mother Frigga was goddess of love and beauty. They were quite a family and she loved Baldur and sought to protect him from any harm. To do this she made everything in the world which was rooted in fire, water, air and earth make a promise not to harm her son. The party pooper was mistletoe – it didn't promise anything. Enter mischievous and unpleasant, shape-shifting god Loki, who sometimes assisted the gods but enjoyed a touch of malicious behaviour. Loki took the mistletoe and made an arrow from its wood. In a rather nasty move, he took the arrow to Hodur, Balder's blind brother, and, guiding Holder's hand, pointed the arrow at Balder's heart. When Hodur let the arrow fly, Balder fell dead. The white berries of the mistletoe became Frigga's tears.

There is another version of the story that has a nice Hollywood ending. Balder is somehow brought back to life and his mother forgives the mistletoe, declaring it from then on to be a symbol of love beneath which anyone lingering can receive a kiss. Back to the dodgy Druids, however, and we're told that the berries of the mistletoe represent the sperm of the gods. This is because a semen-like substance issues from the berries when they are pressed. This gave mistletoe a reputation as an aphrodisiac. If you're a young girl believing in druid lore, you might be a bit wary beneath a sprig of mistletoe because you could be in for a bit more than a kiss.

Oak mistletoe was worn around the neck and used at one time for various ailments including epilepsy, high blood pressure, heart disease, rheumatism and certain tumours. In treatment, powdered mistletoe berries were added to wine, water or milk. However, this plant is highly toxic, so avoid the temptation to try it as a remedy today – we've moved on in medicine since the days of 'Glamorgan Eddie'.

Another legend suggests that mistletoe was a plant of peace in ancient times. If enemies met by chance beneath it in a forest, they laid down their arms and maintained a truce until the next day.

Mineral

Those of a certain age will remember the social phenomenon which came to be known as the Summer of Love in 1967. Hippies around the world, inspired by San Francisco's hairy rock'n'roll dreamers, began congregating in any green open space available to burn joss sticks in the naive belief that the nasty world could be changed for the better. Those participants who weren't too stoned to remember, absorbed elements of ancient traditions and mythology. Perhaps they hoped antediluvian philosophies, arcane superstitions and religions might offer an alternative to politics, war and capitalism. As we've come to learn, such hopes didn't stand a snowball's chance in hell.

However, go to any tourist town today with a decent bookshop, good museum or a cathedral and the remnants of 1967 exist in the form of New Age shops. These are the places where you'll find crystal and gem 'therapies', symbolic jewellery, Tarot cards, African carvings and assorted Buddhas, beads, wind chimes, fake Taiwanese 'native American dream catchers' and, if you're really keen to rekindle that old feeling of being 'far out, maaan', even the odd cheesecloth kaftan or a tie-dyed T-shirt.

The superstitions attached to minerals, gemstones and jewellery go back much further than Haight-Ashbury, 1967. The wearing of jewellery can be traced back many thousands of years. In many parts of the ancient world it was used as a form of currency. A few bags of emeralds or rubies could sustain a ruling family for decades. As today, some jewellery was functional as well as fashionable. Belt buckles and clasps for gowns and togas proclaimed the status of the wearer. Priests, magicians and wise elders would all have their allotted bling to distinguish them from the hoi polloi. As with today's military badges and insignia, such as the civic regalia of a mayor or member of a masonic lodge, jewellery was an instant indicator of who you were. The Romans had specific laws about the wearing of such items. Only approved ranks in the senate or military could wear rings. The Greeks only got their bling out for special occasions, when women would show off their glitter just to remind the plebs who they were.

The colour of stones was also highly symbolic, particularly in ancient Egypt, where each religious deity would be represented by a particular gem or metal.

Gems of many kinds also served, as they still do in the east, to protect against wicked spirits by warding off the evil eye. For many reasons – including good luck, fortune, spiritual significance or healing – popes, bishops, kings and warriors all had their amulets, rings, necklaces and talismans.

Jewellery for prayer

Over two-thirds of the world's religious population employ some type of prayer beads as part of their spiritual practice. One of the most common items of prayer jewellery is the Catholic rosary, a cross or crucifix, a medal, large beads and small beads. There are numerous prayers made by the faithful while working their way through the beads, the basic three being the 'Our Father', 'Hail Mary' and 'Glory Be' prayers. But since the rosary consists of many other prayers it is usually a focus of faith, something tactile you can run through your fingers to meditate on the events in the lives of Jesus and Mary.

Although superstition is frowned upon in Islam, Muslims, too, have prayer beads called *Misbaha* or *Tesbih* (originating from the word *supha* that announces the glories of Allah). They are used as a guide during prayer. Islamic prayer beads are composed of ninety-nine beads, used to recite the ninety-nine names of Allah. Some examples of the jewellery are composed of thirty-three beads that are worked through three times.

Japa Mala is a string of beads commonly used by Hindus, Buddhists and some Sikhs to count mantras (Sanskrit prayers) in sets of twenty-seven, fifty-four or 108 repetitions. *Mala* is a Sanskrit word meaning 'garland'. *Japa* means recitation and is traditionally used as an adjective. Together they describe prayer beads for meditation. They are thought to have their origins in India in the eighth century BC. They help to keep you focused during meditation. The starting and ending point on the *mala* is the large *meru* (mountain) bead used for counting the repetitions.

There is a suggestion that when the Romans arrived in India following the conquest of Egypt by Augustus in 30 BC, they appear to have misinterpreted a Sanskrit word for the Roman word for 'rose'. Upon returning to Rome, *mala* beads were referred to as *rosarium*. Today, in the English language, we've come to know them as rosary beads.

If you're short of beads, you can try prayer ropes. Eastern Orthodox and eastern Catholic traditions still count their repetitions on a rope. The idea was said to have been invented by St Pachiomus the Great (AD 292–348), the founder of Christian cenobitic monasticism (a tradition that stresses community life) in the fourth century, to help illiterate monks with their repetitions of prayers and prostrations.

Orthodox Christians, Buddhists, Sikhs and members of the Bahá'í faith are all known to count repetitions of prayers, chants or devotions, and the beads are often used for protection, meditation or relaxation. They are made of different materials, the properties of which are said to have specific energetic effects. The material used depends on the religious tradition.

Life with the stones

Superstitions about birth stones and crystals are many and complex. Each month of the calendar has a birth stone, but different stones are acceptable across cultures and religions. Although some Tibetan and Indian cultures have a centuries-long tradition of birthstones, the full list jewellery fans will recognise today was probably created as part of a sales campaign by the jewellery-makers Tiffany in 1870. However, there are various mentions of gems and crystals in the Bible, such as Revelation 21:11:

> And he carried me away in the spirit to a great and high mountain and shewed me that great city, the holy Jerusalem, descending out of heaven from God, having the glory of God and her light [was] like unto a stone most precious, even like a jasper stone, clear as crystal.

And in Exodus 28:17–21 the instructions for the expensive breastplate belonging to priest Aaron feature a whole jewellery shop:

> Then mount four rows of precious stones on it. The first row shall be carnelian, chrysolite and beryl; the second row shall be turquoise, lapis lazuli and emerald; the third row shall be jacinth, agate and amethyst; the fourth row shall be topaz, onyx and jasper. Mount them in gold filigree settings. There are to be twelve stones, one for each of the names of the sons of Israel.

These jewels were said to have come from the throne of God. According to the Jewish historian Josephus (AD 37–95), Aaron's breastplate had some powerful magic. Josephus wrote, 'From the stones which the high priest wore . . . there emanated a light . . . a radiance sufficient to give light even to those far away.' There is much dispute over what the actual twelve stones were, due to the confusion over archaic terms and colour references. However, in the most fascinating and thorough book on the subject of stones and gems, *Gems in Myth, Legion and Lore* (Jeweller's Press, 2007), Bruce G. Knuth lists the twelve original gems as: red jasper, light green serpentine, green feldspar, almandine garnet, lapis lazuli, onyx, brown agate, banded agate, amethyst, yellow jasper, malachite and green jasper or jade.

Depending on the month, there are differing groups of birthstones for the cultures listed as Arabic, Hebrew, Hindu, Italian, Polish, Roman and Russian. They include diamonds, bloodstones, rubies, and many more. All are supposed to have differing influences on your life and to bring good fortune in different belief systems. However, over the past century in the west, a more simplified, general list of birthstones has been developed.

MODERN BIRTHSTONES

January: garnet – faith, eternity and truth.

February: amethyst – luck, wit and health.

March: aquamarine – happiness and understanding.

April: diamond – eternity, courage and health.

May: emerald – fidelity, goodness and love.

June: pearl, moonstone – peace, nobility and beauty.

July: ruby – love, enthusiasm and strength.

August: peridot – success, peace and love.

September: sapphire – serenity and truth.

October: opal, tourmaline – purity, hope and health.

November: yellow topaz, citrine – wisdom, courage and sincerity.

December: blue topaz, turquoise, tanzanite – love, happiness and luck.

So far, so good. However, the above list can fluctuate depending on which source we go to, and whose list we decide to rely on. As well as Tiffany's list, in which each stone had an accompanying mystical poem 'by author unknown', the US National Association of Jewellers assembled in Kansas in 1912 with the aim of standardising birthstones. In 1952 the list was updated by the Jewellery Industry Council of America, which added new stones to June, November and October, replaced December's and swapped some stones around for March. The American Gem Trade Association changed the list yet again in 2002. If that wasn't confusing enough, in the UK the National Association of Goldsmiths created their own list in 1937. For a branch of superstition with its roots in the Bible, it looks as if the word of the Lord can easily be overwritten by a few men with an eyeglass and a pair of tweezers.

If you're into astrology, then all this is further complicated as each star sign has different stones. You'll find all you need to know in the works of stones expert Judy Hall, including *The Crystal Zodiac: Use Birthstones to Enhance Your Life* (Bounty Books, 2015).

Crystal therapy: good vibrations?

Crystals of various forms are also popular with New Age therapists, who would probably regard the inclusion of their beliefs under the heading 'superstition' to be offensive. They believe that when crystals are placed directly on the body, they have a powerful vibratory effect that enters you physically. The word 'vibrations' seems to come in for a lot of use in New Age language.

The *Oxford English Dictionary* defines 'vibrations' as 'a person's emotional state, the atmosphere of a place, or the associations of an object, as communicated to and felt by others: e.g, 'I picked up no unusual vibrations as to the envelope's contents.'

For example, purple amethyst crystals are said to hold the vibration of the 'violet flame' that can cleanse your 'negative vibrations' and transmute negativity into the light. Well, that's what they say.

So, if you're feeling low and bereft of spiritual energy, what happens if you visit a New Age crystal 'doctor'? A good friend of mine who practises crystal therapy tells me, 'According to the law of physics, thoughts direct energy and energy follows thought, so crystals help the thoughts connect with the body.' I experienced the therapy myself for an arthritic knee and none of the above occurred, but a steroid injection did the trick. I have yet to be convinced, but we're still friends.

Chakra is a Sanskrit word which means 'wheel'. According to ancient tradition, there are seven main *chakras* located along the spine and extending out of the front and back of the body. Crystal therapy involves placing the 'healing' crystals on the *chakras*. There are different crystals for different conditions. Each *chakra* links with a certain part of the body and an internal organ, the *chakra* providing the organ's functional energy. The theory is that the crystal releases positive energy via the *chakra* and you'll feel better. Needless to say, there is no scientific basis to claims that this therapy works. Controlled tests have been carried out using a mix of crystals and placebos, with even results. Yet the popularity of these superstitious rocks is helped by their endorsement by various celebrities and movie stars.

So what's going on here? Perhaps the imagined effects of crystal healing could be attributed to cognitive bias, when believers want a practice to be true and see only things that back that desire. That said, if the mind has been overcome to such a degree that benefits result, there can be no argument. It seems that superstitions can exert a strong grip on anyone, regardless of their status.

Salt of the earth

Let there be work, bread, water and salt for all.

Nelson Mandela (1918–2013), inaugural address as president of South
Africa, 10 May 1994

It's the most superstitious of minerals and we take it for granted. In many ways salt
is sacred, so culturally valuable that to exist without it would be unthinkable.
Why? Because salt is essential for animal life and saltiness is one of our basic
human tastes. Salt – sodium chloride – is absolutely necessary to the human body.
We're always oozing liquids and they're all salty: blood, mucus, tears, sweat, urine
and semen. Because they flow from us, we're always losing salt. And something
valuable enough to keep us alive means big business. Pepper is a luxury but salt is
a necessity.

Trade in this valuable commodity began with the Phoenicians, and both the
trade and Phoenicia were coveted by the Romans. Thus in 63 BC, the Roman
general Pompey marched into Phoencia in victory, further expanding Rome's
empire. The Phoenicians had been using a lot of salt in creating a rare dye called
Tyrian purple, a substance they made from as early as 1570 BC. It was actually
extracted by salting certain molluscs (shellfish) and was of great value. The colour
did not fade and in fact grew richer when exposed to sunlight. The meaning of
Phoenicia became 'land of purple dye' and the colour was truly special for the
Mediterranean elite. When the Romans conquered the Phoenicians they discovered this secret process. So exclusive was the dye that in the first century BC Julius
Caesar passed a law that no one outside his family could wear purple.

The Romans called salt *salarium* and used it to pay their workers and soldiers,
which, as is widely known, is where our word 'salary' originated.

The Egyptians used natron, a mineral that contains sodium chloride, to prevent
mummified remains from decaying. As archaeology has revealed, it was pretty
effective. Anything that preserves human tissue after death was bound to gather a
lot of mystique.

Salt has been used in religious rites and ceremonies due to its ability to reform after being dissolved. It's been compared to God's unchanging love. There's plenty to say about salt, but let's look at the superstitions.

The most common property attributed to salt is that it brings prosperity. This is why many times people will give it as a gift upon reaching a new year or when moving into a new home.

Another tradition says salt will bring fertility, and some say you should give a bride salt on her wedding day.

Knocking over the salt cellar on the table was said to lead to argument and break up a friendship. It has been suggested that Judas spilled the salt during the last supper, but by throwing a pinch over your left shoulder with your right hand you'll avoid bad luck. Evil was said to exist on the left-hand side, so throwing the salt over that shoulder will send it into the devil's eyes and temporarily blind him from working his spells. In contrast, in parts of Scandinavia, it's OK if the salt you spill is dry because that's lucky – the bad thing to spill is damp salt. In Italy there's another table superstition to go along with spilling salt, as it's equally bad luck to spill olive oil.

Eating another man's salt created a mystical bond between the two of you, and this was a bond which should never be broken.

An old German superstition suggested that any young woman who had laid the table for a meal and forgot to put the salt out must have lost her virginity.

In Greek folklore, salt can be used to get rid of an unwelcome person. All you have to do is sprinkle salt behind that person. The powers of the salt will chase him out and make sure he doesn't return.

It's also an old custom to sprinkle salt in a new home before you occupy it, as the salt will drive any evil out and away from you and your family.

The Japanese believe that you should throw salt over yourself before entering your home on a day when you attend a funeral. This is believed to remove the presence of the dead.

To curtail the power of witches, salt was once sprinkled on the fire by anyone cursed.

It's been known in some cultures that presenting a newborn child with salt will guarantee it whatever it needs in life. People used to hang bags of salt over a baby's cradle to help protect the baby before it was baptised.

You should never put salt on someone else's food – let them salt their own, or you'll bring them bad luck. As the ominous saying had it, 'Help me to salt, help me to sorrow.'

Don't borrow or lend salt. Either give it as a gift or sell it, otherwise you're creating bad luck. It's not only bad luck for the borrower, and it gets worse if the salt is returned. But if you do ever 'borrow' salt and want it back, you must ask if you can 'borrow' it back.

There is an old Christmas superstition about salt. It was common to leave a small heap on your Christmas Eve table. Provided the pile stayed the same and was unaltered in the morning, the year ahead would be OK. If it had altered or, worse still, if some had dissolved, this was considered to be an omen of death.

Birth, marriage and death

Where did you come from, baby dear?
Out of the everywhere into the here.
Where did you get those eyes so blue?
Out of the sky as I came through.
What makes the light in them sparkle and spin?
Some of the starry spikes left in.

George MacDonald (1824–1905), 'Baby' (1871)

Birth, life, death. They belong to all of us, rich or poor. As there will always be superstitions, nowhere will they be stronger than at the moment you come crying into the world.

Those of a certain age, especially in the north of England, may recall that when a baby was due and a pram was ordered it was always delivered after the birth. Delivering it before was considered unlucky.

A silver coin was often placed in a newborn baby's hand. This was something to do with good luck and future prosperity.

It was once commonly believed among mothers that one of the ways of relieving a child's teething pain was by rubbing its gums with your gold wedding ring.

Some of the later rituals – such as 'wetting the baby's head' (usually in the pub) or handing out cigars – carried out by some insensitive fathers who do not have to experience the labour pains suffered by their wives, seem to have faded as the fashion over the past half-century is to be alongside your wife's bed as she gives birth. (In any event, a cigar at a hospital today would get you thrown out . . .)

In recent decades there's been a bit of a jokey superstition held among women that sitting on a seat or chair previously occupied by a pregnant woman means your own pregnancy could be imminent. This begs the question – how would a woman know? There have always been lots of chairs and no shortage of pregnant women. However, discussing this with my wife, I was amazed to discover that in the insurance office she worked in during the 1960s, there was indeed a chair regarded by the female clerical workers as 'the pregnancy chair'. Sure enough, each woman in the office who occupied it, including my wife, became pregnant.

There are many variations on the superstitions about birth and babies mentioned here, which are only a small sample of those found around the world. Throughout history, before we had the medical advantages we now enjoy in the west, birth was a fraught and often dangerous time, so any odd belief and ritual which could lessen the threat was worth trying.

As mothers were about to give birth in ancient Greece the midwives would be summoned. They would carefully examine everything in the room, every corner, to make sure that there were no knots – knots in curtain cords, ropes and sashes, any kind of knot with its superstitious power could be considered a threat to the birth, the mother or the child. For good or for evil, in ancient Greece, odd though it seems, knots had magic. Once the baby was delivered, a protection symbol, believed to be magic, would be made on its forehead to keep the child safe from the ever-present evil eye. There are recent remnants of this practice in Wales, where the baby's head might be smeared with honey. The Welsh also had a super-stition regarding a baby's bath water, which was to be deposited at the base of a tree in leaf.

Another superstition suggested that a baby sleeping in the cradle would be protected from evil spirits if a pair of the father's old pants was draped across it.

If a mother died in childbirth the surviving child could be said to have special healing powers in later life.

What scared both mothers and midwives was the possibility of any harm coming to the baby at the time of the birth. More than the obvious potential medical complications, it was the threat of the supernatural. A woman in childbirth was weak and easy prey for the devil. In medieval times they were also alert to the threat of fairies or demons stealing the child.

Superstition came up with a terrible possibility – that of the 'changeling'. If the supernatural beings or the 'little people' stole the child, they could place another in the crib, one of their own. Mother and baby were constantly watched over to ensure no evil or harm came to them. Fairies were said to like nothing better than stealing a newborn human. This kind of thinking was not only common in the ancient and medieval periods, but continued to the end of the nineteenth century.

AWAY WITH THE FAIRIES

When seventeen-year-old dressmaker's apprentice Bridget Boland of County Tipperary, Ireland, married Michael Cleary in August 1887 she had no idea that she'd become the victim of ancient superstition. During their childless eight years of marriage they lived apart for some time. Michael worked as a cooper in Clonmel while Bridget lived with her parents in Ballyvadlea where she made a living as a milliner and by selling eggs. On 16 March 1895 she went missing. It later transpired that she had been ill for some time; even to the point that a priest was called to give the last rites. It was also believed that the house she had lived in was built on the site of a fairy fort. These are known in Ireland as *raths*, referring to an earthen mound. They are numerous and sacrosanct, as are fairy trees.

Bridget Cleary's charred corpse was discovered on 22 March, buried in a shallow grave. In the ensuing court case it was revealed that her husband and her father were convinced that Bridget had in reality been a fairy changeling. As such, she had to be despatched. Before killing her, they had tried such remedies as holding her in front of a fire to bring out the fairy spirit, and throwing urine at her. Nine people were charged following her disappearance, including her husband. Four were convicted of wounding, and Michael Cleary went to prison for fifteen years for manslaughter. After his release in 1910 he moved to Liverpool and then emigrated to Canada.

Could belief in the fairy folk have survived that long? According to the *Irish Examiner* of 21 December 2012, it survives still. The paper reported the destruction of two fairy forts in Kilmurry, County Cork, offences punished by penalties of 20,000 euros that followed a 25,000-euro fine for a farmer in Kerry for the same offence. Although many people would not claim to believe in fairies, such rural superstition often appears stubborn in Ireland. Even today, some farmers will be reluctant to destroy a fairy fort. As for the changeling myth, this is a common European folk tradition. The Irish version, however, suggests that the bloodline of the fairies could only be maintained if they exchanged an old fairy for a human baby, or a substitute known as a 'stock' which eventually fades away and dies.

Baby blues: a selection of superstitions and rituals

All manner of arcane superstitious rituals and routines was employed in the past at the time of childbirth. Today we anticipate the celebration to come when a woman goes into labour, yet in centuries past, death at childbirth was so common that a mother would have already made funeral plans just in case.

English female monarchs about to give birth had a strange routine once they had settled into the chamber where the child would be delivered. Every piece of visual imagery – particularly tapestries or painted panels depicting animals or mythical beasts – had to be removed in case animal evil might be transmitted to the mother or affect the way the child looked. As with the Greeks, any knots were to be untied.

In the Middle Ages it was common for women to adopt the sitting position in childbirth as this was thought to accelerate the arrival of the infant. The contractions would be carefully counted up to about twenty-five. If no baby had appeared, this would be the time to assist in the opening of the womb. This 'help' was bizarre, to say the least. It could involve not only the untying of knots but an archer firing arrows, the lids of boxes and chests being noisily opened, drawers pulled out and cupboard doors opened. All locks in the house had to be unlocked. If this worked – and one might suppose that the agonised mother would have made a supreme effort with that entire racket going on – then other rituals would follow.

After childbirth, it was also common to place a knife under the bed to assist in easing the pain. Clergyman and poet Robert Herrick (1591–1674), the man who gave us 'gather ye rosebuds while ye may', touches on the knife superstition in his poem 'Charmes':

> *Let the superstitious wife*
> *Neer the child's heart lay a knife:*
> *Point be up and haft be downe;*
> *(While she gossips in the towne)*
> *This 'mongst other mystick charmes*
> *Keeps the sleeping child from harms*

One has to wonder, who is looking after slumbering junior while mum 'gossips in the towne'? There is another version of the knife superstition that places the knife not under the bed but on the doorstep. The devil or any evil spirit cannot pass iron or steel, therefore the child is protected.

Plants such as St John's wort or verbena could be used to protect the newborn. Red verbena was always a divine, supernatural force. Christian folklore suggested this plant was used to staunch Christ's wounds after he was brought down from the Cross. It became known as the 'holy herb', with the Welsh referring to it as 'devil's bane'.

The ancient Egyptians called it the 'tears of Isis', and later dynasties referred to it as 'Hera's tears'. The ancient Greeks dedicated verbena to the goddess of the dawn, Eos Erigineia.

In the far distant days before modern medicine, there seems to have been numerous superstitious ways to protect a baby and help it to grow. The midwife might put a drop of hot water on a child's tongue to guarantee it would speak clearly when grown.

A medieval baby of a well-off mother might have its first bath in milk or wine instead of water.

Although today, for the sake of records, we always weigh a child at birth, in times past this was considered to be very unlucky.

There are so many irrational baby superstitions that it makes one wonder how any of us managed be born and grow up without something terrible happening. So let's thank our lucky stars that the superstitious mothers of the past stuck to the weird rules, including the following:

It was always considered lucky to kiss a newborn baby.

Before placing a silver coin in a baby's hand (or presenting it to the mother) it was once the custom to first hold the coin up to the moon to ensure good luck.

It was considered unlucky to cut a baby's fingernails before it was twelve months old.

An old US custom to predict a child's future: place within its reach a Bible, a silver coin and a pack of playing cards. Watch to see which item the baby selects. The cards mean it will be a gambler. The coin means future wealth and, of course, the Bible means good fortune.

It was bad luck to rock an empty cradle.

Another US belief was that you should never put an old nappy on a baby. The child might become a thief when he grows up. A variation on this was that your baby had to be kept away from mirrors until it was a year old because seeing its own reflection might result in it becoming a criminal.

Pregnant women should never walk across a grave, as this is an omen of death for their child.

It was considered bad luck in the UK to have a child born feet first. This might foretell a crippling accident later in life. You had to rub the baby's legs with bay leaves.

If your baby suffered from colic, it had to be carried around the house three times.

We've all heard the old superstition that runs 'See a pin and pick it up – all the day you'll have good luck.' However, if a woman stuck pins or needles into curtains in the six weeks after childbirth, the baby would end up with bad teeth.

An odd one from Europe: you mustn't pierce the bread of a pregnant woman with a knife or fork or the baby's eyes could be poked out.

You should carry your baby in an upstairs room before you carry it downstairs. You could get around this by holding the child while standing on a chair (don't ask . . .).

Here's a truly weird German one: if there was both a boy and a girl to christen on the same day in the church, the male child should be baptised first. This was further complicated by the belief that using the same font water for the girl as was initially used for the boy meant she would grow up to have a beard. That must explain quite a few circus novelty acts. In Scotland it was believed that children unfortunate enough to die before being baptised would end up as ghosts or wandering spirits. In general, it was thought that once a baby had been baptised, it was safe from supernatural harm.

Another US belief was that keeping water used at baptism and presenting it to the child later in life would make them become a brilliant singer. *X-Factor* success guaranteed.

If a weasel, stoat or ferret jumped over a pregnant woman's stomach, the child would be born with a birthmark. Another animal to avoid was the rat. Having a rat go around or over a mum-to-be's feet? Definitely bad luck.

Predicting a baby's sex today is made easy by technology. However, in the past, various superstitions did the job. In ancient Greece, parents wanting a girl knew it was best to make love while the wind was blowing in a southerly direction. For a boy, it was the north wind. Results for eastern and westerly winds are not recorded so we can only guess at the resulting confused gender problems.

Until the introduction of ultrasound, a favourite sex predictor was to use a ring on a string. This was held over Mum's lump, and if the ring swung from side to side then a girl was due. A boy was indicated by circular motion. In northern England, a version of this superstition substituted the ring and string for a needle and cotton.

Mothers with a burning desire to eat cheese and meat would expect a boy.

Another method of predicting sex was to watch the way the child kicked in the womb. A girl would kick on the right, a boy on the left.

One odd old superstition involved a mother who refused to eat the crusty end of a bread loaf – this signified a girl was due.

Fire and iron were once major weapons against the devil and the fairies at the difficult time of birth. For example, a midwife might carry some fire – maybe a flaming torch or burning piece of wood – in a circle, three times around the bed. The horseshoe above the door was a great protective device against old Beelzebub, but other metals or iron would suffice, such as an open pair of scissors above the cot or handfuls of iron nails placed in strategic locations. You could also use pins, sticking them in a cross shape into baby's clothing.

Outside your home, rowan trees (the mountain ash) were good guards against the supernatural. Also known as the wayfarer's or traveller's tree, British legend had it that the rowan was the tree from which Satan hung his mother (although, as most Bible students will tell you, the devil didn't have a mother, but neither did medieval England have the internet . . .). The tree was handy for travellers because it supposedly stopped you from getting lost.

Reports of fairies entering a dwelling seem thin on the ground, but if these impertinent sprites attempted to come in they could be despatched with a few well-aimed embers from the fire.

Daisies were useful against a fairy kidnap and readily available, so a daisy chain placed around the baby's neck kept the sprites away.

Of course, this selection of birth and baby superstitions is only a sample of the many held throughout the world. You will no doubt have your own or those passed down through family generations.

Jumping the broomstick: marriage and superstition

By all means, marry. If you get a good wife, you'll become happy; if you get a bad one, you'll become a philosopher.

Socrates (c. 470–399 BC)

The words 'love' and 'marriage' seem made for each other. Not everyone agrees, of course. Abraham Lincoln said, 'Marriage is neither heaven nor hell, it is simply purgatory', while that Hollywood star no one can recall ever seeing in a movie, Zsa Zsa Gabor, quipped, 'A man in love is incomplete until he has married. Then he's finished.'

The time of year you decide to marry has always been blighted by superstition. As the Scots used to say, 'Marry in May, rue for aye' (marry in haste and repent at leisure), and it was the month of May the Romans set aside for making sacrifices to the dead. Getting spliced around this time seems a bad idea. When Christianity came along, both Lent, approximately the six-week period prior to Easter, and advent, leading up to Christmas, were also frowned upon for weddings, but these days most people marry when they feel like it.

You may notice that no one tends to get married once the sun has gone down. Ancient superstition suggests that any couple making this error could not only die early but also lose their children.

While marriage has always been popular, divorce seems to have become equally so. In Croatia, the city of Zagreb has its Museum of Broken Relationships, set up by artists and ex-lovers Vistica and Grubisic in 2006. This somewhat poignant showcase of marital failure features all the detritus of a doomed relationship, including mementoes and souvenirs of ill-fated love matches that went tragically wrong. In addition to the well-known superstitions attached to courtship and the big day, around the world all manner of peculiar rituals and customs have developed over the years.

BIZARRE MATING AND MARRIAGE CUSTOMS

At weddings in Puerto Rico, once the knot has been tied and you're at the head table at the reception, you'll notice a doll dressed up like the bride. Around this lone effigy lucky charms and gifts are piled up. Once all the speeches and toasts are over, the items are distributed among the guests.

Hoping for a man to come along, unmarried Armenian women like to send themselves into a dream. This occurs after eating a thick slice of very salty bread. In the dream, a man will bring her water to quench her thirst and this person will be 'the one'.

In the USA, one of the oldest marriage customs from the deep south is 'jumping the broom'. This ritual began a long time ago in Africa. It is thought to symbolise the union of two families, and today it has a darker derivation because of its association with slavery. Most African customs were banned by the slave owners, but this one was considered harmless and survived. The bride and groom jumped over a broom to symbolise moving forward in their new lives together, and the custom remains popular.

The night before his wedding, a South Korean bridegroom's male friends will beat him on the soles of his feet with fish and a bamboo cane. Yes . . . fish. This tradition seeks to establish strength of character, and one would hope the ensuing pain and smell have gone in time for the ceremony.

The role of the clergy at a medieval wedding was simply to bless the couple. It wasn't official church policy until the Council of Trent in the fifteenth century that the priest became involved.

It may be the kind of thing we would associate with strippers in lap-dancing clubs, but Greek brides and grooms take part in the 'money dance' – guests step forward and pin banknotes to their clothes.

In northern Rome, married couples lock up their future love by leaving a padlock on the ancient *Ponte Milvio* (Milvian bridge) over the Tiber. This odd ritual began early this century, inspired by the novel *I Want You*, by Frederico Moccia. Initially, the padlocks were attached by couples as a token of love to a lamp-post on the bridge with the keys thrown into the Tiber. On 13 April 2007 the sheer weight caused the post to collapse. Since then, locks have been attached all over the bridge, including litter bins. The mayor had some steel columns erected for the purpose, but by 2012 it was thought that all this increased weight would cause the old bridge to collapse. The authorities decided to remove all padlocks. Yet the custom has spread to other places in Italy and Europe, and if you feel like locking your love without the weight, there's even an online version at www.lucchettipontemilvio.com.

When it comes to marital compatibility, Indians consult the zodiac. If a bride is born as a *manglik*, or Mars-bearing, superstition dictates that she is cursed and will cause her husband's early death. A Hindu custom designed to break the curse requires the bride to *marry* a peepal or a banana tree (I'm not making this up). After she's married the tree, it is cut down and destroyed and the curse is broken. Alternatively, she can marry a silver or golden idol of the Hindu god Vishnu (which must be a relief for Indian forestry management).

Apparently this bizarre custom is illegal under the Indian constitution, and marrying a tree is perceived to promote a tradition associated with the caste system and untouchability. Tree marriage is believed to violate the rights of women, to say nothing of the doomed trees. A lawsuit is said to have been filed against Indian movie star Aishwarya Rai, a former Miss World, following her marriage to Bollywood star Abhishek Bachchan – though it is unclear how and where the story of her allegedly marrying a tree in order to overcome their astrological incompatibility originated and it has never been proven to be true. Human rights activists were reported to demand she and her family publicly apologise for promoting the caste system, though her father-in-law told the *Times of India* the only person Aishwarya married 'is my son'.

Reflecting their challenging and heroic history, many Russian couples still choose to have their marriage ceremony by the Kremlin wall in Moscow at the tomb of the unknown soldier, the memorial dedicated to Soviet soldiers killed during WWII. Even if they are not actually married there, many engaged Russian couples visit the site to pay homage to those who gave their lives for them. In London's Westminster Abbey, royal brides now have their bouquets laid on the UK's tomb of the unknown warrior on the day following the wedding when all the official wedding photographs have been taken.

Welsh bridegrooms have a tradition of presenting their brides with a carved wooden spoon. The message this presents is that hopefully the couple will never be hungry.

When we look at some of the bizarre demands made of women in various cultures then it shouldn't surprise us if they become annoyed. A marriage is an emotional ceremony and we might expect the odd tear of joy, but when crying becomes mandatory, as it is for China's Tujia people, it's clear that superstition has yet again intervened to take the edge off happiness. The crying ritual of the Tujia people of south-west China's Sichuan Province insists that, for one month before a wedding, the bride-to-be must weep for an hour every day. Yet she may not cry alone, as other women in her family are encouraged to weep as well.

The history of this odd ritual goes back to a time known as the Warring States Period (475–221 BC). A princess of the Zhao state was to be married into the Yan state. As the princess left for the wedding her mother broke down and began weeping at the bride's feet. Because of this first weepy wedding, countless subsequent brides down the centuries have been required to do the same whether they wanted to or not. If they remain dry-eyed they are ridiculed or considered to be of bad breeding and may even get a thrashing from Mother.

In western Sichuan, the practice became known as *zuo tang* (sitting in the hall). The girl would spend an hour a day crying in a hall and on the tenth day be joined by her mother, before the rest of the female family members would come along and everyone would have a good weep together. The whole rigmarole had its own soundtrack; a special song predictably entitled 'The Crying Marriage'. In times past these brides had little choice about who their suitor might be because the grooms were chosen by specialist matchmakers.

Once the crying had stopped, the girls had one last option – they were allowed to verbally abuse the matchmaker, especially if the bloke they'd picked seemed a complete jerk. No doubt if that was the case, they'd really have something to cry about.

Africa has its *Gerewol* (festival for the ladies), and the Wodaabe people have their own spot on their special calendar for 'wife stealing'. In Niger in September at the end of the rainy season the sexually liberated tribe gathers to celebrate *Gerewol*. Extremely vain tribesmen get dressed up in elaborate costumes with special make-up and perform for their potential mates. When the performance is over, the women get to choose the man they like best. The women can have sex before marriage with any man they choose, and can have as many husbands as they fancy.

In the west we have online dating services such as eHarmony, while Indian seekers of romance have Shagun TV, a channel broadcasting profiles of single people in the hopes that someone will call and express the wish to meet them.

In Australia, if you're stranded in the outback, many miles from the big city's urban mores and manners, meeting the girl or boy of your dreams is a challenge. That's where the 'B & S' balls come in. Bachelor and Spinster events, way out in the bush, offer the opportunity for young men and women to meet up. This may seem romantic but marriage may only be a marginal outcome. These young bush folk often travel hundreds of miles to get together, set up camp and party over the weekend and B & S can stand for 'blokes and sheilas', 'beers and sex' or whatever else might brighten up an outback life. According to Australian reports, however, B & S balls are under pressure from rising insurance costs.

Cynical folk might refer to marriage as a 'burden', but in Finland there's a place called Sonkarjävi where they hold the internationally enjoyed *Eukonkanto*, the wife-carrying championships. Believe it or not, this is a kind of race, an obstacle course, in which your fiancée, wife or partner has to be carried on your back. It has a pretty dark superstitious history based on woodland thieves raiding villages and stealing women, but wife-carrying is now practised in Australia, the USA, Hong Kong, Estonia, the UK and other parts of the world. It even has a category in *Guinness World Records*.

Islam views marriage as a religious obligation. It is seen as a contract between the happy couple and Allah. As with other cultures and religions, marriage traditions are different for each branch or sect of the faith. Unlike the staff responsible for western church marriages, Islam has no official clergy to officiate. But as long as a guest or friend has a full understanding of Islam and what is required, they can run the ceremony. Many use marriage officers, a mosque elder called the *qazi* or *madhun*, although Muslims in general are not always married in a mosque.

Initially, men and women are separated during the ceremony. Part of the marriage contract is a statement from the groom to the bride informing her of how much he is giving her as a gift. This is known as the *meher*. The marriage ceremonies are completed with the *Nikah*, according to civil and religious law, with two male witnesses to sign the contract. Words are spoken, such as the bride saying 'I, [name] offer you myself in marriage in accordance with the instructions of the holy Qur'an and the holy prophet, peace and blessing be upon him. I pledge, in honesty and with sincerity, to be for you an obedient and faithful wife.'

The groom will say, 'I pledge, in honesty and sincerity, to be for you a faithful and helpful husband.' The blessing will include a recitation of the first chapter of the Qur'an. The couple may then share a small piece of fruit, such as a date, and happiness can proceed.

Old, new, borrowed and blue

When it comes to available research and publications about folklore, myth and legend, we are well-served in the twenty-first century with diverse sources. However, tribute should be paid to those academics and others who, over a century ago, took enough interest in these subjects to collect and preserve tales and traditions that we today may take for granted.

When looking into wedding rituals and superstitions, two names in particular are worthy of mention: Alfred Trübner Nutt (1856–1910) and Australia's Joseph Jacobs (1854–1916). Together these ardent folklorists spent a great deal of time tracking down the quaint origins of superstitions and fairy tales. Nutt was elected president of the Folklore Society in 1897 and founded *The Folklore Journal* (now *Folklore*). Australian folklorist, literary critic and historian Joseph Jacobs was a writer of English literature who collected and published what would become some of the world's best-known versions of fairytales, including *Jack and the Beanstalk, Goldilocks and the Three Bears, The Three Little Pigs* and others. So when we think back to the popular tales we heard in our rosy childhoods, spare a thought for Nutt and Jacobs. Here's what this dedicated duo had to say in *Folklore* in 1898, about a little rhyme that is undoubtedly recited somewhere in the world every day of the week:

> Something old,
> Something new,
> Something borrowed,
> Something blue.

There is a fifth line to this which today seems obsolete: 'and a silver sixpence in her shoe'.

In this country an old couplet directs that the bride shall wear, 'Something old, something new, something borrowed, something blue.' The 'something blue', I am given to understand, usually takes the form of a garter, an article of dress which plays an important part in some wedding rites as, for instance, in the old custom of plucking off the garter of the bride. The 'something old' and 'something blue' are devices to baffle the evil eye. The usual effect on the bride of the evil eye is to render her fertility to the bride.

This appears to be a British custom, and the four objects added to a bride's wedding outfit are good-luck charms. They can be tokens of love from the bride's relatives, particularly the mother, sister and bridesmaids. The items are presented just prior to the ceremony. A bride can also choose her own lucky charms. Today, 'something old' signifies continuity, 'something new' a positive future, 'something borrowed' can mean borrowing some item – perhaps a piece of jewellery – from friends or relatives who have enjoyed happiness, and 'something blue' symbolises purity, love and fidelity. Since decimalisation, the old 'silver sixpence' is a rarity, but if you have one in your shoe it will stand for fortune and prosperity.

Why do brides wear veils at their wedding? Veils have a long history and their use in weddings may have come into Europe during the period of the crusades. However, the veil and the bouquet that a bride carries could predate the wearing of white. Once again, the ancient Greek and Roman fear of evil spirits and demons comes into play. Before virginal white became the norm, dressing in brightly coloured fabrics such as red and wearing a veil was thought to divert the attention of evil spirits from the bride. Some veils restricted the bride's vision and this was why her father or another person gave her away. The last thing a girl needed was to trip up or collide with something on her walk down the aisle. Bridesmaids wore similar dresses to serve as further decoys for the bride.

In the fifteenth century, crusaders brought back some Eastern customs. The bride was often the subject of a bargain conducted by her father and was only revealed to her husband after the ceremony. Brides also wore orange blossom wreaths in their hair on top of the veil, a fashion which may have led to the tiara some brides wear today. A Muslim girl had to hide her face under her yashmak and, even after the wedding party, her beauty and charm had to remain hidden. In Europe the idea of the veil eventually became the symbol of modesty and purity.

Why is a bride carried over the threshold? This seems to be another medieval custom, based on the superstition that evil spirits could enter the bride through the soles of her feet. She may also have been carried because it was thought that if she tripped on the threshold it would be an omen of bad luck. There is a possible Greek origin in which the girl's love of living in her father's house and her reluctance to leave had to be subdued by the groom literally taking her over the threshold into her new abode. Many ancient marriages were imposed on women who had been kidnapped, and this tradition might represent the bride being picked up and transported to a new life, in other words, 'stealing away'. But this probably has echoes in the fact that the bride and groom 'steal away' before all the other guests leave at the reception.

Why the white dress? Although much has been made about the colour white being virginal and representing purity, prior to Queen Victoria's marriage to Prince Albert in 1840, girls tended to wed in the best dress they had, whatever particular colour. The rich went to the altar in the finest gowns, but it was Victoria who set the trend for the all-white ensemble.

After the wedding comes the bane of all church wardens, the confetti. The name comes from the Latin *confectum*, with confetti the plural of the Italian *confetto*, small sweet. The idea of scattering stuff over people as some form of congratulation hails again from ancient Greece, where it was known as *phyllobolia*, the custom of throwing branches, garlands, fruit and other types of plants. However, there it was also used for different types of events, such as public cere-monies of honour and even funerals. In such large crowds – whether celebrating or mourning – perhaps you couldn't reach out as you would wish and embrace the subject of the procession. Instead, you could bestow some token, such as flower petals or cereals, and at least you were making a connection. In effect, you were throwing handfuls of love, respect, honour or good wishes.

Today, you can keep your vicar happy by not buying the paper confetti but spending a little more on a few bags of dried flower petals. At least they'll do some good in the churchyard.

It's always a great honour and privilege to be asked to become the best man. Before marriage became the more civilised process it is today, men often had to forcefully take their future wives, sometimes by kidnap, particularly if her family disapproved. It was handy to have some help from a trusted friend. The best man tradition may have originated with the Germanic Goths. It was their custom to marry a woman from within the husband's own community. The subject of wedding cakes seems prosaic enough, but yet again this tradition has a colourful past. For example, as with confetti, the Romans would crumble some of their flat, round, fertility-inducing nut-and-fruit wedding cakes and throw the crumbs over the happy couple. Cutting the cake together was a demonstration by the couple of their intention to share everything in life.

Everyone getting a slice of the cake later is a tradition probably started by the Chinese to bestow good luck on everyone involved with the wedding. It is bad luck to refuse a slice of cake for both you and the newlyweds.

If a girl attending the wedding wanted to visualise her future husband in a dream, the best method was to keep her slice of cake and put it under her pillow.

If you've ever wondered why wedding cakes have become elaborate, three-tiered constructions, it has been suggested that the inspiration is the delicate architecture of Wren's attractive St Bride's church in London's Fleet Street.

Finally, there was one ancient English tradition that each wedding guest should bring their own bit of patisserie – a bun or something similar. These offerings would be piled up and the bride and groom would stand at either side of the heap. Providing they could lean towards one another and kiss across the bun-feast without knocking it over, they were in for a long and lucky marriage.

Why are engagement and wedding rings worn on the fourth finger of the left hand? The Romans once believed the vein in this finger went directly to the heart. In medieval times, bridegrooms placed the ring on three of the bride's fingers in turn, symbolising the trinity; God the father, God the son and God the holy spirit.

Today, we have flowers in the bridal bouquet, but in ages past women carried aromatic bunches of garlic, herbs and grains to protect against evil. As people imagined they were becoming less superstitious and as the pong of garlic was hardly conducive to romance, flowers replaced the herbs as they smelled better and symbolised everlasting love and fertility.

A groom wears a flower in his buttonhole in a nod to the days when a knight wore his lady's colours into battle.

The practice we know as the honeymoon originated with the Teutonic people, who liked to have their weddings beneath the full moon. For the full cycle of the moon, thirty days – a period now regarded as a month – following the wedding the bride and groom would drink honey wine.

The lucky chimney sweep

Like many of us today who still have a fireplace, the pagans associated the domestic hearth and the fire with good fortune. This tradition continued into Christian times. The irons used at the fireplace – the pokers, rakes and shovels – were part of the household goods a bride would receive upon marriage. They were a symbol of her new family connections and her new home.

When coal came into use as a regular fuel, it came with its own lucky superstitions and small nuggets of it would be carried by sailors at sea as a link to hearth and home as well as by soldiers who hoped it would help them survive battles. It can also be carried over the threshold for good luck on New Year's Eve.

Therefore, the man who cleaned your chimney – the chimney sweep, with his sooty face and often cheerful persona – became associated with good fortune. Seeing a sweep on your wedding day was a positive omen and even more so if the sweep wished you all the best. There is a legend that a chimney sweep saved the life of King George III by regaining control of his carriage and calming his unruly horse. The king is said to have proclaimed through a royal decree that chimney sweeps were bearers of good luck and fortune, suggesting that the sooty saviours should be invited to weddings and festivals.

Two centuries later, before the wedding of the future queen, then Princess Elizabeth, and Prince Philip, Duke of Edinburgh, on 20 November 1947 at Westminster Abbey, the royal couple were fortunate to get a lucky send-off on their nuptials in front of Kensington Palace from the royal chimney sweep. George III's decree was still recognised as Philip shook the man's sooty hand for good luck and fertility. This tradition has remained popular, and there are plenty of wedding sweep hire services available today that couples can book for their big day. And let's not forget – Dick Van Dyke's chirpy, cod-Cockney sweep certainly brought good luck to the production of *Mary Poppins* (USA, 1964).

Death

If you don't know how to die, don't worry; nature will tell you what to do on the spot, fully and adequately. She will do this job perfectly for you; don't bother your head about it.

Michel de Montaigne (1533–1592), philosopher

Superstitions don't bother dead people. They've gone beyond and, hopefully, wherever and whatever the 'beyond' is, they'll be enjoying some happy relief. Yet as Steve Jobs remarked, 'Even people who want to go to heaven don't want to die to get there.' The superstitions about death only concern the folk around the coffin.

Perhaps no species on earth is more hung up on death than the human race. I have watched cats at the end of their lives, going off into some remote garden corner, knowing it's time to die. Elephants know where their graveyard is. A hedgehog risks crossing a road; *splat*. Abattoirs work around the clock. For animals, life is a blaze of existence and death seemingly comes as naturally as their next meal. But for us wound-up, introspective humans, death is the big final act and, as I'm doing right now, we write about it, ponder over it and, ever since we crawled from the prehistoric ocean, we've surrounded the subject with religious constructs and superstition.

When we are in our twenties or thirties, mortality is something we tend not to think of unless we witness a death. Yet once we've been lucky enough to live past that biblical three-score-and-ten we suddenly realise that the calendar ahead of us is far, far shorter than the one behind.

Perhaps the reason why there is so much superstition around death is down to the fact that, until relatively recently, human life was very short. It was not until the nineteenth century in Europe that we saw the age of the demographic transition from high birth and death rates to low ones. Health slowly improved and populations lived longer, while epidemics like smallpox, typhoid and cholera gradually subsided. In the Middle Ages, men and women were lucky to live to thirty-five. The average life expectancy for a male child born in Britain between 1276 and 1300 was 31.3 years. A man in his fifties would be considered ancient. War, hard physical toil and the plague also cheapened human life. Surrounded by your friends and family dropping like flies, it is hardly surprising that superstition was rife.

As to the idea of an afterlife or a heaven, its origins are vague. When did primitive humanity decide that there was 'something else' beyond life? One suggestion is that perhaps dreams that included the departed may have convinced them that those people were indeed alive in some other mystical dimension. In a much harsher environment, this would have been a great comfort and the idea of an afterlife would have spread rapidly.

There is also uncertainty as to when we began to bury the dead. Skeletons have been found in caves from the Neanderthal period, which would indicate that the practice of burial had not yet begun. However, the unpleasant process of decomposition, and a respect for the dead, must have eventually inspired the common sense of putting a corpse beneath the ground.

It's your (superstitious) funeral

The Victorians appear to have enjoyed the drama of death with a series of grim superstitious moves. Some of these routines still survive today. Clocks in the house would be stopped at the time of death and all curtains drawn. Any framed photos in the house of family or friends would be laid face-down so that the spirit of the dead couldn't enter them. To prevent the deceased's spirit from getting trapped in a mirror these were covered with a black veil or cloth; this superstition dates back to the sixteenth century and the fear that your reflection embodied your soul. When, at the point of death, the soul escaped the body it might be trapped within the mirror and the devil would spirit it away. The Victorians believed that seeing your own reflection in a mirror in a room in which a recent death had occurred, indicated your own impending death.

To inform your neighbours and others that there was a death in the house, a wreath of laurel, yew or boxwood tied with black ribbons was hung on the front door.

It was common practice for Americans and Europeans to carry their dead from the dwelling feet first. This would stop the spirit from having one more look in his home and asking another family member to join him.

Although burial is a more dramatic, open-air ceremony, today, cremation of the dead is increasingly popular. The Bible is not clear on cremation, but it was not always popular in Christian countries, because of the belief in the physical resurrection of the body – no body meant no resurrection, and in 789 Charlemagne made cremation a crime punishable by death. However, the number of corpses in history from plagues and battles often resulted in cremation being the only solution, if only for such emergency situations. Without cremation there was always a chance, following epidemics, of disease spreading.

In Vienna in 1873, Professor Brunetti of Padua, Italy, impressed visiting Sir Henry Thompson, surgeon to Queen Victoria, with his all-new cremation apparatus. Thompson was convinced by cremation as a healthier way of disposing of the departed and recommended it as such when he returned home. The following year Thompson founded the Cremation Society of England, an organisation vigorously opposed by both the government and the Church, who refused the practice on consecrated ground. It seems apt therefore that it was a Welsh druid, Doctor William Price (1800–1893), considered to be a pagan, who finally broke this embargo. In 1884 he cremated his dead baby son, reciting pagan prayers, and was arrested and put on trial. Price argued that there was no existing legislation placing it outside the law. This eventually led to the Cremation Act of 1902.

In Manchester in 1892 one of the first cremation companies was established, with another formed at Maryhill, Glasgow, in 1895. When the feisty and determined 92-year-old Dr Price was cremated in 1893, the ceremony was attended by 20,000 people.

At my own father's funeral, something archaic and vaguely dramatic happened. Before the coffin was about to pass through the curtains for cremation, six elderly gentlemen, none of whom we recognised, some wearing what I at first thought were masonic sashes, encircled it. They held hands, but did not form an unbroken circle, leaving a gap between two men. A short eulogy to their 'departed brother' ensued, before ivy leaves were placed upon the coffin. The men bowed and then returned to the congregation. I collared their leader after the ceremony, and he explained their presence.

They were members of the Royal Antediluvian Order of Buffaloes. This philanthropic benevolent society, sometimes erroneously referred to as the poor man's Freemasons, has its roots in the theatrical community of the early nineteenth century. I knew my father had held a position in one of their lodges, the True Britons' Lodge in Hull, where he was a 'worthy primo'. Members are known today as 'Buffs' and I found their intervention at Dad's funeral quite moving, particularly because he had initiated me into the organisation in 1962, when I was 19. At the time I had found the order and its numerous superstitious rituals absurdly melodramatic. I was more interested in rock'n'roll, not aprons, sashes, blindfolds and secret passwords. To me it seemed like an old man's dressing-up club, a front for some serious beer drinking. I had only acquiesced to my father's wishes to please him, never attending a lodge again. Yet now, almost a quarter-century later, here were these same men placing ivy leaves on his coffin. The circle they formed had a gap in it to signify that one of their brothers was missing. The drinking club motif remained, however; ivy is associated with the Roman god Bacchus. It was often used in hostelry carvings and hung outside pubs, and the Buffs told us it was associated with good luck, but not everywhere. Apparently, at yuletide in some parts of the UK you need to ensure ivy isn't on its own if you're bringing evergreens into the house and should include holly and mistletoe. The Buffs also told me that day that it would protect my father's departed spirit. I hope it did.

The way we see the departed off on that mysterious journey, how we treat their remains, whether in a wooden box on a funeral pyre or neatly stored in a decorative urn, has many variations.

Superstitions often involve death – that's their down side. When sitting around a fire, if you inadvertently place a log that is in some way coffin-shaped and a burst of flame spits from it, this foretells a death. It is also a bad idea to do your laundry on New Year's Day, as this attracts a superstition that you are washing a member of the family out of your life. A bird fluttering into the house is also an omen that someone is about to die.

The use of plants, especially flowers, on graves probably dates back at least to the sixteenth century. Before that time flowers were often woven into a corpse's shroud to cut down the odour of decomposition. Today we express our grief with flowers in a massive way – witness the acres of floral tributes at the death of Princess Diana or following the murder by Isis of 130 innocent people in Paris in November 2015. However, flowers in graveyards were not always popular with the clergy. In medieval times the local priest or vicar kept his graveyard trimmed by allowing farm animals to graze there. An innocent cow or sheep devouring your floral tribute could be upsetting, as was the fact that some plants were not that efficacious to all herbivores. People would build willow and wicker fences around the graves to protect their relative's final resting place. As cemetery burials became more elaborate, the wealthy bereaved of Victorian times echoed those wicker fences with wrought-iron barriers.

Since the late sixteenth century, strewing flowers on graves has been a popular act of homage to the departed. Yet there were parts of Britain where the practice was severely frowned upon, regarded by some vicars and priests as a pagan ritual.

Sprigs of evergreen shrubs such as box and rosemary were often carried by mourners in the funeral cortège because they did not wilt and they symbolised remembrance. As the coffin was lowered into the ground, the sprigs were thrown in on top of it. The Welsh, however, ensured their dead had a more permanent floral display by planting flowers in the grave's topsoil. If you'd passed away in mid-life, you'd get a rose bush. Babies and small children had primroses, daffodils or violets, and if you'd lived to a ripe old age, they planted rosemary.

By the 1890s, there was resurgence in the popularity of flowers with the appearance of wreaths on graves. The use of wreaths for all manner of seasonal celebrations and events dates back to ancient Greece, and today they've become more common as a Christmas decoration. Until recently, many older people in Britain would not consider a wreath on their front door at Christmas because of its association with funerals.

ASHES TO ASHES

Whether or not you're a plain Dawkinsian atheist with no faith but science, you might agree that having the ashes of your cremated loved ones can provide a poignant memento of that person. You may not regard such a practice as spiritual or perhaps even superstitious, but it can serve some purpose as a reminder of our own mortality.

'Ashes to ashes, dust to dust' is a common phrase at funerals, and it may be possible that the tradition of throwing handfuls of dirt on the coffin as the words are spoken could have originated in ancient Egypt when mourners ceremonially cast sand three times upon the body before it was entombed or buried.

Genesis 3:19 tells believers, 'By the sweat of your face you shall eat bread, till you return to the ground, for out of it you were taken; for you are dust and to dust you shall return.'

Early in Christianity, the priest could provide a 'passport' to the next world for the faithful. This would be a document which included the dead person's name, date of birth and death, proof of baptism and communion. This would be placed in the coffin and would hopefully get them into heaven.

In Islam, the deceased is laid in the grave (without a coffin, if permitted by local law) on his or her right side, facing Mecca. Elaborate markers, tombstones or flowers and mementos are discouraged. Rather, one should humbly remember Allah and his mercy and pray for the deceased.

Cremation is the standard way of disposing of the dead among Hindus, Buddhists and Sikhs. In India, the body is cremated on a funeral pyre whenever possible, and in ancient times a deceased man's widow would be sacrificed alive on the burning pyre with their husband.

Can a man's ashes still have some superstitious power long after his cremation? They did in the case of Joe Hill (1879–1915). Born Joel Emmanuel Hägglund in Gävle, Sweden, and also known as Joseph Hillström, Joe Hill was an American labour activist, songwriter, and member of the Industrial Workers of the World (IWW). On the night of 10 January 1914, Hill sought medical help for a gunshot wound. Apparently, he'd been accused of insulting a man's wife and the husband shot him. Elsewhere in that same town that night two men had been murdered in a grocery store. One of the attackers was shot and Hill, hugely unpopular with the authorities, was immediately tagged as one of the grocery murderers. Witness statements were inconclusive, but Hill's alibi for the night was not accepted. The gun used in the raid was never found. Despite a massive campaign before his trial to exonerate Hill, the incident proved a good excuse for the establishment to see off a legendary union activist and organiser. He was executed by firing squad on 19 November the following year.

On the eve of his execution his last words to fellow workers were, 'Don't waste time mourning, organise!' That same night he wrote a poem, one verse of which read:

> *My body? – Oh! –If I could choose*
> *I would to ashes it reduce*
> *And let the merry breezes blow*
> *My dust to where some flowers grow.*

Hill became a labour folk hero and a martyr to his cause. His body was cremated in Chicago and some of his ashes were released to the winds on May Day 1916. The rest were placed into 600 small envelopes and sent around the world to IWW supporters and fellow socialists. Not all of them reached their destination. In 1988 it was discovered that an envelope of ashes had been seized by the US Post Office in 1917 because of its 'subversive potential'. The envelope was captioned 'Joe Hill murdered by the capitalist class, 19 November 1915.' This odd memento found its way into the US National Archives and this was reported in the *New Yorker* magazine and the United Auto Workers' journal *Solidarity*.

Up in arms, the IWW in Chicago began proceedings to reclaim the ashes, and they were duly returned to them later in 1988. The following year, American political and social activist and anarchist Abbie Hoffman suggested that the ashes should be 'eaten' by new 'Joe Hills' such as the UK protest singer Billy Bragg and US singer-songwriter Michelle Shocked. Bragg took Hoffman's cynical suggestion to heart and ate some of Hill's ashes, washed down with some Union Beer. Michelle Shocked's portion of the ashes ended up with Otis Gibbs, an American country singer-songwriter who made the album *Joe Hill's Ashes* in 2010. So, even a dead man's ashes have some lingering superstitious power after all.

Direction of burial

Ancient beliefs dictate the way we are laid to rest. Traditionally, Christianity prefers the burial of bodies in an east–west position – heads to the west and feet to the east. This may originate with pagan sun-worshippers. The Jewish departed are buried facing east in order to face the Last Trump – not 'The Donald': this is the last trumpet, a Jewish idiom for Rosh Hashanah. Genesis 22 is the primary Torah reading for Rosh Hashanah. Abraham was to offer his son Isaac on the altar, an angel intervened and Abraham spotted a male sheep, a ram, caught in the nearby thicket. This was seen as a representation of the sins of humanity. The two horns of the ram were named, the left one as the first trump and the right the last trump. The *shofar* (a ram's horn/trumpet) was seen to play a significant role in the redemption.

Before the time of the religions of the book, it was expected that the body would face the rising sun, an important aspect of pagan sun cults.

Australia's aborigines believe that the sun will rise late in the morning if the dead are not buried with their faces to the west.

CLOSING EYES

A very superstitious reason explains the way in which we adopted the practicality of closing the eyes of a dead person. An open-eyed corpse looking at you was a threat to you and your family. To overcome this, pennies were placed over the eyelids to ensure they were closed. Today, knowing rigor mortis affects the eyes soon after death, we simply close the eyelids down before it sets in. The Greeks and Romans placed a coin inside the mouth (or in the hand) so that the departed soul could pay the ferryman across the river Styx into the afterlife. Without this ticket money he'd have to wait a hundred years to get across. There was a similar tradition in the north of England and Wales, where the coin was supposed to be presented to St Peter once you arrived at the pearly gates and the well-prepared Chinese have been known to bury their loved ones fully equipped with travel currency and even their passports.

THE WAKE

When we have a wake for some departed relative or friend we think of having a few drinks or more and remembering the life of the departed. But this is not the original meaning of a wake. In Victorian times someone sat with the body continually until the time of the burial, not least because it was thought by some to safeguard against burying someone who was not dead (people in a coma often appear dead and could wake up), and, naturally, sitting by the coffin around the clock you'd stay alert, hence the term 'waking'. Surrounded by candles and flowers to mask any unpleasant odours, the body was watched over every minute until burial. In days when travel was more difficult, wakes could last up to five days to allow distant relatives time to get to the funeral. The wake also served as an act of devotion and remembrance.

Anyone who has read the works of Edgar Allan Poe will be familiar with the horror of the premature burial. In the eighteenth and nineteenth centuries this was a widespread fear. Many strange inventions were utilised to warn those left behind if their departed suddenly became conscious again. Odd periscope-type devices were made, utilising mirrors in tubes so that you could look down into the coffin and see the state of the corpse – if decomposition had set in then the chances were he was definitely dead. If not . . .

The most popular device, the safety coffin, was equipped with a coffin bell. The poor corpse had a rope in its hand attached to a bell above the grave. If it awoke, it gave a tug to sound the alarm and, hopefully, if some terrified nearby gravedigger didn't suffer cardiac arrest, they'd come and dig you up.

As an alternative to burial or cremation, there is a tradition among some tribes in Africa of 'smoking' the corpse. For example, Congolese people have been known to keep a fire burning for up to a month above the grave. When the corpse is exhumed, it has become well and truly 'kippered' and is then tightly swathed in lengths of cloth, taken back to the deceased's original home hut and stood in the corner where it can remain for decades to come. A similar practice operates among the Anga tribe of Papua New Guinea's Morobe Highlands. They also smoke cure their dead, placing the bodies on cliffs around the village so they can keep an eye on the living.

Buddhists believe in reincarnation and a funeral is a happy event for them. It frees the soul from the trials of a worldly existence and sets it on the road to nirvana. Depending on the branch of Buddhism, the coffin is taken around the temple three times and may be set down on a bed of flowers surrounded by the mourner's gifts. A monk will read the 'Three Jewels' prayer (seeking refuge in the Buddha, the Dharma – the true Buddhist way of life – and the Sangha, the unity of faith). There's lots of food and music and then cremation, with the ashes preserved in an urn.

Cremation was also the way the Vikings said goodbye to their dead. Their spirits would be carried to heaven in the smoke from the funeral pyre. Afterlife destinations included Valhalla – the place for heroes and those who had lived a good life – and Helheim for those who were not so heroic – even dying innocently of old age could send you to Helheim. The ashes were buried in graves or under piles of rocks along with the deceased's goods and belongings. Like us, the Vikings had graveyards and kept all their dead in one location. The common image of a Viking funeral we have today is of the body being sent out to sea in a blazing longboat, but this was comparatively rare and reserved only for people of great importance. Viking ships were expensive, requiring great skill and a long time to build, and unless you were famous, truly heroic and very rich, such a dramatic funeral was unlikely.

Curse by glamour: Hollywood

In Hollywood, brides keep the bouquets and throw away the groom.

Groucho Marx (1890–1977)

The word 'curse' has long been associated with the supernatural, religion and superstition. According to the *Oxford English Dictionary*, it has several meanings, such as, 'a solemn utterance intended to invoke a supernatural power to inflict harm or punishment on someone or something' or a 'cause of harm or misery'. It's the weapon of choice of witches and wizards. We also use many expletives that are regarded as 'curse' words. But when it comes to superstition, a curse is a result of an individual or group of people innocently or deliberately transgressing some supernatural rule that may result in a series of mishaps, their suffering or even, as many connoisseurs of the unexplained believe, their death.

If you're in the high-profile celebrity bracket, any hint of a curse gets the rumour machine running. For example, there's a rumour about actor Billy Bob Thornton. It suggests that if you've starred with him in a film, then you could suffer an untimely death. If you believe this, you may have been influenced by the fact that Patrick Swayze, Heath Ledger, John Ritter and Bernie Mac suffered this fate and that other Thornton co-stars Shia LaBeouf and Morgan Freeman were seriously injured in separate car accidents. How these superstitions start is a mystery. Looking at this logically, as we're not immortal, then you could say that once we've reached a certain age, everyone around us is bound to die. Does this mean that as individuals we're each the hub of some weird curse? Of course not. And anyone can have a car accident, even people you associate with. But as we shall see, there's much more of this wacky stuff. It makes for good little fillers in celebrity magazines.

When you live your working life in a dream factory, spending your time in character as anyone from a serial killer to a Roman emperor, it must have some effect on your mind. Actors, screenwriters, directors and producers are as prone to superstition and ritual as the rest of us, but the heady romantic air of show business can only enhance the condition and in some prominent cases the results can be very peculiar. Balmy, seemingly un-spooky and sun-kissed though southern California is, it even has a place called the Superstition Hills, a low mountain range in the Colorado Desert, in western Imperial County, southern California.

Even the name 'Hollywood' has an unusual origin. California holly, also known as the Christmas berry (*Heteromeles arbutifolia*), enhances the landscape of the Santa Monica mountains. It has nice red berries in the autumn and winter and a special display of attractive white summer flowers. It can grow over sixteen feet tall and it's easy to cultivate with the California sun and infrequent water. Known locally as 'toyon', in the house it's very decorative for the yuletide season. Like the European holly, it has its superstitions – it is said to keep evil spirits away and bring good luck. That's not to say that Hollywood, under its more derogatory designation, Tinseltown, is bereft of evil spirits or awash with good fortune. Many of those dreaming of the silver screen have ended up pumping gas and parking cars, and many studio heads could give Hitler and Mussolini a good run for their money.

Originally, the place was known as Holly Canyon, and in 1860, the golden age of 'Go west, young man', an immigrant from Odense in Denmark, Ivar A. Weid (1837–1903), arrived. After serving in the Union army during the civil war, Ivar Weid moved to California where he acquired 640 acres of government and railroad land. In the late 1880s he sold some of the land at a thousand dollars an acre, reinvesting the cash in city property. The area Weid lived in became known as Weid Canyon, and, inspired by the holly trees and the beauty of their berries, he is claimed to have renamed the area Hollywood.

Alternatively, the name is associated with H. J. Whitley, who bought 500 acres of land, becoming known as the 'father of Hollywood.' Some sources say that Whitley and his wife, Gigi, came up with the name while on their honeymoon in 1886.

Another claimant is a friend of a friend of Weid's, Daeida Wilcox, who is supposed to have co-opted the name. Beyond this being a fascinating story, it matters little, other than that the 'toyon', or California holly bush, certainly appears to have been very lucky for all of these entrepreneurial pioneers.

By the 1920s, however, collecting the bush's branches had become so widespread in Los Angeles that the state legislature passed a law (Penal Code 384a) forbidding its collection on public land or on any land not owned by the person picking the plant without the landowner's written permission.

California has always been a melting pot for speculators, adventurers, entrepreneurs and, above all, entertainers. It continues to have a very high concentration of the latter. In a world in which you're living on dreams and looking for luck, a good shaman or psychic should give you some comfort. If so, Hollywood, with all its superstition-mongers, is the place.

Sylvester Stallone comes over on TV chat shows as a sound character, good-humoured, a man who doesn't take his projected celluloid images too seriously. His amazing mother, Jackie, still pumping iron in the gym in her mid-nineties, has a different reputation as one of America's top astrologers. She predicted that Sylvester would be a writer, and he believes in his mother's 'craft' to such a degree that he and his wife ensured their son Sage, for the sake of intelligence, would be a Taurus with Libra moon and Leo rising. Sadly, Sage Stallone died of heart failure aged thirty-six in 2012. Tragedy has no respect for fame or celebrity.

Did astrology work for Sly? In some ways, yes. One astrologer warned him against being near heavy machinery and, when he was working out in the gym, a 300-pound bench press fell on him, severing a muscle.

Jackie Stallone's menu of astrological and psychic services now includes a fashionable new pseudoscience akin to physiognomy: rumpology. This involves fortune telling by studying someone's buttocks. One might suppose that, depending upon whose backside you're examining, this could prove to be a much more interesting pastime than palmistry. Rumpology examines your fleshy seating area, the crevice between, and any dimples, warts or other unusual buttography. Mrs Stallone claims that ancient civilisations from the Romans and Greeks and way back to the Babylonians all practised bum-reading.

If you're European and a bit embarrassed by someone looking at your naked derrière, head for Meldorf in Germany where you can check in with blind rump-reader Ulf Buck. He's an arse-trologer who does it all just by feel (http://skepdic. com/rumpology.html).

In the UK, the supreme derrière detective is Sam Amos, and you can get to the bottom of this subject at her entertaining web site www.psychicsam.com. A shower, some deodorant and a pair of clean knickers would seem to be *de rigueur* if you decide to book a session, and it would be good manners to avoid that vindaloo the night before.

The entertaining Stallones and their rump-reading friends seem to be among Hollywood's luckier characters. But stories of the curses suffered by others in the industry take on various forms.

THE OSCAR CURSE OF 'LOST LOVE'

Probably just as many relationships and marriages fail in Hollywood with or without the presentation of an Academy Award. However, superstition or not, it is remarkable that numerous high-profile female actors end up with divorce papers on the mantelpiece alongside that golden statuette.

Anyone with the time and patience to look up female celebrity break-ups on-line will be amazed at how many seemingly firm, devoted marriages and relationships over the past half-century have buckled under the pressures of cinematic life. It appears to happen to Oscar winners, usually female stars. What's become known as 'the lady Oscar curse' even gave the USA its only divorced president. In 1940, actress Jane Wyman married future president Ronald Reagan. In 1948 she won an Oscar for her role in *Johnny Belinda* (USA, 1948). Wyman and Ronnie were divorced the same year. Reagan reportedly quipped to a friend, 'Maybe I should name Johnny Belinda as co-respondent.' Since then there have been many other similar examples. However, these only seem like a 'curse' if you make a list of all the break-ups, and where's the list of male Oscar-winning love cheats? The more likely reason for such domestic splits is the pressurised nature of an occupation where glamour is everything, with your every move tracked by the paparazzi.

The Superman curse

Frank Miller, author of *Batman: The Dark Knight Returns*, *Daredevil* and *Sin City*, stated, 'If people can't stand cartoons about religion, they've got a problem.' Perhaps he was making a reference to the offence some graphic artists have caused to certain branches of faith. Many religious people have a problem about comic-book superheroes. After all, their powers seem almost God-like and their only redeeming factor is that they are usually on the side of the law and the righteous.

When asked what he stands for, Superman tells us 'truth, justice, and the American way.' The 'S' on his manly chest, however, isn't seen as benign by everyone. Followers of David Icke see it as a curled serpent, but as almost every other major figure in the world is claimed by the Ickettes to be a shape-shifting lizard, that's hardly surprising.

Yet perhaps those of faith might be surprised to discover, if indeed they had the time to spare to read as many comic books as possible, that, according to the informative detail on the comic-book fan website www.ComicBookReligion.com, most of the latex-clad, masked and cloaked guardians of humanity do indeed have a faith. Here are a few examples:

Protestants include Spider-Man and Captain America. Batman is listed as 'Episcopalian/Catholic (lapsed)', the Incredible Hulk is also a lapsed Catholic and the same church of Rome can rely on Nightcrawler and Daredevil. Wonder Woman and Aquaman appear as acolytes of a Greco-Roman classical religion. The Atom is Jewish (lapsed), Shadowcat and the Thing are listed as Jewish, and, topping the holy super-league, is Superman; the man of steel is a Methodist.

Due to the modern wonders of CGI this branch of comic-book infantilism has gone way past the printed page stage to the point where Hollywood is spending mega-millions on any caped crusader movie screenplay which comes in. *Iron Man*, *Captain America*, even Thor is in on the act and Spider-Man's web keeps on expanding. But back in the clunky monochrome 1950s, a sequence of odd events began when actor George Reeves (1914–1959) pulled his underpants over his tights as Superman. If the good Lord is against superheroes, then evidence of this lies with the often repeated Hollywood catalogue of dark superstition surrounding Superman.

DC Comics, which owns Superman, has been publishing his comic-book adventures since 1938. Before George Reeves, the first actor to portray the man in the red cape was bit-part, ex-Broadway player Kirk Alyn (1910–1999). *Superman* (USA, 1948) was a fifteen-episode, live-action serial. It told the familiar story of the man of steel's arrival on earth and getting his job as Clark Kent at the *Daily Planet*, where he meets his new friends Lois Lane and Jimmy Olsen. In the first screen outing, Superman does battle with the evil super-heroine, Spider Lady. In 1950, Alyn reprised the role, this time battling ace villain Lex Luthor in a series entitled *Atom Man vs Superman*. I remember it well from the ABC Minors Saturday matinees. I too wore my swimming trunks over my pants and as a cape my dad gave me the flag of South Africa.

George Reeves was a hero. But if any misfortune was to enter his predecessor Kirk Alyn's life, it would never match that of Reeves. Believers in the Superman curse say that after playing Superman, Kirk Alyn's career bombed. Yet, while he was no George Clooney or Brad Pitt, that's not quite true. He made the movie serial *Blackhawk* in 1952 and had several other roles and even played Lois Lane's father in the big-budget 1978 *Superman* (USA) film. His final role was in the 1983 horror movie *Scalps* (USA), and he played himself in the 1988 TV show *Superman Fiftieth Anniversary Special*. And, let's face it – he lived to be eighty-eight.

For a showbiz curse of this kind to gain some traction, it needs consistent, dramatic deadly high points. Everyone points to George Reeves' controversial death by shooting and the tragic paralysis suffered due to a horse-riding accident by probably the greatest of all Superman actors, the late Christopher Reeve (1952–2004; and, no, he wasn't, as some imagine, George Reeves' son).

George Reeves had flown into the role when Alyn was offered the part in the subsequent television series but turned it down. Reeves had been a high-school actor and later a heavyweight boxer who gave up the ring to preserve his good looks. He played the role in the 1951 film *Superman and the Mole Men* (USA), followed by the TV series which ran from 1952 to 1958, *The Adventures of Superman*. Yet popular though he was, once George had hung up his tights he found sustaining his star status difficult. When you've spent eight years leaping over buildings and throwing cars around, people find it difficult to see you as an ordinary Joe.

His fans weren't keen on seeing the man who'd played Superman in a war film, but his acting was fine as Sergeant Maylon Stark in 1953's *From Here to Eternity*

(USA). It is suggested in Allen Coulter's 2006 film, *Hollywoodland* (USA), starring Ben Affleck as George Reeves, that the ex-Superman had his part in the later movie drastically reduced. But this, with so many of these tales, is only a rumour.

The curse took on its sinister aspect after Reeves was found dead in his bedroom on 16 June 1959 from a gunshot wound. Some imaginative websites will tell you that Reeves 'went mad' and jumped out of a window, believing he could fly. The cause of death has officially been registered as a suicide, but a conspiracy theory suggested that he'd been murdered. By whom and for what reason remains unclear. Was Reeves depressed? It seems doubtful. At the time of his death, the show's main sponsor, Kellogg's, had beefed up the budget and another season of scripts had been commissioned for filming later that year. There was even a movie planned, *Superman and the Secret Planet*, the script already written by Jackson Gillis (1916–2010), who would go on to give us *Perry Mason*, *Lost in Space*, *Hawaii Five-O* and *Knight Rider*. In addition, Reeves had also signed to direct a movie in Spain. Hardly the scenario to inspire suicide but, then again, what do we know?

As well as Kirk Alyn, who enjoyed his long life, two other actors who played Superman, Bud Collyer (1908–1969) and Lee Quigley (1976–1991), are always said by conspiracy-mongers to have 'died untimely deaths'. Collyer played Superman on the radio in 1940, later voiced a series of Superman cartoons and had a highly successful showbiz life as a game-show host, although he did die with Alzheimer's disease aged sixty-one. Untimely? Aren't all deaths 'untimely' for those of us left to grieve?

Lee Quigley's is an altogether more tragic case. In the big Christopher Reeve movie in 1978, Quigley, who was British, played the role of the baby Superman, Kal-El, who arrives on earth from the planet Krypton. You don't get a much earlier start in acting than playing a baby, but he never acted again. Quigley died at the age of fourteen after inhaling solvents.

Away from TV and Hollywood, let us not forget the six-foot-four-inch-tall Bob Holiday (b. 1932), who played Superman on Broadway in the acclaimed 1966 Hal Prince musical *It's a Bird, It's a Plane, It's Superman*. Holiday has played the part more than any other Superman actor, in over 140 performances, making many live appearances in character. He is also the oldest surviving, live-action Superman. He went on to be a very successful captain of industry, building holiday homes in Hawley, Pennsylvania. No curse there, then.

It was on 27 May 1995 that Christopher Reeve suffered the terrible riding accident that left him paralysed from the neck down. He died after a well-publicised and heroic struggle on 10 October 2004 from heart failure stemming from his medical condition. His widow, Dana, died from lung cancer two years later aged forty-four. She had never been a smoker. Followers of the 'curse' see this as further proof of dark supernatural influence.

Margot Kidder, the actress who played Lois Lane opposite Christopher Reeve, went missing for four days in 1996 and lived as a homeless person on the street. She was saved by a family who found her in their backyard and was taken to a medical centre where she was diagnosed as bi-polar. Kidder had been involved in a car crash in December 1990, after which she was unable to work for two years, causing her financial problems.

So, if there's a curse, what about subsequent actors who've played the man of steel? Dean Cain (b. 1966) was Superman in the TV series *Lois and Clark: The New Adventures of Superman*. At the time of writing, he seems to be doing OK. The same can be said for Brandon Routh (b. 1979), the star of the 2006 film *Superman Returns* (USA). However, his co-star as Lois Lane, Kate Bosworth (b. 1983), is said by followers of the 'curse' to have blamed her split with Orlando Bloom on her role in the film.

Tom Welling (b. 1977) has been nominated for plenty of awards for playing Clark Kent and Superman in the 2001–2011 TV series *Smallville*. Truth, justice and the American way seem to have served him well, allowing for his divorce in 2015.

The latest recruit for curse-ville is Britain's Henry Cavill (b. 1983). Cavill played Superman in the 2013 film *Man of Steel* (UK/USA), a huge commercial success and the highest-grossing *Superman* film of all time. The world of superheroes seems to be his natural habitat, as he returned in *Batman v Superman: Dawn of Justice* (USA, 2016) and has been named as part of the cast for the upcoming films *Justice League*, parts one and two (USA, planned for 2017 and 2019).

So what does this all amount to? Had Superman actors been remotely superstitious following the suicide/murder (?) of George Reeves, arguably, the man of steel would have remained between the covers of DC Comics, to be overshadowed by the equally muscular *Batman*.

Toxic torment: the curse of the conqueror

Oh people, know that you have committed great sins. If you ask me what proof I have for these words, I say it is because I am the punishment of God. If you had not committed great sins, God would not have sent a punishment like me upon you!

Genghis Khan (1162–1227)

Ill omens and curses may have been the province of witches and superstition in the past, but in the high-octane world of entertainment ordinary men and women can innocently set a curse in motion simply through bad planning and a lack of attention to potential consequences. In retrospect, some will choose to interpret such calamities as supernatural, but often these chains of events are down to simple cause and effect.

In the world of movie making there are a dozen painfully remembered disasters for every classic Oscar-laden hit. *Citizen Kane*, arguably the greatest movie ever made, cursed its creator, Orson Welles, for the rest of his life.

When Terry Gilliam tried filming *Don Quixote*, his unfinished film, *The Man Who Killed Don Quixote*, came to represent the essence of film-making bad luck. On the first day of shooting in 2000, it became clear that the Spanish location, Bardenas Reales, was noisily hampered by nearby NATO aircraft flying on target practice missions. Gilliam forlornly hoped that in post-production he could remove the noise. On the second day of shooting a huge hailstorm and flash flood ruined equipment and altered the appearance of the location, preventing further scenes from being filmed. Then the film's elderly star, Jean Rochefort (b. 1930), suffered a herniated disc and had to leave the set. The dream was over and a fifteen-million-dollar insurance claim ensued.

Yet Gilliam got over this debacle. Compared to a much bigger movie made forty-six years earlier, his problems were minimal. *The Conqueror* (USA, 1956) was to be the epic story of Temujin, who would become better known as twelfth-century warlord Genghis Khan. The man who bankrolled this disaster would also have his own life filmed in 2004 as *The Aviator* (USA), starring Leonardo de Caprio. Billionaire industrialist Howard Hughes (1905–1976) not only built airplanes but loved movies, and his massive wealth allowed him to indulge his passion.

Starring in *The Conqueror* would appeal to an actor of epic stature. Despite his non-Mongolian looks, John Wayne imagined he was born to be a cinematic Genghis Khan. The costly adventure that ensued has gone into Hollywood history as probably the worst, most badly written, directed and miscast turkey ever made. By 1980, ninety-one of the 220-plus crew had been diagnosed with cancer, forty-six of them dying of the affliction (one committing suicide on learning of its severity) that also killed star, director and producer.

John Wayne was a superstitious man. He would fly into a rage if anyone left a hat on a bed; it was an omen of bad luck. Even when dining with his family, no one was allowed to pass the salt to the Duke. It was placed on the table within his reach and only he could pick it up.

He had a particular dislike of suede shoes. Michael Caine tells the story of meeting Wayne in Beverly Hills when the Duke gave him some acting advice, 'Speak low and don't say too fucking much. And never wear suede shoes.' Intrigued, Caine asked why. 'Because one day a guy in the next stall in the toilet recognised me and turned towards me and said. "John Wayne, you're my favourite actor!" And he pissed all over my suede shoes. So don't wear them when you're famous, kid.'

John Wayne didn't have much time for Shakespeare, but he admired Winston Churchill so much he had every book the great man had ever written. He also admired Dickens and in particular *David Copperfield,* to the point that every time he agreed to a business proposal, he would exclaim, 'Barkis is willing!' (this is what Mr Barkis says when announcing his eagerness to marry Peggotty).

Even Wayne could never have imagined what a cinematic rat's nest of ill omens he was entering with *The Conqueror*. In 1955, he had accidentally come across a deliberately discarded, clunky script written by English writer Oscar Millard (1908–1990). Wayne had a vision of potential cinematic immortality in what he wrote.

The screenplay had been intended for Marlon Brando, who had just hit the big time in 1954 with *On the Waterfront* (USA). Brando passed on the opportunity. Dick Powell, the eminent director of RKO pictures, had seen the script for *The Conqueror* and thought its deliberately antediluvian, cod-classical dialogue totally absurd and threw it in his rubbish bin. While he was out of his office, Wayne arrived and retrieved the screenplay. He was impressed. When Powell returned, the Duke was already quoting Millard's lines. Powell pleaded with the big man, but

Wayne was convinced – he would be Genghis Khan, end of story. And as Powell would state later, 'Who was I to turn down John Wayne?'

An epic like *The Conqueror* today would cost upwards of sixty million dollars. Even in the mid-1950s, the movie's budget of six million dollars was enormous. Howard Hughes saw the story as a romantic, sweeping, Cinemascope epic, and the people at RKO (the same studios that made *Citizen Kane*) had to do their master's bidding. Powell now faced the challenge of turning John Wayne into a Mongol warlord.

It was OK in those days to 'black up', so Wayne was plastered with yellow skin make-up, his eyes pulled back with rubber bands to achieve a Mongolian look. As well as nurturing an inscrutably wispy, Fu Manchu-style moustache, he also removed his eyebrows and the make-up department found him some false eyelids. Voila! One Mongolian warlord. Of course, it might have helped if more than two members of the huge cast were actually Asian (and if more than one of them had got a line of dialogue), but this was Hollywood. As for the female lead, any suggestion that the Irish-Swedish, heavily lipstick-ed and pale-faced redhead Susan Hayward, playing Wayne's love interest, Bortai, had never been anywhere near Mongolia was overlooked.

Hayward knew from the start what a barrel of gunge she'd fallen into and spent much of her time between takes bursting into laughter at each line of baroque dialogue. Two years later she'd receive an Oscar for her part in the 1958 film *I Want To Live!* (USA). Other cowpunchers included Lee Van Cleef and John Hoyt, who had starred in the TV western series *Gunsmoke* and must have balked at his role in *The Conqueror*. He'd not only been a part of Orson Welles's Mercury theatre but was an alumni of Yale University and his talents included a superb impression of Noël Coward. Other substitute Mongolians included TV favourites Pedro Armendáriz and Thomas Gomez.

Filming began in May 1954, but not in the sweeping grasslands of Mongolia that Genghis Khan would have recognised. Director Dick Powell opted for Utah's Escalante Valley, which looked nothing like the Gobi desert. The previous year, 135 miles away from the shoot, the US Atomic Energy Commission had exploded eleven nuclear bombs at Yucca Flats in Nevada under the codename Operation Upshot-Knothole. The blasts included a 51-kiloton bomb named Simon and a 32-kiloton bomb called Harry (known later as Dirty Harry). The local town of St

George was coated in grey ash. Whole flocks of sheep died, but the government blamed cold weather.

Between January 1951 and July 1962, a hundred atom bombs were tested in the Nevada desert. These were accompanied by massive and deadly clouds of fallout. Borne on the desert wind, the 1953-fallout dumped on the shooting location of *The Conqueror* – Snow Hill Canyon. None of this bothered the Duke, the rest of the cast or crew. They spent over three months in the area, breathing the deadly dust and drinking the local water. The government said that the area around the town of St George, where the crew were filming, was completely safe. Wayne was so dismissive of any danger he would show visitors to the location the fascinatingly high readings on the Geiger counter. (As he might have drawled, 'Ain't no commie-killin' atoms gonna down a Mongolian cowboy . . .')

Worse still, Howard Hughes thought it would add some visual authenticity to the interior studio shots if he had several truckloads of the radioactive desert earth dumped back on the Hollywood set. Hundreds of animals, including a bear, goats and a panther (not only not native to Mongolia but it attacked Susan Hayward), had to be stabled out in the desert, with Texan longhorn steers doubling for Mongolian oxen. Dozens of the portable huts used by nomads, Mongolian yurts, were constructed in Hollywood and driven out to the desert. A massive army of carpenters and technicians was driven each day in school buses from their motels. For the Mongolian hordes, Native Americans from nearby reservations were hired – ten dollars a day on foot, twelve if you brought your horse.

The end result was not only a critical disaster, but a total embarrassment for all concerned, not least Wayne himself, who later was said to shudder even at the movie's name. The full story of the film is hilariously told in Harry and Michael Medved's book *The Fifty Worst Movies of All Time* (CBS, 1978). There may have been slicker and more expensive disasters since, such as *Batman and Robin* (USA, 1997) or *Battlefield Earth* (USA, 2000), but such films never had the tragic carcinogenic aftermath of *The Conqueror*.

The dialogue alone sends you into paroxysms of laughter. Wayne exclaims at one point, 'While I live, while my blood burns hot, your daughter is not safe in her tent!' A. H. Weller in the *New York Times* wrote, 'This Genghis Khan is merely Hopalong Cassidy in Cathay. Should get a few unintentional laughs.' Another critic quipped that a film couldn't have been miscast any worse if Mickey Rooney had been chosen to play Christ in *King of Kings* (USA, 1961). Wayne wanted to hold the premiere in Moscow, saying it would be a 'peace gesture and cultural tribute', but, after the Russians had seen the film, they turned the offer down.

The man-made curse of the nuclear tests provided a grisly aftermath with the high rates of fatal cancer in the cast and crew. In 1963 Dick Powell died with lymphatic cancer, followed by leading lady Susan Hayward with brain cancer in 1975 and, four years later, John Wayne expired with stomach cancer on 11 June 1979. When Pedro Armendáriz was diagnosed, just after completing *From Russia With Love* in 1963, he committed suicide. Many of the Native Americans who served as Mongolian warriors eventually had cancer and John Wayne's son Michael died from the illness in 2003. As for the five thousand hapless residents of the town of St George, today they are known as the 'downwinders' and their cemetery is filled with the graves of cancer victims, with new victims diagnosed every month. Of course, we could argue that back in 1956 everyone smoked. However, maybe the US government had a lot to answer for. In an article in *People* magazine dated 11 November 1980, a scientist from the Pentagon's defence nuclear agency said, 'Please, God, don't let us have killed John Wayne'.

For weirdo billionaire Howard Hughes, however, *The Conqueror* was one of the two films he watched over and over again in the reclusive darkness of his penthouse suite at the Xanadu Princess Resort hotel in the Bahamas. The other was a Rock Hudson movie, *Ice Station Zebra* (USA, 1968). This strange man ate nothing but chicken and chocolate, surrounded himself with boxes of Kleenex, never took a bath, or used the toilet or cut his nails, and legend has it that at the repeated nightly screenings of *The Conqueror*, his projectionist was made to wear a blindfold. Considering the film today and what it grimly achieved, perhaps that projectionist got the better deal.

Don't mention Mac**** and 'break a leg'!

Out, out, brief candle! Life's but a walking shadow,
a poor player that struts and frets his hour upon the stage
and then is heard no more: it is a tale told by an idiot,
full of sound and fury, signifying nothing.

William Shakespeare (1564–1616), act five, scene five, the 'Scottish Play' (1599–1606)

'Double, double, toil and trouble . . .', 'By the pricking of my thumbs, something wicked this way comes . . .' Ah, the thespian life. Actors are a superstitious bunch. And little wonder.

Acting is like time travel. One night you're a Tudor king, the next a medieval Danish prince or a Roman emperor. Your career can start or end on that stage, so every bit of luck is needed and that means each premonition or omen is respected. That's what drama demands. So here's a few theatre superstitions you'll need to stand by if you ever tread the boards.

Well-wishers should never wish a cast good luck before they go on. 'Break a leg' is the only acceptable substitute. This saying has a variety of possible origins. In ancient Greece theatre audiences didn't applause by clapping hands as we do today. They stamped their feet. So maybe if you stamped very hard there was an increased – if distant – possibility you'd break a leg. In Elizabethan times, the act of bowing was to 'break the leg'. There was a practice in vaudeville of keeping actors just offstage (to 'break the leg' of the curtain was to enter the playing space, and that meant they got paid). Understudies for parts could jokingly say 'break a leg' to the lead players in the vain hope they might do just that, giving the job to the stand-in.

I suppose it's OK now for me to type the word 'Macbeth', but under no circumstances must Shakespeare's play be mentioned outside the performance itself in the theatre. It must always be referred to as either the 'Scottish play 'or the 'bard's play'. Otherwise you're in trouble. The lead character is often referred to as the Scottish king or Scottish lord. In US theatres, the play is often called 'Mackers' or 'MacB' and Lady Macbeth is simply the 'Scottish lady'.

There are stories dating back to the seventeenth century of unexplained deaths and sudden collapses as *Macbeth* was being performed.

It has been said that the three witches' incantations may have been taken by the bard from active witchcraft and that Shakespeare did actually get the routine from a practising witches' coven. When they saw his work performed, they were unhappy with his lines and cursed the play. Alternatively, the theatre prop master in Shakespeare's time purloined a real cauldron from a group of witches and the result was the curse. Other suggestions are that the bard himself placed the curse on the work so that only he could direct it or that he was disappointed by the less than appreciative response to *Macbeth* from King James I and for the rest of his life Shakespeare himself referred to it simply as the 'Scottish play'. We may never know, although some actors, like the late Sir Donald Sinden, disregard the superstition completely.

So, if you do make the error of saying 'Macbeth' in the theatre outside of a rehearsal or performance, what's the antidote? Go outside, spin around three times, spit over your left shoulder and say something rude or vulgar or quote a line from the bard's other works, such as, 'If we shadows have offended,' from *A Midsummer Night's Dream*. And don't forget to say 'Macbeth' three times before you come back in. Who would have thought acting could be so complicated?

The ghost light is another superstition that does have a practical purpose. In ancient Greece the first known actor was Thespis (hence 'thespian'). It's said Thespis still haunts the theatres of the world and can be a disruptive and calamitous influence. When a theatre is 'dark' (empty), a single light is always left on above the upstage centre to ward away any evil power. More practically, when stagehands and staff arrive they can see their way to finding the main light switches.

'Bad dress, good opening' suggests a bad dress rehearsal will become a good opening night. If nothing else, such faith after a bad run-through at least gives actors a glimmer of hope.

Wearing blue is to be avoided, although that isn't such a prominent superstition today. In Shakespeare's time and long before, blue was the most expensive dye for any costume. So some acting companies who were dying the death on stage often added a touch of blue to make the audience and critics think they were better off.

As with sailors on ships, whistling by actors in the theatre is also discouraged. The mechanical aspects of theatre – scenery, ropes, tackles and backstage rigging – often attracted sailors to work in theatres, and they would sometimes quietly signal one another when changing scenes with a whistling code. If anyone whistled who was not involved with shifting, heaving and lowering, this could be misunderstood and an accident could occur.

There have been some actors in the past who believed that you could learn your lines faster if you slept with the script under your pillow. Writers, however, will tell you it doesn't work.

And never give an actor a bouquet of flowers before a performance. It's bad luck. It's OK to shower them with blooms at the curtain call, but before the show it can have a bad effect on the performance.

At the end of the day: superstition or stupid-stition?

> Superstition is a part of the very being of humanity; and when we fancy that we are banishing it altogether, it takes refuge in the strangest nooks and corners, and then suddenly comes forth again, as soon as it believes itself at all safe.

> Johann Wolfgang von Goethe (1749–1832) *The Maxims and Reflections of Goethe*

There are many, many more superstitions which could have been included in this book. We probably missed the one you were most looking for, your particular favourite.

What is it with seven years of bad luck when we break a mirror? Where does that come from? In ancient times, before mirrors were made of silvered glass, they were made from highly polished metal. Naturally, they were unbreakable, probably only suffering a dent if they fell to the floor. The new technology of glass mirror-making opened up in fifteenth-century Venice, where only the very rich could afford a looking-glass and any domestic skivvy hapless enough to break one could be 'sentenced' to seven years of indentured household labour. Well, that's the story, anyway. But isn't this what we say about every superstition? 'The story goes' or 'there was a myth' and 'legend has it'?

And what about the umbrella? It was a sunshade for the pharaohs, but now we're lumbered with superstitions like these: it is bad luck to give an umbrella as a gift; if you drop an umbrella, do not pick it up. Instead, have someone else do it for you or you will have bad luck; if a single woman drops an umbrella, she will never marry; if an umbrella is opened outside when it is not needed, rain will follow, and if opened indoors it could knock something over, poke someone in the eye and, in any event, why would you do it? It would make you look stupid.

In the final analysis, do black cats bring bad luck? Not really. They are, however, in certain circumstances difficult to see and easy to trip over. As for them becoming the familiars of witches, this was down to the weird, twisted imagination of sadistic, quasi-religious fanatics building their reputations as witch-finders. I have three cats, two domesticated (Flossie and Dusty) and a feral rogue (Tommy, who is as sooty black as they come). Is he mysterious? Yes, he is, and every time he comes in from his adventures for a feed I count that as really good luck.

There is of course rationality behind many superstitions. Walking under ladders proves this. Yet if we're thinking about bad luck in a modern society we can get it in so many superstition-free ways. 'One for the road' in the pub, then getting behind the wheel in your car. Not washing your hands after visiting the toilet. Unprotected sex with a stranger. Keeping a gun in the house; sooner or later that'll bring bad luck. Not looking both ways when you cross the road. Applying for yet another credit card or voting for the wrong political party. Checking your horoscope and plotting your life by it. The list is endless.

Yet many of us indulge in seemingly pointless rituals, even though we imagine ourselves to be rational. I have my 'lucky' fountain pen. I always have two boiled eggs and a slice of toast for my lunch on Thursdays. I lay out my wallet, glasses and wristwatch in a certain pattern when I go to bed at night. I'm still fearful if there's a knock at the door but there's no one there when I open it. It happens. Cats caterwauling in the garden in the early hours sound darkly ominous, even though I know it's just a couple of randy toms from down the street. Is there something wrong with me?

Obsessive compulsive disorder (OCD), when we perform rituals over and over again in an unnecessary interference with everyday life, can sometimes stem from superstitions. Think about the movie, *As Good as It Gets*, starring the inimitable Jack Nicholson who has to have the same table in his local café for breakfast every day, the *same* breakfast and, on his way, he avoids the gaps between paving stones and uses a fresh bar of soap every time he washes his hands. If you suffer with OCD, then you feel the need to worry about something or other in order to prevent that something from happening.

Throughout this book I've approached superstitions and their tangled roots and branches in what I hope has been seen as a spirit of cynical fun. I may well, in some sections, especially in the area of faith and religion, have offended some readers. But as most faiths preach tolerance and compassion, the faithful are at liberty to consider me an irresponsible sceptic and a fool and, as no animals were harmed in the production of these pages, let me be a test of your faith in seeking your forgiveness.

I have used the word 'however' quite a lot because the subjects have required it. So here's a final 'however'. Despite clinging to the slippery raft of reason, I still realise that there are aspects of our universe which defy explanation. Coincidence and synchronicity; the way animals know when you're coming home; how pigeons find their way back across continents; was there ever life on Mars? and who threw that pair of worn-out Nike trainers up on that telegraph wire? The Brazilian lyricist and novelist Paulo Coelho de Souza (b. 1947) is the recipient of numerous international awards and he seems to me a wise man. If superstition has anything to do with destiny, I doubt it. Coelho wrote:

> I can control my destiny but not my fate. Destiny means there are opportunities to turn right or left but fate is a one-way street. I believe we all have the choice as to whether we fulfil our destiny, but our fate is sealed.

Yes, it sounds ominous, but it is a thought worthy of consideration. So if you're turning left or right or going straight ahead, fate is taking you somewhere. Don't let a ladder, a black cat, a hooting owl, a magpie or a cracked pavement put you off. You've decided where you're going. Have a safe journey and don't forget your umbrella.

Bibliography and further reading

Considering the length and nature of this book, I have not opted for detailed footnotes and endnotes in the generally accepted academic manner, and where possible I have referenced sources in the text as the work progressed. To provide a full list of both the various books and online sources accessed over several months of writing would consume many pages. The following selection will give the reader a brief overview of the numerous publications and sites dealing with superstition.

Adkins, Roy and Lesley, *Jack Tar: The Extraordinary Lives of Ordinary Seamen in Nelson's Navy*, Little, Brown, London 2008

Ali, Abdullah Yusuf (translator). *The Holy Qur'an*, Wordsworth Classics, 2000

Bénabou Roland, Vindigni, Andrea and Ticchi, David, *Religion vs Science*, Princeton University, 2013

Brewer, E. Cobham, *Brewer's Dictionary of Phrase and Fable*, Wordsworth Edition, 1993

Brown, Raymond Lamont, *Phantoms, Legends, Customs and Superstitions of the Sea*, Patrick Stephens Ltd, 1972

Campbell, Joseph, *Creative Mythology: The Masks of God*, Penguin, 1976

Campbell, Joseph/Bill Moyers, *The Power of Myth*, Doubleday, 1998

Chapman, Colin, *Shadows of the Supernatural*, Lion Publishing, 1990

Crippen, T. G., *Christmas and Christmas Lore*, Blackie & Son Ltd, 1923

Darnton, Richard, *The Great Cat Massacre and Other Episodes in French Cultural History*, Basic Books, Perseus, 2009

Ellis Davidson, H. R., *Scandinavian Mythology*, Hamlyn, 1969

Engels, Donald W., *Classical Cats: The Rise and Fall of the Sacred Cat*, Routledge, 2001

Ferm, Vergilius Ture Anselm, *A Brief Dictionary of American Superstitions*, Philosophical Library Inc, 1965

Finn, Julio, *Musical Heritage of Black Men and Women in the Americas*, Interlink Publications, 1992

Frazer James George, *The Golden Bough: A study in Magic and Religion*, Macmillan, 1976

Hole, Christina, *The Encyclopedia of Superstitions*, Barnes & Noble, 1996

Hurston, Zora Neale, *Folklore, Memoirs and Other Writings*, Library of America, 1995

Opie, Iona and Moira Tatem, *A Dictionary of Superstitions*, Oxford University Press, 1989

Pickering, David, *Dictionary of Superstitions*, Cassell, 1995

De Rosa, Peter, in *Vicars of Christ: The Dark Side of the Papacy*, Poolbeg Press, 2000

Rogers, James, *Dictionary of Clichés*, Facts on File Publications, 1985

Roud, Steve, *A Pocket Guide to Superstitions of the British Isles*, Penguin Books, 2004

Roud, Steve, *The Penguin Guide to Superstitions of Britain and Ireland*, Penguin, 2006

Saul, Nigel, *A Companion to Medieval England 1066–1485*, Tempus Publishing, 2000

Timpson, *John Timpson's Book of Curious Days*, Jarrold Publishing, 1996

Tunstall, Jeremy, *The Fishermen*, Granada Publishing, 1962

Vindigni, Andrea and Ticchi, David, *Forbidden Fruits: The Political Economy of Science, Religion, and Growth*, New Version, March 2015. Also: *Religion and Innovation*, Princeton University, www.princeton.edu/~rbenabou/PP-Article_7.pdf

Waring, Philippa, *A Dictionary of Omens and Superstitions*, Souvenir Press, 1978

Zuckerman Phil, *Society Without God: What the Least Religious Nations Can Tell Us About Contentment*, NYU Press, 2008

Websites

If you are looking for superstitions on the internet, there are countless sources covering those from around the world. Some interpretations of the same practice or belief differ widely from others, but this is to be expected in such an imprecise subject. The following is a small sample of those accessed – all links working at the time of writing.

www.allaboutturkey.com/superstition.htm

www.educationuk.org/global/articles/uk-superstitions

www.factmonster.com/spot/superstitions1.html

www.firewolfsmagic.com/witchcraft/superstitions

www.historic-uk.com/CultureUK/British-Superstitions

https://islamqa.info/en/97221

www.islamreligion.com

www.lastprophet.info

mentalfloss.com/uk/animals/28064/8-weird-superstitions-about-cats

www.myjewishlearning.com › . . . › Jewish Magical Practices & Belief

www.nanations.com/jesuits/religion_superstitions.htm

www.oldsuperstitions.com

www.philosophicallibrary.com

www.pitt.edu/~dash/superstition.html

psychiclibrary.com/beyondBooks/superstition-room

www.roman-empire.net/religion/superstitions.html

Skepdic.com

http://www.thereligionofpeace.com/pages/Muhammad/superstition.aspx

'UK Superstition Survey', Richard Wiseman, www.richardwiseman.com/resources/superstition_report.pdf

www.webmd.com/mental-health/features/psychology-of-superstition

Unusual festivals

Around the world, there are literally hundreds of traditional festivals which have ancient roots and superstitious connections. Listing them all would require the proportions of a guidebook. Perhaps the most recognised UK gathering (other than Glastonbury) is the annual sunrise on the winter solstice at Stonehenge, Wiltshire. It comes complete with all the robes, prayers and incantations you would expect from some ersatz pagan past, although the so-called 'druids' are straight out of Hammer Films' central casting. But it's fun, spiritual, and highly superstitious, an essential hangover from the golden days of hippiedom.

Pagan festivals for witches

Samhain (Halloween), 31 October

Yule, winter solstice, 19–22 December

Imbolg, 1 or 2 February

Ostara, vernal equinox, 19–22 March

Beltane, 1 May

Midsummer, summer solstice, 19–22 June

Lammas, 1 August

Mabon, autumn equinox, 19–22 September

Burning Man

An annual gathering at Black Rock city, a temporary community erected in the Black Rock desert in Nevada. The event is described as an experiment in community and art. Nothing to do with the Wicker Man.

GREEN MAN

An independent music and arts festival held annually in the Brecon Beacons, Wales.

THE SMITHSONIAN FOLKLIFE FESTIVAL

Held outdoors on the National Mall in Washington, D. C., during the last week of June and first week of July. If superstition's your thing, this is the place to be.

www.festival.si.edu/visitor-information/general-information/smithsoniane.

GREEK SUPERSTITIOUS FESTIVALS

www.greeka.com/greece-culture/traditions/

Traditional Greek festivities include name day celebration, engagement, carnival, Clean Monday, Easter, Greek Independence Day, the Oxi Day (when Mussolini was refused permission to occupy parts of Greece), and superstitious events dealing with the evil eye (*mati*), spitting, black cats, hobgoblins, Tuesday the 13th and the celebration of the expression *piase kokkino* (when two people say the same thing together they immediately say '*Piase kokkino*' – 'red touch' – they touch one another and then have to touch any red item they can find). Well, Greece is the cradle of civilisation, after all.

WEIRDLY CURIOUS: BRITISH FESTIVALS

There are numerous superstition-driven events throughout Europe which are just as peculiar as the UK's, but once again there are too many to list. However, these are a few of the five hundred and more curious and eccentric annual events you'll find throughout the UK. There is an excellent, thorough and fascinating calendar of these and many more which has been assembled by Woodlands junior school in Kent: http://resources.woodlands-junior.kent.sch.uk/customs/curious/may.html

It has been pointed out to me by my wife that, with few exceptions, these festivals are male-dominated in their origins and enactment. 'A bunch of drunken blokes messing about' is her astute observation. I'll not argue with that. Meanwhile, the following few examples will provide confirmation that whatever we thought was barking mad about the Middle Ages, it still exists in Britain and long may it continue to be so.

TWELFTH NIGHT

Bankside, London

Marking the biblical day of Epiphany, this appears to vaguely resemble a religious event. However, this twelfth-night celebration has heavy pagan overtones dating back to pre-Christian midwinter feasts.

OBBY OSS

Padstow, Cornwall, 1 May

Probably the oldest and weirdest dance festival in the country, rooted in a Celtic festival held in honour of the sun god Bel (look him up!). The old 'oss is represented as a black horse who attempts to pull women under its cape as a fertility rite. Oh, any old excuse . . . The blue 'oss represents peace.

DARKIE DAY

More controversial and arguably politically incorrect, Padstow also celebrates Darkie Day (now known as Mummers Day), on 26 December and 1 January, when locals sing traditional songs and black up. Some say it celebrates the end of slavery, but with its shades of the minstrels and Al Jolson, it's debatable.

KETTLEWELL SCARECROW FESTIVAL

Yorkshire, August

This is the day scarecrows are supposed to take over, and the straw-filled figures are made to look like public figures, anything from a member of the monarchy to Jeremy Clarkson. Similar events occur in Guernsey, Herefordshire and Norfolk.

www.kettlewellscarecrowfestival.co.uk

HAXEY HOOD

Lincolnshire, 6 January

This violent and bizarre event goes back seven centuries and began when a Lady de Mowbray was out riding and a gust of wind blew her hat off. A bunch of farm lads retrieved it and she dubbed the man who handed it back to her as 'lord of the hood'; the hapless labourer who had been too embarrassed to give her the hat became the fool. The ancient event is re-run annually on the twelfth night of Christmas, started by the fool from a stone in front of Haxey parish church. Violent and scary.

UP HELLY AA

Shetland, January

It looks exceedingly Norse and feels very primeval and pagan, but the Vikings of Lerwick in Shetland are a comparatively recent tourist attraction. Whatever the weather, they celebrate a fire festival held on the last Tuesday of January, complete with processions with flaming torches, horny helmets and shields, big beards and a burning ship.

DUNMOW FLITCH TRIALS

Great Dunmow, Essex, July

Every four years, married couples from all over the world appear before a group of judges who have to be convinced that the wedded couples have never transgressed, fought or argued in twelve months. The winners get a joint of bacon (the flitch). A procession then proceeds through the village with the winners held aloft on the men's shoulders. Why? Don't ask.

www.dunmowflitchtrials.co.uk

HUNTING OF THE EARL OF RONE

Combe Martin, Devon, May, spring bank holiday

It doesn't get much weirder or more ancient than this four-day event. Allegorical characters search the streets for the earl of Rone until they 'find' him on Monday night. The humiliated earl, sitting backwards on a donkey, is paraded through the streets, 'shot', knocked off his mount and then tossed into the sea.

www.earl-of-rone.org.uk

WELL-DRESSING

Derbyshire

Well-dressing is one of Derbyshire's and the Peak District's best-known, most popular and colourful customs. It dates back hundreds of years, and though there have been religious associations, the true origins remain unknown.

FIREBALL WHIRLING

Stonehaven, Aberdeenshire, 31 December

Stonehaven folk take the Scots tradition of Hogmanay much more seriously than their inland cousins. In the sharp winter cold, just before midnight on the last day of the year, over thirty townsfolk with local bagpipe bands amble through the streets swinging enormous balls of fire about their heads. This all concludes with the fireballs being hurled into the North Sea and the people go from house to house for a glass of whisky as they begin 'first footing'. Stonehaven is proud that the event has only been cancelled twice – during WWI. A great way to get a hangover.

SWEEPS FESTIVAL

Rochester, Kent, first weekend in May

Another throwback to pagan traditions celebrating the tradition of chimney sweeps who welcomed the arrival of summer so that they could clean the sooty chimneys.

DWILE FLONKING

Lewes, Sussex

Usually outside a local pub, the Lewes Arms, a dishcloth soaked in ale is produced on the end of a stick and then lobbed at a ring of players. Contesting players include pub regulars and the Lewes operatic society. Once again, why? Well, why not?

Skipton Sheep Day

Skipton, Yorkshire, July

To acknowledge Skipton's farming heritage, sheep and lambs are let loose on the high street to race. There are accompanying events such as sheepdog duck-herding to cow-milking, and the obligatory vintage tractors.

www.sheepday.co.uk

International Festival of Worm Charming

Blackawton, Devon, May

The worm charmers encourage people to wear fancy dress, with maypole and Morris dancing. Contestants patrol around a 'secret' field, indulging in this ancient art. Cider is liberally consumed and any drink poured on the ground must also be drunk to prove it won't harm the worms.

www.wormcharming.co.uk

Shrove-tide football

Ashbourne, Derbyshire, Shrove Tuesday and Ash Wednesday

Dating back to Elizabethan times, locals play this odd game with an oversized football. The town is the entire playing field. This all ends up as an unruly brawl to the point where you'd better park your car elsewhere and shopkeepers have to board up their premises against potential damage. If you're going to attend, be very careful.

www.ashbourne-town.com/events/football

Gurning World Championship

Egremont, Cumbria, September

Can you pull a world-winning ugly face? Oddly enough, this grimacing championship event dates back to 1266. If you're proud of looking hideous, this is your event.

www.egremontcrabfair.com

The Great Wrekin Barrel Race

Shropshire, September

The challenge is to race to the summit carrying a water-filled barrel. If you're fit you can get up there in less than twenty minutes, allowing for a potential hernia. It all began two centuries ago at the Wrekin Wakes, when barrels of ale were taken to the top of the hill for a celebration. As if beer drinkers needed an excuse . . .

www.wellingtonunderthewrekin.co.uk

Cheese Rolling

Gloucestershire, late spring bank holiday, May

As many as 15,000 turn up for this strange 'sport', but the rigours of twenty-first-century health and safety may yet intervene due to the dangers of rolling or slipping down a grassy slope with a terrifying 1:2 gradient in pursuit of a rolling cheese. If you win, you get a big cheese. Or a visit to A&E. Don't wear your best trousers.

www.cheese-rolling.co.uk

Nutters' Dance

Bacup, Lancashire, Easter Sunday

Here we go again with the blacking-up routine when eight men with blackened faces, wearing clogs with wooden bobbins tied to their knees (for percussion), indulge in non-stop dancing for seven miles through the streets waving flowered garlands. The original nutters, or Britannia Coconut Dancers, were a troupe of coal miners or mill workers whose blacked-up faces represented their mining heritage. Other sources indicate that this could be a connection to seventeenth-century Moorish immigration. Others say it's all to do with warding off evil spirits. Whatever it is, it makes the Monty Python 'fish slapping dance' seem like *Swan Lake*.

Acknowledgements

Material from the UK Superstition Survey reproduced with kind permission from Professor Richard Wiseman.

Material from Vergilius Ferm originally published in *A Brief Dictionary of American Superstitions* reproduced with kind permission from Philosophical Library Inc.

Material from Barbara Frale's The Chinon chart, *Journal of Medieval History* (volume 3, issue 2, 2004) reproduced with permission of Taylor & Francis Ltd.

Material by Donna Henes reproduced with kind permission from the author, www.DonnaHenes.net

Material from Shing Tat Chung's www://superstitiousfund.com reproduced with permission by the author.

Material from Philippa Waring's *Dictionary of Omens and Superstitions* reproduced by permission of the publisher, Souvenir Press Ltd.

Material from *Religion and Innovation* by Roland Bénabou, David Ticchi and Andrea Vindigni (Princeton University 2015) reproduced by permission of Professor Roland Bénabou.

Material from Fr. *John Hardon's Sexual Pleasure outside Marriage* reproduced by permission of John O'Connell, mirafica.com.

Material on St. Nicholas included with permission of Fr. Gerardo Cioffari, www.stnicholascenter.com.

Excerpt from Albert Einstein's *Religion & Science* (1930) included by permission of the Albert Enstein Archives, The Hebrew University of Jerusalem.

Index